# GROWING SCHOOLS

# GROWING SCHOOLS

## Librarians as Professional Developers

Debbie Abilock, Kristin Fontichiaro,
and Violet H. Harada, Editors

 **LIBRARIES UNLIMITED**

AN IMPRINT OF ABC-CLIO, LLC
Santa Barbara, California • Denver, Colorado • Oxford, England

**Library of Congress Cataloging-in-Publication Data**

Growing schools : librarians as professional developers / Debbie Abilock, Kristin Fontichiaro, and Violet H. Harada, editors.
   pages cm
Includes bibliographical references and index.
ISBN 978-1-61069-041-6 (pbk.) — ISBN 978-1-61069-042-3 (ebook) (print)
1. Teachers—In-service training—United States—Case studies. 2. Teachers—Training of—United States—Case studies. 3. Educational technology—Study and teaching Case studies. 4. Information technology—Study and teaching—Case studies. 5. Technological literacy—Study and teaching—Case studies. 6. School librarian participation in curriculum planning—Case studies. 7. Academic libraries—Relations with faculty and curriculum—Case studies. 8. Libraries and teachers—United States—Case studies. 9. School libraries—Information technology. I. Abilock, Debbie, editor of compilation. II. Fontichiaro, Kristin, editor of compilation. III. Harada, Violet H., editor of compilation.
LB1731.G77 2012
370.71'1--dc23          2012016191

ISBN: 978-1-61069-041-6
EISBN: 978-1-61069-042-3

16  15  14  13  12    1  2  3  4  5

This book is also available on the World Wide Web as an eBook.
Visit www.abc-clio.com for details.

Libraries Unlimited
An Imprint of ABC-CLIO, LLC

ABC-CLIO, LLC
130 Cremona Drive, P.O. Box 1911
Santa Barbara, California 93116-1911

This book is printed on acid-free paper ∞
Manufactured in the United States of America

# CONTENTS

# INTRODUCTION

*Editors' Note:* Amidst the turmoil of constantly shifting reform initiatives and diminishing budgets, librarians are struggling to legitimize their contributions to school communities. What is emerging from the chaotic landscape is the power and promise of librarians as professional developers. In this volume, we showcase a range of stories that capture the voices of librarians, district directors, and library educators who have cultivated these learning gardens. The introduction provides glimpses of the wonderfully diverse narratives that unfold in the volume. Each story is unique in terms of context, goals and audience. Strung together, they present a compelling portrait of gardeners who have planted seeds and nurtured growth in a range of landscapes. Their candid narratives of successes and obstacles challenge the reader to take risks and reap their own harvests. As a fitting counterpoint to the introduction, Carol A. Gordon and Ross J. Todd provide encouraging evidence from their New Jersey study that school librarians are receiving administrative support to foster this new leadership skill.

## Cultivating Learning Gardens Through Professional Development

### Violet H. Harada with Kristin Fontichiaro and Debbie Abilock

In Peter Brown's picture book, *The Curious Garden* (Little, Brown 2009), Liam lives in a gray city devoid of nature. When he finds a staircase and ascends, he discovers an abandoned railway track. There, amid the railroad ties, he notices a few spindly plants reaching for the sun. Where others might see desolation, he sees possibility. Returning repeatedly to nurture the struggling shoots, he transforms the site into a brilliant green garden.

As the national economic recession continues, we see that school librarians are also struggling in their gardens. Acquisition budgets are reduced, support staff is eliminated, and some have been given the daunting responsibility of covering multiple sites.

Just one of those conditions might cause a school librarian to succumb to hopelessness, to accept this gray, unfriendly terrain. But we have noticed something different. Rather than accept a barren landscape, librarians are focusing on possibilities for growth. They water the handful of plants reaching for the sunlight, believing that their effort and contributions will improve the schools and schooling of the students they serve. In many cases, they are intensifying their efforts in professional development—because it works. This book and our work in schools supports these gardeners because we believe passionately that professional development is a cost-effective, meaningful way for school librarians to grow the capacity of school staff to provide great instructional opportunities for students.

Some readers may be questioning this statement. Perhaps like the three of us, you remember (or perhaps you've chosen to forget) most of your professional development (PD) experiences. Sadly, when we talk with librarians, everyone remembers an agonizing, seat-time experience dutifully attended and silently endured. Others were less painful—a welcome break from your daily schedule, interesting but unrelated to your own needs. The snacks might have been memorable, bonding with faculty was fun, but nothing "grew" from your attendance. Perhaps once or twice you gained a seed of inspiration and were inspired to try some new idea or lesson when you returned to your library, although there was no one to turn to when you had questions or got stuck. Only rarely might a workshop intrigue you to the point that you couldn't wait to return to work, nurture those seeds, share your success with others, and collectively watch the flowers grow. As diverse as workshops, presentations, and staff development days (or weeks) appear on the surface, we're guessing that most of your experiences had three things in common: you had little input into their design or focus, it was up to you to apply what you heard, and you had no substantive access to that PD expert when things didn't work out.

When we began interviewing school librarians about conducting professional development for their own faculty, we heard many commendable examples of librarian-teacher collaborations but without an explicit intention of incorporating professional learning. There were seize-the-moment "one shots," one-time workshops by school librarians when an opportunity presented itself (e.g., "My principal offered me thirty minutes of a staff meeting.") and examples of just-in-case mini-lessons (e.g., "I showed the new faculty how to access our databases for future projects.") These workshops were usually episodic rather than systematic, opportunistic rather than sustained, and "just-in-case" rather than closely connected to daily practice.

Many of you may already be doing what we think of as concierge PD, the one-to-one learning and teaching with a collaborative partner that is grounded in active listening and a trusted relationship. In this case, you see PD as an extension of what you do day in and day out in your school.

Perhaps you are reading this book because you yearn to learn more about how you can harness the power of professional learning to make a difference with your staff. Or maybe you picked up this book because you're being pushed into an unfamiliar role: instead of being presented *to*, you are the one who is being asked to lead professional development sessions for your staff and colleagues—and you're nervous or fearful or, maybe, even unwilling. You worry that your colleagues may come to your sessions feeling as you have felt during those one-shots, and you want to push past that to create something meaningful—but how?

How, indeed—especially now, when today's schools are experiencing unprecedented reform? Job responsibilities for educators are expanding faster than the job descriptions can be rewritten. Teachers are expected to add the skill set of a special educator or gifted and talented coordinator to their toolkit, becoming skilled at differentiation and response to intervention. Counselors now go beyond classroom skills presentations and host clubs. Even as school librarians in England resist "redundancy" layoffs and a single librarian of record is charged with an entire district in California, we see a promising opportunity for our profession. While previously you might have had little or no involvement in professional learning initiatives, or may have only been expected to demonstrate the latest upgrades to expensive databases, you might now be approached by your administrator to become a partner in school reform and in the professional learning needs of a building or district (Danielson 2007; Zmuda and Harada 2008). It's also important to note that a critical skill for all new librarians in the *ALA/AASL Standards for Initial Programs for School Librarian Preparation* (NCATE 2010) is not only to participate but to lead professional development.

It's tough to grow under these conditions, when changes come our way so rapidly. But growth is *the* reason for professional development.

## TRADITIONAL PD: WHY DOESN'T IT WORK?

Andy Hargreaves (1995) says that professional development often fails because it does not "acknowledge the personal identities and moral purposes of teachers or the cultures and contexts in which they work" (13–14). Whether the professional development is fashioned as a brief interlude or extended over a period of time, problems manifest themselves when the efforts are disconnected from the purposes and contexts of the real work that educators do and provide no appropriate follow-up during implementation (Guskey 2000). A seed without soil to grow in will not germinate; at issue is a fundamental lack of understanding about how adults learn best.

## THE NEED TO KNOW THE ADULT LEARNER

Adults bring a rich background of experiences, knowledge, skills, interests, and competences to any new learning experience (Early and Bubb

2004). Because of this, they command an active role in their own learning (Smylie 1995). Peter Early and Sara Bubb (2004) highlight the following characteristics of adult learners:

- They are largely self-directed and require a climate of trust, openness, and respect to learn effectively.
- Their previous experiences are too significant to ignore and must be implicit in the process.
- They need to accept the need to learn.
- They prefer learning that incorporates problem-solving strategies.
- Their commitment to learning depends on its practical relevance. (18)

Yet a gardener knows that each plant grows best under certain conditions; a gardener learns to match soil, light, and water to that plant's needs. Working in a learning mode with other adults, then, requires nimble thinking and a deft hand that can reinforce prior understandings, draw the learner into new experiences, and make connections among ideas.

## WHAT MAKES PD WORK?

How do we translate what we know about adult learners into practice? Stop for a moment and consider the best professional development in which you participated. What made it resonate with you? Recently, Kristin Fontichiaro asked a room of school librarians to identify what were the qualities of their best professional development experience (Figure 1).

---

### Figure 1: Librarians Tell Us What Professional Development Looks Like

**Relevant**
- reflected what I do every day
- implementable on Monday morning
- connected abstract concepts to concrete practices
- matched the learning preferences to the participants
- had a takeaway that I can try
- maximized buy-in
- had relevance for all participants
- excused participants for whom the session lacked relevance

**Varied**
- organized in a range of groupings, pacing and energy level, degree of challenge, format and medium
- provided choices
- was teacher-led

**Responsive**
- provided midstream feedback

---

- scheduled at times when the staff was not already overburdened (e.g., right before conferences or report cards)
- incorporated proactive evaluation and asked questions like, "Did this work? What could we do differently?"
- didn't require homework that burdened already overextended teachers
- considered differentiation by ability level
- was fun
- got you energized and enthused

**Allowed for time and practice**

- modeled how we should work with students
- assumed that some changes would take time to implement
- provided opportunities to practice what I was learning

The librarians' responses in Figure 1 correlate with the principles that notable researchers in the field of education have identified as key to improving instruction and raising student achievement (e.g., Darling-Hammond and Richardson 2009; Supovitz, Mayer, and Kahle 2000; Garet et al. 2001; Perez et al. 2007; Weiss and Pasley 2006). Figure 2 summarizes these principles.

### Figure 2: Principles of Effective Professional Development

- The driving goal of all professional development is learning.

- School improvement will result from improving the skills and abilities of the faculty.

- Explicit learning goals are embedded in all learning experiences.

- Learners understand pedagogical strategies when they can apply them to their disciplines.

- Learners are capable of making significant decisions and choices about their own learning.

- Learners have different stages of concern about a change that must be recognized and respected.

- The design of learning experiences must be guided by coherence and relevance.

- Both formal and informal environments can support learning.

- Interventions facilitate the learners' evolving stages of concern about change, needs for information, assistance, and support.

## WHY SHOULD LIBRARIANS NOW TAKE THE LEAD IN PD?

Limited funds coupled with societal reappraisal of the nature of expertise has driven schools to turn inward, looking for collective responsibility for staff development and grassroots talent to grow institutional capacity and continuous improvement within local professional learning communities.

As school librarians we are "in position" to lead professional development because we service the entire school network beginning with the students and faculty and extending beyond to families and communities. We possess an objective "whole school view" (Dees et al. 2010, 10); we are not bound to or biased toward specific grade levels or departments (Gilmore-See 2010). Unlike outside consultants, who are strangers stepping into an unfamiliar culture of teaching and learning, we know the current system, values, and key players. We possess a deep understanding of the personal and political struggles that can impede effective transformation. We also recognize the need for respectful introduction and implementation of change in what is often a fragile, people-centered workplace. Instead of presenting abstract ideas about teaching and learning, we can connect those ideas directly and concretely to specific classrooms, students, and teachers. By embracing the American Association of School Librarians' *Standards for the 21st-Century Learner* (2007), we model lifelong learning for our students and staffs. To succeed as staff developers, we facilitate the building of teams that work and learn from each other regularly. Along with knowledge of standards and curricula that define the school program, we demonstrate pedagogical skills in cultivating learning environments where goals are clear and rigorous and participants discover and construct personal meaning. We have the gardening tools necessary to nurture the growth of others.

## ORGANIZATION AND CONTENT OF THE BOOK

There is no one set of conditions under which every plant will thrive. Some prefer warmer temperatures, some cooler. Some like more humidity, some less. Some flourish when drenched with water; others sip demurely. Some will only grow if aggressively pruned; others not. Similarly, there is no one best approach to professional development. The chapters in this book reflect a range of processes and techniques that have worked in different contexts and for different learning goals. Our hope is that you apply these insights to your own learning journeys. We organized the chapters loosely by themes so that the echoes of richly diverse voices find musical counterpoints throughout the book. We invited all authors to narrate their journey of trials, errors, and successes, teasing out how their experiences might be applicable to others' situations. Collectively they represent K–12 public and private institutions, district and regional units, and universities across the United States and Canada. To provide you with a glimpse of the stories, here are snapshots of the themes and topics covered.

## Creating a Sense of Play in Personalized PD

- *Kelly Ahlfeld* describes how she devised the Exploratorium as a "hands-on learning with a hands-off approach," inviting teachers to discover the wonders of web tools at Mettawee Community School in Vermont. In a playground atmosphere, teachers select the tools they wish to explore, experiment, and share their experiences with each other. Her classroom colleague, *Jennifer Bloomingdale*, provides a collegial perspective.

- Inspired by Helene Blowers's "23 Things" and the California School Libraries' "Learning 2.0" projects, *Susan Geiger* and *Anne Arriaga* created a series of online tutorials on Web 2.0 tools for teachers at California's Moreau Catholic High School. *Jackie Siminitus*, who coordinated the Learning 2.0 initiative, follows this chapter with a short piece on how the Learning 2.0 tutorials have been adopted and adapted across the nation.

- Using a fishing metaphor, *Connie Williams* of Petaluma City Schools in California describes how she "reels in" teachers to take a bite of 2.0 technologies that fit her new school's culture and goals. Her play-and-practice approach, which was also inspired by "23 Things," includes tips on using 2.0 tools in daily classroom activities. As an introduction to this section, *Mike Eisenberg* at the University of Washington emphasizes that it is the school's priorities and program that guide the school librarian as "information manager."

## Promoting Evidence-Based Practice

- *Catherine Lewis* of Mills College identifies key design elements of lesson study and how it positions educators to become leaders of continuing improvement. *Anne Stokes* of Edgewood School in New York recounts the intense and rewarding nature of lesson study as she collaborated with teachers on the construction, delivery, and review of specific lessons.

- Shifting from the building level to a district initiative, *Pamela Kramer* and *Linda Diekman* discuss a PD initiative focusing on outcome-based teaching and assessment for learning in Illinois's DuPage Library System. They tell the story from two critical perspectives: Kramer as one of the program designers and Diekman as a librarian-participant.

- *Judith Sykes* presents a compelling case for conducting action research through her various leadership experiences as a school principal and as a district and a provincial administrator in Canada's Calgary school system. *Violet H. Harada* from the University of

Hawaii follows this chapter with brief examples of how teams of librarians and teachers can effectively apply action research to improving teaching and learning in individual school contexts.

## Building Professional Learning Communities

- Professional learning communities often begin with successful one-on-one collaborative experiences. *Judi Moreillon* of Texas Women's University passionately promotes instructional co-planning and co-teaching. She reflects upon her past collaborations and frames them as an effective job-embedded form of professional development.

- As big picture people on the school campus, *Carolyn Kirio* and *Sandy Yamamoto* describe how they became part of a leadership team to establish and grow a school-wide learning community at Kapolei High in Hawaii.

- Moving from routine announcement sessions to forums for critical issues, *Christopher Harris* highlights how restructuring district meetings have fostered a professional learning community among New York's Genesee Valley librarians. His colleague *Brian Mayer* comments on the type of district support that facilitates community building.

- *Tish Stafford* thoughtfully chronicles how librarians in Maryland's Cecil County evolved a professional community based on assessment and reflective practice to help students become more critical users of information.

- *Kristin Fontichiaro* from the University of Michigan shares how she has learned to deepen her teaching to grow community among pre-service librarians and educators through various Web 2.0 tools. Her student *Mariah Cherem* discusses how one of those strategies, Diigo groups, resonated beyond the classroom.

## Diverse Participants, Diverse Purposes

- As a result of her experiences with pre-service teachers at the University of Georgia, *Elizabeth E. G. Friese* emphasizes the importance of approaching mentoring as a co-learning adventure. In her supporting commentary, *Kim Dority*, founder of G. K. Dority & Associates, agrees that mentoring is not so much about "knowing it all" as it is about growing along with your colleagues.

- *Marilyn Kimura* details her long-term school-wide training of parents, teachers, teaching interns, and administrators to facilitate literary discussions in a Literary Club for mixed-age students at Nueva School in California. *Nancy Kranich* from Rutgers University describes how a librarian can use these same facilitation skills to moderate community issues, faculty decision-making processes, and other difficult discussions.

- Collaborating with administrators and teachers, *Susan Smith* fostered a team approach to integrating information literacy at Harker School in California. She describes how training and strategic implementation have positioned information skills as central to the school's mission.

- Capitalizing on the successful integration of technology at New Canaan High in Connecticut, *Michelle Luhtala* recounts how she "took the show on the road" via webinars to reach national and international audiences that now include librarians, educational technologists, administrators, academic faculties, graduate students, and private industry professionals.

### Ending at the Beginning

- *Debbie Abilock*, consultant on school library media and literacy, adds a postscript to our book, which reflects the Taoist maxim that "a journey of a thousand miles begins with a single step." She returns to our roots of professional development, the humble one-shot session, and suggests techniques to improve this format. In preparing for and implementing sessions that introduce factual, conceptual, or procedural knowledge about new programs and instructional approaches, she stresses the importance of knowing and nurturing the adult learner's needs and experiences.

## AUDIENCE FOR THE BOOK

Our focus has been to address practitioners at the building and district levels, who may already be engaged in professional development or who want to get involved in designing such initiatives to develop learning gardens in their schools. Pragmatic questions addressed in the various chapters include:

- Why should I get involved in designing and implementing professional development?

- What do I need to know?

- How do I do it?

- How do I know if I've done it?

- How can I get better at it?

Secondary but equally critical audiences include a range of educators, who organize professional learning experiences for school librarians including instructional college librarians, building-level principals, state and district personnel, library educators, and cross-level teams from pre-K through college. In addition, potential readers might include professionals in nonprofit initiatives that work with K–12 libraries and vendors who sponsor webinars.

## VALUE OF THE BOOK

While there are many books, articles, and online resources on professional development for K–12 schools in the general field of education (e.g., Guskey 2000; Danielson 2007; Darling-Hammond and Bransford 2005; Marzano 2007) there are very few resources on this theme that directly address the potential role of the school librarian as a staff developer. In recent years, related articles have appeared in *Knowledge Quest, School Library Monthly* (formerly *School Library Media Activities Monthly*), *Teacher Librarian,* and *Library Media Connection.* However, these are necessarily brief pieces that provide seeds of promising practices. This is a first book on professional development for school librarians that provides in-depth narratives of the design and implementation processes. The intent is to have practitioners, who have successfully implemented a range of professional learning options, share their stories of tilling the soil, germinating seeds of interest, and tending to tender shoots until they grow into strong new practices. In the telling, they go beyond the "what" of their stories to delve more deeply into the "why" and "how" of individual experiences that emerge as the substance of best practices. Along the way, sidebar panels present brief commentary and counterpoint.

## LET THE ADVENTURE BEGIN!

It has taken decades, but educators are finally realizing that adults learn best under the same conditions that are advocated for students. Effective professional development "requires moving from replication to reflection; from shallow and fragmented to deep and integrated; from learning separately to learning together" (Hawley and Valli 1999, 134). If we want our young learners to survive and succeed as self-initiating and creative problem solvers, who will responsibly develop better lives for themselves and for the global community, the professionals charged with guiding our young students must experience this same transformative learning. Regardless of how schools are formed or reformed, structured or restructured, the renewal of staff members' professional skills is fundamental to improvement (Guskey and Huberman 1995). Thomas Guskey (1995) emphatically states:

> We cannot improve schools without improving the skills and abilities of the teachers within them. . . . We must see change as an individual process and be willing to invest in the intellectual capital of those individuals who staff our schools. . . .

At the same time, we have to see it as an organizational matter, too. The key is finding the optimal mix between macro-level concerns and micro-level realities. (118–19)

We believe that professional learning should be a unique opportunity for self-discovery for everyone involved. For creators of professional development, the challenge is to guide learners to improved practice and a shared ownership in the experience. Join us in these tales of librarians working to grow capacity in their schools. See the tools in their gardening sheds, and compare them to the ones you see in your own. Then, as in *The Curious Garden*, see the possibilities, not the barriers. Strategic optimists make good gardeners.

## REFERENCES

American Association of School Librarians. 2007. *Standards for the 21st-Century Learner*. Chicago, IL: American Association of School Librarians. http://www.ala.org/aasl/standards (cited September 6, 2011).

Brown, Peter. 2009. *The Curious Garden*. New York City: Little, Brown.

Danielson, Charlotte. 2007. *Enhancing Professional Practice: A Framework for Teaching*. 2nd ed. Alexandria, VA: Association for Supervision and Curriculum Development.

Darling-Hammond, Linda, and John Bransford, eds. 2005. *Preparing Teachers for a Changing World: What Teachers Should Learn and Be Able to Do*. San Francisco, CA: Jossey-Bass.

Darling-Hammond, Linda, and Nikole Richardson. 2009. "Teaching Learning: What Matters?" *Educational Leadership* 66, no. 5 (February): 47–53.

Darling-Hammond, Linda, and Gary Sykes, eds. 1999. *Teaching as the Learning Profession: Handbook of Policy and Practice*. San Francisco, CA: Jossey-Bass Publishers.

Dees, Dianne, Alisande Mayer, Heather Morin, and Elaine Willis. 2010. "Librarians as Leaders in Professional Learning Communities through Technology, Literacy, and Collaboration." *Library Media Connection* 29, no. 2 (October): 10–13.

Early, Peter, and Sara Bubb. 2004. *Leading and Managing Continuing Professional Development: Developing People, Developing Schools*. Thousand Oaks, CA: Sage.

Garet, Michael S., Andrew C. Porter, Laura Desimone, Beatrice F. Birman, and Kwang Suk Yoon. 2001. "What Makes Professional Development Effective? Results from a National Sample of Teachers." *American Educational Research Journal* 38, no. 4 (Winter): 915–45.

Gilmore-See, Janice. 2010. "Staff Development: Teacher-Librarians as Learning Leaders." In *The Many Faces of School Librarianship*, edited by Sharon Coatney, 115–22. Santa Barbara, CA: Libraries Unlimited.

Guskey, Thomas R. 1995. "Professional Development in Education: In Search of the Optimal Mix." In *Professional Development in Education: New Paradigms and Practices*, edited by Thomas R. Guskey and Michael Huberman, 114–31. New York: Teachers College Press.

Guskey, Thomas R. 2000. *Evaluating Professional Development*. Thousand Oaks, CA: Corwin Press.

Guskey, Thomas R., and Michael Huberman. 1995. *Professional Development in Education: New Paradigms and Practices*. New York: Teachers College Press.

Hargreaves, Andy. 1995. "Development and Desire: A Postmodern Perspective." In *Professional Development in Education: New Paradigms and Practices*, edited by Thomas R. Guskey and Michael Huberman, 9–34. New York: Teachers College Press.

Hawley, Wills D., and Linda Valli. 1999. "The Essentials of Effective Professional Development: A New Consensus." In *Teaching as the Learning Profession: Handbook of Policy And Practice*, edited by Linda Darling-Hammond and Gary Sykes, 127–50. San Francisco, CA: Jossey-Bass Publishers.

Marzano, Robert J. 2007. *Art and Science of Teaching: A Comprehensive Framework for Effective Instruction*. Alexandria, VA: Association for Supervision and Curriculum Development.

National Council for Accreditation of Teacher Education. 2010. *ALA/AASL Standards for Initial Preparation of School Librarians*. Washington, DC: NCATE. http://www.ala.org/ala/mgrps/divs/aasl/aasleducation/school library/schoollibrary.cfm (cited September 7, 2011).

Perez, Maria, Priyanka Arnand, Cecilia Speroni, Tom Parrish, Phil Esra, Miguel Socias, and Paul Gubbins. 2007. *Successful California Schools in the Context of Educational Adequacy*. Washington, DC: American Institutes for Research.

Smylie, Mark A. 1995. "Teacher Learning in the Workplace: Implications for School Reform." In *Professional Development in Education: New Paradigms and Practices*, edited by Thomas R. Guskey and Michael Huberman, 92–113. New York: Teachers College Press.

Supovitz, Jonathan A., Daniel P. Mayer, and Jane B. Kahle. 2000. "Promoting Inquiry-Based Instructional Practice: The Longitudinal Impact of Professional Development in the Context of Systemic Reform." *Educational Policy* 14, no. 3 (July): 331–56.

Weiss, Iris R., and Joan D. Pasley. 2006. *Scaling Up Instructional Improvement through Teacher Professional Development: Insights from the Local Systemic Change Initiative*. Philadelphia: Consortium for Policy Research in Education (CPRE) Policy Briefs.

Zmuda, Allison, and Violet H. Harada. 2008. "Reframing the Library Media Specialist as a Learning Specialist." *School Library Media Activities Monthly* 24, no. 8 (April): 42–46.

# "Clone the School Librarian": Evidence of the Role of the School Librarian in Professional Development

## Carol A. Gordon and Ross J. Todd

What do good school libraries look like? The question was posed by the New Jersey Commissioner of Education in 2008 in a meeting with Rutgers University's Center for International Scholarship in School Libraries (CISSL). The New Jersey Association of School Librarians (NJASL) joined CISSL in exploring the dimensions of the commissioner's question to shape the purpose of the study:

1. To construct a picture of the status of New Jersey school libraries.

2. To understand the contribution of school libraries to the New Jersey educational landscape.

3. To understand what inhibits and enables school libraries.

4. To make recommendations to sustain and continuously improve school libraries.

A two-phase study revealed that school libraries contribute to education through information service roles, reading and literacy initiatives, general school services, school leadership, and extracurricular activities. Data collected in Phase 1 (2009) from an online survey covered this range of school library functions from 765 school librarians.

Phase 1 findings show:

1. 63% of school librarians provide professional development in relation to information literacy;

2. 72.8% provide professional development in relation to information technology in their schools;

3. 96.1% meet with principals every year and 51.7% meet with them more than five times a year;

4. 74.4% meet with curriculum supervisors; 24.3% meet with them more than five times a year; and

5. 38.3% meet with their superintendent during the school year.

These results demonstrate that the librarian as professional developer is neither novel nor new; rather, many are already engaged in professional development in information literacy or technology. The statistics regarding meetings with administrators and curriculum leaders suggest that librarians are seeking opportunities to connect their expertise and programs with larger initiatives. In addition, findings showed that 98.9 percent of school librarians hold a membership or affiliation with at least one professional organization and 83 percent belong to more than one professional organization. This speaks positively about librarians' commitment to their own learning and skill development, essential if they are to develop and maintain expertise that can be shared with colleagues. On average, school librarians reported three discrete professional development activities for a total of 2,261 collaborations annually.

In Phase 2 (2011) CISSL researchers conducted focus groups in twelve schools that reported high levels of collaboration between the school librarian and classroom teachers. The groups in each school consisted of the principal, classroom and specialist teachers, and curriculum/instructional supervisors. Three questions structured the dialogue:

1.  In what ways, if any, does the school library contribute to school learning?

2.  What do students actually learn through their interaction and engagement with the school library?

3.  What is it about this school that has enabled the school library to reach this status?

Findings reveal that a collaborative school culture supports the school library as a pedagogical center. Principals

- endorse a whole school, 21st-century learning environment where educators model collaboration for students as they collaborate;

- encourage a culture of innovation, risk taking, and high expectations; and

- acknowledge the actions school librarians take to shape a school culture of deep learning.

Teachers report that:

- the school library conducts substantial, cost-effective, hands-on professional development through the cooperative design of learning experiences. The substance of this professional development includes inquiry-based instruction, integration of technology and learning, the effective use of both print and digital information, and engagement with information;

- school librarians have instructional expertise; and

- the school library offers a learning environment that is not based on the right answer prompted by rote learning, but on a more complex model of teaching and learning that is exploratory and highly motivational.

The data from this study strongly indicates that the professional development role of the school librarian is embedded in instructional best practice, whether that instruction is focused on students or faculty. When educators were asked what they would change about their school library, the answer was unanimous: "Clone the school librarian."

## REFERENCES

Todd, Ross J., Carol A. Gordon, and Ya-Ling Lu. 2010. *One Common Goal: Student Learning. Report of Findings and Recommendations of the New Jersey Library Survey, Phase 1.* Center for International Scholarship in School Libraries. Retrieved December 7, 2011, from http://cissl.rutgers.edu.

Todd, Ross J., Carol A. Gordon, and Ya-Ling Lu. 2011. *One Common Goal: Student Learning. Report of Findings and Recommendations of the New Jersey Library Survey, Phase 2.* Center for International Scholarship in School Libraries. Retrieved December 7, 2011, from http://cissl.rutgers.edu.

# CHAPTER 1
## PLAYFUL EXPLORATION

*Editors' Note:* In this chapter, Vermont school librarian Kelly Ahlfeld reflects on how she has learned and examined new technologies for potential use in her practice. Seeing informal time set aside for play and experimentation as key, she and her colleagues develop the Exploratorium model of self-directed professional development. With a focus on experimentation and exploration, Exploratorium proves to succeed in ways traditional PD did not. Classroom colleague Jennifer Bloomingdale discusses the impact of Exploratorium on her practice.

# Hands-on Learning with a Hands-off Approach

## Kelly Ahlfeld

## INTRODUCTION

We are more than ten years into the 21st century, and our students need teachers who exemplify the values and skills of global, interconnected, and innovative learners. The ISTE National Educational Technology Standards for Students include creativity, information fluency, collaboration, and critical thinking among its goals (International Society for Technology in Education 2007). To support these goals, ISTE created the National Educational Technology Standards for Teachers, which include inspiring innovation and creativity, designing digital-age experiences and assessments, and modeling digital-age learning and digital citizenship (International Society for Technology in Education 2008). With the Common Core State Standards on the horizon as well, teachers and librarians must be ready to guide our students on this challenging journey. In order to teach students for the 21st century, we must be learners first.

Yet many hard-working teachers feel overwhelmed with so many day-to-day responsibilities that they have little time for learning how to integrate technology, and they feel left behind in our digital age. According to the Partnership for 21st Century Skills (2011), professional development is one of four key support systems for students' 21st-century outcomes, but offering effective professional development for teachers in technology is easier said than done. A few years ago, several colleagues and I asked ourselves whether our professional development gave adequate support to teachers so that they could define, explore, and implement skills of creativity, collaboration, and integration of technology. Our professional development experiment, titled "Exploratorium," and our experiences may inspire you to examine how you lead, partner, and support the growth of the adult learners in your school.

## SETTING THE STAGE

The story begins at the Mettawee Community School in rural Vermont, a public PK–6 school with approximately 190 students. Our principal is a strong advocate for teachers and lifelong learning, and our staff appreciates her talent, hard work, and rigorous professional development in the form of courses, conferences, and workshops. We have a built-in time for professional development during the winter because our school dismisses students at 11:30 to use the local ski mountain and skating rink while teachers stay for PD time until 3:00. Our staff members enjoy working together and being silly together (more on that later!).

When our professional development experiment began in the fall of 2008, my position as Librarian and Technology Coordinator was four days a week, with Fridays off, and our school had a few tech tools for students. We offered a lab of ten eMacs, one or two eMacs in each of our classrooms, a document camera, a Smartboard, one digital video camera, and two carts of AlphaSmart word processors. Our equipment was in good shape, and we finally had a stable wireless internet network. We had a technology committee, a cadre of tech pioneers and leaders who integrated technology tools like iMovie and WebQuests in creative and interesting ways, but about two-thirds of our teachers had not used or even heard of such then-emerging tools as Facebook, blogging, Skype, or digital video cameras. YouTube was something most had only glanced at a few times.

## WORKING HARD . . . BUT TECHNOLOGY INTEGRATION NOT IMPROVING

As the librarian and technology coordinator, I struggled to keep up with the challenges of teaching fourteen library classes, maintaining the library and equipment, and helping teachers integrate technology. I could see that many of the ideas and suggestions I did pass on to teachers were out of context, not immediately relevant, and forgotten quickly. Frustrated by my lack of progress in integrating technology into the classrooms, I tried offering technology workshops featuring a variety of tools to see if a more structured setting would translate into more and better integration into instruction, but I found that these demos and practice sessions with "cool tools" burned bright then fizzled out when teachers were back in their classrooms. I yearned to go beyond my gadget demonstrations to help teachers incorporate technology to improve their students' learning. Fortunately, an opportunity soon presented itself; best of all, it came from my teacher colleagues themselves.

## EXPLORATORIUM IS BORN

Three of our most tech-savvy teachers were debriefing what they'd learned at a technology conference and they were reflecting on the excitement they felt when they were able to use new tools with their students. The conversation turned to how they had become our school's tech pioneers. One teacher suggested that experimentation was the driving force; they had become tech-savvy because they all enjoyed exploring and playing with computers and that they used their leisure time to try things, fail, and then try other things. The light bulb went on for us: protected time and a desire to play were the missing links between those who integrated technology and those who didn't. If time to play was really the key, we wondered how we might change our PD structure to provide this. We all began to talk excitedly about how to start from the point of view of each teacher and redesign our workshops. It seemed that the usual bounce effect, or surge in energy and enthusiasm from the conference, was about to spread through our school and make some real change in our teaching! Exploratorium was born.

## PITCHING THE PLAN: PROCESS, NOT PRODUCT

Our next step was to formulate a plan and bring it to our principal. It was tricky to find the right balance between exploration and accountability. At first, I erred on the side of open exploration, but one of my teacher colleagues pointed out that we needed some accountability in order to keep people on track and provide some structure. We decided that teachers would be asked to choose a tool to explore based on something they'd like to do differently in class. They would have time to explore that tool, experiencing all the success and failure that would accompany it, and then share their experiences. Sharing ensured accountability; sharing experiences rather than a finished product ensured that failure was perfectly fine, as long as teachers took a risk and tried something new. This authentic accountability, coming from one of our own, carried more weight than it would if we were complying with an outside mandate. We were accountable to ourselves and our students, and that was exciting and motivating. The process-versus-product decision was something I insisted on. I wanted our teachers to focus on trying and failing rather than feeling the pressure of presenting the best project. I believed it was the key to helping the teachers who feared technology (not to mention presenting to their colleagues) to become less intimidated and enjoy this new teaching challenge.

## THE ROLE OF THE PRINCIPAL

Despite the staff time needed to explain district initiatives in writing and math, to implement a new spelling program, the usual administrative announcements and other colleagues who wanted to share their experiences from a variety of conferences, our principal chose to dedicate three of our afternoon in-service sessions to our self-guided, hands-off professional development idea. I credit her leadership and vision with many positive things in our school, and her support of our grassroots venture is another example of how administrators are almost always essential if teachers are to both lead and implement new initiatives. Even the most supportive of administrators have to consider a variety of variables in new projects, however, and we were careful to create a plan to which she could say yes. We had a plan for each session laid out before we approached her. We also presented our idea in terms of getting the most value out of the original money spent on the conference by pointing out that hands-on training would be the most sustainable result from the original conference. The accountability of teachers sharing their ideas helped her to justify three in-service sessions. The fact that we shared our experiences with our superintendent along the way also created a project she could feel enthusiastic about. When we got the chance to move forward from her, we were pleased and enthusiastic but we also felt pressure to make sure we provided something engaging and useful for our adult learners!

## RESPECTING TEACHERS AS LEARNERS

Teacher-learners are hard-working educators who devote hours outside of the school day planning their classes, and who attend courses and conferences during their vacations. I wanted to make sure they felt respected and in control of their learning so that they would be more likely to buy into our project. I had a hunch that more individualization of learning might be a key factor; I had some survey data about technology that I had collected in order to make tech purchasing decisions. That data showed me there was a small segment of teachers who craved new and different equipment and already had ideas about how they wanted to use it, and there was a larger group who was completely satisfied with very little equipment and could not imagine what additional items they would need. I observed that teachers became uncomfortable or even anxious when teaching with technology: Would it work? Would the students handle using equipment well? Would students misbehave if problems occurred and it took too long to figure out how to fix them? Many of our teachers worried about using technology because they perceived they would not know more than the students. Through conversations with the tech committee and in the classrooms and hallways, I gained an understanding of the range of our tech-emotions, from fear/avoidance to excitement/early adoption. I knew we would need to meet our teachers where they were by personalizing their learning and setting individual goals.

Our Friday winter in-service sessions include twenty-five full-time faculty members, including classroom teachers, a music and PE teacher, special educators, the school nurse, and our principal, who was a great model for us, because she was excited to try something new herself. With the diversity of job descriptions and comfort levels with technology in mind, we created a three-part workshop. For the first session, we asked each teacher to identify a learning experience for students that they'd like to enrich—they would dream a dream that had nothing to do with technology and everything to do with content mastery. During the first and second sessions we would show them some interesting tools that might help them accomplish those visions and consult with them about what they might like to try. They could work alone or in groups. We would encourage both mistakes and failures as ways to learn. Finally, at the last session, they would formally share what they tried and learned but would not need to present a finished product.

## OVERCOMING PLANNING CHALLENGES

We faced two practical planning challenges: equipment and scheduling. Since we had no idea what teachers would choose to do ahead of time, we prepared for the possibility that we might have to purchase more equipment or software during the next few weeks of Exploratorium. We would also need to be ready to provide support and tutoring for any number of tech tools. Our principal supported us in multiple ways: she cut through red tape and freed up money midyear for anticipated new equipment purchases; empowered teachers by supporting their interest in setting up a YouTube account to try uploading video (the site was not blocked, but they felt more comfortable knowing in advance that she would support the move); and she lightened my work load by enlisting help with some of my library clerical responsibilities so I would have more time to support our teachers.

We planned three sessions for our learners. At the first kick-off session, teachers would dream up ideas and learn about the variety of tools from which they could choose. Before the middle session, the main try-and-learn session, teachers would e-mail me their ideas so that I could suggest tools and plan for equipment purchase and tutoring. The final session would be our sharing time. There were several weeks in between each session in order to give the planners and the learners what we felt was so crucial in our design from the beginning: time.

## THE INITIAL KICK-OFF: DREAMING AND PLANNING

I felt the kick-off session was very important to our goal of making real change in people's attitudes about technology. A problem arose, in that my part-time position meant that the Friday in-service days were not scheduled workdays for me; on those days, I had the job of a mom driving kids to the ski mountain! We had decided that this experiment was too important to let the limitations of scheduling be a barrier, and most of our plans worked around that challenge. For the opening session, however, I did not want to miss being there. I decided that I could find a way to "attend" while also introducing some fun technology. I wanted to model getting out of my comfort zone and taking a risk, so I used a Flip video camera to create a very silly video. At the time, most of my fellow teachers had never used the Flip camera. This way I could be with them virtually to explain this new professional development that they would try. I appeared in several different costumes, describing my whereabouts as "an undisclosed location" each time, and then finally getting down to the serious explanation of how our plan would work. The response from teachers was very positive; in fact, I think they focused more intently on the video version of me than they would have if I had been there in person!

The video got the first Exploratorium session off to a positive start with its message of celebrating mistakes and taking risks. The video version of me provided our teachers with a road map for their journey with checkpoints along the way, and they began dreaming. Some teachers decided to work alone, but many created small groups of like-minded colleagues. The library served as the center of operations, and for the opening session, we provided an area with lists of ideas and websites, some photographs of equipment, and a variety of actual equipment we owned to handle and try. Many teachers were inspired to use digital video in some way; they had really enjoyed the opening session video, saw that it was easy for me to use, and they wanted to incorporate that medium into their classes. One teacher even joked with me that she would be quitting teaching to become a YouTube sensation! Already we had our first challenge: we owned only one Flip camera, so we knew we would need to make some purchases right away. Teachers brainstormed during the session and continued to think more after the session was over. Some teachers e-mailed me immediately with their project ideas; others took longer. In my initial e-mail planning conversations with all of them, they were directed to ask themselves teaching questions first, such as: How can I get more of my students excited about reading? How can I have students learn from each other in math? How can I make the countries we are studying more real? The technology stemmed from the teaching idea. Once the e-mails started to arrive, I made a checklist to ensure that each teacher had a dream to pursue before our hands-on session a few weeks later.

There was an interesting variety of projects in those e-mails. One group of primary teachers wanted to evaluate the Scholastic e-book product *Book-Flix* in order to determine whether we should purchase it. They read some research on the program and checked pricing and licensing agreements. They got a trial license and tested it out with students, conducting a survey with the students to find their reaction to it. Ultimately they came up with a recommendation to purchase it. Although this project was not cutting-edge technology for some of us, for these teachers it represented a chance to take a leadership role with technology and, more importantly, to make pedagogically relevant selections that would benefit students. *Bookflix* was one of those products mentioned in past e-mails from the library, but not something that had much meaning to them without the time to see it in action, so it was "my" idea, not "theirs." One of the members of the team had seen her daughter use it with her own students and wanted to use Exploratorium time to find out more. Once they had explored and evaluated it themselves and included students in that process, they were truly invested, and it has been a thoughtfully utilized literacy tool in our school ever since. The *BookFlix* team's experience taught me a valuable lesson as a librarian: my colleagues must find value in a tool themselves and have time to see it in action in daily classroom experience in order to utilize it most effectively; e-mail alerts of new products are not meaningful without the teacher's vision of their students in mind.

Many teachers' projects involved ways to leverage the power of digital video in their classes, an idea that was new to many of us. One 1st grade teacher incorporated video into her "Royal Reader" ceremony, using the video to assess and celebrate young readers' fluency as they took their turn as the class "Royal Reader." A 2nd grade teacher started a collection of student-authored math tutorials in which students taught each other math concepts such as measurement and computation concepts. His idea was to have a ready video library for students who would benefit from extra review or learning visually. In hindsight I realize that he started our own little Khan Academy! A 3rd grade teacher used video in her class to create a play in which students modeled effective conversational and writing techniques. Another 3rd grade class transformed their field trip by turning over cameras to the students and giving them the chance to decide what was important to film. Finally, our principal got into the digital video act, learning how to start a YouTube channel and uploading her video. She experienced a valuable lesson in the risks of Web 2.0 when she received inappropriate comments from a stranger about her video, which brought home for her the importance of digital citizenship education for our students.

Our learners had the time to try projects that demanded more spare time than is usually available to teachers. Two 6th grade teachers wanted to learn Skype's free web-based videoconferencing tool and try Skyping people they knew in countries the 6th graders were studying for geography. One of our kindergarten teachers was interested in motivating some of her reluctant writers, so she registered for ePals and started the long process of finding a matching school and project; the results were some very excited kindergartners writing and illustrating mini-autobiographies for their kindergarten e-pals in Texas, then receiving and reading the life stories of the Texas friends, many of whom spoke Spanish at home. Our music teacher embarked on a self-taught course in Garage Band and iPods in order to provide her students with a new way to compose music. Our Physical Education teacher tried using digital video to enhance her students' fitness, and found that the students responded in a focused way to their fitness goals when they were able to video themselves and assess their progress. She also experimented with a Wii gaming system fitness program and found that students' wait time and the virtual aspect might actually make PE less fun. Students would be spending *less* time exercising and more time in line! Our school nurse even got into the act and created her own wellness blog for the adults in the building to support each other's health and exercise goals during the winter.

List of projects in hand, my job was to make sure they got the most out of our precious window of time for hands-on learning. Using follow up e-mails and face-to-face conversation, I then tracked the various projects and needs of my colleagues.

With my principal's support and funding, I bought equipment and tested out the web-based tools teachers wanted to use. You could consider grant-writing as an alternative if technology funds are not available.) In some cases, I suggested the tool teachers could try; in most, they already had one in mind. If there was a need for a quick tutorial, I wrote one and sent it via e-mail. For example, I let the 6th grade teachers know the equipment they would need for Skype, showed them how to create an account and get audio and video going when Skyping. It was a time crunch to prepare everyone in time for our middle work session, but it was exciting and fun to know I was working toward concrete interests and teachers' goals, rather than creating a workshop that might only interest one or two people.

After the first session, I e-mailed the following to my colleagues:

> Hi folks!
>
> Wow! What a great Exploratorium it sounds like it was! Thanks so much for all of your energy and enthusiasm. You guys are just the greatest bunch to work with ever. I appreciate receiving e-mails with all of your dreams in them, or reports that you're still dreaming and will let me know. Great! You'll get a response from me today about your project and some thoughts I have and this will help me to get going and get prepared for you!
>
> Some of you have already taken steps toward what you want to do, e-mailing people you're going to connect with, coming up with ideas, even putting yourselves on YouTube! That was awesome! If

you haven't taken steps yet, that is exactly right too; you can per-
colate on your idea and we'll start up on the next Exploratorium
session.

Thanks again for being such great teachers and fearless models of risk-
taking!

Kelly

I could tell that they were committed with e-mails like these:

I have ordered a full trial version of Timez Attack (multiplication
computer game) from its author.

I am having my kids do an evaluation of the game. We will consoli-
date our findings and present our recommendations (via a yet to be
determined format) at a future date, after the "evaluation cycle."

Here's what I'd really love to do. . . . I'd love to bring in a Wii Fit and
have it project on the big screen for my classes to participate in.

However, my big dilemma is that I don't have a Wii Fit. Do you
know anybody that does? I think my nieces and nephew got one
for Christmas, so I'm going to check with them to see if I could borrow it. . . . but I really need to borrow one in order for my project
to work. . . . so let me know if you know anybody that has one. . . .

If this doesn't work, I was thinking that we could possibly have different students demonstrate different jump rope skills on the flip
video. We could then use it for demonstration purposes for our
Jump Rope unit, and then finish with our Jump Rope for Heart
event.

I am thinking of doing a few small projects such as using the flip
camera for our weekly Royal Reader.

I loved your video. It was worth it for all of us that you left your comfort zone.

This kind of energy translated quite well to the next session.

## SECOND SESSION OF EXPLORATORIUM: NOISY, HECTIC, AND FUN

The middle session of Exploratorium was noisy, hectic, and fun, as all good
learning tends to be. For this session, I wanted to be there in person, so I
found a substitute to handle my ski mountain duties for the day. As I think
back on this experience, the one sound that comes to mind most clearly is
laughter. One group started Skyping for the first time in the library, shout-
ing, "Are you there? I can hear you but I can't see you! What do I push to
see you?" then erupted into laughter. Meanwhile, another group was filming
itself in a skit, and then sitting down to work through the Flip software.

Our *BookFlix* team was listening to books, calling the Scholastic salesperson to get a quote, and writing up a survey for their students. Other teachers worked alone or in pairs in their classrooms, sifting through the complexities of putting a course on Moodle or creating the look of their first blog. I ran from place to place, checking for questions or troubleshooting technical difficulties. In truth, most of the time the teachers did not need me; they figured things out for themselves and learned a lot more in the process. Just as I have found with my elementary school students, the best learning happens with me checking in on the side, rather than standing up in front of students talking at them.

## THE FINISH LINE: SESSION THREE

The final sharing session sparked inspiration in colleagues as they listened to each other's creative projects. Since some teachers had worked alone on their projects, the social component of the sharing session not only provided the accountability we wanted but also gave them a collegial opportunity to share learning experiences. Everyone received a small prize for playing, then the big prize was unveiled—digital video cameras for every grade level, the *BookFlix* subscription, and a commitment to purchase laptops for each teacher at Mettawee over the next three years. The final session was a celebration of their willingness to work hard at something new, and it was definitely a party atmosphere.

## THE GLOW OF SUCCESS

Our hopes for Exploratorium had come to fruition. Our teachers gave me feedback that they definitely experienced a higher level of engagement in their professional learning. One teacher noted that it "increased her confidence," while another liked "the creativity and flexibility" of this kind of learning. A colleague who lives in a rural area appreciated the time given to her during school to explore because she had no internet access at home, so Web 2.0 learning on her own time was impossible. One teacher liked the combination of "freedom to explore, but also a goal and a deadline to keep me organized." Many said they enjoyed this kind of learning and would like to do it again.

Because teachers started the first session off with a pedagogical goal rather than the technology, they were able to get excited about learning a tool that they strongly believed would fill their teaching needs. This also allowed them a clear way to determine what tool would be relevant or irrelevant, workable or impractical. In addition to higher engagement, all of our teachers gained some measure of confidence in their tech abilities, and most increased their technology problem-solving skills as they encountered all of the typical challenges of working with electronic machines. Most importantly, they definitely got the message that they could try something new and feel rewarded, even if it didn't work out according to plan.

## AFTER EXPLORATORIUM

Although our winter in-service time was now over, I continued to see positive effects from the experience. With the positive message of "it's OK to fail—try it" entering slowly into the school culture and their confidence growing, teachers began to expand what they were willing to try in their classrooms. Our 5th grade teachers wanted to improve their students' writing and presenting skills as exemplified by the state standard, so they took advantage of an offer by our US senator to Skype with their class. Each student wrote and presented a question for the senator, practicing their writing skills and their ability to make a presentation in front of an adult who was very important to our state.

I was looking for a chance to make connections outside of our school, and our primary teachers wanted a way to show their students the real-world application of learning writing skills, so we embarked on "Blogging Buddies," weekly blog entries created by 1st and 2nd graders, with commenting provided by college students enrolled in a local college's teacher prep program. Our students loved having a big buddy who read their writing every week, and they really understood that their writing was important and that it communicated a message to others; for their part, the teacher prep students got a chance to see what real 1st and 2nd grade sentence structure, grammar, and spelling look like.

A 5th grade teacher wanted to spark more discussion in her literature circles, so she set up a wiki to see if the power of social networking and computers could energize her students' conversations; she was pleased with the results and has used a wiki for all of her language arts studies ever since.

A district initiative to pursue more formative assessment was a challenge to one of our 4th grade teachers until she tried having her students film each other on the Flip video answering their assessment questions. In all of these cases, the teachers started with their challenge and then considered what might be a useful way to meet the challenge with technology. They had learned to expand their horizons through their professional development practice.

With expanded horizons came expanded purchases. It was an exciting new world, knowing that our purchases stemmed directly from teacher's immediate interests in making change in their classrooms. In the time since our Exploratorium, we have purchased more Flip video cameras, several Kindles, more document cameras, projectors for each classroom, iPads, a microphone for podcasting, and enough netbooks to have a one-to-one laptop set-up in 5th and 6th grade, close to one-to-one ratio in 4th grade, and another cart of netbooks for the lower grades to share. The initial promise of laptops for every teacher was met as well. In two short years we have become equipment-rich compared to the days of the Exploratorium.

## WHERE DID THE MONEY COME FROM?

The money to do this came from a variety of sources. Some of it represents a shift in priorities to technology in our schoolwide plan and thus the budget line items; some came from reallocating funding once spent on software and videos as we continued to transition to free Web- or cloud-based tools and resources. We became more savvy and aggressive in seeking (and winning) grants, and we were able to leverage our technology success with students to win more grants. We also used more down-to-earth sources like the points earned through our grocery store chain incentive card! From all of these efforts, we have grown from a place that hoped just to get teachers to experiment with new technology, to a place that has teachers who are ready to put the new technology right into the students' hands.

## THE LIBRARIAN'S CHANGING ROLE

My role changed during the Exploratorium as well. Before our experiment, I sometimes felt like a professional nag, throwing tools in front of my colleagues and expecting them to try them, feeling disappointed in my efforts if they did not. During Exploratorium I became more of a travel agent, giving them a map to their destination of choice, providing directions and checkpoints, obtaining tickets for them, even riding along on the bus and narrating. Sometimes the trip would go in a different direction, or the transportation might fail us, but they always made their final destination, because that was improving their teaching for students. The journey always improved their skills as a teacher. On a personal level, I much preferred adding value to something they had chosen rather than asking them to find value in every presentation about technology they attended.

Of course, not every minute of our professional development was packed with value. There were limitations of time and resources. Because I could only attend two of the three sessions, I wasn't able to give on-site immediate support in that first session. On the other hand, my absence in the initial session may have provided freedom and independence for those learners who might have felt constrained by or dependent on my suggestions. Some teachers challenged themselves less than others, but I believe all of them made progress from their varied starting points.

## SINCE THAT FIRST EXPLORATORIUM

Unfortunately we weren't able to set aside the time the following year for a similar hands-on learning time during winter in-service. The demands of other professional development initiatives had to take precedence for that year. Exploratorium continued to have a positive effect on our thinking in general, however. Although we couldn't repeat the Exploratorium session the next year, we did try other transformative professional development sessions, such as asking two 5th grade students to train teachers to use the Nintendo DS to improve spelling and computation practice. We wanted to find new ways to have our students take charge of their own learning, and we thought teaching adults would be a great place to start. The positive experience of differentiation we had in Exploratorium led us to see the benefit of carving out release time and individualized instruction for teachers when tackling new initiatives like a new learning management system or online assessment for students. Exploratorium had changed our way of thinking about training and learning in general.

## YEAR THREE: MOVING ON: EXPLORATORIUM 2.0

This year, my school brought back hands-on professional development with Exploratorium 2.0. Once again, it was teachers who wanted to share their enthusiasm from a technology conference who inspired our return to self-directed learning. One colleague suggested that the format and framework of Exploratorium would work well, rather than a standard presentation on tools they had learned about at the conference. We lobbied our principal for the time, and after agreeing that all projects would be approved to ensure that they were in sync with our district's goals, our principal again devoted three sessions of winter ski in-service time. After several years of expanding technology, my hours had been expanded as well, and now that I was a full-time employee, I could be there in person to arrange challenging technology trips for all of my teachers. Even better, three other teachers were travel agents along with me. In this round, we asked our teachers to step up their game from last time. Following our superintendent's district goal for personalized learning for every student, teachers again started with their students in mind, or even one student in mind, and came up with a learning challenge they wanted to solve. Although I think they enjoyed me more on video, I was pleased to be there this time to start them on their journey. After a fun introduction, three of my colleagues offered presentations on possible tools in the area of math, science/social studies, and language arts. We asked that teachers pilot their project with students this time and share their experiences using a Google Doc (http://docs.google.com), an online collaborative word processing tool, so we could reflect and comment to each other. It was amazing to think how far we had come that we knew all of our teachers could use this collaborative tool easily. Just as in our previous Exploratorium, the bottom line was that the process and learning were more important than having a "successful" product. We asked them to share what worked and what didn't so that their colleagues could benefit from their advice.

The results this year were terrific. A kindergarten teacher who had students with handwriting issues did a pilot test of the iPad's handwriting apps to see whether daily use for several weeks would make a difference, and it did. A 4th grade teacher met the needs of some of her gifted students who wanted to publish their writing by learning to use *Mixbooks*, a free web-based publishing tool with which students can write, illustrate, and publish a book online. One teacher who is a bit timid and reluctant with new tools decided she would attack that weakness and find every possible pedagogical use of a document camera in her classroom, use it almost daily if she could, until she amassed data on its usefulness for her students and got over her fears of setting up new equipment in her classroom—she accomplished both. Two teachers wanted to find out more about using a Wii remote and some software as an inexpensive way to create a Smart Board and then see what changed for their students' math and language arts learning. That project started a wave of enthusiasm among our teachers for this new technology, and it is a grassroots effort; I still have not had time myself to learn how to use it.

Overall, a major part of the success of the Exploratorium is that it fit right in with our sense of community: we supported each other in taking risks and trying something new. We were empowered as teachers and trusted to know what was best for our students and classroom.

Perhaps my favorite part of this year's Exploratorium was the sharing session. One of my colleagues had the idea of using the last session to share, but not to share in front of each other. While we did see the value of coming together, she felt that people would not have as much time to discuss the various projects if we used the time to have mini-presentations. As a relatively shy presenter herself, she also felt many of the teachers would be focused on having to get up in front of the room and present, and that would detract from their attention for other presentations. So we agreed that teachers would all share at the same time, but would do it via Google Docs. For our three-hour time together, teachers spent the first hour writing their own reflection, answering a series of questions. I circulated through the building, solving any technical glitches that came up. For the next two hours, teachers would be asked to read at least three other reflections and comment on them. The session was a huge success. Teachers enjoyed the freedom to sit in their own classrooms, not on the spot to present, perhaps sitting with a friend or two while they reflected. Almost every teacher ended up reading and commenting on all of their colleagues' work rather than sticking with the minimum. And, most importantly, some fantastic conversations arose about our students' learning, practical issues, recommendations for purchase or training, and there were lots and lots of compliments to each other. I don't think these conversations would have happened if we had tried presentations or if we had asked teachers to do the reflections and commenting on their own time outside of school. There was an element of freedom and fun to this virtual conversation that allowed all of us in our own classrooms to talk to each other across the hallways, each of us munching on a snack, or taking small breaks to make photocopies, enter grades, or walk to a friend's room and laugh about the instant messaging aspect of the whole afternoon.

This spring, in response to teacher requests, I have partnered with a local college to offer a one-credit course about transforming teaching for the 21st-century classroom. It was generated by a need from a colleague, it was designed in-house, it is based on pedagogical challenges, and it will proceed in a hands-on manner. The Exploratorium model seems to be a structure that continues to work for us.

Challenge and opportunity are words that perfectly describe our current era of education. When we challenged ourselves to engage in a new kind of professional development at my school, we created new opportunities for learning and growth. Most importantly, we moved past a sort of boundary with Exploratorium, and I can tell we'll never go back. There has been a cultural shift at our school that has led to new conversations, new purchases, new ways of teaching our students. It is my belief that the pedagogy-based, homegrown, hands-on aspects of Exploratorium will remain a part of our professional development program. Perhaps most importantly we have a new attitude: one that favors risk taking, experimenting, and traveling in new directions.

## REFERENCES

International Society for Technology in Education. 2007. *National Educational Technology Standards for Students.* Retrieved December 28, 2011, from http://www.iste.org/standards/nets-for-students/nets-student-standards-2007.aspx.

International Society for Technology in Education. 2008. *National Educational Technology Standards for Teachers.* Retrieved December 28, 2011, from http://www.iste.org/standards/nets-for-teachers/nets-for-teachers-2008.aspx.

Partnership for 21st Century Skills (P21). 2011. *Framework for 21st Century Learning.* Retrieved December 28, 2011, from http://www.p21.org/overview/skills-framework.

## Acknowledgment

The author would like to express gratitude to all of her colleagues at the Mettawee School and particularly principal Nancy Mark and her colleagues involved in Exploratorium 1 and 2: Jennifer Bloomingdale, Diane Mach, Mark Rampone, and Cindi Roberts.

# Tips for Starting Hands-on Professional Development

- **Start with a grassroots interest.** What do your pioneer teachers know that would be great for others to learn? What are the interests of your colleagues?

- **Dedicate the time for teachers to explore and play.** Doing so gives a message that their learning is important; asking teachers to learn on their own time means that only those who love to play with technology will do so.

- **Build in time for preparation.** Allowing teachers to choose their own projects means you will need time to provide equipment, software, and introductory tutorials.

- **Give up your own need for control.** Allow teachers to explore tools they think will work for them, rather than your own favorites.

- **Have a system for checking in with learners to see how they're doing and what support they need.** Go to them and ask because they may be too busy working hard at their daily job of teaching to come to you.

- **Create an atmosphere of risk taking.** Emphasize the process and the learning rather than the product at the end.

- **Ensure accountability** with some form of sharing at the end, but ensure that sharing failures is just as acceptable as sharing successes.

- **Consider the option of inviting teachers to create the projects on their own,** without the students, at least the first time you try. Many teachers don't enjoy being out of control or failing in front of their students. Think about allowing teachers to try their first project in a way that feels comfortable and safe for them. Once you've tried that, teachers will feel more comfortable doing a pilot project with students.

- **Celebrate the learning process of each learner** when sharing is done.

- **Keep the momentum going.** Look for other opportunities to provide hands-on, individualized learning for your adult and kid learners!

– Kelly Ahlfeld, Librarian/Technology Coordinator

From *Growing Schools: Librarians as Professional Developers* edited by Debbie Abilock, Kristin Fontichiaro, and Violet H. Harada. Santa Barbara, CA: Libraries Unlimited. Copyright © 2012.

# Exploratorium: A Teacher's Perspective

Jennifer Bloomingdale

After completing two rounds of the Technology Exploratorium, once as a participant and the second time as a leader, I believe it was one of the most effective professional development opportunities I have ever been a part of.

I loved the idea from the start. The biggest thing for me was that there was time built in for discovery. It allowed us to brainstorm with our coworkers, and then time to actually plan and implement our ideas. I tackled two different projects: exploring my options for creating a class wiki and learning how to use iMovie. I spent a good amount of time exploring the different wiki sites and creating accounts at each. It would have taken me weeks to explore a little bit here and there, but with the time provided through the Exploratorium I was able to do a lot of it in one afternoon.

This "wiki play" inspired me to develop Wiki Literature Circles, which became the center of the literacy program in my classroom. For iMovie, it gave me time to get comfortable with main aspects of the program so I could edit movies for my students. I was able to use this across the curriculum. I began creating movies for when I was going to be absent, using content from Discovery Streaming. I recorded any presentations my students did and then merged them into one full movie that we could view as a class, and students used it to create Book Trailers. It became a very important tool in my teaching. That one professional development experience led to some major changes in my classroom, which I continued to develop and fine tune over the next two years.

Another aspect that I really liked about the program was that it allowed for differentiation. All of the teachers in the building were at different places with their technology integration. The Exploratorium allowed us each to think about our own classroom goals and what we were comfortable with trying. While everyone was pushed to do something out of their comfort zone, I think it helped that everyone was being asked to take a risk and that it was ok that my risk was going to be different from everyone else's. We talk about this all the time within the context of our classrooms, but many times professional development is "one size fits all." By differentiating for all of the experiences, it allowed the teachers to get the most out of their time and the professional development.

In both of our Exploratorium years, I enjoyed hearing what everyone had done and what their experiences were. I think a key component for our success was that we didn't necessarily have to show a finished project, but that we talked about what we noticed in our classroom and if we would continue developing the project.

I thought the strategy that we used for sharing in the second year, using a shared Google Doc for communication and sharing, was highly effective. As someone who doesn't really speak up during faculty meetings, the Google Doc allowed me to really think about what I wanted to say and then comment on everyone's project. Many conversations might not have happened if we had all tried to share verbally in that same amount of time. In many cases, conversations that were started on the Google Doc were continued face-to-face throughout the next week.

# CHAPTER 2
# HUMANIZING ONLINE LEARNING

*Editors' Note:* When California school librarian Susan Geiger realized that her school's rapid deployment of a 1:1 student-laptop program coupled with a bewildering flood of Web 2.0 tools had created both faculty apprehension and a fertile ground for technology training, her library team enthusiastically market a series of playful online tutorials for all the adult learners, followed up by weekly personal help in the library and "drive by" troubleshooting in staff and administrative offices. The fruits of the professional respect she garners with PD that cost the school less than $500 have begun to pay off in opportunities for richer curricular planning.

Concluding the chapter, Jackie Siminitus, whose work inspired Susan and Anne, offers further insights into the design and delivery of online PD based on her own extensive experience as co-developer of the California School Libraries' Learning 2.0 project for school librarians. In turn, these tutorials were based on the original tutorial created for her public library by Helene Blowers, now Director of Digital Strategy and IT at Columbus Metropolitan Library in Columbus (OH), who created the first 23 Things tutorial for the public library in which she worked.

## The 24th Thing:
## How a Web Discovery PD Program Redefined Our Library's Role Within the School

Susan Geiger with Anne Arriaga

## SHINY NEW TOOLS

We had survived the first year of a 1:1 laptop rollout in the 2007 school year. Most of what we had worried about had proven to be no problem. We had worried about charging and whether the laptops would fit on classroom desks—neither proved to be an issue. Teachers worried about classroom management until they realized they could just ask students to close their laptop lids. We were facing problems we hadn't considered: bandwidth issues associated with increased network use and printing volume. Still, things were going well overall.

Our freshmen and sophomore students had taken to their laptops almost without effort. This fall the juniors would come on board, with only the seniors still using the 36 desktop computers in our library lab area. One nagging concern still remained for me: the varying levels of technology confidence of our staff. Some teachers embraced technology while others held their laptops at arm's length as if they were alien objects. I felt it was finally time to take action on my long-held belief that the school needed systematic, practical, hands-on professional development that focused on the application of technology to learning if our school was to address the wide discrepancies in learning.

## WAY BACK WHEN

Moreau Catholic High School began introducing technology in the early 1990s. Like many schools, we began by putting computers in the library and in two student computer labs, which were supervised by the computer science department. Next the technology department created a small technology lab for teachers' use and placed desktop computers on the teacher's desks. Staff development was "owned" by the technology department, which focused on early adoption of administrative tools such as Pearson's PowerSchool, a web-based student information system displaying real-time grades, homework assignments, and attendance records to students and parents.

Of course, some learning applications were introduced. The technology coordinator, Shawna Martin, taught individual staff members how to generate rubrics and how to design WebQuests, which were structured inquiry-oriented online activities. I was very invested in providing web access to resources so, in the mid-1990s, a group of students and I created the school's first website.

While demand for resources and services grew, access to technology was severely limited. Our old library had eighteen desktop computers, not enough for a class, and the computer labs were always booked. Teachers with several sections of the same course encountered difficulties getting all sections consecutively into the labs. The IT department's needs assessment revealed intense teacher frustration; faculty wasn't interested in further training until they had access to enough computers for all their students. This led to the school's decision to renovate the library and develop a 1:1 laptop program.

Indeed, the decision to become a laptop school was in many ways an administrative leap of faith. Despite extensive planning, they had many remaining questions about technology diffusion—but they weren't willing to wait for all the answers. Lauren Lek, the assistant principal for curriculum and instruction, showed a video at a staff meeting about learning to fly an airplane while flying an airplane, her way of acknowledging the absurdity of expecting instant technology integration while simultaneously delivering staff development.

Lek, a young and technologically savvy administrator who was getting a doctorate in educational technology, was eager to share what she was learning and modeled the authentic use of technology in her interactions with faculty. She routinely posted meeting agendas in Google Docs, requiring people to sign up for a Google account in order to view them. During one faculty meeting, she suggested that groups of teachers organize and share the results of a brainstorming session on how to use technology in the classroom using online mapping software. Teachers were expected to use their laptops in ways they might replicate with students.

Shaped by Lek and Martin, the school's philosophy toward technology was generally progressive. Early on, Martin implemented iChat, in-house instant messaging software for Mac computers, so that students, faculty, and administrators could communicate freely with each other on campus. Previously a teacher, she was open-minded about how technology might be deployed in service of learning. She configured the network so that access to the web was generally unfiltered and educators were able to request that websites be unblocked as needed. Categories such as online gambling and pornography sites were filtered, but whole categories of tools were not. Streaming media like YouTube and social networking tools such as Diigo, Twitter, and Facebook were available on the school network with the assumption that these had educational value.

Our newly renovated and enlarged library, furnished with LCD projection screens and flat-screen televisions, had opened the same year as the laptop program. Since the library was the largest academic space in the school and was open until 5:30 every afternoon, it became the logical place for group work to take place. As a result of giving laptops to freshman and sophomores, faculty had begun to assign group projects that took advantage of the programs available in the Mac iLife suite. My assistants or I were available and able to help students with software or networking problems as well as their research tasks after school, so students now saw the library, not the IT department, as the frontline for tech support. I was edging the library towards a learning commons model in which students would think of our facility as a technical support center and production space, as well as a place for their research and reading needs.

## MY OWN CRASH COURSE

I had spent the year before the laptop rollout aggressively working on my own professional growth, subscribing to blogs and Nings and then using the information and links I found to expand my own online Professional Learning Network (PLN). I began pushing relevant Web 2.0 resources and tools to the school's early adopters via e-mail. Using Bloglines, a blog reader, to aggregate all of the blogs I was following, I could click a button and send a significant blog post to selected teachers or administrators along with my comments. I sent relevant executive summaries of newly released white papers announced on Gary Price's Resource Shelf (now InfoDocket.com) blog to our economics teacher. I found statistical data, reports, and studies of other 1:1 programs for our administrators and content-area resources for departments or individual teachers. Since my suggestions were tailored to their interests, pedagogy, and curriculum needs, teachers and administrators began to see me as a resource expert. As the conference co-organizer of Internet@Schools, a K–12 subconference held in conjunction with the Internet Librarian and Computers in Libraries conferences, I was being exposed to powerful and creative uses of technology within school, academic, public, and special libraries. The more I understood the new technology landscape, the easier I found it to connect ideas I had heard at conferences, read in magazines, or learned from my PLN with our school's situation.

My hope was that eventually teachers would develop their own PLNs, but waxing lyrical about my own Twitter network wasn't going to make that happen. My own learning experience was showing me that it would take multiple exposures, time, and recognition of a need before networked learning became habitual. I began targeting marketing to specific groups and individuals. Responding to the school's push toward e-learning resources and teacher-driven rather than textbook-driven curriculum, a number of math teachers became interested in joining Escape the Textbook, a vibrant community of math teachers on EdWeb. I scoped out subject-specific groups in Diigo such as Resources for Languages, and then encouraged the modern languages teachers to join.

## SPEED BUMPS AND MISFIRES

Students in the yearbook and journalism classes had begun Adobe InDesign but, in general, teachers were not familiar with Mac software and applications since prior to this the classroom computers were all PCs. Therefore, the year before the freshman and sophomore classes were given laptops (2006), administrators gave Macs to a small pilot group of influential educators in hopes of jumpstarting technology use among faculty. This group, called the Trailblazers, received training provided by Apple. When laptops were distributed to the entire faculty midyear, school-wide trainings continue to concentrate almost exclusively on Mac applications. Teachers grew comfortable with the iLife suite, and some used iPhoto, iMovie, and GarageBand for their own productivity. However, since the Apple trainers hired by the school came from a K–8 background, their teaching examples were not always tailored to our pre-collegiate population. Anyone who does training with high school faculty knows that when you explain how to teach a technology tool using examples of 3rd graders, you've lost your audience.

Of course, as a result of Lek's administrative leadership, most teachers were *aware* that they should incorporate a broader range of tools into their teaching. I began to see more assignments that required students to use technology but noted that teachers didn't necessarily grasp the impact that the tool would have on a project or how a type of tool could relate to the purpose of the project. Our printers jammed for a few weeks as one teacher after another jumped on the comic strip "bandwagon," assigning Comic Life for relevant and not-so-relevant projects. One teacher assigned both Comic Life and an essay for the same project; she wasn't sure if comics "counted" as a credible learning tool, nor was she clear on how to assess their quality. Another teacher misjudged how long it would take when she asked students to create and edit a ten-minute iMovie. Although the laptop rollout was successful with the freshmen and sophomores, the administration and I wanted to broaden the faculty's understanding of the range of learning opportunities. How could teachers begin to alter their instruction to maximize the value of a 1:1 initiative given their problematic technology fluency?

As a way to build teaching fluency, administrators asked lower-division teachers who had embraced technology to demonstrate content-specific applications to upper-division teachers in their department. Since upper-division teachers had, as yet, no practical experience using laptops in the classroom (juniors and seniors didn't have their laptops yet), they had little background understanding of how to apply these models to their own curricular needs. Even more problematic, our early adopters were still novices, looking for tools that would adapt to their current lesson plans. They were not prepared to model or discuss how technology could change—or was changing—

---

**Design Tip: Questions to Teach Teachers to Ask Themselves about a Tool's Relevance to the Purpose or Content of an Assignment**

- Have you used this tool yourself?

- What will you have to teach students so that they will use the tool effectively?

- Does the tool make some aspect of learning clearer or easier?

- What educational value will the tool add to the learning process?

- How does the tool encourage collaboration and sharing that was not possible before?

- Are you familiar enough with the tool's affordances and benefits to create a rubric to evaluate student products?

their teaching. The idea for departmental sharing was a good one, but the timing was off. These departmental teaching events did little to advance the hoped-for organic diffusion of technology into teaching and learning.

## DIAGNOSTICS AND REPAIRS

Lek's lead in modeling technology use and the library's success in helping students troubleshoot their tech problems crystallized my thinking about our potential role in sustained, school-wide technology-focused staff development. As I observed the struggle to incorporate technology, it became obvious that the school's training had leapfrogged some very basic skills in the heat of rapidly deploying new technology. We were focused on transforming teaching practice although some teachers were not yet comfortable with basic features on their laptops, some were not aware of the variety of Web 2.0 tools available, and many were not taking advantage of the school's networked environment.

As we helped individual teachers in the library, we noticed that some otherwise excellent teachers were unfamiliar with copying and pasting text or images into a document or creating and manipulating files. Others needed help customizing toolbars with frequently accessed sites and organizing applications on their desktop. At some point everyone had probably received a basic introduction to many of these simple procedures but, without sustained use or real needs, the lessons had not been internalized. By assuming that the faculty had a basic level of computer expertise and focusing instead on specific educational applications, we had inadvertently let some teachers drop through the cracks. While it was not a large group of teachers, it was a very important group to reach. Our experienced faculty, now feeling like novices, was uncomfortable making these changes. They saw little reason to abandon the traditional, paper-based teaching that had worked well—and that they knew to be the bread-and-butter of most college classes.

Did they need a wider range of teaching examples and learning models than the school community could provide? After all, I had learned so much from my own PLN. I reasoned that, if they first became more comfortable with their laptops, they might be more receptive toward investigating the multitude of Web 2.0 tools. Their need for PLNs would grow as they wanted to incorporate technology in more meaningful ways. They would want to find others facing similar challenges. In short, one of my goals became how to help my faculty learn the basics so that they would reach out both within our community and beyond for learning partners, mentors, and experts.

## THE SPEEDWAY TEAM

For my professional development initiative to succeed, support from my library personnel would be critical. Fortunately I had a perfect library team with complementary skills already in place. My assistants Anne Arriaga and Connie Stanton were, if anything, more technically adept than I was. Anne, a new hire, was a student in the San Jose State University online graduate school. She brought infectious enthusiasm and awesome organizational skills to the team. Connie, who has been with me for many years, approached technology fearlessly and continuously conveyed confidence in others' capacity to take the same risks. My long-time relationship with the faculty, a strong rapport with our administration, and a deep understanding of the school's culture rounded out the team's strengths.

The library team had another goal beyond teaching the basics and exposing faculty to PLNs: we believed our *entire* school needed to become a learning community. Like the faculty, the classified staff and administration were experiencing their own technology challenges, as they transitioned to an unfamiliar operating system. While a school-wide learning community with faculty, staff, and administrators on equal footing as learners would be a cultural shift, my team believed that this was the direction that networked technology and tools were taking us anyway. Our team felt that they had the capacity to help everyone feel OK about not knowing all the answers, asking questions, and trying new things. We decided to include everyone in the training.

## REDESIGNING THE CHASSIS

I read about a program known as "23 Things," created by Helene Blowers (2006) at the Charlotte and Mecklenburg County Public Library to help her library staff experiment with emerging technologies and social networking tools. I learned that the California School Library Association had modified Blowers's *Learning 2.0* into *School Library Learning 2.0* for librarians. Then, at the Internet@Schools Conference in Monterey (2008), I heard Jackie Siminitus (see her essay at the end of this chapter) describe Classroom Learning 2.0, targeted to teacher learning. It occurred to me that we could revise the design of her short tutorials to deliver professional development that met our entire school's needs. We would use the same framework, modified for our users, to systematically strengthen technology skills, model use of tools in learning, and expose our faculty, administrators, and staff to resources, services, and social networks in an experimental, playful way.

Our initial planning was shaped by CSLA's Management/User's Guide (http://cslausersguide.csla.net/), a roadmap for managing this type of online tutorial. We chose Edublogs, a WordPress blog platform, to create our 23 Things main blog because it was free, had no ads, was targeted to educators, and was well supported by Sue Waters and the Edublogs team. After reviewing CSLA's *Classroom Learning 2.0*, which is licensed for reuse and adaptation under a Creative Commons License, we began to change the look and feel to match our school community so that our users felt that these exercises had been created especially for them. Some changes, like designing a logo (Figure 2.1) and making sure that the graphics in the main blog featured pictures of the school, were cosmetic. However, the content needed to be rewritten. Anne and I sat together with our laptops on-and-off for about six weeks and went through the CSLA *Classroom Learning 2.0* tutorials word-by-word to create the Moreau Learning Web 2.0 (Figure 2.2).

Figure 2.1: Moreau Logo

We followed the blog format of CSLA's tutorial but edited the text, changed the structure, and replaced several Web 2.0 tools that were out-of-date. Our tutorials covered a variety of Web 2.0 tools such as RSS feeds (a tool that allows information from another website to be updated automatically on a personal web platform), wikis, social bookmarking sites, photo sharing sites, and image generators. They needed to *experience* the excitement of learning rather than approach these tools with an analytical educators' lens. Since our emphasis was on adult learning, we encouraged participants to explore areas of personal interest; anything from food blogs to dog rescue. Like Blowers's 23 Things, each page began with an overview of the Web 2.0 tool followed by practice exercises, examples of the tool, and ways in whe tool might be incorporated into classroom learning.

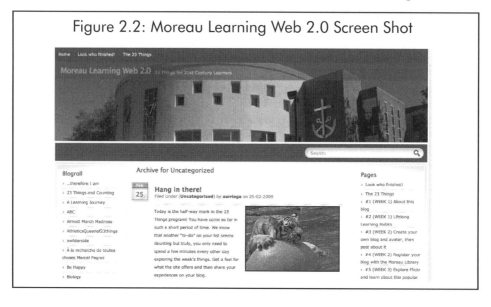

Figure 2.2: Moreau Learning Web 2.0 Screen Shot

Self-discovery and reflection are prominent features of 23 Things. Therefore the first task is for participants to set up a blog in Edublogs, create an avatar image to upload, and begin to narrate their exploration and experimentation.

These blogs were linked from the main site so that participants would be able to follow each other's progress. As they progressed through the tutorials, faculty and staff read each other's blogs, recognizing a sense of community and developing a spirit of cooperative problem solving.

We seeded the discovery tasks with curricular examples from as many departments and classes as we could, then suggested how teachers might apply the "things" in a section of our blog called "Curriculum Connec-tions." In the wiki exercise, we linked to class wikis for science, Span-ish, American history, 10th grade English and a government class. For Flickr's curriculum con-nections, we proposed digital equivalents of presentation formats like magazine covers and poster displays using image generators like Flickr Toys and collage-creators like Glogster.

Play is a compelling feature of 23 Things. In the playful spirit of the original, we added an avatar of Father Moreau (Figure 2.3), our school's founder, intoning "23 Things is good for you." Just as we enjoyed explor-ing 2.0 tools to personalize Moreau's tutorials, we wanted our participants to enjoy experimenting by branding their blogs with unique avatars and mounting banner images after learning to create them in our tutorials.

Once our tutorial was finished, our next undertaking was to provide pow-erful incentives to participate. Our faculty and staff were all very busy teach-ing, coaching, and moderating various club activities, so we needed to make

> ### Design Tip: Make Tasks Lean, Clear, and Focused
>
> We now know that we should have limited each tutorial to one task per week; setting up a blog was difficult enough without also ask-ing participants to create an avatar. Scrutinize each tool, justifying its value to curriculum thoroughly before including it. If you are un-able to both justify and explain a tool clearly, eliminate it.

> ### Design Tip: Don't Measure Success by Adoption of a Single Tool
>
> After 23 Things ended, our participants did not continue to maintain and add to their blogs. While the blogs had been a good vehicle for reflection *during* the PD, faculty didn't turn them into professional reflec-tion blogs. An important lesson here is that tools can be project specific and then retired. That doesn't mean that faculty isn't reflect-ing on their practice. Within our classroom management system, faculty is sharing and reflecting; Moodle is serving a similar, albeit less public, purpose.

the case that they would find their involvement both useful and fun. We also wanted people to buy into a full nine-week commitment, since they would need that time to explore, learn, and reflect.

We added two compelling incentives: T-shirts and jeans. Unless you work at a school with a strict dress code, you might not realize that wearing casual clothing would be seen as a significant privilege by teachers. We designed black T-shirts with the school's logo and the tag line, "23 Things for 21st-Century Learners," both to give teachers cachet with students and to appeal to the sensibilities of the faculty and staff who would wear them. By relaxing our dress code so that all participants could wear jeans and T-shirts every Friday and by financing the T-shirts, our assistant principal of curriculum gave us exactly the support we needed, assuring us that we would have a strong turnout.

---

## Figure 2.3: Playful Learning with Father Moreau

**For this discovery exercise, we want you to have even more fun than you're already having!** Find a few fun images or text generators to play around with and write a post in your blog about one of your favorites and display the result. Often adding the image you mocked up to your blog is as simple as copying and pasting the image into your blog. If not, you may just need to save the picture to your desktop and then add it to your post by using the "tree button" in edublogs to insert an image. If you're having difficulty getting your image added to a post in your blog, ask the library for help.

### Discovery Exercises:

1. Play around with some image generators and find one that you like.

2. Post the image you created in your blog.

Note: Be sure to include a link to the image generator itself, so other participants can discover it too.

Take some time and have fun with this exercise. And remember to be tasteful too!

* To create images, visit FD Flickr Toys, Comic Strip Generator, and/or Image Chef.

### Discovery Resources:

Try searching for image generators using Generator Blog. And check out more image generators on the MCHS Learning Wiki!

If you like this exercise you can take it to the next level and turn your images and/or photos into music videos or cartoons. Check out the MCHS Library's examples:

We picked an all-day professional development session on curriculum mapping as a strategic time to introduce our program. Administration gave us twenty minutes, so Anne produced a humorous video featuring administration, staff, and faculty from all areas of the school answering the question, "Do you have 23 Things?" We filmed ourselves asking them the question and their funny answers. For example, one teacher replied resignedly, "I have 23 essays to grade? Is that what you need?" Nobody was familiar with the 23 Things program, but everyone was now curious about it. Our faculty is collegial and enjoyed seeing themselves and their colleagues on screen; the film focused on potential participants, not on the library. We followed the film with a Letterman-style "Top Ten" slideshow illustrating reasons why someone would want to participate. The faculty learned that the program was online, self-paced, and should only take about fifteen minutes a day at a time of their choosing. Not only were these attractive selling points compared to traditional staff development, they "fit" our goals of individual growth among a community of learners. The last slide announced the surprise dress code incentive—it was the clincher!

During the four weeks before the program began, we marketed 23 Things at least once a week. Once we had about a third of the ninety computer-using faculty, staff, and administration signed on, we made and e-mailed a link to the entire faculty of an Animoto video featuring participant photos set to music (http://animoto.com/play/GELCej3H1bINDp04jdbzdg). Not only were we modeling a tool, but we were also tapping into peer pressure; soon we were up to seventy-seven faculty, staff, and administrators. We wanted to take a group photo of them wearing their T-shirts (Figure 2.4) for the school's website, but it was impossible to gather everyone together during the school day, so we scheduled several photo shoots in the library and created a mash-up with Photoshop, demonstrating another fun technology.

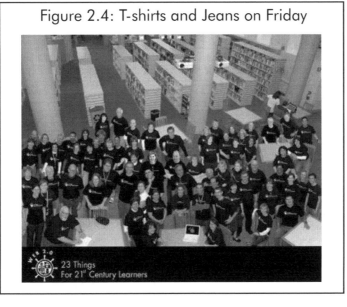

Figure 2.4: T-shirts and Jeans on Friday

Our standard mode of communication was e-mail, a comfortable tool for even the least tech-savvy adult. The IT team created a single 23 Things e-mail address, which enabled us to present ourselves in a unified way in all communication, as well as on all the Web 2.0 examples we created and displayed. This single "persona" solidified our internal unity, reinforced our library "brand," and helped others think of us as a team.

## A HYBRID MODEL

During the first week of the program we established "Tech Fridays" and invited participants to come to the library at any time during the day for treats and assistance. We baked on Thursday nights to provide treats for the following day. Some only took a cookie and left, but they saw us assisting their peers. Others had questions and would stay for their entire prep period. The first two weeks were pretty intense since all participants needed help creating a blog, understanding the format of the program, and building an avatar.

Just thinking of a clever name for a blog caused some anxiety. There were names that reflected participants' ambivalence, like *Rowing Upstream*, *Kicking and Screaming*, *It's Me and I'm Just Learning*, and *I'm a Techie (with Training Wheels)*. The age and experience range was also reflected in blog names; one teacher named her blog *Born Analog* while another used the title *Born Digital*.

The original 23 Things had been de-

---

### Design Tip: Simplify Sign-Ons

Adult learners lose their usernames and passwords almost as often as students. If your IT department doesn't want to create a script so that your faculty and staff can log in to a common password-protected page and authenticate sign-ins from there, either suggest that people use the same login for every site, or create a hard-copy list of the 23 Things tools and have people write their usernames and passwords next to each tool. If you get super-sick of the problem, buy a password manager like RoboForm 2Go for each member of your staff and hope they won't lose the thumb drive.

---

signed as an online learning program, while ours was a hybrid of online learning and face-to-face interactions—a design change that was key to our success. Often all three of us were visible working in the library, often with more than one teacher or staff member (Figure 2.5).

We would greet questioners with enthusiasm and listen carefully. Whether it was how to embed a video into a blog or how to close a window, we offered the same nonjudgmental support. We tried to both acknowledge the challenges and ease their fears. As a dyslexic, it was easy for me to empathize with others' frustrations and stumbling blocks. I would share what I had found confusing and, if I didn't know how to do something, I said I would find out. Interactions were informal and nonthreatening. People learned to trust us because we were coaches and partners; our goal was their achievement.

Since staff and administrators had office responsibilities and couldn't always conveniently come to us, we went to them. We called it "Roadside Assistance." We would drop by offices and, if an administrator had a few moments, we would comment on a great-looking avatar, or admire how attractive the blog appeared, or answer a question on how to embed a picture.

Figure 2.5: Connie Stanton, a Library Assistant, Helping a Teacher

We began to notice that teachers were in the library on other days besides Friday. One teacher liked working on her blog in the library during her prep time and even after school because it took her out of her office routine and gave her the confidence to "get something done" with tech support nearby. It was something she wanted to accomplish because the PD had pulled her out of her comfort zone—something she strived for with her own students.

The success of the program depended on our accessibility and on-the-spot help when participants encountered a roadblock. Our takeaways from this include recognizing the power of as-needed, individualized learning in which librarians are experts, but not the only experts. Group discovery was happening naturally and,

> **Design Tip: Assign Help on the Fly**
>
> Our original plan was to divide participants up among the library team with each of us responsible for a group of learners. While we would have gotten to know a smaller group of adult learners more intimately, we realized almost immediately that just-in-time learning demands just-in-time help—no one appreciates cooling your heels waiting for the "assigned" person.

at one time or another, everyone shifted either into the role of learner or teacher. We knew that this was an effective approach with students, but now we realized that it had equal value for adult learners. This has permanently shaped our thinking about PD; all our staff development features easy availability and immediate help.

## KEEPING THE TRAFFIC MOVING FORWARD

Every week, we crafted a blog post highlighting accomplishments, the link to which was e-mailed to every member of the school community regardless of their participation. While we were certainly cheerleading the participants so that they wouldn't become discouraged, we were also nurturing the idea that everyone was part of our learning community, whether they were observers or participants.

Humor continued to be an important ingredient in our communication. One of the first images used in our blog was a line-drawing of a man labeled "you" with a life preserver labeled "me" jumping from a diving board into a pool called "WEB." When it became obvious that the investment of time we were asking from our teachers was going to exceed the fifteen minutes a day we had so blithely promised, we got plenty of jibes along the lines of, "Only fifteen minutes a day, yeah right!"

Our time estimate was unrealistic because we hadn't factored in participants' basic comfort level with their laptops. For example, some people didn't know how to use keyboard shortcuts or how to modify their browser, while others were very adept. We continue to see that people's confidence in navigating their laptops pays off in terms of their curricular integration of technology.

Very few were able to keep up with the weekly tutorial tasks. While we had not expected this, we encouraged participants to continue at their own pace no matter how slowly. Each week we featured a different teacher's blog in our status post to the community. By celebrating every accomplishment with equal fervor both in person and online, our communication created buzz around the program. It was the main topic of conversation on campus and, sadly, the few faculty and staff who were not involved felt left out. One participant told us that at faculty lunch time, people would compare their progress: "I'm on step 13." Students seeing teachers wearing their 23 Things T-shirts on Fridays would ask, "What are you learning today?"

## LAST LAUGH (NOT)

Not everyone completed all twenty-three tasks in nine weeks. We were only able to officially recognize those who did, presenting them with a "23 Things Superstar Badge" at our year-end staff luncheon. Nonetheless, looking and feeling extremely silly, we composed and performed a cheer using borrowed pompoms from the athletic department as a tribute to all of our faculty and staff. Amid the ensuing laughter, everyone celebrated our collective hard work.

---

**Design Tip: Adapt PD to New Needs**

Tools change rapidly and, given the smaller number of potential participants (we have little personnel turn-over), the extensive revision that would be necessary to update our 23 Things isn't a wise use of our time. In fact, perceptions about the library have shifted. Even without the cookies, faculty has begun to "drive by" us every day. You need help organizing a complex group assignment with multiple parts? Come to the library, we will help you set up Diigo groups to utilize social bookmarking. Looking for an alternative assessment for your US Constitution unit? Come to the library, and we can show you how a wiki can give you the data you need.

---

## IT'S OUR JOB

Since the focus of 23 Things was self-discovery, blog posts were often personal. We learned that a particular history teacher is very passionate about travel and enjoys spending time with his grandchildren. We learned about one of our administrator's favorite holidays. We learned about the personal learning styles of our faculty by watching how they approached the tasks. A few faculty members were entirely independent; we learned of their progress through their posts. We connected with them by responding to their posts and featuring their blogs in our weekly updates. This was a group we would target later on as technology leaders. By watching and listening, we were able to share the frustrations and accomplishments of participants and forge personal relationships.

Building on the relationships we created during the 23 Things and the school's move toward teacher-driven curriculum, we have subsequently been collaborating with several teachers on substantial long-term assignments. One is a world history research project assigned by the chair of the social studies department. She had worked with the library team to design her 23 Things blog and was used to coming into the library with questions. When she approached us for help preparing her students for a particular research project, we jumped at the chance to contribute. We had read "Teaching Students to Form Effective Questions" by Tish Stafford in the Sept/Oct 2009 issue of *Knowledge Quest* in which she created a special presentation for her classes. [See Chapter 10 for Stafford's own professional development journey.]

While we were pleased that some teachers turned to us when designing their curriculum, we felt that others still seemed confused about our role within the curricular life of the school. We did want to make sure we held on to the time slot during the all-day staff development that begins each semester at Moreau Catholic, so we decided to create a presentation for the entire faculty highlighting some of our collaborative endeavors with teachers. We called it "It's Our Job" (Figure 2.6). We invited the teachers we had worked with to participate in the presentation and share their experiences working with us. While the faculty enjoyed our presentation, it was the testimonials from other teachers that really made an impact on our audience.

---

### Figure 2.6: Final Slide of "It's Our Job" Presentation

You Dream It . . .
We will build it for you.
We will help you use it.
We will learn something new together.
This is our job.

---

For weeks after our presentation, faculty came into the library asking various questions followed by, "It's your job!" One social studies teacher explained how this slogan changed her view of the library. "Understanding the library's role opened up the possibilities for me as a teacher to incorporate technology tools into my classes without feeling that I had to be an expert. For example, I don't know how to use Glogster, I come down to the library, and you help me learn it. You find and add informational resources to our online platform (LibGuides) and that becomes our textbook."

## THE 24TH THING

We believe that the 24th thing is the solid connection we have built between professional development and the librarians. The library is the road to professional development and personal learning, whether we are connecting teachers to individuals in their field or providing targeting learning sessions (Figure 2.7) at meetings. It's our job. We have been asked to develop all-day summer PD training for one department and are being presented with a wealth of future possibilities because we have redefined our role within the school community and shaped how professional development will be approached in the future.

## A GPS TIP FOR OTHERS ON THIS ROAD

To some librarians reading this story, it may seem as if we've focused on technology and abandoned the traditional roles of a school librarian. In our view, as our laptop school embraces hybrid instruction using Moodle, the school library needs to respond to the new needs of our learners and teachers. We're not sure which came first, but we've seen a connection between participating in 23 Things and a growing adventurous attitude. By supporting risk taking, teachers become independent and experienced users of computers and new technology. For the school librarian who has been swinging wide the doors to professional learning, the opportunity to influence teaching practice and the curriculum is within reach.

We have enhanced traditional library services and resources by integrating them into both the virtual and physical classroom. If teachers want to include resources and tools in their Moodle courses, we provide LibGuide training for teachers so that they can partner with us in creating interactive online research guides and subject-specific pathfinders linked to our eBook and database resources as well as to the videos, images, RSS feeds, surveys, and other tools that they learned about in 23 Things.

During our now regular professional development day slot, in order to make our role as co-teachers transparent, we debuted our library instructional offerings as a course catalog (http://bit.ly/pMa0pa) modeled after that of Wyoming Seminary's Kirby Library. We used Yudu, a free eBook publishing format, because it allowed us to produce a professional-looking document that mirrored our school's course catalog for students. The library's version includes everything from basic freshman orientation to note taking and works cited creation using NoodleTools, from presentation skills to advanced Google searching techniques.

Figure 2.7: Anne Arriaga (left) and Susan Geiger (right)
Participating in a Curriculum Meeting

As a result of including staff and administration in our PD, our relationship with administrators has changed. They see the library team as problem solvers and partners in school-wide initiatives. Recognizing that our incoming 9th grade tech camp training needed to be updated, we volunteered to revamp the entire curriculum and created an online course that featured screencast videos for teachers and students to follow.

Following the success of the new Tech Camp model, we have taken on other projects at the request of our administration. Our assistant principal of instruction asked for an online tutorial for first offenders of our academic integrity policy, so we built a self-guided tutorial on Moodle featuring instructional content and interactive quizzes. We included videos of teachers explaining the difference between group work and copying, and students giving advice on how to respond when approached inappropriately by peers to share work.

Since the school is implementing e-portfolios for students, we created a model resource site with research resources, e-portfolio examples, and a training module for teachers on using Google Sites for e-portfolios. Cumulatively our work has positioned the library team as the training experts within the community. Our 23 Things is referred to by our faculty, staff, and administration as a transformative experience not just for individuals, but for our school.

# The Model for Susan and Anne's Tutorial

Jacquelyn (Jackie) Siminitus

When offering a professional development course, it is useful to **know your audience**. For example, do you already have a pool of PD participants or are you offering something new, where potential participants will need incentives or encouragement of some sort? The Learning 2.0 courses are all online and self-paced. Individuals or groups can participate. When a school or district offers the course, participants will probably expect time off, hands-on workshops, and possibly a certificate of completion. On the other hand, participants who take the initiative to complete the course on their own time because they want to learn the new tools need only to know the course exists, and they are off and running. It is important to realize that self-starters are in the minority; most beginners need a lot of incentives including "lab time" to learn alongside colleagues. Accept this and you won't be disheartened by those who do not get to the finish line!

The **top desired goal** of the online PD courses is to prepare and build teacher librarians as **technology leaders** on campus. The general public and many fellow educators associate the school librarian's role with reading and books, not necessarily instruction, online resources, professional development, or collaboration. A secondary goal is to provide teacher librarians with useful, creative and fun tools to enhance teaching and learning. Both goals contribute to a school's move into 21st-century learning.

Originally we didn't anticipate that those who successfully complete the course would be able to immediately offer a similar course or series of workshops to fellow teachers—but this has proved to be common. In other words, the online tutorial became a train-the-trainers model. We also found that the online learning experience gave educators a valuable taste of how today's workforce learns new material and how many graduate schools are educating their students. Large corporations with national or global workforces were the first to move training to online courses or tutorials. In doing so, they saved millions if not billions of dollars a year in both productivity and travel costs. Graduate school programs followed the corporate lead with online programs that drove down their costs, and quickly and efficiently provided equal access to specialized knowledge. Susan's strategy of offering "roadside assistance," T-shirts, Tech Fridays, and treats was an effective way to bridge the differences between the public and private sector. It is wonderful to see how a strong school library team can transform a school.

Learning 2.0 is divided into nine weeks or 23 "things." The modules begin by laying out the concept of lifelong learning and explaining the framework of what participants need to do. The first real assignment is to create a basic no-frills blog and to post a message. Each assignment after that is meant to build familiarity with and ownership of their blog. For example, creating and adding an avatar is an exercise in identifying, copying, and pasting html code. The photo assignment asks participants to upload an image, introducing them to the blog picture tool. In many cases, participants don't use simple blog features like using bold, underline, or links until several weeks later. While participants proceed at different rates and with varied problem-solving skills, all who finish experience a strong sense of accomplishment, a desire to celebrate and to share their excitement.

Ideally, the Learning 2.0 tutorials are meant to be taken with a group of fellow participants, so they can comment each other's blogs. Identifying with cohorts is a powerful support mechanism, whether the group is from one school, district, state, or country! When the California School Library Association (CSLA) offered the first tutorial (summer 2007), a team of five "peer cheerleaders" volunteered to follow blogs and provide fun, positive comments. Participants responded enthusiastically to these coaches. The CSLA co-developers sent welcome and congratulation messages at the start and finish, then wrote news items for the association's listserv and monthly journal. They also set up a curriculum wiki for participants to contribute to for an assignment related to wikis.

About 10 percent of our membership participated over that first summer from homes spread across the state. The leadership group learned a lot that first year, including that most individuals really like an immediate payoff; they are less reticent if they are learning in a social setting that is fun. Marketing strategies, regular reminders, interim celebrations, and the creative use of new media messages also keep the energy level high. For more ideas, see our Users Guide at http://cslausersguide.csla .net/.

Nonetheless a sizeable group of participants from that first year still have parts of the course on their "to do" list. During the following school year we saw an increase of group participants as part of district-led professional development initiatives. When a school or district decides that all their librarians or library staff will take the course as their PD goal, fun and motivation increases; more participants finished that second year because everyone was cheerleading each other after school in a lab setting with refreshments, as well as online.

In 2010, led by Connie Williams who has authored another chapter in this book (Chapter 6), the CSLA 2.0 team offered a teen- and teacher-tested version of the 23 Things focusing on digital citizenship and online manners called Tools2Create (http://tools2create.pbworks.com). Designed for middle school and high school students and for after-school programs, this second-generation of tutorials keeps evolving.

In 2011, Dr. Lesley Farmer developed another professional development tutorial for CSLA called "Digital Citizenship" (http://ecitizenship.csla.net) with the goal of teaching educators and their students "to use technology safely, responsibly, critically, and pro-actively to contribute to society."

Finally, to understand how these tutorials have grown from a single public library to worldwide adoption, read Helene Blowers' advice on making the most of 23 Things, at http://www.schoollibraryjournal.com/article/CA6600689.html.

# CHAPTER 3
# CONTINUOUS IMPROVEMENT,
# LESSON BY LESSON

*Editors' Note:* Introducing this chapter is Catherine Lewis, a distinguished research scholar at Mills College, where she directs two federally funded studies of "Lesson Study"—a collaborative, teacher-led approach to improving instruction. Lewis hails from a family of three generations of public school teachers, and her writings and videotapes, including *Lesson Study Step by Step: How Teacher Learning Communities Improve Instruction* (Heinemann, 2011) and *Can You Lift 100 Kilograms?: The Lesson Research Cycle* (Mills College Lesson Study Group, 2000) have introduced educators on four continents to Lesson Study.

Anne Stokes, an elementary school librarian in Scarsdale, New York), details how she is learning to lead from the middle during the intensive Lesson Study process of framing deep conversations about pedagogy and student learning around a single "research lesson." Throughout the three phases—planning a lesson, observing students respond to that lesson, and analyzing student learning—Anne's full participation in collegial planning and learning and in peer observations brings her credibility as a teaching partner. She reflects on how her new expertise and deepening faculty relationships can facilitate future professional learning for and with her colleagues.

# Introduction to Lesson Study

## Catherine Lewis

In Lesson Study, teachers collaboratively plan, observe, and analyze actual classroom lessons, building shared knowledge about teaching and learning. Lesson Study is the heart of professional development in Japan, and has spread rapidly around the world since the first English-language videos and descriptions became available (see http://www.lessonresearch.net for a sampling).

Lesson Study is a cycle of four basic activities. First, teachers engage in "curriculum study"—they study curriculum and research that illuminate the content to be taught or issues in teaching and learning more broadly. In the case described by librarian Anne Stokes, the teachers had a mutual interest in the inquiry process and wanted to use its methodology to reshape their classroom instruction. The next step in the Lesson Study cycle is that teachers collaboratively plan a lesson designed to bring to life what they learned during curriculum study; in this case, teachers aimed to help students develop skills and habits of scientific inquiry as they investigated ants. In the third step of the Lesson Study cycle, one team member teaches the collaboratively designed "research lesson" (so called because it allows teachers to study student learning), while the others observe and record students' learning. Finally, in step four, team members conduct a structured post-lesson discussion, reporting observations of student activity during the lesson and drawing out the implications for design of the lesson and for teaching and learning more broadly.

Although many US teachers have written about their Lesson Study work, this may be the first account written from the perspective of a librarian. Anne Stokes provides compelling examples of why librarians will want to participate in this classroom-focused, collaborative, educator-led form of professional learning. Educators in this Lesson Study group learned fascinating lessons about the design of inquiry science lessons—and about teaching and learning more broadly. For example, they learned that placing many pictures of ants on the table shared by a small group of students was not as effective as placing one picture, since sharing a single picture prompted students to converse rather than talk in parallel. Using the Lesson Study process, the educators in this group developed and tested ideas about the experiences and teaching models that would help students *wonder about* and question their observations.

Lesson Study is not just about observing a lesson and improving it—although it is about that. Lesson Study supports educators to become leaders of continuing improvement at their schools. Lesson Study builds a collaborative school culture, in which teachers look at practice together, carefully observe student learning, and use their observations to keep improving instruction. In this chapter, Anne Stokes provides a view into the beginnings of a culture of Lesson Study as it emerges at a school.

# My First Lesson Study: A Collegial Approach to Professional Development

## Anne Stokes

I am the librarian at an elementary K–5 school of approximately four hundred students. It is one of the five elementary schools in our district. Situated in a relatively affluent suburban community in New York State, our school has a large English Language Learning (ELL) population with students from all over the world. The library offers a mixture of fixed classes with opportunities for flexible scheduling. The school has a vibrant Teachers' Institute in which teachers, guest lecturers, and occasionally administrators run professional development (PD) classes. Teachers participate voluntarily according to what they feel they need and what works with their schedule. I have taken many institute courses and have co-taught some. One such course was Lesson Study.

Lesson Study is designed to improve instruction and, through better instruction, to improve student learning. We use a modified version of Japanese Lesson Study (Lewis and Tsuchida 1998; Stigler and Hiebert 1999), a systematic study of teaching practice through close examination of what is called a "research lesson." Teams of teachers focus on both how a teacher presents material and more importantly how the students learn it. Participants are extremely attentive to all aspects of the Lesson Study cycle: planning, teaching, revising, reteaching, and assessing their lesson. Throughout the cycle the team reflects on the design and implementation of the lesson, on how it fits within curriculum, as well as how and what the children are learning. To an outsider the focus may seem to be on a single lesson, but there are much larger benefits to the teacher and school that include a better understanding of how to teach various subject matter, expertise in observing and gathering important data on students, growth of peer-to-peer faculty accountability, and the development of connections with one's colleagues as part of a community of learners.

Lesson Study reminds me of my weekly training sessions as a pre-service teacher. We would share experiences with our mentor and carefully examine why we were doing what we did. The gratification and insights that I gained from reflective learning has guided my professional work as a teacher and a teacher-librarian. I believe that Lesson Study experiences will have a similar long-lasting impact.

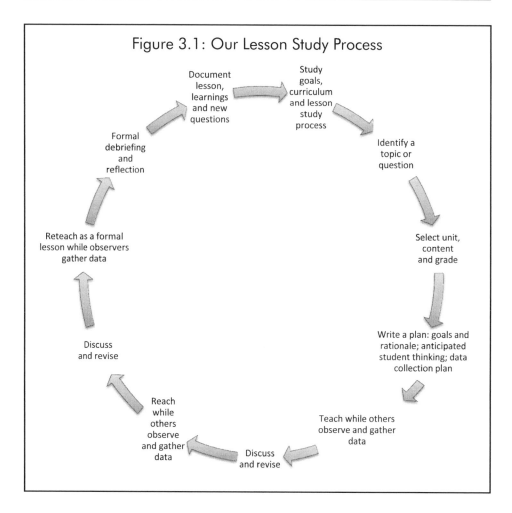

Figure 3.1: Our Lesson Study Process

I was intrigued by the interest that was generated when Lesson Study was introduced in the district's Teacher Institute. Generally I want to participate in new professional directions, especially when teachers will devote time and attention to them. If I build collegial relationships during PD work, I find that my cohort-teachers are more open to collaboration and innovation afterwards. An added benefit of collaborating in PD, of course, is that it serves to coordinate the work that the teachers and I do with students.

Our district employs district-level helping teachers who are responsible for coordinating curriculum and helping site-based teachers with curriculum implementation in different subjects. When a new math helping teacher joined our faculty, he spoke highly of Lesson Study as a deeply enriching form of professional growth. He had studied its use in Japan and showed videos of teachers using it. During his first year he helped groups study lessons in mathematics but, in the second year, several teachers in my building, including myself, asked him to help us broaden Lesson Study into other areas of the curriculum. Since teachers in Lesson Study groups meet formally and informally quite often, it was an advantage for us to be from the same building.

## DEVELOPING LEARNING GOALS

At the beginning of the 2009–2010 school year our entire faculty met to work on building-level goals that would mesh with the district-wide goals developed previously by administrators and the Board of Education. All teachers would be expected to implement these building-level goals in their own way. Since Lesson Study is grounded in learning goals for students, teachers who were involved with Lesson Study would use them as the foundation for the specific lesson they created. Our principal's enthusiasm in and discussion of Lesson Study showed that he expected everyone to learn about it, even teachers who did not participate in a group. Indeed

---

### The Role of Administration in Growing Site-Based Leaders

My administrator's curriculum leadership both supports my work and serves as a model for my own participation. When he sees a positive direction for the school, he rolls up his sleeves and gets to work. He is there when we brainstorm the direction of a study or, if he hasn't been able to be involved in early planning, he is sure to inquire about the direction that a group is taking. Whenever he sees that people are struggling with a topic, he will suggest others to consult. Since he is very familiar with the professional library, he will often ask to sign out a book in the name of the teacher he is helping.

---

he and two helping teachers were course leaders of the large Lesson Study class we had formed as part of the Teachers Institute. Out of this class smaller Lesson Study groups would eventually form.

A Lesson Study goal or focus may remain the same for an entire school year or it may be a broader, multiyear goal with different yearly subgoals. In our case the entire faculty developed a building-based, long-term goal and subgoal that the Teacher Institute's Lesson Study class then used to guide their work.

---

### Building-Level Goals

**Goal:** To develop a student-centered learning community that fosters children's abilities to think critically and creatively, communicate their understanding, and reflect on their learning.

**Subgoal:** To develop student-centered lessons in a learning environment that promotes risk taking.

---

The building-level goal and subgoal fit nicely into the district's goals of critical and creative thinking. They also matched my library goal to encourage inquiry-based learning. I want students to be able to use the resources of our library to pursue their own curiosity.

## LEARNING ABOUT LESSON STUDY

Once we finished creating building-level goals, the Teacher Institute's Lesson Study class began to meet after school. To ground ourselves in this new pedagogy, we read and discussed several articles and saw some video clips of teachers developing and studying lessons. We watched the same math topic being taught in several different ways and then discussed how we had seen children learn the same material differently in each teacher's lesson. While I found the videos somewhat didactic, they did convey the attention to detail and the reflective attitude that we would need to develop to do our own Lesson Study. Equally important, they documented the improvement in children's ability to think mathematically, a result of thoughtful, child-centered teaching.

During this exploratory stage, both individually and collectively, we began to ask ourselves, "Which lesson do we want to use?" By January we had evolved into groups by interest. My group consisted of five teachers: a kindergarten and a 1st grade teacher; a "teacher in charge" who was formerly a 1st grade teacher now working under the principal; a science helping teacher who had taught older students; and me, the librarian who was also a former elementary-classroom teacher. We met during lunch and after school about seven or eight times. Most meetings were about an hour, although, occasionally, they were longer. While there was no formal facilitator, each meeting had an agreed-upon focus. The principal gave the classroom teachers release time with assigned substitutes. I had to reorganize my time by rescheduling classes or having the library aide take the class.

I had worked closely with one teacher in our group for several years and, as we all shared our ideas and our curiosity about how children learn and question, I became confident that we would all learn to work well together on the same goal. This is essential since Lesson Study assumes that all members are equal, that decisions will be developed through consensus, and that everyone is equally responsible for the outcomes. Ultimately our team would need to debrief a polished lesson and explain the rationale for all our teaching decisions in front of the entire Teacher Institute Lesson Study class. To insure collective and individual accountability, our team would develop a minutely detailed lesson plan that included carefully thought-out replies to students' anticipated responses. The lesson would be taught, revised, and retaught in front of many colleagues before we delivered our final, public lesson. Eventually each team within the Teacher Institute Lesson Study class would complete this process, so that everyone would see many polished lessons. Each group would write up the rationale for the lesson, its place within a curriculum unit, and its alignment with state standards. These write-ups would be placed in binders for others to refer to, use, or modify.

## OUR FOCUS ON INQUIRY LEARNING

There was a wide range of interests among the groups in the Lesson Study class. One team wanted to study how to teach children about the physical features birds use to eat, while another wanted to focus on electromagnets, and a third wanted to study the teaching of a specific reading skill. While members of my team had been drawn to Lesson Study for different reasons, we found that we had a common interest in inquiry learning. One teacher had been part of a district-wide committee on inquiry. Yet another had gone to a science inquiry workshop at the Exploratorium in San Francisco and wanted to implement what she had learned. A third wanted to explore what she perceived as a contradiction between what she had read about inquiry and what she felt she knew about early childhood development. The previous summer I had taken a course with Dennie Palmer Wolf on building a climate of inquiry through genuine, intentional questioning. I shared the desire to focus even more deeply on how children asked questions, especially at the primary level. I was gratified that my group settled on an inquiry approach in the primary classroom.

However, our mutual interest in the inquiry process needed further focus. After we had browsed through the district binder of inquiry lessons, the group agreed that our lesson should be grounded in a curriculum unit so that we could reuse it in subsequent years. Our first challenge was to select both the content and grade level, either 1st grade or kindergarten. I felt that I could support any content at either grade as long as the topic would support my interest in how children develop questions. After some debate the group narrowed the choice to questioning in kindergarten science.

Bearing in mind that inquiry is a *method* of investigation that is applied to the study of a topic, we began to discuss what we wanted to learn about questioning. We asked ourselves what we already knew, or thought we knew, about young children's ability to ask questions. Weren't children always filled with questions? I offered that, when I ask a group of kindergarten students if they have questions, they often respond by telling me a story about an event in their life. This proved to be a common experience; it seemed that many kindergarten students find it difficult to differentiate between a question and a statement.

We wanted to help children ask richer questions. For example, 1st grade students are familiar with red and green light questions, ideas introduced to us by Amysue Kenney, a social studies helping teacher. Red light questions give answers; they revolve around a fact and end the conversation. For example, "What color is an ant?" is a red light question. A green light question extends the conversation and leads to asking more questions. For example, "Why does an ant make tunnels?" Although we wanted our classrooms to be places where students felt comfortable asking *any* question, we wondered if we could deepen kindergarteners' inquiry thinking by helping them learn to ask more green light questions.

Two of us had attended a Lincoln Center Institute workshop in which "noticing" was identified as preliminary to curiosity and inquiry. We had been using this technique, asking students what they noticed, during discussions in our classes. I shared that, when I ask young children about the book jacket, I find that many are willing to notice details, even when they are reticent to ask a question or make a prediction. However, after they have contributed observations, these students seem to move more organically into asking *why* certain characters or objects are depicted in a certain way. Perhaps, I wondered with our group, there was a way to structure the development of better questions using noticing techniques.

What approach could we take that used observations to develop inquiry? Would we want to set up a "Discovery Center" to feature an object that students could notice and then observe more deeply again? That seemed logical to me, but the rest of the group wasn't convinced. We brainstormed other ideas but, since nothing seemed to resonate with everyone, we set a deadline to return with materials that might help the group make a decision. I had recently placed Georgia Heard and Jennifer McDonough's book, *A Place for Wonder* (2009), in the professional library and read most of it. At our next meeting I suggested that we could apply some of the authors' suggestions about wondering and questioning to shape our Lesson Study. Another teacher concurred, saying that she had just ordered *A Place for Wonder* based on her experience reading other titles by Heard. With recommendations from both of us, the group agreed to familiarize themselves with the book. Concurrently we would reread the relevant New York State Standards.

## HONING OUR INQUIRY

At the following two meetings we narrowed our focus. We decided to concentrate on an upcoming inquiry-rich kindergarten science unit called *Pets, Creatures, and Other Small Animals*, since it involved observing small animals in the classroom, an activity that naturally evokes children's curiosity and questions. In this unit students study ants and ant farms in order to understand the needs of living things, their life cycles, and how to take care of animals in captivity. By the end of the unit the students are asked to relate caring for ants in the classroom to caring for small animals at home or at a neighbor's.

Much of what is studied in kindergarten is interconnected. For example the year-long kindergarten goals of cooperation and working in groups connect with the library's goals of cooperating with others, learning the various library procedures, and treating people and materials gently and with respect. While my participation in a Lesson Study team would not, in itself, require a group to insert library skills into a lesson, this unit was rich in library research tasks as well as inquiry learning. Students are introduced to the research techniques of drawing and labeling diagrams and making models and drawings, as well as listening to and doing research using nonfiction books, a process of locating, finding, and using information. After we reviewed the New York State Standards, district- and building-level goals, and the unit goals I'd copied for our team, we were able to articulate interdisciplinary Lesson Study goals including understanding the difference between fiction and nonfiction and using library resources to ask and answer questions. If we could plan an introductory lesson for this unit that encouraged students to ask questions that they could later investigate, I felt confident that important library goals would be included throughout.

---

### Lesson Study Unit Goals

**Science Goals**
- To help children understand that each animal has properties, which enable the animal to meet its needs

- To help students understand that each kind of animal goes through its own stages of growth and development during the life span of the animal

- To help children value and respect life in the natural world

- To help students learn the proper care of, and importance of humane treatment for, the small animals they work with in school or keep at home

**Interdisciplinary Goals**
- To help students understand the difference between fiction and nonfiction

- To help students with diagramming skills (pictures with labels)

- To help students begin to use nonfiction books to find information

---

Now we knew that we had to design an introductory lesson to encourage children to wonder and to ask questions about ants. What questions could the students generate on their own initiative? How could our lesson drive children's inquiry throughout the unit?

## PLANNING A LESSON

We had been meeting sporadically throughout the school year but, at the beginning of March, we recognized that we had better schedule the planning meetings, debriefing sessions, and two practice lessons so that we could present the formal lesson in April in front of the entire Teacher Institute Lesson Study class. Working backwards from mid-April, we scheduled five planning meetings to be held in the library and two practice lessons that we would deliver in the other kindergarten classes, spaced so that we would be able to refine our lesson between each session.

The instructional videos we had seen in the fall showed several different teachers presenting the same lesson. In our case the kindergarten teacher wanted to present all three lessons to the kindergarten classes, and, after some discussion, we agreed. If I were doing this Lesson Study again, I would argue more forcefully for at least one session in which she would observe another teacher deliver the lesson. While she was able to practice teaching the lesson several times, it did not give her the opportunity to observe another teacher presenting the lesson, nor was she able to observe the children's responses, which are only partially captured through videotaping. Since Lesson Study is a cycle of inquiry, both of us will have other opportunities to repeat this process using the insights we've accumulated.

What materials did we need for the lesson? Kindergarten children like to imagine themselves in different occupations: role playing is an important aspect of early career awareness. If students were to think like scientists, they needed the "props" of a scientist. The kindergarten teacher owned a lab coat and the children could wear parents' old white shirts as lab coats. Like scientists, students would become close observers. They'd use the classes' magnifying glasses to notice small details, cardboard "spy glasses" made from toilet paper rolls to isolate specific viewing areas and eyeglass frames without lenses to reenforce the general concept of noticing. The kindergarten teacher thought the parents would be glad to help find enough old shirts for the entire class and round up the toilet paper rolls and eyeglasses.

Beyond devising a detailed lesson, we must anticipate what students will be doing and saying and how the teacher will respond. In retrospect our first attempts to suggest questions kindergarteners might ask sounded like a list of curriculum questions a teacher would ask. We asked red light questions such as, "What body parts can you see?" "How many legs does it have?" "How long do they live?" "What is the purpose of each body part?" "Can an ant hear?" "What food does it eat?" "Where does it live?" "Can they be held without being hurt?" "Can we use our senses to closely observe the ants?" So we then asked more green light questions such as, "Why does an ant carry its food?" "Why does it carry so much food in one trip?" "How does it build its home?" "How does it move?" "How do ants work together?" "How does the ant colony work together?" "How are they born?" We were able to develop a more realistic set of children's questions as we taught the practice lessons.

At our next meeting we were bursting with ideas about potential follow-up activities. Typically Lesson Study team members see many possible activities that *could* be done, if only more time became available. After some intoxicating brainstorming, we refocused on the one lesson we *would* teach. The kindergarten teacher had her house invaded by ladybugs. She had taken many pictures of the ladybugs and become fascinated by them, so she proposed that her experience should become part of our introductory lesson.

Other team members were more reticent; they felt we should center our lesson on ant farms and work down to the close observation of individual ants. Our decision to go with her idea was a significant team compromise, which we realize, in retrospect, diffused the focus of our lesson design.

The plan we developed had the kindergarten teacher describing the invasion of ladybugs and how she and her own children used a magnifying glass to observe them closely. While showing photographs on her Smart Board she would ask children to brainstorm what they noticed. As the children noticed the parts of the ladybug, the teacher would label them on the Smart Board. Then children would divide up in three groups with an adult at each table. They would look at ant pictures using their various "noticing" props and then observe a single live ant in a magnifying box. Lastly we would show them ant farms with tunnels forming, which had been started the previous week in first-grade classrooms. The adult at the table would record questions that the children asked throughout this process (Figure 3.2).

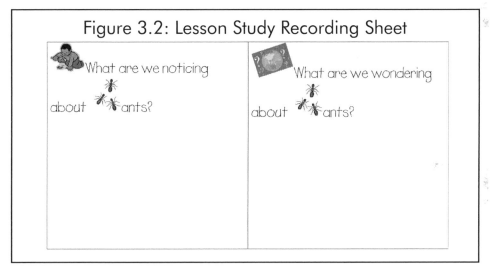

Figure 3.2: Lesson Study Recording Sheet

What are we noticing about ants?

What are we wondering about ants?

Once the lesson had been framed, we divided the responsibilities. Each teacher had materials to obtain. Some needed to follow up on the props; some needed to order the ants. My job was to find books and pictures of ants. I found over twenty pictures of different kinds of ants and ant colonies along with a set of library books on ants. These books would be put in a basket devoted to ant books after the first day of the lesson and would remain in the classroom for the duration of the unit. I also located a "Big Book" on ants that would be used later in the unit.

By the beginning of April our materials were gathered. We knew when the ants would arrive, and we had a broad outline of what we would do. Previously we had been looking at the goals of the unit, but we were now able to articulate lesson goals connected to the school's Lesson Study subgoal to promote risk taking and also to the yearlong goals of kindergarten that incorporated our building-level goals.

---

### Lesson and Year-Long Goals

**Lesson Goal**

To help students develop the inquiry skills of:

- Noticing and observing
- Wondering and asking questions

**Year-Long Goals**

- To develop a student-centered learning community that fosters children's abilities to think critically and creatively, communicate their understanding, and reflect on their learning
- To give students the skills necessary to work collaboratively
- To take risks and ask questions about what they are interested in
- To help students develop the inquiry skills of noticing and observing, and to wonder and to ask questions.

---

## WRITING THE LESSON SCRIPT

We needed a script to test on our first class, so the kindergarten teacher and I began to outline what she would say and to anticipate what the children would say. We took what the group had worked out as the outline of the lesson and fleshed out the wording she would use. Working from notes taken at our previous meetings, the two of us distilled our group's thoughts and recommendations into a workable script. As you look over our lesson plan script (see Appendix 3A) you'll see that we wanted to model questioning repeatedly. We pored over our lesson to identify every opportunity for the teacher to say what she was wondering and to turn students' statements into wonder questions.

We made a number of procedural decisions as we wrote. Since the students were accustomed to being divided into three groups for other activities, we had them divide into these same groups so that they would transition easily from the whole group mini-lesson to their individual observations of ants. One question that stymied us initially was whether we should sit at the tables with students, or whether teacher aides could do this. We reasoned that, since our team members would not be in this classroom in subsequent years, we would ask the classroom teacher to sit at one table and teacher aides to join the other tables.

After the students had completed some close observations of ants in small groups, we planned to bring them back together to share and chart their questions on the Smart Board. As the children reviewed some of the table pictures now on the Smart Board, we would record their new wonderings and questions to refer to during later investigations. We thought about having the students sort their questions into groups (e.g., questions about body parts, eating food, behavior) but decided that, since this involved new content and skills, this should be done as a separate lesson.

## TEACHING AND REVIEWING THE LESSON

As the kindergarten teacher taught the first lesson, we were responsible for gathering multiple kinds of evidence. Afterwards our team would review all this evidence, and then revise the script for the next trial lesson. One group member filmed the lesson, while another took still photographs. Two other members of the group observed and recorded what the teacher and children said, respectively. The last member of our Lesson Study team timed each section to be sure that we had allocated time effectively. Early in our planning we had gotten permission to run the trial lessons in several kindergarten classrooms, so these teachers also observed the lesson. We were eager to have them critique our lesson with fresh eyes and welcomed the additional insights they might have about their students.

Immediately after the first lesson, we debriefed with the kindergarten teachers. We learned that, at the table supervised by the kindergarten teacher of that class, students were generating observations and questions independently. If a key concept did not occur to children during the lesson, she knew it would be introduced later in the unit by posing questions that students could investigate like, "I wonder what ants eat?" On the other hand, the teacher-aides had no knowledge of the goals of the lesson, so they had been answering some of the questions themselves and leading students toward specific observations. Recognizing that this had occurred, the kindergarten teachers offered to replace all the aides at the tables for the next two lessons. If this modification worked well, they would commit to team-teaching the lesson this way in the future.

Later that afternoon our Lesson Study group sat down to review all our data. At the tables we had given students enlarged photos of ants so they could identify body parts in still photos before they were given the live ants in boxes. I had collected many good pictures of ants but didn't consider that the sheer number of pictures would present a problem. Faced with so many pictures on their table, children had a hard time focusing on any one picture. Since all the children were not looking at the same picture, they spoke in parallel rather than conversing with each other. We narrowed down the pictures to six per table, so each child would be looking at a single photo during the next lesson. I saved the remaining pictures for a future bulletin board display.

After our second practice lesson and our review of the second set of detailed observations, we smoothed some of the transitions and made sure our activities fit the allotted time. The detailed notes and suggestions from this second lesson were equally invaluable in making decisions on how to modify the script of what the teacher says and how the students realistically respond.

## THE FORMAL LESSON AND DEBRIEFING

Finally we were ready for the formal lesson in front of our Teacher Institute Lesson Study classmates who would all watch each other's lessons. We gave them an outline of the lesson including the anticipated responses, as well as the questions on which we wanted their observations to focus:

---

### Questions for Evaluation

**1. What was the quality and quantity of students'**
- Noticing / observing?

- Wondering / asking questions?

**2. Were students able to**
- Work collaboratively?

- Take risks and ask questions about what they are interested in?

---

In addition, they receive a Lesson Study protocol, which provides a framework and method for recording what they see. As tempting as it might be to focus on their colleague's instruction or to survey what all students in the class were learning, observers are instructed to record the cycle of learning for only one child or a small group because the most important factor in Lesson Study is a child's learning. Was the child learning to question? Our protocol underscores the importance of remaining in one place watching a small group, since we felt that big bodies moving from group to group would be especially disruptive for kindergarteners.

---

### Observation Protocol

Dear Observers:

Thank you for coming to our research lesson today. Please adhere to the following observation protocol.

1. Please plan to stay for the entire lesson.
2. Please read the lesson plan carefully to understand and assess the intent and goals of the lesson.
3. In order to preserve the integrity of the lesson, please do not help or interact with students.
4. During the small group activity, please observe only one table carefully to see how they react to different aspects of the lesson. Please stay on the periphery of the room and minimize your movement.
5. Please take detailed notes on the lesson plan to refer to during the post-lesson discussion later this afternoon.

Thank you again.

Sincerely,

Primary Research Team

---

It was crucial that Lesson Study observers did not interact with the students, but we anticipated that this might be difficult for teachers and students who knew each other. Therefore we explained to the students at the beginning of the lesson that the teachers were there to observe and that, after giving them a wave, students were not to talk to them until after the lesson. We had done a great deal of preparation and pedagogical thinking. Now it was time to learn what the students were learning!

The formal debriefing with the entire Teacher Institute Lesson Study class was conducted after school on the day of the lesson. Our team sat at a long table facing the class. Our role was to explain what our process had been before and during the lesson, and how we now perceived the result. The class members would let us know what they had observed in the students in relation to our stated goals. They were expected to give detailed answers to the evaluation questions we had asked them.

The Lesson Study leader began by framing the discussion. He reminded the whole group of our focus and what we were seeking to learn from their input. He reiterated the building-level goal that our faculty had developed earlier that year. After his introduction, the kindergarten teacher spoke about how she perceived the lesson. Generally the students had behaved normally even though there were a large number of adults in the room. One child had completely stopped talking and, when asked directly if she had an observation or a question, just looked at her teacher and shook her head as if to say, "Don't even ask." Perhaps with so many strange individuals in the room, the Lesson Study format had inhibited her from taking any risks. If so, her teacher expected that, with time and experience with other Lesson Study trials, the student would grow more comfortable with observers in her classroom.

One of the luxuries of Lesson Study is the opportunity to do the same lesson multiple times in slightly different ways, rather than tabling a lesson for an entire year before teaching it again. Our team explained the modifications and improvements we had made after each practice lesson. For example, in our first

> ### Catherine Lewis on Cultural Differences Among Teachers
>
> "As I listened to Japanese teachers debate whether it was more important for students to acquire correct scientific knowledge or to practice scientific processes, I imagined how different the situation would be in the U.S. if teachers with opposing viewpoints planned, viewed, and discussed lessons together" (Lewis 2002).

lesson all the scientific tools were on the table together. For the second and third lessons we introduced each tool sequentially. First the students put on their lab coats, and then they observed with their "glasses" on. After that, we handed them the "spy glasses" and finally we gave them the magnifying glasses. We had learned that students needed time to explore each tool separately prior to using it to observe the ants.

We had hypothesized that students would produce multiple observations before their questions emerged—and this proved to be correct. In all three classes the students made statements and observations until the teacher's own modeling suggested to them that they could turn their observations into questions. For example, if the child says, "Look at the tunnel," the teacher might reply, "I wonder *why* there is a tunnel?"

While each member in our group had different perspectives about teaching inquiry, we all came away with renewed respect for how difficult it is for students to wonder and ask questions in a new situation. I've learned that students need to observe or read about a subject, or notice aspects of the subject, before they can transition to wondering. Subsequently I have been using this in planning curriculum units with other teachers, suggesting that they read many picture books or show a video, bring in a number of images or do an experiment, before they expect students to do inquiry learning. Of course, some students are quicker to question, but others may stop at observations and need prompting to begin to ask questions. Further, if the teacher charts the students' questions on large paper or a Smart Board, students can learn to develop better questions from each other.

During our debriefing observers asked us if all student questions are equally important; aren't some questions really statements in disguise? We acknowledged that this is true but also explained that we wanted to promote risk taking. To me this goes to the art of teaching. If one doesn't "allow" a certain question, students can sense that it is somehow incorrect; this can quickly stifle curiosity and risk taking.

The observers were impressed with the pacing and the management of the lesson. Each successive layer seemed to add to students' excitement: listening to a story about ladybugs told by their teacher; becoming scientists who looked at pictures of ants; observing an individual ant; and finally noticing how ants behave in an ant farm. The observers remarked that children grew more focused and the conversation grew more intense with each new experience. By the time the ants in the magnified boxes were introduced, students were animatedly talking to one other, pointing out what they saw (Figure 3.3).

In contrast, observers described the conversations about the six enlarged photographs at each table as weak and diffused (Figure 3.4). They suggested that fewer photographs would have prompted interactive conversations rather than parallel monologues, since students would have a common frame of reference and listened to each other more closely. Then, when the pictures were redisplayed on the Smart Board, they felt that a more thoughtful whole-group discussion would have resulted. To compare and analyze too many items can be confusing for a child of any age, something I'm now more conscious of in my own lessons.

Figure 3.3: A Kindergarten Boy Closely Observes His Live Ant

The observers also identified one element of our lesson that seemed to be irrelevant to our goals. During the introduction the teacher emphasized recording observations by labeling the parts of an insect. Since the students weren't going to record anything later, the observers questioned if this was necessary for this lesson. We acknowledged that the scientific process of recording and labeling the parts of their ant should be extracted from this lesson and taught later in the unit.

Another of the observers' insights had to do with the role of the kindergarten teachers at the tables who were both facilitators and recorders simultaneously. Since the essence of inquiry learning was being demonstrated during the table conversations, observers recommended that the teachers should be free to listen carefully and respond appropriately. To me, this is a dilemma. We want a careful record of what happens as we teach, but it isn't feasible to both record evidence of inquiry and coach the students at the same time. Filming the tables has tremendous potential as a documentation tool, but film is time consuming to review and edit. This year, for example, I was one of the few teachers that was able to look at all the video footage and hear the audio recordings.

At another juncture, the observers wondered if there were instances when it was appropriate to answer student questions. For example, students thought that the blue ant food in the ant farm was water—or maybe ice. Should the teachers have immediately disabused the students of the notion that the blue substance was water? One of the kindergarten teachers had the students hold the farm so that they could determine that it wasn't cold and, therefore, couldn't be ice, but all students didn't make that connection. As much as we want student to ask questions to be answered later, the observers' consensus was that the students should have been told that the blue material was ant food, so that they would not assume that ants could live in water or ice. The process of determining which questions should be answered immediately and which should not could be the beginning of another Lesson Study cycle.

We had hoped that our planning would have resulted in more student-generated questions. However, the observers who taught older students shared that even their students had trouble forming questions to drive an inquiry. Children simply need time to observe and build background knowledge. The observers concluded that these children didn't have the vocabulary and prior knowledge they needed to ask more questions. Richer questions would be generated after the students had observed the ants more, had begun to read about ants, and had learned some new vocabulary.

Everyone was intrigued with the engagement that emerged when students used the scientific tools. While our previous experience made us confident that students would enjoy taking on the role of scientists, we were gratified that the tools had reinforced our observation goals so well. We watched children experiment with moving the magnifying glass closer and further away to sharpen what they were observing. How narrowly could they focus on individual parts? Students were engaged for more than forty-five minutes and, even without their scientific instruments, they continued to find and study ants in the schoolyard during the recess that followed the lesson.

The debriefing ended as formally as it had begun with an observer summing up the discussion. While Lesson Study might strike one as overly precise and formal, I found it immensely gratifying to work through a lesson so thoroughly over time, and to hear observations about learning and individual children that supported the teaching decisions we had made. My reward for all the hard work was a broader knowledge of how children learn.

### English Language Learners (ELL) Turn and Talk Strategy

Pairs of students take turns responding to a question with each other, and then each shares their partner's idea with the entire class. Half the class is responding while the other half is actively listening. This can be particularly helpful to those students who are shy about speaking to the entire class, or those who are just learning English (ELL)—or when everybody wants a turn to speak!

Although we would not revisit this lesson until the following year, our group discussed how we would change it. Since the leap between the ladybug sequence and the ants was confusing, we would provide more time with the ant farms in the classroom before the lesson. This would give students time to build up prior knowledge and watch ants develop their tunnels. Initially we would work on whole-class observations to develop noticing skills and vocabulary. We would record their observations, vocabulary, and any questions on chart paper to post in the classroom. Note taking and labeling would be reserved for lessons later in the unit. We would be more selective in our choice of photographs, looking for ones that portrayed specific aspects of ants that we wanted to reinforce. We would direct students' table conversations more precisely using the ELL "turn and talk" strategy, which would encourage all students to speak.

Figure 3.4: Students Scrutinize Photographs of Ants and Share Their Observations

Questions would be honored and recorded, but the expectation would be that deeper questions and speculations would come later. As the unit progressed, "class questions" could help frame students' research progression of finding information in nonfiction sources. Given this strong group of teachers, I realized that we were as likely as not to "overplan," trying to teach too much at one time. Perhaps I could help them learn to slow down, creating what Heard and McDonough call "a landscape of wonder" (2009, 6).

## THE WRITTEN RECORD OF OUR LESSON STUDY

Part of my role in this group was to convene meetings and assist in the development of the lesson plan. Although not everyone could attend every meeting, we kept minutes to record our foundational agreements, which enabled us to keep the momentum going. We have many video clips and photographs of our work. We placed the minutes, lesson plans and recording sheets, copies of the photographs, and a bibliography of both professional and student books in a binder that will be used when we revisit the lesson next year and could be disseminated to others who want to investigate this unit.

At the end of this process we were asked to present our material to an outside group that was evaluating our entire school for evidence of meeting the district's goal of critical and creative thinking. I put the videos and photographs into a keynote presentation that our group shared with the evaluators. As we showed how we helped students learn to be scientists, to observe and wonder and begin to develop critical questions, we also demonstrated how our own critical thinking grew as we examined the lesson from many different angles, evaluating every aspect prior to teaching it, and then reflecting and revising the lesson again.

During the presentation we were asked what Lesson Study did for the school community. For me it has not only helped nurture teacher collaboration and mutual support among group members and within the Lesson Study class but has also impacted professional practice throughout the entire school. The intellectual energy that infuses Lesson Study is respected and supported by the whole faculty, since they want to achieve the same student goals that our team has identified.

I gained a great deal from Lesson Study. By working intensely on a unit, I came to know a group of teachers in a way that would otherwise have taken years. I can appreciate the intensity with which they go about planning lessons. Having observed their strengths, expertise, and teaching styles, I feel confident that I can approach them with pedagogical questions. In turn, teachers now approach me for insights on students or teaching. When investigating materials they need to support other units, they are more likely to ask me to research other materials that are available, rather than just using what they have at hand. Of course, my specific knowledge of this curriculum unit and these teachers means that I can support student learning better than I could in the past.

I have begun a new Lesson Study with a different group of teachers including a 5th grade teacher, a principal, and an ELL teacher. Once again, we are all equal participants in the group, focused on the development and delivery of a specific lesson within a curriculum unit. Our cycle of reflection will sharpen our teaching and enrich our students' learning. We are considering how to use Shaun Tan's graphic novel *The Arrival* (2007) to help the students understand the emotional impact of being an immigrant. Should we integrate the novel into our current study of immigration? Should we use it as a means to introduce immigration? Might we use a graphic form to assess the students' learning? How can we be sure that the students are experiencing the impact we feel when we read the novel? At this point we have decided that we will study graphic novels prior to studying immigration. We know we want the students to study a specific immigrant group and create a graphic display of the country of origin, the means of travel, and the immigrant experience in the new country to present to their peers. Our next job will be to decide which lesson will be "The Lesson" to be observed by our entire Teacher Institute Lesson Study class.

## REFERENCES

Gawande, Atul. 2011. "Annals of Medicine—Personal Best: Should Everyone Have a Coach?" *New Yorker* (October 3): 44–53.

Heard, Georgia, and Jennifer McDonough. 2009. *A Place for Wonder: Reading and Writing Nonfiction in the Primary Grades*. Portland, ME: Stenhouse.

Lewis, Catherine. 2002. "Everywhere I Looked—Levers and Pendulums." *JSD* 22, no. 3 (Summer): 59–65. http://www.learningforward.org// .cfm?articleID=393.

Lewis, Catherine C., and Ineko Tsuchida. 1998. "A Lesson Is Like a Swiftly Flowing River: How Research Lessons Improve Japanese Education." *American Educator* (Winter): 12–17, 50–52. http://www.lessonresearch .net/.pdf.

Stigler, James W., and James Hiebert. 1999. *The Teaching Gap: Best Ideas from the World's Teachers for Improving Education in the Classroom*. New York: Simon & Schuster.

Tan, Shaun. 2007. *The Arrival*. New York: Arthur A. Levine, Scholastic.

Wolf, Dennis Palmer. 1987. "The Art of Questioning." Academic Connections (Winter). http://www.exploratorium.edu/IFI/resources/workshops/artof questioning.html.

## Appendix 3A
## Final Lesson: Introduction to the Study of Ants

Kindergarten Teacher: Ms. Magnani Date of Lesson: April 15, 2010
Edgewood School

Research Team: Ellen Anders, Jen Kiley, Jeanette Magnani, Nancy O'Rourke, Anne Stokes

**Unit Goals:** Classroom Pets: *Live Science Pets, Creatures and Other Small Animals*

- To help children understand that each animal has proper-ties that enable the animal to meet its needs
- To help students understand that each kind of animal goes through its own stages of growth and development during the life span of the animal
- To help children value and respect life in the natural world
- To help students learn the proper care and importance of humane treatment for the animals they work with and the pets they own

Interdisciplinary Goals:

- To help students understand the difference between fiction and nonfiction
- To help student develop observation skills
- To help students with recording skills including pictures with labels
- To help students begin to use non-fiction books to find information

**Lesson Goals:**

To help students develop the inquiry skills of:

- Noticing and observing
- Wondering and asking questions

To encourage the year-long goals:

- To develop a student-centered learning community that fos-ters children's abilities to think critically and creatively, com-municate their understanding, and reflect on their learning.
- To give students the skills necessary to work collaboratively
- To take risks and ask questions about what they are interested in

**Relationship of the Lesson to the New York Standards:**
Describe the characteristics of and variations between living and non-living things.
Major Understandings:

1.1a Animals need air, water, and food in order to live and thrive.

1.1c Nonliving things do not live and thrive.

1.1d Nonliving things can be human created or naturally occurring.

Describe the life processes common to all living things.
Major Understandings:

1.2a Living things grow, take in nutrients, breathe, reproduce, eliminate waste, and die.

Recognize that for humans and other living things there is genetic continuity between generations.
Major Understandings:

2.2a Plants and animals closely resemble their parents and other individuals in their species.

Describe how the structures of plants and animals complement the environment of the plant or animal.
Major Understandings:

3.1a Each animal has different structures that serve different functions in growth, survival, and reproduction.

Describe the major stages in the life cycles of selected plants and animals.
Major Understandings:

4.1a Plants and animals have life cycles. These may include beginning of a life, development into an adult, reproduction as an adult, and eventually death.

4.1f Each kind of animal goes through its own stages of growth and development
during its life span.

Describe basic life functions of common living specimens (e.g., guppies, mealworms, gerbils).
Major Understandings:

5.1a All living things grow, take in nutrients, breathe, reproduce, and eliminate waste.

5.1b An organism's external physical features can enable it to carry out life functions in its particular environment.

5.2c Senses can provide essential information (regarding danger, food, mates, etc.) to animals about their environment.

**Materials:**

White lab coats (Students will use an adult white shirt)

Magnifying glasses

Cylinders (e.g., toilet paper rolls)

Eyeglasses

Photo of a ladybug

Insect boxes with ants

Ant farms

Clipboards and recording sheets for teachers

Photographs and drawings:

Photos Used

**Ants build a bridge out of themselves if they have a gap to cross.**
Huang Meng, T. "Ants build a bridge." Beer, A-J. *Ants*. Danbury: Grolier, 2008, p. 6.

**Foraging ants form a row on the way to a source of food.**
Tweedy-Holmes, K. "Foraging ants form a row." Beer, A-J. *Ants*. Danbury: Grolier, 2008, p. 30.

**An ant's outer covering is made of a tough substance called chitin, which is a type of sugar.**
Yaroslav. "An ant's outer covering". Beer, A-J. *Ants*. Danbury: Grolier, 2008, p. 13.

**Two worker ants communicate by using their antennas to pass on special chemicals called pheromones.**
Photos.com. "Two workers ants communicate." Beer, A-J. *Ants*. Danbury: Grolier, 2008, p. 29.

**An ant is covered in tiny sensory hair.**
Zuckerman, J. "Ant covered in tiny sensory hair." Beer, A-J. *Ants*. Danbury: Grolier, 2008, p. 14.

**Ants can communicate by touching their feelers together.**
Stickland/Visuals Unlimited. "Ants communicate." Heinrichs, A. *Ants*. Minneapolis: Compass Point Books, 2002. p. 8.

**The ant's body has three main parts.**
Beatty, B. " The ant's body". Heinrichs, A. *Ants*. Minneapolis, Compass Point Books, 2002, p. 7.

**An ant's nest has many tunnels and chambers**.
Moffett, M./Midden Pictures. "Ant nest with tunnels and chambers." Heinrichs, A. *Ants*. Minneapolis: Compass Point Books, 2002, p. 11.

**Ants eat a small mammal**.
Kuhn, D. "Ants eat a small mammal." Heinrichs, A. *Ants*. Minneapolis: Compass Point Books, 2002, p. 15.

**A tropical leaf-cutter ant carries a piece of leaf back to the nest.**
Thom, R./Visuals Unlimited. "Tropical leaf-cutter ant carrying leaf." Heinrichs, A. *Ants*. Minneapolis: Compass Point Books, 2002, p. 16.

**A honey ant filled with honey.**
Australian Picture Library/Corbis. "A replete honey ant swollen with honey." Heinrichs, A. *Ants*. Minneapolis: Compass Point Books, 2002, p. 20.

**Slave-maker ants carry stolen young back to the nest.**
Moffett, M./Midden Pictures. "A slave-maker ant." Heinrichs, A. *Ants*. Minneapolis: Compass Point Books, 2002, p. 23.

**A colony of leaf-cutter ants.**
Mitchell, R., and Linda M. "Colony of leaf-cutter ants in Texas." Heinrichs, A. *Ants*. Minneapolis: Compass Point Books, 2002, p. 27.

**Some ants are as large as half your middle finger.**
Atkinson, K. Oxford Scientific Films. "Ant as large as half your middle finger." Hartley, K., and C. Macro. *Ant*. Des Plaines: Heinemann Library, 1998, p. 8.

**Young queens and male ants fly off to start new nests.**
Taylor, K. "Young queens and male ants fly off to start new nest." Hartley, K., and C. Macro. *Ant*. Des Plaines: Heinemann Library, 1998, p. 10.

**The ant queen lays eggs in the ground.**
Goetgheluck, P. "Queen lays eggs in the ground." Hartley, K., and C. Macro. *Ant*. Des Plaines: Heinemann Library, 1998, p. 11.

**Ant larva make a hard cocoons around their bodies.**
Milkins, P. "Larva makes a hard cocoon around its body." Hartley, K., and C. Macro. *Ant*. Des Plaines: Heinemann Library, 1998, p. 12.

**Worker ants cut open cocoon to release ants.**
Thomas, M. "Worker ants cut open cocoon to release ants." Hartley, K., and C. Macro. *Ant*. Des Plaines: Heinemann Library, 1998, p. 13.

**Many millions of ants are part of the cleanup crew.**
Ziegler, C. "Many millions of ants are part of the tropical forest cleanup crew." Markle, S. *Army Ants*. Minneapolis: Lerner Publications Company, 2005, p. 3.

**Soldier ants protecting their colony from insect enemies.**
Wild, A. "Soldier ants protect their colony from insect enemies." Markle, S. *Army Ants*. Minneapolis: Lerner Publications Company, 2005, p. 23.

**Bulldog ants inside a tunnel.**
Sisson, R. "Bulldog Ant inside a tunnel." National Geographic Stock. Stewart, M. *Ants*. Washington, DC: National Geographic, 2010, p. 10.

**An underground ant's nest.**
"Underground Ant Nest." De Agostini Picture Library. Getty Images. Stewart, M. *Ants*. Washington, DC: National Geographic, 2010, p. 11.

Appendix 3A continues on the next page with the Lesson Plan Script.

# Lesson Plan Script

| Learning Activities, Teacher's Questions and Anticipated Students' Reactions | Teacher Support and Things to Remember | Observation Notes |
|---|---|---|
| **1. <u>Introduction</u> (Steps 1, 2 & 3 - 20 min.)**<br>**T: Children watch what I am doing. See what you can notice. Who do you think I am today?**<br>Teacher models her clothing and puts on her name tag.<br>*S: A scientist, a doctor, a dentist.*<br>**T: A scientist! How did you know that?**<br>*S: Because scientists have white coats.*<br>*   Looks like a lab coat.* | Name tag in pocket | |
| **2. <u>Modeling the Procedure</u>**<br>Teacher models her observation of a ladybug. (noticings/observations)<br>**T: I have a story to tell about ladybugs.**<br>**T: Why do you think I wanted to be scientist today? Something special happened at my house. I noticed these ladybugs in my house and I was so excited. (Teacher continues story about finding ladybugs.) Do you want to see them?**<br>**T: I didn't catch it, but I have a picture of it. I started to notice and wonder about ladybugs.**<br>Teacher displays picture on Smart Board.<br>**T: I began to notice things about them. My family and I got down on the floor and watched carefully.**<br>Teacher circles parts of body while saying:<br>**T: I noticed antenna, eyes, color, spots, shape, legs, antenna, and body.**<br>**T: We turned one on its back and we noticed wings under the shell.**<br>**Why do you think they have wings? Shells?**<br>*S: To protect them!*<br>Teacher models her questions. (questions/wonderings)<br>**T: I noticed all these awesome things and then what do you think happened? . . . I had lots of questions about ladybugs.**<br>**Why were the wings underneath the shell?**<br>**Why did they need shells?**<br>(After children try to answer the questions) **But we don't really know that.**<br>**Why are the ladybugs in the house?**<br>**Are all the ladybugs the same color?**<br>**Do they have the same number of spots?**<br>**There are so many things that I don't know and want to find out.** | Photo of ladybug on the Smart Board<br><br><br>Blue marker on photo | |

From *Growing Schools: Librarians as Professional Developers* by Debbie Abilock, Kristin Fontichiaro, and Violet H. Harada, Editors. Santa Barbara, CA: Libraries Unlimited. Copyright © 2012.

| Learning Activities, Teacher's Questions and Anticipated Students' Reactions | Teacher Support and Things to Remember | Observation Notes |
|---|---|---|
| **3. <u>Launching</u>**<br>Teacher models tools of a scientist and reveals what is in her pockets.<br>**T: Are you ready to be scientists?**<br>**Good scientists notice things and ask questions.**<br>**Scientists have tools.**<br>**Here are some of the tools that you will use.**<br>Teacher shows the toilet paper roll "telescope"<br>**T: Why would I use this?**<br>*S: Telescopes help you zoom in to things.*<br>Teacher shows eyeglasses.<br>**T: Why would I use these?**<br>*S: To see things better.*<br>**T: It reminds me to look carefully.**<br>Teacher shows magnifying glass.<br>**T: Why would I use this?**<br>*S: Make things look bigger.*<br>Teacher shows empty bug box.<br>**T: Why use this box?**<br>*S: It keeps the bug inside the box.*<br>*It gives it a home.*<br>*It makes it look bigger- easier to see.*<br>**T: What else could you observe in this box?**<br>*S: spider, ants, beetles*<br>**T: There is another thing that scientists do besides observing and questioning things – they need to remember what they see and observe.**<br>**How can they do that?**<br>*Various responses.*<br>*S: Paper, pencil, crayon*<br>Teacher displays chart on Smart Board.<br>**T: We need to draw and write what we are noticing about the ladybug.**<br>**T: What did I notice?**<br>*S: Legs, Wings, Antenna …*<br>Teacher quickly draws legs and labels with initial letter and/or word.<br>**T: What did I wonder?  What questions did I ask?**<br>*S: Were the wings black?*<br>*S: Why were the bugs in your house?*<br>Teacher continues to draw, write and uses question mark. | Tools: Magnifying glass, eyeglasses, toilet paper roll, bug box<br><br><br><br><br><br><br><br><br><br><br><br><br><br><br>Chart with noticing and wonderings with ladybugs on Smart Board | |

| Learning Activities, Teacher's Questions and Anticipated Students' Reactions | Teacher Support and Things to Remember | Observation Notes |
|---|---|---|
| **T: Today teachers will record what you say. Your job will be to notice and ask questions about the ants.** **Who's ready for the mission? Today we're not going to study ladybugs. Today we are going to study another bug that I have seen outside and inside my house . . . ants!** **First you will put on your lab coats, and put your name tag on your lab coat.** **Next you will use your tools and see what you can observe about ants and what questions you might have about the ants.** **We are going to go back to our tables. There will be a teacher at each table. Tell your teachers what you notice and what you are wondering.** Teacher directs students back to tables. | | |
| **4. Practice (18 Min.)** (8 minutes) Children go to tables and put on lab coats and name tags. Tools are distributed and children try each of them out. At each child's seat there is a photo turned upside down. The children are asked to turn over the photos. **T: What do you notice?** **T: What questions do you have about ants?** Teachers allow students to observe. Teachers record children's observations and questions. If necessary, teachers may suggest the following to prompt observations: **T:** Observation Questions **What body parts can you see?** **Mouth? Eyes? Antenna?** **How many legs does it have?** **What are they doing?** **What else do you see?** Wondering Questions **Can ants hear?** **What food does it eat?** **How does an ant carry its food?** **Where does it live?** **How does it move?** **How long do they live?** **How are they born? From eggs?** (5 min.) Children will be given bug boxes with an ant in each. | Charts on clip board Tools at tables Photo at each place Bug boxes | |

| Learning Activities, Teacher's Questions and Anticipated Students' Reactions | Teacher Support and Things to Remember | Observation Notes |
|---|---|---|
| **T: What do you notice?** <br> **T: What do you wonder?** <br> Teachers record children noticing and wonderings. <br> Ant Farm <br> (5 min) <br> Each table will be given an ant farm to observe. <br> **T: What do you notice?** <br> **T: What do you wonder?** <br> *S: How do they get through?* <br> Teachers record children noticing and wonderings. | Ant farms | |
| **5. <u>Sharing</u> (5 min.)** <br> Bring students together and share their observations and questions. <br> Teacher displays the photographs on the Smart Board. <br> **T: Great Job! You had so many observations and questions!** <br> **Let's share. What did you notice?** <br> *S: Students share some of their observations.* <br> **T: What did you wonder about?** <br> *S: Students share some of their questions.* <br> **T: Our next job will be to take all our observations and questions and organize them. Then we will try to find the answers to our wonderings. But right now you have worked so hard, I think it is time for a snack and recess.** <br> *S: I'm going to look for bugs!* | Photo collage on Smart Board | |

# CHAPTER 4
# EVIDENCE OF LEARNING

*Editors' Note:* This chapter highlights how a district initiative in Illinois helped school librarians design outcome-based learning plans and use the assessment of student learning to communicate the value of librarian-teacher partnerships. Pam Kramer, as one of the project managers, describes how a hybrid form of professional development was conducted with the assistance of academic partners from neighboring institutions of higher learning. Linda Diekman, as one of the participants, provides vignettes of how the training influenced her practice and bolstered her confidence in assuming a leadership role in her school community. Together, they capture how evidence-based practice benefits both students and instructors.

## Building Evidence-Based Practice: Moving from Circulation Counts to Assessing for Student Learning

### Pamela Kramer and Linda Diekman

For more than a decade school librarians have been struggling to convince administrators that they are an important part of the educational team in schools. Yet with the demands of No Child Left Behind, the emphasis on high-stakes testing, and diminishing funding for schools, librarians have been caught in a net of competing forces. In Illinois, most librarians knew about information literacy standards through training sessions with the *Linking for Learning, the Illinois School Library Media Program Guidelines* (ISLMA 2005b). To collect data on the school library's role in promoting student achievement, our state had also contracted Keith Curry Lance to conduct a study that resulted in *Illinois Study: Powerful Libraries Make Powerful Learners* (ISLMA 2005a). Although principals, curriculum directors, and superintendents had been introduced to the study, they indicated that the information was too general. While they might extrapolate from the *Illinois Study* that more visits and interventions by school librarians could be positively correlated with test scores and student achievement, the data did not dig down to the local level.

## IDENTIFYING THE NEED

Administrators wanted more specific evidence of how libraries contributed to student learning in their own library programs. While teachers were planning strategically and providing data for decision making, school librarians were still collecting data on how many books were checked out and how many classes used the library. Clearly there was a disconnect between what school librarians were communicating and what administrators wanted to hear. Librarians were measuring what they did; administrators wanted to see concrete evidence of the impact of the teaching. Librarians were saying, "I taught web evaluation to all of the sixth graders" and "All the seniors had information literacy training from me," when administrators wanted to know what was actually being taught and how well students were learning critical skills through the library's instructional program—for example, what percentage of the students were able to identify the accuracy and authority in web pages.

As the youth consultants for the North Suburban Library System (NSLS) and DuPage Library System (DLS) in Illinois, Sharon Ball and I (Kramer) realized that we needed professional development that would empower school librarians to plan strategically and measure student learning. Collecting evidence to strengthen teaching and learning would also provide librarians with vital information to communicate the value of their programs to stakeholders. DLS, which is located in northeast Illinois, primarily west of Chicago, serves 138 libraries including 11 academic and 28 public libraries, 27 private schools, 42 individual school districts, and 30 special libraries in 391 different buildings. NSLS, located north and northwest of Chicago, serves over 650 different buildings, including 49 public and 72 special libraries, 97 individual school districts, 33 private schools, and 27 academic libraries.

In 2007, Sharon and I applied for a Library Services and Technology Act (LSTA) grant to provide specialized training for school librarians. Prior to writing the proposal, we conferred with Elizabeth "Betty" Marcoux from the University of Washington and Violet Harada from the University of Hawaii about initiatives they had coordinated that included strategic planning for librarians. We believed that librarians had to learn not only how to collect, interpret, and use the data but also how to communicate the results to stakeholders who make decisions about funding and staffing. Therefore, we also consulted with Steve Mongelluzzo, a communications trainer, on a marketing component for the project. Mongelluzzo had previously conducted media training for Illinois librarians and had also been involved in message development for *Powerful Libraries*. As part of the grant-writing process, Sharon and I also studied anecdotal information from Illinois librarians and administrators and data from state testing scores as well as the professional literature on assessment for school libraries (Harada and Yoshina 2005; Geitgey and Tepe 2007; Todd 2003; Wiggins and McTighe 1998).

We ultimately received a $46,000 LSTA grant for the training project entitled, "Here's the Evidence: School Librarians Help Students Achieve." The aim of this professional development was to design and implement evidence-based practice in school libraries and to disseminate this information to other stakeholders in the school community. This chapter describes the development, implementation, and outcomes of the project from the perspective of one of the two grant managers (Kramer). To track how the training influenced actual practice, the chapter includes anecdotal commentary from one of the cohort members (Diekman).

## DEVELOPING A FOCUS

Sharon and I identified three major goals for participants: to develop a strategic approach to planning and assessment, to apply outcome-focused lesson planning, and to communicate findings to stakeholders. We selected these goals because we realized that the instruction being provided through many of our libraries was marginally connected to the classroom. Teachers did not always view library instruction as critical to the standards they were struggling to achieve with students. We believed that school librarians could produce more compelling evidence of their value as teaching partners if they engaged in strategic planning and assessment, designed outcome-based instruction, and honed their communication skills. These concepts are explained below.

### Strategic Planning and Assessment

Librarians have to speak the same language and have the same goals as their teachers if they wish to be key instructional players in their schools. Strategic planning requires that librarians support the school's mission and goals. They must work closely with teachers to identify major learning targets based on classroom observations of student performance and test scores, and devise learning strategies to improve student achievement. Strategic planning focuses the energies of a school and district so that stakeholders are striving toward a shared vision. Importantly, this type of planning demands a continuous assessment of progress that centers on student learning.

### Outcome-Based Instruction

Outcome-based teaching challenges instructors to identify "what the students should know and be able to do at the end of the learning experience" (Harada and Yoshina 2005, 14). Wiggins and McTighe refer to this as a "backward design process" (1998, 9). This planning process emphasizes targeting the desired end results, determining what evidence of achievement looks like, and, finally, creating the actual learning experiences. Based on the assessment of results, teachers and librarians develop intervention strategies to differentiate and individualize instruction for students needing additional help.

## Communication Strategies

In addition to planning and implementing outcome-based teaching, school librarians need to develop skills in communicating the results to teachers, administrators, and other decision makers. Sharon and I realized that school librarians were not always perceived as valued partners in the instructional landscape of their buildings. Therefore, massaging the message became an important component of the training.

## ORGANIZING THE TRAINING

We wanted to provide ongoing online support as well as face-to-face training in this project. To help with the online portion, Sharon and I enlisted academic partners from three local institutions of higher education, who worked closely with school library preparation programs: Don Adcock and Chris Balsano from Dominican University, Barbara Fiehn from Northern Illinois University, and Gail Bush from National Louis University. The partners agreed to assist in planning the project and offering consultative support to participants during the upcoming school year.

After we received the grant, we were on a very tight timeline. Beginning in October 2007 we selected the participants, issued contracts to trainers Marcoux and Mongelluzzo, and set tentative training dates. Since we were working with school librarians, the project activities had to conclude by the end of the 2007–2008 school year. To be selected as one of the cohort members, a librarian had to be certified with at least two years of experience in a school library. Applicants also had to have collaborative instructional experience with teachers. We asked that applicants submit a letter of support from a principal or superintendent and agree to attend all the scheduled events. Sharon and I created lists of school librarians in our respective systems that would make good candidates. The goal was to have a balanced representation from the primary, middle/junior high, and high school levels.

The cohort consisted of twenty-eight librarians, fourteen each from NSLS and DLS. Several school librarians reported that just being selected as a cohort member increased their status in their buildings! Each librarian received copies of *Assessing Learning* (Harada and Yoshina 2005), *Understanding by Design* (Wiggins and McTighe 1998), and *Winning Media Interviews* (Mongelluzzo 2005). They also received flash drives to store their work, journals for their personal reflections, and portfolios for their notes and papers. The original timeline included four days of training, with the academic partners providing consultative support in between the face-to-face sessions. However, once the training began, we modified the original schedule based on participants' needs for more assistance with various aspects of assessment (we elaborate on this later in the chapter). Figure 4.1 represents the final schedule.

# Figure 4.1: Training Schedule

| Timeline | Focus | Topics covered |
|---|---|---|
| December<br>Session 1: full day | Overview | • Defining assessment<br>• Identifying tools and measurements in schools<br>• Video presentation from Violet Harada<br>• Group time to discuss assessment tools and ideas<br>• Beginning to think strategically |
| December<br>Session 2: full day | Connecting and planning | • Identifying teacher-collaborators<br>• Connecting classroom and information literacy standards<br>• Discussing qualitative vs. quantitative assessment<br>• Targeting learning priorities according to your school's agenda<br>• Examining types of assessment instruments<br>• Discussing how to interpret and use assessment data<br>• Group time to begin reviewing sample forms and share possible project ideas |
| December – January | Preliminary collaboration on-site | • Identifying and connecting with school mission and goals<br>• Targeting building level needs<br>• Brainstorming with collaborating teachers about potential lessons and standards they need their students to achieve |
| January<br>Session 3: full day | Assessment tools and techniques | • Examining strategies to collect assessment data<br>• Learning how to analyze data<br>• Creating timelines for how and when to conduct on-site assessment<br>• Group time to exchange strategies and timelines by grade levels |
| January - April | Implementation of plans on-site | • Continuing work with teachers<br>• Conducting lessons<br>• Collecting data and beginning the analysis of data |
| March<br>Open House at each system | Individualized assistance | • Consulting with academic partners<br>• Reviewing data collected<br>• Receiving assistance with analysis of data |
| April<br>Session 4: full day | Communication strategies | • Knowing audiences and their needs<br>• Using message worksheets<br>• Exploring delivery techniques<br>• Refining impromptu speaking techniques<br>• Group time to develop and practice messages<br>• Practicing with the whole group |
| June<br>Session 5: half day | Celebration and reflection | • Reviewing debriefing questions<br>• Sharing projects<br>• Reflecting on accomplishments and next steps |

From *Growing Schools: Librarians as Professional Developers* edited by Debbie Abilock, Kristin Fontichiaro, and Violet H. Harada. Santa Barbara, CA: Libraries Unlimited. Copyright © 2012.

## IMPLEMENTING THE TRAINING

Betty Marcoux served as lead trainer for the two sessions in December with the project managers and all the academic partners in attendance. The first session began with an overview of the entire project. We discussed the differences between assessment and evaluation and asked the participants to identify the measurement tools and tests that were currently used in their schools to document student achievement. In an afternoon web conference, Violet Harada (2007) covered the following key concepts that connected assessment with strategic planning:

- Focus on the connections between classroom standards and information literacy standards.
- Assess what matters to teachers and administrators.
- Target skills that your students lack and that teachers are struggling to teach.
- Adjust instruction in the library to meet the identified needs of students.

In the first session, we stressed that the goal of planning strategically and thus assessing strategically was to show that every professional in the school is responsible for student learning. Assessment provided a means of measuring progress and improving instruction. Assessment was an integral part of the learning process; therefore, planning with the specific outcomes in mind was essential to good teaching. Teachers and school librarians, working together, should determine the intended outcomes before deciding on the lesson strategies.

On the second day, Marcoux fielded questions from the participants and recapped and reinforced some of the work of the previous day. In addition, the cohort reviewed the Illinois Learning Standards and information literacy standards to identify areas of alignment between the classroom and the library. Participants used I-SAIL (updated 2009), an online resource created by the Illinois School Library Media Association to match teaching targets with classroom learning standards. I-SAIL links the Illinois learning standards, the *National Educational Technology Standards for Students* (International Society for Technology in Education [ISTE] 2007), and the *Standards for the 21st-Century Learner* (American Association of School Librarians [AASL] 2007) so that librarians can see where their standards connect with standards in the subject areas. Marcoux also urged the cohort members to clearly understand the mission and goals of their own districts and schools when they began their collaborative work with a teacher. For example, if improvement in reading scores was the school's target goal, then how could a collaborating librarian support that goal?

During the two sessions, cohort librarians examined a range of tools to measure student learning such as pre- and post-tests, graphic organizers, exit slips, and rating scales. They also explored the use of interviews and surveys to assess how students perceived their own work. In addition, the librarians studied how the quality of student performances might be evaluated as applications of learning to new situations. Although several school librarians wanted to assess their collaborative projects through elaborate statistical research, we cautioned everyone to start small—begin with one teacher, focus on one lesson, and use one measurement tool or strategy. The cohort's assignment before the next session in January was to identify a single teacher and begin collaboration on an outcome-based lesson or short unit. To plan strategically, we advised the participants to first examine the mission and goals of the school and the school's improvement plan. Working with teachers, the cohort members were to identify targets that related to the school's learning priority areas as well as to the ISTE and AASL standards and to brainstorm how they might focus their instruction to meet these targets.

After two days of training, there were mixed reactions from cohort members. Some jumped right on the idea of strategic planning and succeeded in identifying and working with school partners in the ensuing weeks.

---

### Linda's Commentary

In Fall 2007, I participated in a full-day workshop on assessment presented by Violet Harada and Joan Yoshina at the AASL conference in Reno, Nevada. During that workshop, I met Pam Kramer and expressed my interest in being part of the "Here's the Evidence" grant program. Upon my return home, I contacted Sharon Ball, the youth consultant of NSLS and, again, indicated my desire to participate in this training. I was intrigued about the whole idea of measuring my impact on student learning, but I wasn't really sure where to begin. The structure provided with "Here's the Evidence" was what I needed to change my practice. While nervous about what collaborative project to select for the assessment grant, I decided to take the advice of the grant leaders and "start small and start friendly."

The 5th grade teacher I approached was enthusiastic about having me teach note taking as part of a larger research project. Note taking was a critical element of the project. With the emphasis on identifying main ideas and important facts, paraphrasing, source citation, and organization, this activity supported the school's focus on Reading and Language Arts performance. I designed a checklist that targeted the areas we thought were important (Figure 4.2). We wanted students to paraphrase, to write one fact per note card, and to cite their sources. After the pretest, I shared the results with the teacher. We used the data to identify students who needed additional coaching in specific areas. The teacher was thrilled to receive this feedback. Within the week, the two other 5th grade teachers asked me to do the same lesson and assessment with their classes. This is when assessment made sense for me. I realized that by speaking the language of teachers and helping them accomplish their goals, I could accomplish mine, to develop the abilities of our students to acquire, evaluate, and use information.

## Figure 4.2: Note-taking Checklist

| My notes should be | This means that . . . | Student evaluation | | | Teacher evaluation | | |
|---|---|---|---|---|---|---|---|
| | | Always | Sometimes | Never | Always | Sometimes | Never |
| Related to my explorer | My notes are about my explorer and have accurate information from a print or online source. | | | | | | |
| Complete | My notes cover all of the research topics on the outline. | | | | | | |
| From a reliable source | I have recorded the source of my information on the note card. | | | | | | |
| "Short and sweet" | My notes are written as phrases. | | | | | | |
| One per card | My notes are written one fact to a card. | | | | | | |
| Meaningful to me | My notes are written in my own words and I understand every word I have used. | | | | | | |
| Well organized | I have used the correct colored card to record my information. | | | | | | |

For several cohort members, however, the notion of the librarian assessing for learning was new and daunting. They thought of assessment as evaluation and felt it was the teacher's responsibility to examine student work for grading purposes. They were accustomed to "cooperating" or "coordinating" with teachers who assumed total responsibility for the lessons. The librarians' past teaching responsibilities had been restricted to locating resources. However, as a result of the discussions, these librarians slowly realized that their previous interactions with teachers lacked alignment of classroom and library learning goals. They also recognized the need to embrace a wider view of the school's goals including documenting evidence of student learning.

## ESTABLISHING ONLINE SUPPORT

As the grant managers, Sharon and I realized that communication in between the face-to-face sessions was going to be critical. For this purpose, NSLS created an online "Community of Practice" (CoP) with their proprietary software. Using the online CoP for threaded discussion forums, Marcoux, the academic partners, and the grant managers provided support to the participants and eased concerns about expectations. For example, several cohort members struggled with the idea of changing how they collaborated with teachers. They were unsure about who should lead the assessment and how assessment should occur. Marcoux and the academic partners suggested ways to identify the specific learning goals by examining standards and simple strategies such as exit passes and checklists to assess for student performance. In reassuring the librarians, Marcoux acknowledged that change was hard, and she encouraged them to persevere.

## USING FEEDBACK TO MODIFY TRAINING

The third training session in January was originally going to be a half-day of assessment techniques and a half-day of communications training. Based on the online conversations we were having with some of the librarians and mindful of their job commitments, we recognized that they needed more time to exchange views on how to implement strategic planning, outcome-based learning, and assessment. Since we had money left from the grant, we decided to reschedule the communications training and added an additional session in April for it.

At the January session, Marcoux organized the cohort by grade levels with at least one academic partner assigned to each group. She had three groups—elementary, middle/junior high, and high school—with two of the partners sharing the high school group. To assist the groups in developing assessments for outcome-focused instruction, Marcoux designed a grid with the following questions. In responding to the questions, librarians had to consider how their teaching aligned with the school's instructional priorities and to the national learning standards accessed through I-SAIL.

- What am I going to assess?
- What standard(s) is/are a part of this assessment?
- Why am I assessing for this?
- Who is going to be assessed?
- How am I going to assess for learning?
- What is my assessment timeline?
- What do I plan to do with the results?

As a team, the grant managers and the academic partners continued to provide online support as the librarians worked through their outcome-based lessons and assessments between January and April. From the onset of the training, cohort members also raised questions about the evidence folders they were supposed to produce at the end of the school year. These digital folders would include lessons with examples and assessments of student work. To assist members in planning for and organizing their folders, one of the academic partners created a reporting template and posted it to the CoP (Figure 4.3).

## Figure 4.3: Template for Creating an Evidence Folder

**Name of school librarian**

**Name of school**

**Check grade level**

☐ Elementary  ☐ Middle  ☐ High

**I. Mission statements**

District statement

School statement

Library statement

**II. School improvement plan – what are your school's major targets?**

**III. School/library connection I**

[Brief description of how instruction in the library connects with the school's learning targets]

**IV. Lesson exemplars**

[Sample of lesson taught in the library that connects with the school's learning targets]

1. Lesson objective – what am I going to assess?
2. Why am I assessing for this?
3. Who/what is my assessment target – grade level, subject area, curricular unit?
4. Outcomes: What must students be able to demonstrate at the end?
5. Which Illinois Learning Standard is part of this lesson?
6. How am I going to assess for this? How will student performance be measured? What instrument/s will I use?
7. Instructional procedure: How will this lesson be delivered? What will instructors do? What will students do?
8. When will I do the assessment? Timeline?
9. What do I plan to do with the results?
10. Assessment instrument

[Attach your assessment instrument as a separate document if possible]

**V. School/library connection II**

[Brief description of how this particular lesson connects with the school's learning targets]

**VI. Student work**

[Samples of student performance]

**VII. Compiled assessment data**

[Compiled data that summarizes what students learned from the lesson]

**VIII. Student feedback**

[Sample commentary from students if possible]

**IX. Teacher feedback**

[Sample commentary from instructors if possible]

From *Growing Schools: Librarians as Professional Developers* edited by Debbie Abilock, Kristin Fontichiaro, and Violet H. Harada. Santa Barbara, CA: Libraries Unlimited. Copyright © 2012.

## LEARNING FROM PEERS

While the grant managers and academic partners provided online assistance as requested through the CoP, we were also pleased that two high school and two middle school cohort members and one academic partner met twice in a Meebo instant messaging chat room. We had encouraged experimentation with technology, and it was exciting to see cohort members taking the initiative to "try something for fun." They discussed how different data collection tools might be used in their situations and exchanged ideas about having students keep logs of what they had learned. One librarian introduced the possibility of working with two teachers and creating a control group. Her colleagues reminded her of the "small and simple" guidelines we had provided. As the group discussed the issue of assessing and documenting what students were able to do, one participant noted that she had started collecting learning data and found it very useful in improving her teaching. Another librarian noted that not all the projects had to be big and involved. The group also agreed that by exploring and experimenting, they were learning from the results regardless of their success. At the end of the sessions, one person commented that the online chats had focused her thinking and allowed her to learn from her peers.

## PROVIDING INDIVIDUALIZED ASSISTANCE

We originally planned for three two-hour meetings in February and March in addition to the four days of training. While we had envisioned these sessions as opportunities for the group to network and address issues as they arose, we realized that it was not practical to ask cohort members for more release time from their schools to travel to a single site. While the geographic area covered by the two systems was relatively small, the time to travel to one or the other location in metropolitan area traffic was great. Therefore, to make it convenient for cohort members to get face-to-face help from the academic partners, DLS and NSLS decided to scrap the two-hour meetings and each scheduled an open house at their system's headquarters with at least one academic partner present. Attendance at these open houses was voluntary.

In early March, cohort members were invited to come to their system's headquarters for this extra help and support one day after school between 2:00 p.m. and 6:00 p.m. Eight came to DLS and two to NSLS. From the perspective of the participants who attended, the time was well spent as they each received individualized help from an academic partner. For example, one librarian was struggling with analyzing the pre- and post-data she had collected. An academic partner helped her to interpret the results and consider options for documenting her evidence of student learning.

## REFINING COMMUNICATION SKILLS

The additional session in April was devoted to communication training. In his presentation, Mogelluzzo emphasized the following points:

- Know your audience. Be sensitive to their concerns, needs, and interests.
- Identify and state your key points as they relate to that audience.
- Know what you want the audience to do with the information they receive. It may be as simple as stopping by the library to see the finished student products or as complex as funding support for new databases.
- Explain the benefits or consequences of the action to the stakeholders and community.
- Connect the action to what matters to the stakeholders; speak their language. Include short stories, quotes, and anecdotes in the message. These examples allow you to personalize the message and connect with the listener.
- Create a sound bite or a memory hook that the listener will take away. Examples: "It's not your mother's library" or "Libraries don't cost; they pay."

Mongelluzzo used a simple worksheet to help the librarians prepare succinct and attention-getting messages (Figure 4.4).

---

### Figure 4.4: Worksheet for Designing Messages

Topic: _____    Audience: _____

Key points:

Action(s) I want the audience to take:

Benefit(s) or consequences to the audience (from taking that action):

Memory hooks (stories, examples, quotes, analogies, metaphors, etc.):

Sound bite:

---

Cohort members also learned how to prepare "elevator speeches" that were no longer than a minute in length. Mongelluzzo advised librarians that when someone asks how you are doing, jump on the opportunity to share something about the success of your program, how and what students are achieving, and exciting new resources available through your library. He challenged the group to always communicate evidence of what the library program is contributing to the whole school program.

## ASSESSING FOR LEARNING

Prior to the final session in June, the academic partners conducted exit interviews by phone and e-mail with members of their groups. The partners structured their interviews around the following questions (Figure 4.5).

---

### Figure 4.5: Exit Interview Questions

1. On a scale of 1 to 5 (1 being "not at all" and 5 being "significantly"), how has your level of communication with stakeholders changed since you began the project?

2. Which stakeholders have you interacted with most? Rank them from 1 (least) to 3 (most).

3. What changes in the interactions have you observed?

4. What grade levels did you impact?

5. Do you plan to use this strategic process again next year?

6. If yes, which part will you use?

7. How has participation in this project made a difference in your school and library program?

8. What were the biggest challenges?

9. What were the best things about participating in this project?

10. Other comments you would like to make?

11. Do we have your permission to quote you in promotional and reporting materials?

---

The information collected was sent to Marcoux who compiled a report that she presented to the cohort members in the June session. A total of nine elementary, eight middle/junior high, and eight high school cohort members completed the project and submitted "evidence folders" using the template we had provided (refer to Figure 4.3). I received these electronic files through e-mail and forwarded them to Sharon as well. Of the original twenty-eight participants, one left her school position in December and two librarians did not complete the evidence training because of personal commitments.

There were two levels of assessment going on in this professional development: the assessment of how participants were incorporating key concepts in instructional planning, and the assessment of how well K–12 students were learning from the instruction provided by the librarians. Sharon and I coordinated the first level of assessment with Marcoux's assistance. Librarians provided the second level of assessment — evidence of student learning — through documentation in their evidence folders.

**Linda's Commentary**

After going through the communications portion of the training, I now always have an elevator speech ready. In the time that it takes to ride an elevator, I can relate a student success story. For example, when a school board member visited the library to look at the new OPAC software, I filled him in, not on the features of the software, but on the number of 5th graders who had demonstrated they could compile a bibliography. As a result of my participation in "Here's the Evidence," I knew that I could not let an opportunity pass to inform a stakeholder about the impact I was having on student learning. The message at the top of my mind was the recent student successes with this portion of their research project and how that fit into our overall emphasis on Reading and Language Arts performance. He was impressed that these successes were happening in the school and that I was collaborating with teachers to meet learning standards. Now when someone asks, "How are things going in the library?" I have an elevator speech. My answer? "Just great! Did you know that 90 percent of the 5th graders attained 'master storyteller' status last week?" People can't help but stop and have a conversation, and I can elaborate on the accomplishments of our students.

## ASSESSING FOR LIBRARIANS' APPLICATION OF TRAINING

An examination of the evidence folders revealed that twenty-three of the projects directly aligned with the local school improvement plans. They covered fifteen different Illinois Learning Standards. Some projects were cross-disciplinary and targeted multiple standards. Most of the projects incorporated portions of Illinois State Goal 5, which was the research goal. The following are examples of projects reported:

- **An elementary project on graphing was a critical fit between classroom and library.** Computer literacy skills, such as creating a graph, were connected with math skills needed for success on the Illinois State Achievement Tests (ISAT). This activity that connected with ISTE and AASL learning standards helped students develop media literacy as they designed their own graphs and tables.

- **A secondary project connected directly with the school's goals to improve critical thinking skills in science.** The librarian supported the interpretation and analysis of scientific literature by providing access to reliable and current online articles and helping students retrieve information from them. She also assisted students of various reading abilities to comprehend and evaluate the information, providing particular attention to the needs of special education students.

- **A high school project focused on students taking notes for position papers in US government.** The librarian helped students apply methods of social science inquiry by guiding them to derive and support conclusions with evidence from their research.

- **Two projects fell short of librarians collaborating on achieving the school's learning targets.** In one case, the librarian worked in isolation on website evaluation. Although she indicated that this skill could be used across the curriculum, there was no evidence that she had achieved faculty support for this goal. In a second project, we could not easily identify the specific learning goals or the connection to the school's targets.

The interviews that the academic partners conducted confirmed what cohort members had shared at earlier sessions. For one, the members mentioned how important it was to start with the goal in mind. They reaffirmed that assessment and documentation did not have to be complex and time consuming. They all agreed that collecting evidence of student performances made them accountable for learning in their schools. The librarians reported that encouraging changes were happening in their schools. One middle school librarian noted that she had won building-level support for helping students become more competent users of information:

> One of the school goals for next year is to build a more cohesive approach to information literacy during the students' time at the school from 6th grade to 8th grade. I hope that evidence I collect will help to create buy-in from faculty and expand the collaborations into other areas and disciplines.

Another middle school librarian reported that working on the project helped her identify a critical learning need and resulted in collaborative support to meet that need:

> One unexpected piece of information I learned as I worked with my 8th graders was that most of them had never written an actual research paper before. I have spoken with the building principal and several teachers, and we will be working to create a continuum of projects to ensure that all students will have done several research papers before they leave middle school.

Cohort members indicated that collaborative planning and assessment for learning benefitted both the teaching partners and the students. The following reflection summed up this sentiment:

> The teacher involved in this project was completely open to change and ready to make adjustments to the course as well as to individual lessons within the course. We worked together to identify goals for

the project, evaluate how the student works were progressing, and determine what skills the students were lacking in order to create better products. The teacher was enthralled by *Assessing Learning: Librarians and Teachers as Partners* and began marking pages and strategies almost immediately upon seeing the book. When she became discouraged because student work wasn't what she hoped for (they were second semester seniors, after all!), we were able to work together to explain to students that substandard work was not an option. She said that working with me was like "pressing the easy button" because when she would get overwhelmed, we'd simply sit down and work through the problem together. For me, this was an amazing experience because I was able to see the students grow from being barely able to choose a topic to being fully capable of producing professional presentations for business leaders. Several teachers on the adjudication panels stated that more students this semester 1) were better prepared, 2) included detailed research, and 3) presented professional final projects.

## ASSESSING K–12 STUDENTS' LEARNING

The assessment of student learning, based on collaboratively planned lessons with classroom teachers, was the ultimate goal of the training. The objective was to have individuals collect data they could use to improve teaching and learning in their schools. The assessment tools ranged from students creating simple sticky notes that flagged key ideas to pre- and post-tests that required more detailed comprehension of information. The instruments included student-created graphs that displayed how students organized and communicated what they learned as well as short questionnaires that allowed students to reflect on what they were learning and how they felt about their learning. The librarians also used entrance and exit slips, evaluations of note cards and bibliographies, and even simple drawings by non-English-speaking students showing their grasp of math concepts. Here are two examples of assessment techniques used and the assessment results.

An elementary librarian used sticky notes with first graders to assess their ability to make meaningful connections to literature, i.e., text-to-self, text-to-text, and text-to-world. Stories were read to the children over five weeks. The youngsters discussed each story, identified the main idea, and shared the connections they made to each literary work. They wrote their connections on sticky notes and posted the notes on a wall chart under the categories of text-to-self, text-to-text, and text-to-world. At the beginning of the five weeks, 54 percent of the students could make relevant connections. By the end of the five weeks 75 percent could complete this task proficiently. In the Illinois reading test, all of the students showed gains in their ability to create extended literary responses in which they identified the theme of a story and made meaningful connections.

A middle school librarian focused on students' effective use of online databases. The librarian and teachers had previously observed that students were not using the library's databases to do their research. With support from the teachers, the librarian conducted instructional sessions on database searching for several ongoing classroom projects. She documented the students' increased use of different resources including databases in a pre- and post-survey (Figure 4.6). The results were shared not only with students and teachers but also with the administration to justify the expense of database licenses.

## Figure 4.6: Student Use of Different Sources for Research

| Source | Pre-instruction (# of students using) | Post-instruction (# of students using) |
|---|---|---|
| Books | 94 | 83 |
| Encyclopedias | 84 | 68 |
| Magazines | 47 | 93 |
| **Databases** | **10** | **90** |
| Web sites | 75 | 81 |
| Wikipedia | 60 | 63 |
| Internet [Google] | 94 | 85 |

## Linda's Commentary

Students used the note-taking checklist (Figure 4.2) from the pre-assessment as a self-assessment before turning in their note cards. This allowed for students to edit their notes before turning them in for grading. I used the checklist again for the final assessment. Using the same assessment tool allowed me to compare the results and track student progress. My collaborating teacher included note taking as an item in the grading rubric for the project. How did the students do? There were marked improvements on the following criteria:

1. **Using one's own words:** in the pre-assessment, almost 30 percent of the students copied all information. In the post-assessment, 100 percent of the students put facts in their own words some or all of the time.

2. **Paraphrasing:** in the pre-assessment, about 50 percent of the students could paraphrase accurately. In the post-assessment, over 90 percent were able to do this some or all of the time.

3. **Using note cards:** in the pre-assessment, 17 percent of the students were able to properly use the format for note cards. In the post-assessment, 100 percent of the students were able to do this some or all of the time.

4. **Citing sources:** in the pre-assessment, 68 percent of the students were able to correctly cite their sources. In the post-assessment, 94 percent were able to this some or all of the time.

## COMMUNICATING THE EVIDENCE TO STAKEHOLDERS

In their exit interviews, the librarians concurred that having evidence of student performance was critical in educating administrators, teachers, and other stakeholders about the librarian's contributions to the learning process. They reported that stakeholders responded positively to evidence-based communication. For example, one cohort member reported that "showing the learning impact got us back our aides." Another librarian reported, "The project got us on the radar with the new principal." Still another participant said, "We have validity with a new superintendent who is all about the data." Six months after the project ended, we sent a follow-up survey asking the same questions we had used in the exit interviews. About half of the cohort members indicated that they were continuing to use the strategic planning process and assessments.

Although Sharon and I had hoped to compile the training materials into a single document for distribution to a wide group of stakeholders, the two library systems could not financially support additional activities. Nonetheless, we have continued to carry the message about the value of assessing for student learning and collecting evidence for advocacy to various professional library groups, and authored several publications on this theme (Kramer and Ball 2008; Kramer and Diekman 2010; Kramer 2009, 2010).

In reflecting on their experiences, cohort members commented on the challenges they experienced by venturing into uncharted territory and the time invested in experimenting with outcome-based planning and assessment. In spite of the difficulties they encountered, they were overwhelmingly positive about how this training opportunity influenced their practice. As evidenced in the examples below, their comments reflected a newly discovered confidence and a sense of empowerment:

- "Thanks to the grant, I am growing. It's exciting!"

- "I was glad to hear the results of the Illinois study [*Powerful Libraries*]. 'Here's the Evidence' feels like we are completing the picture."

- "I am now speaking the same language as the teachers with my focus on student achievement."

- "I saw how my input influenced a classroom teacher to improve assignments."

- "My participation in this grant resulted in my being viewed as a valued resource and collaborator by my peers."

Since the conclusion of the project, some schools have new administrators and several school librarians have moved on to new jobs. From conversations with them, we learned that cohort members have continued to implement evidence-based practices whether they have remained in their positions or moved on to new posts. They realize the importance of focusing on student learning and reporting evidence of that learning on a regular basis, not just in times of crisis for libraries. They recognize the need to persistently communicate this message. They strongly believe that the real winners in all of this are the students.

## Linda's Commentary

I continued to utilize assessment strategies in both collaborative projects and isolated library skill lessons. I shared the evidence of student learning with classroom teachers, administrators, and parents at every opportunity. One of those opportunities was in the interview process for a position in a school district closer to my home. From the reaction of the interview committee it was clear that I was the only candidate who was able to articulate her impact on student learning. I got the job. When I started the position at my new school, there was an unspoken assumption that I would be focusing on student achievement along with teachers. From the first day, I have been the one at the planning meetings asking, "How will we know what the students have learned? What's our evidence?"

Assessment has improved my practice by focusing my attention on what students are actually learning in our time together. Because I detail the unit's learning outcome and set specific learning targets for each lesson within the unit, my instruction is more focused. I am better able to meet my students where they are in their learning by utilizing pre-assessment data. When I collaborate with teachers, I am able to build in more continuity from unit to unit because the assessment data tells me what skills students still need to master. Assessment has become the cornerstone of my work.

When I realized the difference that incorporating assessment made on my teaching practice and in my library program, I felt compelled to share the information with others. Since 2008, I have presented on assessment and related topics at more than a dozen local, state, and national conferences for school librarians. These presentations vary from one-hour overviews to full-day workshops. I emphasize identifying student needs, capitalizing on opportunities to document student achievement, designing assessment instruments, giving feedback to students, and preparing impact statements for stakeholders. As I share how I incorporate assessment as a way to gauge student learning, other librarians realize that, they too, can make changes to their programs. For example, one attendee stated, "I am going to use the 'I will learn . . .' statements on lessons this week." Another commented, "I don't have to do it [assessment] on Monday, I just have to start with one teacher on Monday!"

These workshops cause a ripple effect. Each workshop participant affects the performance of potentially hundreds of his or her own students each year. One attendee commented, "I will look at the tools for assessment and map out improved instruction." Another said, "With the variety of assessment tools presented I will be better able to reflect on my teaching methods and change . . . to better meet the needs of my students." One added that her participation in the workshop would "impact student learning in numerous ways . . . [It] will motivate me to do better and do more with the students."

## CONCLUSION

Reflecting back, Sharon and I listened to the concerns of our librarians and wanted to offer something that only a multiple-session experience could provide. What we finally developed was an ambitious venture that could not have happened without the cooperation of specialists, academics, and national leaders. I believe what we shared with the librarians was cutting-edge thinking about their role.

I now realize that there were things that could have been done better. In working with our academic partners, for example, we might have requested more detailed documentation on their sessions and exchanges with participants. We might have made site visits and encouraged greater use of the CoP. But in the end when we read the evidence folders, Sharon and I were impressed by how well nearly everyone applied the ideas and strategies introduced in the project. We saw school librarians grow professionally and assume leadership roles both in the cohort and in their schools. We experienced the power of peer groups learning from one another. School librarians often feel alone in their schools. This project not only delivered new approaches to make learning relevant, it provided opportunities for librarians to grow these ideas with their colleagues.

While I have since retired, I believe that what we were training our cohort to do is the very thing all school librarians must embrace in today's schools. Illinois recently adopted the Common Core Standards, which will require that everyone in the schools speak the same language and share a common agenda for student learning. These new standards require that students identify, critique, use, and apply information. These are the very standards that librarians have promoted for years. It is the perfect time for librarians to become indispensable to learning in their schools.

## REFERENCES

American Association of School Librarians (AASL). 2007. *Standards for the 21st-Century Learner.* http://www.ala.org/aasl/standards (cited March 12, 2011).

American Association of School Librarians (AASL). 2009a. *Empowering Learners: Guidelines for School Library Media Programs.* Chicago, IL: American Association of School Librarians.

American Association of School Librarians (AASL). 2009b. *Standards for the 21st-Century Learner in Action.* Chicago, IL: American Association of School Librarians.

Geitgey, Gayle A., and Ann E. Tepe. 2007. "Can You Find the Evidence-Based Practice in Your School Library?" *Library Media Connection* 25(6): 10–12.

Harada, Violet. H. 2007. "Assessing for Learning." Presentation for "Here's the Evidence: School Librarians Help Students Achieve" sponsored by North Suburban Library System and DuPage Library System, Illinois, December.

Harada, Violet H., and Joan M. Yoshina. 2005. *Assessing Learning: Librarians and Teachers as Partners*. Englewood, CO: Libraries Unlimited.

Illinois School Library Media Association. 2005a. *Illinois Study: Powerful Libraries Make Powerful Learners*. Canton: Illinois School Library Media Association.

Illinois School Library Media Association. 2005a. 2005b. *Linking for Learning, The Illinois School Library Guidelines*. 2nd ed. Canton: Illinois School Library Media Association.

Illinois Standards Aligned Instruction for Libraries. *Home—ISAIL*. 2009. http://isail.wikidot.com/system:list-all-pages (cited September 12, 2010).

International Society for Technology in Education. 2007. *National Educational Technology Standards for Students*. http://www.iste.org/standards/nets-for-students/ nets-student-standards-2007.aspx (cited May 26, 2011).

Kramer, Pamela. 2009. "Evidence = Advocacy." *ISLMA News* 21(3): 1.

Kramer, Pamela K. 2010. "Why School Library Information Specialists Need to be Concerned about Assessment." *Linking for Learning, Illinois School Library Media Program Guidelines*. 3rd edition. Canton: Illinois School Library Media Association.

Kramer, Pamela, and Sharon Ball. 2008. "LSTA Grant Update: Here's the Evidence, School Libraries Help Student Achieve." *WebJunction Illinois*, June 19. http://webjunctionworks.org/il/blog/index.php/2008/06/19/lsta-grant-update-heres-the-evidence-school-librarians-help-students-achieve/ (cited May 25, 2011).

Kramer, Pamela K., and Linda Diekman. 2010. "Evidence = Assessment = Advocacy." *Teacher Librarian* 37(3): 27–30.

Mongelluzzo, Stephen. 2005. *Winning Media Interviews: Sure-fire Tactics to Get Your Messages Out*. Vernon Hills, IL: Raisbeck-Marr Publishing.

Todd, Ross J. 2003. *Student Learning through Ohio Libraries: A Summary of the Ohio Research*. http://www.oelma.org/StudentLearning/documents/OELMAResearchStudy8page.pdf (cited April 15, 2011).

Wiggins, Grant, and Jay McTighe. 1998. *Understanding by Design*. Alexandria, VA: Association for Supervision and Curriculum Development.

## A Special Note

Sharon Ball, my partner in this project, was an outstanding educator and skilled grant writer. She succumbed to cancer in 2009 after fighting a valiant battle against the disease throughout our work on this initiative. Linda and I keenly felt Sharon's presence as we relived our project experiences in writing this chapter. She was a wonderful friend and mentor to so many of us. We miss her deeply.

—Pam Kramer

# CHAPTER 5
# LEARNING THROUGH ACTION RESEARCH

*Editors' Note:* Judith Sykes describes how action research has played a critical role in her professional work in Canada first as a school library district specialist, then as a school principal, and presently, as a provincial library manager. At each point in her career, she shares how hunches about library programs evolved into critical questions about quality services, how these questions determined what data to collect, and what actions to take based on the findings. Throughout the chapter, she outlines the crucial steps involved in conducting action research and the importance of allowing questions to drive professional growth. Violet Harada follows with examples of collaboratively undertaken action research from schools in Hawaii. She explains how teachers and librarians move their curiosity about how things might work better into a more formal and systematic approach to finding out how reflective practice can transform teaching.

## Action Research: Professional Renewal as Living in the Question

### Judith Sykes

Action research is a systematic approach to problem solving and understanding phenomena in depth that can be woven into the fabric of everyday work patterns and routines. It connects educational practice with educational theory (Farmer 2003). One of the more significant qualities of action research is that it invites the building-level professional to accept more responsibility for her personal learning and growth (Mertler 2006; McNiff 2002). By envisioning teachers as researchers rather than as the researched, it democratizes the research process. The intent of action research is to enable the professional to "live in a question" for a period of time and ultimately define ways to improve practice (Pascarelli quoted in Sykes 2002, vii).

Action research is a process of defining a question related to one's practice, then designing, executing, reflecting upon, and changing that practice as a result. It combines studying and reviewing literature, collecting and analyzing quantitative and qualitative data, and structuring action plans to create continuous cycles of informed professional renewal. Individuals (educators or students), schools, school districts, and even states or provinces can adopt the methodology of action research. As such, it lends itself to mobilization—indeed, action and transformation—in enabling schools and school libraries to support and advance the learning of each student. Developing skills and strategies for formulating questions, amassing data, structuring events, and analyzing results can lead to profound professional renewal and more responsive service to the students and learning communities one serves. Figure 5.1 captures the spiraling process of action research.

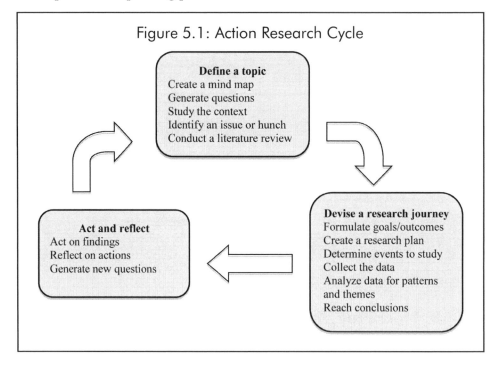

Figure 5.1: Action Research Cycle

**Define a topic**
Create a mind map
Generate questions
Study the context
Identify an issue or hunch
Conduct a literature review

**Devise a research journey**
Formulate goals/outcomes
Create a research plan
Determine events to study
Collect the data
Analyze data for patterns
and themes
Reach conclusions

**Act and reflect**
Act on findings
Reflect on actions
Generate new questions

When I reflected upon how action research enabled me, over and over, to engage in professional renewal, I thought back to three key phases in my professional life. The first came when I was a district school library specialist in the second largest metropolitan school board in Canada. At that time, I was completing graduate studies with the University of Portland. I was also co-chairing the chief superintendent's School Libraries of the Future Task Force that developed the document entitled, *School Libraries Supporting Quality Learning* (Calgary Board of Education 1999). This work led to the revision of district school library operational policy.

Later, I moved on to the role of school principal. It seemed natural for me to engage the skills and processes of action research to mentor the school community and embed the library within a process that was transformative. It helped me take the best of what was foundational and work with my school staff to examine a range of internal and external data sources and literature to build a shared vision for the school and for the school library to be a part of that vision. The process also involved the co-creation of action strategies that were constantly revisited, questioned, and reflected upon. Action research encouraged individuals and groups to try new ways of doing things so that actual transformation of practice could be developed rather than mandated.

As the provincial library manager since 2008, I have coordinated the Alberta Education's School Library Services Initiative (SLSI). Once again, I have drawn on action research skills and processes to engage stakeholders and experts in reviewing provincial school library services and revising provincial school library policy, guidelines, and resource supports. What follows is a summary of my journey.

## ACTION RESEARCH AS A SCHOOL LIBRARY DISTRICT SPECIALIST

My first foray into action research was as a district school library specialist studying the future of school libraries in 1996. The district encompassed over two hundred K–12 schools at the time. As a specialist I worked with all of the school libraries, coordinating the production of the *Recommended Resource Listings K-12*, and *Core Resources for Collection Development*, in English and French. These projects required identifying, evaluating, and selecting learning and professional resources in all formats for the Integrated Media System (IMS) and revising processes for school involvement in evaluating learning resources for the listings.

As a specialist, I also established networks of practice through chairing professional development activities with all departments in the unit — math, science, English — modeling the work a teacher-librarian would do within a school. For the school libraries, I focused on creating communities of practice through area "network meetings" involving school library teams that consisted of various mixes of school administrators, teacher-librarians, teachers, library technicians, and assistants. We invited guest speakers and introduced a range of issues for dialogue. I also established "Teachers as Readers" groups and workshops and kept everyone informed about professional opportunities through a monthly bulletin.

### Focus for Action Research

My major assignment was jointly coordinating the chief superintendent's Libraries of the Future Task Force with a high school teacher-librarian. The task force had been commissioned by the chief superintendent to explore the future of school libraries in the district, create a vision document and an action plan, and recommend revisions to the board policy on school libraries. A diverse group of key stakeholders comprised the task force including system and school personnel, students, and community representatives.

The work of the task force presented me with a focus for my action research in my master's studies at the University of Portland. As I chaired meetings and listened to the participants, I was able to reflect upon the task force dialogue with a critical eye as a participant/observer. I kept a reflective journal to document the events in which I participated. These notes helped me identify key patterns and themes emerging from the discussions.

## Developing a Mind Map

To begin the preparation of writing questions for my research focus, I brainstormed what I knew or assumed I knew using a graphic organizer (mind map) that was framed around the following:

- What stands out for me about my role as an action researcher (e.g., ability to create actions to impact students)?
- What are some assumptions that I believe I need to examine or test (e.g., what is a trend)?
- What questions do I have about some of these assumptions?
- What will stand the test of time?
- What are some things I must consider as I begin to move into the role of action researcher (e.g., learn more about reflective journaling as an impetus to action)?

## CREATING RESEARCH QUESTIONS

The development of good questions is foundational to action research. I took key discoveries from my mind maps and created questions to guide the research. Jamie McKenzie states that "questions and questioning may be the most powerful technologies of all" (1999). McKenzie's "questioning toolbox" (1997) provided expert guidance in my formulation of questions. He created charts detailing seventeen types of questions with explanations, examples, and mind maps. These ranged from basic planning questions and probing questions to essential questions. He also presented additional questions to promote divergent, critical, and analytical thinking and learning. I used McKenzie's categories of questions with teachers and students as I mentored them in their own research journeys. Questions I explored together with educators included:

- What kind of place will the school library of the future be?
- Will it be a place or a center of knowledge construction? Will it be a place of connection?

- Will it be a physical or virtual space or a blend?
- What educational designs or practices are relevant? What needs to transform?
- If over twenty years of research (e.g., Lance and Loertscher 2005) clearly demonstrates that quality school libraries advance student achievement, why are school libraries being cut back or even closed?
- How do libraries become learning centers?
- What are the desired elements of a school library transformed to a learning center? What needs to change? Why?
- How can you transform your library's services?
- How will you know you have been successful?

## KNOWING YOUR CONTEXT

Once a series of questions propels the action researcher, the context of the work needs to be established to define the size and the scope of the exploration. Action research projects frequently examine a classroom, a group of students, or a portion of a school such as the school library. The beauty of becoming an action researcher is learning how to reflect upon your contextual data to gain insight and meaning in shaping professional decisions and actions, to compare and contrast your learning with other researchers and what experts in the field are doing, and to advance your practice with information and confidence in the steps you devise to take.

### Beginning with an Issue

After studying the many questions generated around the future of school libraries, particularly in our district, one question clearly stood out and became the focus for my research. This question was borne of a hunch that had been nudging my thoughts along—the notion that school libraries of the future needed to be vital constructivist centers of learning in both a real and a virtual place where students constructed knowledge from ideas and information. The hunch came from my many years as a teacher-librarian, where I collaborated with teachers to co-create engaging learning experiences around the provincial program of studies. I wanted to ask questions about how to develop libraries as critical centers of learning, and I was prepared to be challenged by ideas I had not previously considered.

## Constructivism

Constructivism emphasizes learning as creating one's own knowledge. Through a continuous process of experiencing new ideas and events, people question and assess what they already know and reconcile these experiences with past knowledge. By doing this, they discard irrelevant notions and expand personal knowledge (Brooks and Brooks 1999). In schools that are based on a constructivist philosophy, students engage in the study of problems and issues that challenge them to think creatively and deeply and to reflect thoughtfully on what they are doing. The instructor's role in such an environment is to listen carefully to students' questions, to facilitate learning that strengthens students' ability to integrate new information, and to encourage more questions.

This curiosity drove my research and helped me focus during times when I found myself veering off into areas that didn't pertain to this particular study. I realized that the next steps would be exploring the literature about teaching and learning in the school library, engaging the district stakeholders in discussions about how libraries might make a significant difference in learning, and analyzing results from data gathered to recommend actions to support the vision.

## REVIEWING THE LITERATURE

To explore the topic of constructivist school libraries, I invited the task force to consult a range of authoritative sources. Our key literature included the works of librarians Walt Crawford and Michael Gorman (1995) on the critical mission and purpose of all libraries. We read pieces from futurists such as Nicholas Negroponte (1995), Derrick de Kerckhove (1995), and David Shenk (1997). We reviewed articles and books by Doug Johnson (2007) and Jamie McKenzie (1996) on education and the impact of new and emerging technology. It was important for us to also read works from school library leaders such as Keith Curry Lance and David Loertscher (2005), Barbara Stripling (1997), Ken Haycock (2003), and Dianne Oberg (1997; Oberg, Hay, and Henri 2000) on school library pedagogy and the crisis in school library development and student access. Critical understandings that emerged from our readings included the following:

- Librarians should take pride in the field of librarianship and value the library's central mission, which is providing equity of access and fostering knowledge and understanding, not simply storing and dispensing data and information (Crawford and Gorman 1995).

- Citizens must be critical thinkers and ethical users of information. To produce such citizens, libraries must move from an industrial age mentality with factory models of living and learning to supporting collaborative, global cultures in a digital age (Negroponte 1995; de Kerckhove 1995; Shenk 1997; Johnson 2007).

- Access is not restricted to libraries as physical spaces but must expand to virtual services that enrich intellectual access to ideas and dialogue. Students must not only locate information but they must construct knowledge by analyzing information, evaluating it, creating new knowledge, and communicating it. This vision becomes the focus of the 21st-century school library—to prepare students to become information-literate citizens (Stripling 1997; Haycock 2003).

## DETERMINING A FOCUS: FORMULATING GOALS, OUTCOMES, AND A PLAN

What our task force had read and reviewed in the literature affirmed what I had been envisioning. It expanded my personal knowledge about learning and teaching, and I discovered new directions to explore, such as the importance of leadership around the wise use of technology as a critical direction for school librarians. I felt ready to decide on my major research goals, the anticipated outcomes, and a plan for gathering data. I formulated four overarching questions to frame my research:

- What defines an excellent school library of the 21st century?

- What is important about the relationship of school libraries to learning and teaching?

- What might be impediments in providing equitable access to excellent school libraries for all students K–12?

- How might some of these impediments be overcome?

I organized my data-gathering action plans around "events" such as interviews with experts in the field (telephone, e-mail, in person), focus group meetings with the school district task force members, and student focus groups (video recordings).

## Collecting and Analyzing the Data: Acting on Findings

As I collected data through these events, I kept field notes that documented the dates, times, locations, persons involved, and other details. I then analyzed the emerging data through a simple form of coding using a different color to highlight key words and phrases in the data that matched my four key research questions. This color-coding helped me to identify five key patterns and themes across the different target groups:

- Application of constructivist learning in school library learning experiences

- Equity of access to information and ideas for all students to achieve academic success

- Qualified school library personnel to guide and facilitate student learning

- Community involvement in school library programs

- Impact of technology in school library programs

The recommendations derived from the above themes ultimately resulted in a new district vision for school libraries that was published by the task force in *School Libraries Supporting Quality Learning* (Calgary Board of Education 1999). Earlier vision documents had focused on the school library largely as a repository for information and resources. The new vision challenged our stakeholders to perceive the school library as a highly interactive learning and teaching environment. It promoted the library as the center, or heart, of the school where collaborative practices helped students become information-literate learners. To support this constructivist vision of learning, we included best practice models with real-life examples of learning experiences in a school library (i.e., examples of project-based learning). Figure 5.2 summarizes the key elements of action research practiced at the district level.

Implementing the new vision required that the district revise its school library policy. The task force co-chair and I worked with the policy division in updating the board library policy, and schools began using it to reexamine their school libraries. This came at a time when the district was moving toward site-based management. With budget cuts in education, it was clearly a challenge to develop program-based budgets, partnerships, and accountability measures for school library services.

## Figure 5.2: Summary of Action Research at the District Level

**Mind map used:**
- Web with reflective questions

**Questions:**
- What defines an excellent school library of the 21st century?
- What is important about the relationship of school libraries to learning and teaching?
- What might be impediments in providing equitable access to excellent school libraries for all students K-12?
- How might some of these impediments be overcome?

**Hunch:**
- School libraries of the future are going to be vital constructivist centers of learning.

**Brief list of literature consulted:**
- Crawford and Gorman, Negroponte, de Kerckhove, Shenk, Johnson, McKenzie, Lance and Loertscher, Stripling, Haycock, Oberg

**Goals:**
- Description of an excellent school library
- Importance of information literacy
- Factors leading to erosion of school libraries
- Proactive solutions to mitigate erosion

**Types of data collected:**
- Expert interviews, telephone/email/ in person surveys, three stakeholder focus groups (task force, stakeholders, students)

**Patterns/themes discovered:**
- Implementing learning founded on constructivist theory
- Involving community in understanding and participating in school libraries
- Promoting the leadership role of qualified school library personnel
- Developing equitable access to quality school libraries
- Adopting wise use of technology

**Conclusions:**
- Shared vision of the future role of quality school libraries in advancing student learning—recognizing that this will be a challenge to achieve
- Recognition that realizing the vision will require new models of staff development, professional networks, and collaboration and teamwork among stakeholder groups

**Reflections:**
- Action research has a snowball effect where the original questions lead to many more research questions

**Changes in practice as a result of the research:**
- Experimenting and examining new models
- Using the richness of qualitative and quantitative data and its analysis in professional growth

As a district specialist, I had been able to use action research with the task force to formulate a vision and inform policy. However, I realized that the real issue would be actualizing the vision at the school level. Knowing this, I decided to make the career move from a district specialist to a building-level administrator. I wanted to see if I could help to bring about the type of change I envisioned as a district specialist. This move required that I serve first as an assistant principal. I found this to be an invaluable opportunity to work with fifty other schools in the area. I was able to create a School Library Network involving school library teams. Members of the network helped develop the monthly meeting agendas. We invited guest speakers, read and exchanged views on articles dealing with best practices, and introduced "hot topics" first in table groups and then as a large group. We discussed issues that had surfaced from the data collected for the district's vision document, e.g., training and hiring accredited school library personnel, understanding our evolving roles and responsibilities as librarians, unlearning old understandings or perceptions, and broadening stakeholder in-servicing based on current best practices in the field.

## ACTION RESEARCH AS A SCHOOL PRINCIPAL

Once I had satisfied the board requirements to gain administrative experience, I applied for and obtained a position as a school principal. I adjusted my contextual lens to the inner workings of a school and how the library could be embedded within the overall school plan and its student learning outcomes, targets, and measures. As an action researcher, new questions were forming in my head. With the economic climate I faced and the decisions I would have to make, could I provide my students and staff with a 21st-century school library program? How could I manage this? How could sustainable steps to implementation be collectively developed? The context included each classroom, each student and teacher, and a unique program that emphasized a learning approach centering on technology and the fine arts (visual arts, music, drama, dance, and film). How could the school library support the arts and technology and each student's success in achieving the outcomes of the provincial programs of study?

### Beginning with an Issue

At the school level, the issue was to take the district vision of the school library as the learning and teaching heart of the school, engage the learning community in a guided conversation around it, and develop a shared vision with staff, students, and parents. The vision would fuel action plans that infused the school library program with the arts and technology as part of the larger school development plan. My hunch was that collaboratively transforming the library into a vital center of constructivist learning would positively impact student learning. At this point, the school had lost its teacher-librarian, and a half-time library assistant managed the library. The library was used for occasional book exchanges, but not learning and teaching. The library assistant was highly enthusiastic, supportive, and involved as over time we transformed the library.

## Reviewing the Literature

My staff and I immersed ourselves in professional learning community (PLC) teams (DuFour et al. 2004; Anderson, Herr and Nihlen 1994), exploring literature pertaining to the arts (Suzuki, McConnell and DeCambra 2002; Gelb 2000), brain research (Jensen 1996; Sylwester 2003; Wolfe 2001), curriculum innovation (McKenzie 1996; Johnson 2007; Sykes 2002, 2006), and school library programs (Alberta Learning 2004). Our goals were to prepare actions and strategies to impact each student's learning, to integrate the arts and technology throughout our curriculum, and to transform our school library from a place that simply provided books and other resources to a constructivist learning center. Not all of the PLC teams focused on school libraries; some focused on leadership, the arts, assessment, and new curricula in math and literacy. Faculty members selected which teams to join based on their interests. Everyone was expected to share their ideas, research, and recommendations with the entire staff to create our school action plans. Some of the critical understandings we gleaned from the literature reviews included the importance of shared leadership, mentorship, and data-driven decision making to build consensus, and best practices focusing on accountability and outcome-based budgeting. It was fortuitous that my area principals' group was also studying accountability for learning (Reeves 2004) and how understanding accountability methods and procedures for improving learning and teaching were foundational to the action research process.

## Determining a Focus: Formulating Questions and a Plan

To examine our school plan—a collaborative, annual process that involved the entire staff—we focused our work on nurturing an environment of inquiry. We used both qualitative and quantitative data to gather evidence of work accomplished and stakeholders' perceptions of achievements. The qualitative data were derived from assessments of classroom and library projects; surveys and focus groups of students, staff, and parents; and information gathered for the Provincial Accountability Pillar (more details on the Pillar are available at http://education.alberta.ca/admin/funding/accountability.aspx). Quantitative data sources included the Provincial Achievement Tests and report cards. In particular for the library, Provincial Achievement Test (PAT) questions focusing on inquiry, such as questions pertaining to social studies topics or literary analysis, were closely examined. The range of data enabled us to examine key student learning outcomes and strategies that were aligned with the provincial programs of study. The school library plan was embedded in the larger school plan, and thus its strategies were dedicated to the same student learning goals and outcomes.

## Collecting and Analyzing the Data—Acting on Findings

After studying all of the data collected, the PLC team focusing on the school library prepared outcomes to share with the staff. One of the school's overarching goals was having "students achieve academic success by engaging in the inquiry process." The school library team proposed the following strategies in support of this goal and ways to measure progress.

### Action Strategies

- Form a PLC for information literacy that addressed teaching strategies and assessment around identified PAT gap areas for inquiry-based learning.

- Advance student information literacy skills by working with faculty and the district school library learning leader on inquiry projects.

- Expand upon collaborative, inquiry-based, arts-infused, and technology-supported learning to develop information literacy across the curriculum.

- Build upon success noted in PAT in subject areas taught through inquiry and address students' need for more time to successfully accomplish tasks.

- Plan and deliver parent education sessions in literacy (e.g., web awareness session).

- Extend leadership and mentorship opportunities for staff, students, and parents in areas that enhance awareness and increase effective use of the school library.

- Provide more opportunities for staff to increase student access to the library for knowledge construction with support and just-in-time professional development.

- Write more grants and expedite budget expenditures for resources in digital media to enhance students' skills in gathering, organizing, and presenting information effectively.

### Ways to Measure Progress

- Raise June PAT scores by 13.4 percent in areas supported by inquiry-based learning in the core subjects and also raise Grade 3 reading scores by 6.7 percent.

- Increase satisfaction ratings regarding expansion of inquiry projects in June school surveys.

- Review and analyze how inquiry-based projects might have impacted achievement test results in November and March report card data.

- Analyze anecdotal files and recorded observations to determine impact of inquiry-based learning experiences.

- Analyze results relating to school library services in the Accountability Pillar.

- Review and reflect on decisions and actions recorded in library PLC meetings.

- Evaluate library inquiry-based projects and note number of projects developed.

- Document topics and numbers in attendance at parent education sessions.

- Collect survey data on how students use or would like to use technology in school and at home.

By implementing the above action strategies and ways to measure progress, we were able to correlate our data and note a steady increase in student success on the achievement tests. We also documented positive gains on report card grades and a growth in the number of inquiry-based projects developed. Although the school did not have a teacher-librarian, two teachers voluntarily stepped into the role of teacher-leaders in the library. Working as a team with the library assistant, the teachers increased the number of collaborative learning and teaching projects so that teaching teams eventually involved all students in at least two projects each year. This change process took almost eight years of continual renewal, data examination, and collaboration to achieve. The students were also very involved with leaders from each classroom providing input into ways that the library might evolve into a learning commons. Figure 5.3 summarizes the key elements of action research implemented at the school level.

As other teachers observed how the school library PLC team used action research to focus on issues and to collect and use data to make improvements, they were inspired to adopt the methodology in their own practice. Several of them not only used action research to improve their classroom teaching but they also incorporated action research in their graduate studies. One of the teachers, who had been a teacher-leader in the library, became an area learning leader while earning a master's degree in technology. She is presently a doctoral candidate studying the impact of technology in learning. Three other teachers adopted action research in pursuing their master's degrees and are now principals or assistant principals.

## Figure 5.3: Summary of Action Research at the School Level

**Mind map used:**
- Webs, notes with reflective questions, ideas

**Questions:**
- What defines an excellent school library for our school?
- How does what we do in the library help our students' learning?

**Hunch:**
- Transforming the school library will enhance student literacy and the co-construction of knowledge as well as support arts-based learning

**Brief list of literature consulted:**
- DuFour, Focus on Inquiry (Alberta Education), Gelb, Johnson, McKenzie, Reeves, Suzuki, Sylwester, Wolfe

**Goals:**
- Description of an excellent school library
- Importance of information literacy
- Proactive solutions to transforming the school library
- Connection between the library and the arts program

**Types of data collected:**
- Student achievement data (provincial tests, classroom assessment, report cards), Accountability Pillar (staff, student, parental survey)

**Patterns/themes discovered:**
- Implementing learning founded on constructivist theory infusing arts/technology
- Involving community in understanding and participation in school libraries
- Promoting the leadership role of qualified personnel in school libraries
- Developing equitable access to quality school libraries
- Adopting wise use of technology

**Conclusions:**
- A dynamic school library program is possible even in a small school with tight funding

**Reflections:**
- Leading a staff in new directions takes daily coaching, mentoring, modeling, dialogue, encouragement
- Transformational change occurs over time

**Changes in practice as a result of the research:**
- Being more patient with the rate and pace of transformational change; yet knowing how to balance that against providing the best program possible for each student every day

From *Growing Schools: Librarians as Professional Developers* edited by Debbie Abilock, Kristin Fontichiaro, and Violet H. Harada. Santa Barbara, CA: Libraries Unlimited. Copyright © 2012.

While my school had made steady progress in establishing a dynamic library program, not all schools in our city or province were able to transform their school libraries as envisioned in the *Quality Learning* document (Calgary Board of Education 1999) or in *Achieving Information Literacy: Standards for School Library Programs in Canada* (Asselin, Branch, and Oberg 2003/2006). In 2008 Alberta Education decided to examine the state of school libraries throughout the province. They created a position for a school library services manager, and I was offered the post. I wondered if I could take what I learned at the district and school levels and apply it to the provincial level. Once again, I started to formulate questions. If the school where I served as principal could progress the way it did with the library, why couldn't all schools? Didn't all students need to benefit from learning supported by transformed school library services? Was the vision reflected in the 1999 district document and the revised 2006 Canadian national standards still relevant in 2008? Would they be relevant twenty years from now?

## ACTION RESEARCH AS A PROVINCIAL LIBRARY MANAGER

My contextual lens shifted once again when I became the provincial library manager in 2008. Now I had to consider all schools in the province and recognize that each school had its own unique context—public, separate, Francophone, charter, and private. This work required that I review K–12 school library services and support resources across the province. Broadening and narrowing my focus was an important skill that I had acquired through the action research paradigm.

### Beginning with an Issue

I was excited to discover that the emerging perspective of the library as a learning commons (Loertscher, Koechlin, and Zwaan 2008) aligned perfectly with the concept of school libraries as constructivist learning centers. A learning commons recognizes that both students and faculty have diverse and evolving needs and provides flexible physical spaces to accommodate these needs as well as access to information anywhere, anytime. This perspective supports learning and teaching innovation in collaboration with staff, students, other libraries, and the community. Considering the diverse school contexts in the province, I had a hunch that schools were at varying stages with school library services, constructivist learning centers, and school library transformation; however, I did not have the data to substantiate this hunch.

### Reviewing the Literature

As I had done at the district and school levels, I initiated a literature review that included examination of *Achieving Information Literacy, Standards for*

*School Library Programs in Canada* (Asselin, Branch, and Oberg 2003/2006), the American Association of School Librarians' *Standards for the 21st-Century Learner* (2007), and other research-based guidelines for school libraries, as well as studies relating to school library collaboration with other libraries. I included studies by multiple teams of researchers that had documented the correlation of student access to school library services on tests and literacy scores.

Our review of the research on transforming a library into a learning commons was particularly relevant to the data we collected and the recommendations we ultimately presented. Through our readings, we discovered that some metaphors for the school library learning commons included the learning laboratory, studio, or even "great room" in the school and community. The commons was viewed as both a physical space and a virtual environment. The key to the commons was intellectual engagement with information and ideas to inform critical and creative thinking. Importantly, the commons encouraged dialogue and collaborative knowledge construction. No matter what format the written word was published in—think print to e-book—the learning commons fostered exploration, critical responses to readings, and the development of joy in reading. The research also recognized the role of emotions as a critical link to learning, hence the value of nurturing healthy relationships and connections. While staffing and leadership for the learning commons varied, it should ideally include teacher-librarians, technology teachers, and teacher-leaders in instruction. Administrative vision and support were crucial. Other partners that nurtured the learning commons were library technicians and assistants, who supported students and teachers, and community librarians, who worked with schools to create life-long readers and library members.

## Determining a Focus: Formulating Questions and a Plan

The System Improvement Group, Accountability and Reporting Division of Alberta Education, created a provincial school library survey to gather current information on K–12 library staffing and facilities, and access to technology, resources, and services. The goal was to develop an inventory of the current state of school libraries in Alberta. A critical part of the design process was having the the School Library Advisory and Inter-branch Committees review drafts of the survey questions.

As the provincial library manager, I worked closely with the School Library Advisory Committee. This advisory committee participated in the focus groups for advisement and review of initiative actions that included the literature and research, policy review, and design of the provincial school library survey. The committee was also involved in the study and compilation of the work of four subcommittees preparing resource supports for the initiative. Comprising the committee were representatives from the College of Alberta School Superintendents, Alberta Teachers' Association

Specialist Councils, Alberta School Library Council, Educational Technology Council, Alberta School Boards Association, Association of School Business Officials of Alberta, Library Association of Alberta, Alberta Library Trustees Association, Alberta Association of Library Technicians, Alberta School Councils' Association, Alberta Regional Library Systems, University of Alberta, and teacher-librarians from northern and southern Alberta.

## Collecting and Analyzing the Data: Acting on Findings

Superintendents were informed about the survey before it was officially disseminated to the principals in all Alberta schools. The feedback from principals confirmed the need to revise Alberta Education's 1984 *Policy, Guidelines, Procedures and Standards for School Libraries in Alberta*. A gap analysis of the survey results prepared for the consultation process revealed three key themes: planning for student learning through library services, pedagogical support for student learning, and students' seamless access to physical or virtual school library services. A document entitled *Transforming Canadian School Libraries to Meet the Needs of 21st Century Learners: Alberta Education School Library Services Initiative Research Review and Principal Survey Themes* (Alberta Education 2010), provides a detailed analysis of the data. Some of the key responses to each of themes and the recommended strategies follow.

### Planning for Student Learning

Principals' responses indicated that

- 58 percent did not have a current plan for school library services;
- 64 percent did not have a budget plan;
- 66 percent did not have a collection development plan; and
- 80 percent did not link student learning outcomes to the school library in the annual school plan.

Recommended strategies to strengthen library involvement in student learning included:

- creating awareness for and implementing the perspective of the school library as a learning commons;
- providing models of resource support and budgets for libraries functioning as a learning commons;
- addressing how to link student learning outcomes to school library access;
- developing student learning rubrics and/or continuums to facilitate the linkage to student learning outcomes;

- studying how school-based assessment data correlates with the development of a learning commons; and
- promoting new research partnerships with the district or universities to study the impact of a learning commons on student learning.

## Pedagogical Support for Student Learning

Principals' responses indicated that

- 30 percent had no staff with any form of library training attending the library;
- 35 percent used a library technician or clerk to attend the library;
- 35 percent used a library assistant/clerk to attend the library;
- 57 percent did not report any co-planning and teaching between the classroom and the school library;
- 74 percent had less than 0.5 FTE assigned to a teacher to coordinate library services; and
- 90 percent did not have a teacher-librarian.

Recommended strategies to gain greater pedagogical support for learning included

- identifying key personnel essential in a learning commons team and building capacity around understanding the roles and responsibilities of all staff in supporting student learning; and
- developing innovative in-service models that address the interdependence of a learning commons team in co-planning and teaching, promoting recreational reading, and addressing reference needs.

## Students' Seamless Access to Physical and Virtual Library Services

Principals' responses indicated that

- 21 percent only opened the school library at selective times throughout the week;
- 70 percent did not have an online catalogue; and
- 71 percent did not have a school library web page.

Recommended strategies to improve access to both physical and virtual services included

- clearly defining "seamless access" as both physical and intellectual access for all students;

- ensuring that each learning commons becomes a portal to the world and allows any time, any place, any pace learning; and

- developing and highlighting innovative student learning models in the physical and virtual learning commons.

The data-driven recommendations have informed the collaborative revision work currently underway on the school library services policy. Consultation with the School Library Advisory Committee and its executive boards has been critical in the process of updating the policy. Appendix 5A documents the questions framing their work.

In studying the data, we realize that a variety of support resources will be essential to provide students with seamless access to library services in every school. These resources must include student learning models, innovative strategies for improved access to K–12 library services across the province, and in-service models to build capacity for school library service development. The SLSI will also explore sharing licensing for digital resources with Municipal Affairs (public libraries) and Advanced Education and Technology (post-graduate). Figure 5.4 summarizes how action research was conducted at the provincial level.

---

### Figure 5.4: Summary of Action Research at the Provincial Level

**Mind map used:**
- Webs, notes with reflective questions, numerous writing drafts

**Questions:**
- What defines an excellent school library for our province that is based on best practice, innovation (the emergence of the school library learning commons) and the current changing environment)?
- How can we demonstrate the connection between school library services and the impact on each student's learning?
- How can we link school development goals to the school library goals and action planning?
- How can we foster collaborative teamwork for school library transformation within schools and within the community?

**Hunch:**
- The transformation of school library services to a learning commons perspective will create both dissonance and resonance as stakeholders struggle together to support student learning.

**Brief list of literature consulted:**
- Koechlin/Loertscher/Zwann, Haycock, Lance, Canadian Association of School Libraries, American Association of School Libraries, Ontario Association of School Libraries

(continued on page 114)

**Goals:**
- School library transformation to a physical/virtual/intellectual learning commons
- Critical importance of the school library learning commons perspective to student success
- Ideally led by teacher-librarians: explore shared models of creating leaders to establish learning commons
- Proactive solutions to transforming school library services: developing leadership, teams

**Types of data collected:**
- Provincial survey (on-line)
- Focus groups
- Committees (both advisory and working groups)
- Consultations with experts
- Communications with colleagues in government and library field

**Patterns/themes discovered:**

Capacity building needed for:
- planning for student learning through library services
- pedagogical support for student learning
- students' seamless access to physical or virtual school library services

**Conclusions:**
- Belief that a school can develop a dynamic school library learning commons through collaborative teams focusing on student learning outcomes

**Reflections:**
- Leading a province in new, transformative directions takes coaching, mentoring, modeling, dialogue, encouragement, patience

- Transformational change takes time but there must be impetus to begin and accountability to sustain

**Changes in practice as a result of the research:**
- Learning to become more patient with the rate and pace of large scale transformational change; knowing how to balance that with providing the best supports for varied and unique situations

## CONCLUSION

My experiences with action research at each major stage of my career have strengthened my conviction that this form of intentional reflection tests and affirms a person's beliefs and assumptions. I discovered that the process of questioning opened avenues to even more challenging questions for me. In this chapter, I stressed the importance of knowing the literature and collecting rich data that helped us understand and derive conclusions about the questions we asked. We started with hunches and evolved them into foci for the research. The process of knowledge construction was collaborative—all of my work involved teams, task forces, and committees. I learned the critical importance of honoring open and honest dialogue and providing encouragement through modeling, coaching, and mentoring.

I also came to realize that substantive actions take time to implement. Change requires patience and persistence. There is a tension between dissonance and resonance inherent in this process. Transformation causes us to rethink and question the way we have always done things, and this causes dissonance. However, as we work through the action research process and examine and engage in research and evidence, develop a shared vision, and incorporate our learning and reflection into informed actions, we move back to resonance.

As action researchers, we assume the roles of both the participant and the observer as we live in and reflect upon our actions. Through this introspective and deliberate process, we discover strategies that improve practice and allow us to view issues through divergent lenses. By using the tools of action research, we personalize what is learned in our day-to-day environments. Living in a question ultimately leads to living in the next one(s), generating a snowball effect. Action research empowers us to live and act through inquiry.

## REFERENCES

Alberta Education. 2010. "Transforming Canadian School Libraries to Meet the Needs of 21st Century Learners: Alberta Education School Library Services Initiative - Research Review and Principal Survey Themes." http://education.alberta.ca/department/ipr/slsi.aspx (cited March 9, 2011).

Alberta Learning. 2004. *Focus on Inquiry*. http://education.alberta.ca/media/313361/focusoninquiry.pdf (cited June 6, 2011).

American Association of School Librarians. 2007. *Standards for the 21st-Century Learner.* http://www.ala.org/ala/mgrps/divs/aasl/guidelinesand standards/learningstandards/standards.cfm (cited March 9, 2011).

Anderson, Gary L., Kathryn Herr, and Ann Sigrid Nihlen. 1994. *Studying Your Own School, An Educator's Guide to Qualitative Practitioner Research.* Thousand Oaks, CA: Corwin Press.

Asselin, Marlene, Jennifer L. Branch, and Dianne Oberg, eds. 2003, revised 2006. *Achieving Information Literacy: Standards for School Library Programs in Canada*. Ottawa: Canadian School Library Association.

Brooks, Jacqueline Grennon, and Martin G. Brooks. 1999. *In Search of Understanding: The Case for Constructivist Classrooms.* Alexandra, VA: Association for Supervision and Curriculum Development.

Calgary Board of Education. *School Libraries Supporting Quality Learning.* Calgary, Canada: Calgary Board of Education, 1999.

Crawford, Walt, and Michael Gorman. *Future Libraries: Dreams, Madness, Reality.* Chicago: American Library Association, 1995.

De Kerckhove, Derrick. *The Skin of Culture: Investigating the New Electronic Reality.* Toronto, Canada: Somerville House, 1995.

DuFour, Richard et al. 2004. *Whatever It Takes: How Professional Learning Communities Respond When Kids Don't Learn.* Bloomington, IN: Solution Tree Press.

Farmer, Lesley S. J. 2003. *How to Conduct Action Research: A Guide for Library Media Specialists.* Chicago: American Association of School Librarians.

Gelb, Michael. 2000. *How to Think Like Leonardo da Vinci: Seven Steps to Genius Every Day.* New York: Dell.

Haycock, Ken. 2003. *The Crisis in Canada's School Libraries: The Case for Reform and Reinvestment.* Toronto: Association of Canadian Publishers.

Jensen, Eric. 1996. *Brain-based Learning.* Del Mar, CA: Turning Point.

Johnson, Doug. 2007. *The Indispensable Librarian: Surviving (and Thriving) in School Media Centers.* Worthington, OH: Linworth Publishing.

Lance, Keith Curry, and David V. Loertscher. 2005. *Powering Achievement: School Library Media Programs Make a Difference: The Evidence Mounts.* 3rd ed. Salt Lake City: Hi Willow Research and Publishing.

Loertscher, David V., Carol Koechlin, and Sandi Zwaan. 2008. *The New Learning Commons: Where Learners Win! Reinventing School Libraries and Computer Labs.* Salt Lake City: Hi Willow Research and Publishing.

McKenzie, Jamie. 1996. "Libraries of the Future." *School Libraries in Canada* 16(2): 6–9.

McKenzie, Jamie. 1997. "A Questioning Toolkit." *FNO* 7(3). http://www.fno.org/nov97/toolkit.html (cited May 10, 2011).

McKenzie, Jamie. 1999. "Beyond Technology: Questioning, Research, and the Information Literate School Community." *FNO 9*(3). http://www.fno.org/nov99/techquest.html

McNiff, Jean. 2002 *Action Research: Principles and Practice.* 2d ed. London: Routledge Falmer.

Mertler, Craig A. 2006. *Action Research: Teachers As Researchers in the Classroom.* Thousand Oaks, CA: Sage Publications.

Negroponte, Nicholas. 1995. *Being Digital.* New York: Vintage.

Oberg, Dianne. 1997. "Ways of Demonstrating That School Libraries Make a Difference in Learning." *LRC Newsletter* (Fall): 18–22.

Oberg, Dianne, Lyn Hay, and James Henri. 2000. "The Role of the Principal in an Information Literate School Community: Cross-Country Comparisons from an International Research Project." *School Library Media Research* 3. http://www.ala.org/ala/mgrps/divs/aasl/aaslpubsandjournals/ slmrb/slmrcontents/ volume32000/principal2.cfm (cited March 9, 2011).

Reeves, Douglas B. 2004. *Accountability for Learning: How Teachers and School Leaders Can Take Charge*. Alexandria, VA: Association for Supervision and Curriculum Development.

Shenk, David. 1997. *Data Smog*. San Francisco: Harper Edge, 1997.

Stripling, Barbara. 1997. "School Libraries: Catalysts for Authentic Learning." *School Library Media Quarterly* 25(2): 89–90.

Suzuki, David T., Amanda McConnell, and Maria DeCambra. *The Sacred Balance: A Visual Celebration of Our Place in Nature*. Vancouver, Canada: Greystone Books.

Sykes, Judith. 2002. *Action Research: A Practical Guide for Transforming Your School Library*. Greenwood Village, CO: Libraries Unlimited.

Sykes, Judith. 2006. *Brain-friendly School Libraries*. Westport, CT: Libraries Unlimited.

Sylwester, Robert. 2003. *A Biological Brain in a Cultural Classroom: Enhancing Cognitive and Social Development Through Collaborative Classroom Management*. 2nd ed. Thousand Oaks, CA: Corwin Press.

Wolfe, Pat. 2001. *Brain Matters: Translating Research into Classroom Practice*. Alexandria, VA: Association for Supervision and Curriculum Development.

## Appendix 5A: Stakeholder Consultation with the School Library Advisory Committee

During the winter of 2010, a stakeholder consultation with the School Library Advisory Committee and their executive boards was held to review a draft of the revised policy, and a consultation report was prepared detailing and analyzing data. Further consultation with School Library Advisory Committee stakeholder groups on the draft revised *School Library Services Policy and Guidelines* occurred January through April 2010. School Library Advisory Committee members submitted reports to Alberta Education from their association/organization executives framed around a series of guiding questions. A summary of the consultation and a draft of the revised *School Library Services Policy and Guidelines* endorsed by the School Library Advisory Committee were submitted to Alberta Education in 2010.

1. What does your representative group support in the draft revised Library Access Policy?

Comment on ensuring student access to:

- Library services in a transformed physical and virtual space—is there another word besides "library" we should use? Does "library" suggest only a physical space?
- Information
- Guidance from trained library staff

Comment on what your representative group response supports in developing and implementing a school library strategy that supports a school's education plan, specifically:

- The learning needs of the students served;
- The context of the school(s) served;
- A shift to a learning commons perspective;
- The principal's role in developing a school library strategy;
- Developing student outcomes, targets, and measures that align library services access with the school's own student outcomes, targets, and measures;
- Reporting student outcomes, targets, and measures that align library services access with the school's own student outcomes, targets, and measures at a school or jurisdictional level;
- Roles and responsibilities of a school library team; and
- Selection of print and electronic resources for students and teachers.

2. Using the above frame of reference, what does your representative group find challenging to support in the draft Library Access Policy?

3. If the policy were effective and well implemented with a well-designed library strategy enhancing student learning, student achievement at the provincial level should rise. What measures, if any, need to be in place at the local level to ensure effectiveness? What indicators of success would be evident at the school level?

4. Does the draft revised policy provide a balance between student access to library services and direction to school authorities?

5. What additional advice do you have regarding student access to library services, information, and guidance from trained library staff for Alberta Education at this time?

# School Librarians as Action Researchers

Violet H. Harada

School librarians are well suited to be action researchers. Carol Gordon (2009) states that the collaborative nature of the classroom teacher/librarian relationship in planning and instruction is ideal for the collaborative tendencies of action research. Equally important, by engaging in action research, librarians and teachers model the very process of inquiry that they strive to promote with their students. In short, both students and instructors are doing research in a school community where action research is happening.

## WHAT'S INVOLVED

Action research begins with a deep self-questioning process to identify a researchable question. It involves the following key components:

- clear definition of the problem or situation to be addressed
- selection of appropriate actions or interventions based on the problem definition
- identification of techniques for data collection
- implementation of the planning-action-evaluation spiral

Figure 5.5 provides elements of the process and examples of questions that action researchers need to ask.

These components are not necessarily linear; as unplanned changes and events occur, the researchers should be able to reflect on these occurrences and consider revised options. Marian Mohr and colleagues emphasize that action research "both shapes and is shaped by its context" (2004, 25). Unlike experimental research, which does not permit adjusting variables during the trial period, action research recognizes that a midphase change may positively influence the results. As researchers identify and better understand the assumptions underlying the schools in which they operate, they strive to uncover the relationships and tensions at work, and make changes for the better.

## WHAT IT LOOKS LIKE IN PRACTICE

Over the last decade, I have been a university partner with teams of librarians and teachers at elementary schools that were searching for better ways to incorporate inquiry-based learning into the curriculum (Harada 2005). The teams used the following data-gathering procedures to determine results: (1) samples of students' work, (2) reflection logs written by students, (3) teacher and librarian lesson plans, and (4) informal notes and anecdotal logs maintained by the instructional partners. Here are snapshots of action research conducted in three of the schools.

### Figure 5.5: Key Elements of Action Research and Related Questions

| Key Elements | Examples of Questions |
| --- | --- |
| Formulation of idea | What are my underlying assumptions?<br>What will I try in order to improve my practice?<br>What will be the observable change from this proposed intervention? |
| Exploration of idea | How will this proposed intervention impact what is happening at my school?<br>What do I already know about this intervention?<br>How can I find out more about it? |
| Planning the research | How do I involve students and colleagues in the study?<br>How can I develop benchmarks to guide my progress?<br>How might this change be measured or observed?<br>What data would be most appropriate to collect?<br>How will I document the process? |
| Implementation of research | What does the data tell me?<br>Was my research design appropriate for what I wanted to address? |
| Reflection and next steps | Was the intervention effective? How do I know this?<br>How do I communicate results to key audiences?<br>What should be the next actions?<br>What new questions do I now have? |

## School A

*Focus.* The team included a 6th grade teacher and the librarian. They formulated the following questions to guide their inquiry: (1) What are effective intervention strategies to help students understand a process approach to information searching and use? (2) How might students assess their own learning throughout this process? The team spent more than a semester working with students on two mini-research projects.

*Findings.* A combination of guided practice, immediate feedback, and conferencing was deemed "highly effective." Instructors and students singled out conferencing as most essential. In addition, both students and instructors repeatedly mentioned the positive results of working together to construct and use rubrics.

*Action taken.* The team worked on another extended project with the students later that year. They intentionally built more modeling and practice sessions in both the library and the classroom. Since students were working on group projects, the teacher and librarian scheduled regular conferences with the different teams to provide feedback and support as needed. Working with the students, the teacher and librarian refined the rubric being used to assess student performance at different points in the research process. In addition, the librarian shared what was happening with other teachers at the upper grade levels. She facilitated discussions about how similar strategies might be incorporated in projects with these teachers in the upcoming school year.

## School B

*Focus.* The team included the librarian and a teacher, who taught a mixed class of 5th and 6th grade students. They studied the effectiveness of journal writing as a strategy to build deeper student understanding about the research process. They worked with students over a six-month period and implemented two social studies projects.

*Findings.* The team discovered that 75 percent of the students improved in expressing their understanding of the research process between the first project conducted early in the school year and the second project completed at the midpoint of the year. Figure 5.6 provides examples of Student X's journal entries on information searching and taking notes during the second project.

---

### Figure 5.6: Sample of Student X's Journal Entries on Information Searching and Note Taking

*Scan through all of your resources. Take your time while doing this. While skimming you tag important sections then it will be easier to go back to that page and find information. Always look at your questions because they give you clues about what to look for. Take notes by writing keywords first, then long answers. Don't copy your answers out of the book because the teacher knows what kind of work you do and you will have to redo it anyway.*

---

*Action taken.* Toward the end of the school year, students in this class decided to share what they had learned about the research process with 4th grade students at the school. They revisited the logs they had written and discussed what they had learned. In teams, the students prepared slide presentations on critical things they had discovered about how to search for and use information. In May, the librarian invited these students to share the slides with the 4th graders. The older students titled their presentation "Tips to Success When You Get to the 5th and 6th Grades." The librarian and teacher continued to incorporate journal writing as an effective tool for self-assessment in subsequent years.

## School C

*Focus.* The librarian and a kindergarten teacher wondered: as part of an inquiry process, could students at this young age accurately identify major steps involved in finding answers to questions? The context for this study emerged when students found a strange bug on the playground and wanted to learn more about it. The students' questions fueled the ensuing investigation. At the end, they shared their findings with the rest of the school by producing a two-minute video that was aired on the school's closed circuit network.

*Findings.* As a result of the bug project, students also created a class concept web of the inquiry process (Figure 5.7). The web reflected students' awareness of the following aspects of the process:

- Prior knowledge must be considered as part of an investigation.
- Questions (i.e., wonderings) shape an inquiry.
- Information may not be easily found.
- Ethical management of information is critical.
- Knowledge gained should be shared with others.

*Action taken.* For the remainder of the school year, other students in the school recognized these kindergarteners as the bug experts on campus. When students found strange bugs on the playground, they asked the kindergarteners to search for and share information about the insects. The young researchers eagerly accepted these challenges. As the school year progressed, they became more adept at knowing where to search for information and how to communicate their newfound knowledge. The teacher had the students reexamine and expand on the class concept map as they worked on additional projects in science and social studies that year. She and the librarian continued to use concept mapping as an effective strategy to organize and synthesize information with students.

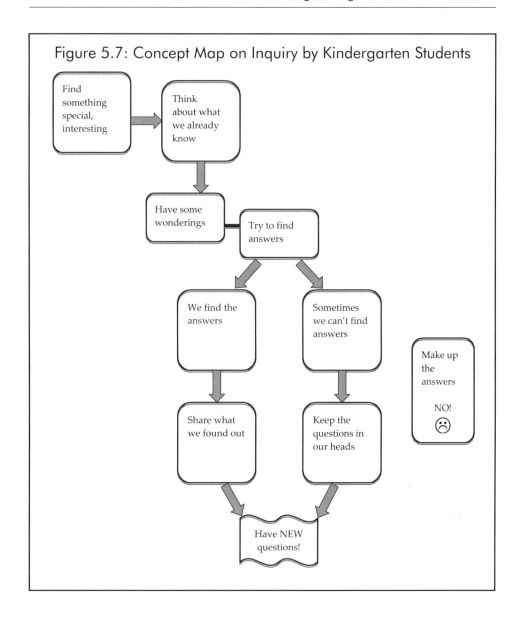

Figure 5.7: Concept Map on Inquiry by Kindergarten Students

## TAKING UP THE CHALLENGE

The goal of action research is "changing practitioners' practices, their understanding of their practices, and the conditions in which they practice" (Kemmis 2009, 463). When school librarians incorporate action research into their teaching and share action research with colleagues, collaboration becomes the context for leadership and change. It's a practice worth the challenge!

## REFERENCES

Gordon, Carol A. 2009. "An Emerging Theory for Evidence Based Information Literacy Instruction in School Libraries, Part 1: Building a Foundation." *Evidence Based Library and Information Practice* 4(2): 56–77. http://ejournals.library.ualberta.ca/index.php/EBLIP/article/view/5614/5320 (cited September 21, 2011).

Harada, Violet H. 2005. "Librarians and Teachers as Research Partners: Reshaping Practices Based on Assessment and Reflection." *School Libraries Worldwide* 11, no. 2 (2005): 49–72.

Kemmis, Stephen. 2009. "Action Research as a Practice-Based Practice." *Educational Action Research* 17, no. 3 (September): 463–74.

Mohr, Marian, Courtney Rogers, Betsy Sanford, Mary Ann Nocerino, Marion MacLean, and Sheila Clawson. 2004. *Teacher Research for Better Schools.* New York: Teachers College Press.

# CHAPTER 6
# REINVENTING OUR ROLE

*Editors' Note:* As the inundation of Web 2.0 tools threatens to overwhelm even the most purpose-driven educators' efforts to incorporate technology, Mike Eisenberg introduces the added challenge of prioritizing: why a school librarian leader must shape her library's allocation of time, resources, and efforts, including the provision of professional development in technology, to the school's priorities. Connie Williams follows by reflecting on how she has designed relevant and thoughtful professional development in the past and how the paradigm shift that new technologies affords has presented her with further challenges in her new school, as she struggles to rank her priorities in the face of budget cutbacks, time constraints, and other education initiatives.

## On the Role of the Teacher-Librarian as Information Manager

Mike Eisenberg

In order to systematically address the teacher-librarians' role in information management, it's essential to first set the context for that role. Context begins (and ends) with the needs of students, and in the middle includes the chosen instructional and curriculum goals, objectives, and program of the school as well as its logistics of the setting (number of students, classroom teachers, grades, schedule, organization of the school, etc.). The teacher-librarian (TL) and the library information and technology (LIT) program have a fundamental role in learning *regardless* of the learning focus of the school—e.g., standards and tests, inquiry-based learning, and one-on-one laptops. Furthermore, the practice of teacher-librarians themselves setting library program goals and program must stop. There's a lot of talk in our field about collaboration, but the most important collaboration that can (and must) take place is for the library information and technology program to be the *school's* program through TL collaboration with the school community. The goals and emphasis of the LIT program should be collaboratively determined on an ongoing basis—through leadership teams, the LIT program advisory committee, and regular meetings with administrators.

I refer to this as "pie-chart planning." In a nutshell: The mission of the LIT program is to ensure that students are effective users and producers of ideas and information. The program can fulfill this mission through (1) information and technology literacy learning, (2) reading advocacy, and (3) information management. The percentages of time and effort allocated to each of these functions should be based on the needs of the students and the school. The allocations should be set before the beginning of the school year and then revised and adjusted each marking period collaboratively by teacher-librarians and the school community as noted above.

The elements and options associated with the first two options—information and technology literacy learning and reading advocacy—are fairly well known and established, even as they are changing due to significant changes in technology, access, collections, and facilities. The third function—information management—may be less clear. Consider this function as the "information infrastructure" in the school—similar to the information management unit in businesses and organizations. Most businesses have CIOs—chief information officers—who oversee the information operation and various systems, resources, and staff. There is no CIO at the school building level, but there should be, and the teacher-librarian can fulfill that role. That means overseeing all the information systems (network, websites, print library collections, learning resources, textbooks, online resources, etc.) and making sure that the staff, systems, and resources are focused on meeting student and teacher needs. It also means providing support and professional development to other teachers as needed.

I can hear the outcry that we don't have the time, staff, or support to do this. "I can't even get the books back on the shelves." But remember, we've changed the way decisions are made about LIT program priorities as well as how time, effort, and resources are allocated. Therefore, now the TL can work collaboratively with administrators and decision-making teams to decide on priorities and see that the program has the support elements to deliver on the priorities. And, of course, it also means giving up low-priority program elements and reallocating existing resources (particularly TL time).

One brief example: in Shady Grove Middle School (Gaithersburg, MD) (grades 5–8), the top educational priority for the year is meaningful integration of technology into classroom instruction and learning. This comes from the district, but is also embraced by the building leadership team, teaching staff, and administrators. Established goals for the school year include student use of computers and networked resources in everyday, classroom learning. The #1 priority for the LIT program (including the teacher-librarian and technology teaching assistant who is now assigned to the LIT program) is to maximize the amount of access to a computer and the Internet for each student. An equally important priority is to support every classroom teacher in setting up a class website that guides students through subject area content, resources, exercises, and assessments.

To meet these priorities, the reading advocacy program will be scaled back drastically for this year including maintenance-level collection development and having classroom teachers assume reading promotion responsibilities. The information and technology literacy program will be directly tied to the technology priorities of access and classroom instruction. As part of the information management function, the teacher-librarian focuses on managing existing laptop and desktop resources, purchasing as many new devices as possible, and surveying the students (and parents) to create an inventory of devices, operating systems, software, and Internet access available to students outside of school. The survey also inventories devices that students would be able to bring to school if encouraged to do so. The teacher-librarian will work with the administration and leadership team to develop a plan to maximize student availability and access.

In addition, the LIT program will oversee implementation of a system to create the classroom websites and coordinate classroom instruction (e.g., Moodle). The teacher-librarian will hold a series of professional development sessions focusing on the pedagogical use of the system, the use of e-books and online resources in instruction, and online assessment. The TL will either teach these sessions or arrange for others to do so. The TL will also establish two support communities: online and in-person (before or after school) for posting, sharing, and discussing best practices and concerns.

This example shows a LIT program and teacher-librarian directly focused on school priorities, essential to the school's achieving those priorities, and recognized as such. It also shows the potential scope of the information management role. Lastly, it demonstrates how systematic, pie-chart planning can deliver a dynamic and flexible program that helps to make the difficult decisions allocating staff, resources, and systems to meeting priority student needs.

# They Call it Learning

Connie Williams

## PRACTICING A CRAFT

Every summer for many years, a friend of the family, a retired teacher, could be found hip deep in the cold water of the Rio Grande, his fishing line splayed out into the river, and the sun reflecting off the rushing water. It took such patience and practice to wade out there and cast the perfect arc of his line so that it sunk right where he aimed. And he'd wait and wait. He might reel one in and pocket it into his creel or come home empty handed but at peace. Through long Oklahoma winters he'd sit contentedly making flies, each one directed to a different kind of fish, each a work of art. When asked why he did this—plan, create, practice, perfect his craft—especially since it didn't always result in bringing home any fish, he'd say: "Well, you know, they call it fishing. Not catching." What an amazing thought: Practice, not just results. Every day I hear the words "results" and "student achievement," but did we practice our craft? Did I help someone improve their teaching?

I got to thinking about fishing a as model of deep and satisfying professional learning. What I'd really like to be able to say to my administrators or to a visitor who drops by when the library is brimming with students chatting, reading, or doing homework, is that a colleague and I are working together to improve a lesson for next week. "You know," I'd say, "right now we're learning, not teaching."

## THE SCHOOL CONTEXT

I began my teacher librarian career in a junior high of just over one thousand students covering 7th and 8th grades. It is one of two junior high schools in the district, with each junior high school feeding into their own high school. We are a most fortunate district in California with incredible community support: each secondary school has a teacher librarian because our community passed a parcel tax that pays for two librarian positions and money for materials. The other two positions are supported by district funds and their support for the school libraries. Petaluma is a town that maintains, and is proud of, its agricultural history even as it seems to be moving closer to becoming a "telecom" valley. Our students come from a variety of backgrounds, and diversity is embraced.

## MY FISHING BEGINS

I began my learning journey during the twenty years I spent in junior high. There are those who praise me for having "survived" junior high for all those years, and those who say I must have been crazy. I reckon that I've been a little bit of both. During those twenty years in one school, I slowly built a set of faculty expectations about working with the library that shaped the school culture. New teachers would slide right in to that culture when I introduced myself and the library team, what we had to offer, and how we'd love to work with them on any assignment.

Creating a reflective and collaborative climate takes time, and, while it's mostly a matter of everyone taking baby steps, I believe that it's important that the librarian take that first one. I offered my services in person—one teacher at a time, one lesson at a time, and even one list of new titles at a time. These small steps do lead into longer and more involved lesson planning and eventually to a professional learning culture that permeates the entire campus.

One of my most satisfying multiyear collaborations emerged from a conversation with a science teacher about feeling professionally stale. When the County Office of Education (COE) offered a school-team computer workshop, Carol and I signed up to create technology-infused lessons together, knowing that the COE's IT leader would be on hand to help us over the learning curve. After creating podcasts, refining our video editing skills, and acquiring some new lesson-design ideas, we developed a simulation in which students would learn important science content, think through alternative approaches to a problem, and create a presentation to influence a defined audience.

We based this unit on a real situation: our school was moving to a new site. The district facilities designer explained to our classes that the planning team was required to prepare an environmental report for the three sites selected by the Board of Education. Their proposal would consider ways to mitigate the impact of potential natural disasters such as tsunamis, mudslides, earthquakes, and floods. Since the facilities planners actually had to research and calculate systematic responses to these disasters—and since these were topics within our Life Science standards—we reasoned that our students would treat their research as an authentic challenge. They would be motivated to learn about these disasters thoroughly, develop a considered opinion, and defend their choice passionately in front of a board using audio, video, posters, PowerPoint, and other presentation tools. After we identified several state standards that could be met including those in science, technology, language arts, and English Language Learning, I agreed to teach propaganda techniques (media literacy), information gathering and keyword searching, note-taking and attribution, and how to use the technology tools. Carol taught the science content, which she delivered in a variety of interesting and unique ways—via video, hands-on labs, discussion, lecture, and experiments. We both taught mapping and other skills relating to site planning.

Our scenario involved significant preparation, but we were energized and eager to come to school and work with our students. We prepared our lures: lessons where we taught skills and content and classes where we facilitated discussions. We came to understand how much we were learning—by ourselves and from each other. There wasn't time for "professional development," and it wouldn't have been tailored to exactly what we needed anyway. This seat-of-the-pants, self-designed, peer-to-peer collaborative learning allowed us to take the best of what we both knew, research what we didn't just when we needed it, and design lessons that ignited students' learning.

Year after year we would change and tweak how we cast our lines, learning from our mistakes and experimenting with alternatives. Indeed, the results of year three were far superior to year one; student projects contained far more clarity, science content, analysis, and reflection.

Well, a year later, site chosen; we moved into the new school. the new school was finally built on one site. We knew that the curricular framework we had developed was solid, but it was time to find another Rio Grande to fish. So, we went back to the standards, back to looking at the issues of the day, new technologies, and the interests of the students. A recent measure on our local ballot proposed that our county ban genetically modified organisms (GMOs) in foods. Hearing students mirror voters' passion about this controversy, we decided that "GMO free" would work as a research topic. I attended technology workshops to help me narrow down the choice of possible presentation tools and then returned to teach Carol what I had learned. Since online tools had gotten easier to use, we could concentrate on the content and thinking skills. We implemented our new project: a simulation in which students had to convince their peers to "vote" yes or no on our mock election for a GMO-free county.

As others learned about the projects that Carol and I were doing, interest in technology-rich lessons grew. I began working with the teacher of English Language Learners (ELLs) to design lessons for *Dia de los Muertos*, which would result in hands-on presentations that taught other students about the history and culture of the Mexican Day of the Dead. When they accompanied their students to the library presentations, other teachers saw the technology in action and began to request that I plan and teach technology lessons with them. At the same time Carol was leading technology diffusion through personalized professional development within the science department. More confidently, more consistently, and more effectively each time, we fished and waited and fished again, building on successes emerging from the classrooms.

## WHAT WAS I WAITING FOR?

After twenty years in junior high, I was offered an opportunity to move to the high school. This move meant that I was leaving a school with only two grades to one with four, and to a much larger library, campus, and number of faculty. I jumped at this chance to reinvent myself—but it was quite a change! I arrived on campus well into the first semester. Not only was I the new kid on the block but I was entering an established culture and first semester classes that were almost half over.

Rather than tackle these challenges head on, I spent time watching, listening, and getting to know the students, faculty, administration, and staff. I participated in as many activities as possible. While I reorganized the library as an open and inviting space, I didn't make major changes to what was expected of the program.

Over time, this cautious approach paid off. As I helped students, I became familiar with teachers' assignments and handouts, teaching styles, and teacher expectations. I got a sense of the outcomes teachers were expecting and, by attending team and department meetings, learned that many were, in fact, unhappy with some of their results: perfunctory essays, plagiarism, and little, if any, attribution. (Of course I had already seen those papers as they came out of the printer by my desk.) In spite of teachers' directions to use the databases or the resources specifically picked for an assignment that I'd added to the library's website, student work showed an overreliance on Wikipedia, few citations, and careless, shallow writing. This was my challenge and my opportunity—one that I know is absolutely not unique to my school.

As it turns out, it's not unique to high school either. I occasionally substitute as a reference librarian at Santa Rosa Junior College. Predictably I answer questions on locating sources, citing them, and searching databases. One evening at the desk, I was reading our local paper's tribute to the tenth anniversary of the Jean and Charles Schulz Information Center at Sonoma State University. One article quoted students' responses to the question, "What do students have to say about library instruction at Sonoma State?"

> "Library instruction opened my eyes to a whole new world. I wish I would have learned all this in high school; it would have saved me from doing so much extra work."

> "I wish I had a class like this earlier. I found it exciting to come up with ways to become more familiar with the concepts and techniques of research."

Shortly afterwards, Nancy Persons, a librarian at Santa Rosa Junior College, confirmed how widespread these sentiments were. When she asked her one-unit library skills class what they wished they had known earlier about the library and its services, they responded:

"I would have liked to have known how important proper citations are to a research paper and what are good resources [*sic*]. I didn't know that there was a database on the library website to find periodicals. So what would be helpful is if a teacher would say what kind of resources they want and how to find them in the library."

"I wish instructors had mentioned the plethora of databases that can be accessed through the JC [Junior College] because I spend most of my time searching Google for sources and half the time can't even find a good source and waste more time trying to adjust my search and avoid websites that have nothing to do with my topic or offer little to no information on it."

"I wish that my instructors had told me about all the resources the library has. Most of my teachers have never even mentioned the library."

From years in teaching junior high, I was well aware that citation, database use, and search strategies were three vital skills I should be teaching. Even more important, students need to see that teachers value these skills and give them time to practice them. Let's face it, I thought: I'm going to hear these college lamentations every year until my students learn these skills as a core part of their high school education. As a long-standing Pollyanna, I was sure it could be done, but I was realistic enough to know that I didn't stand a chance alone.

My "a-ha" was that if my colleagues gained confidence in using our new databases, the online catalog, and some practical or creative Web 2.0 tools—and if they recognized the necessity for accurate attribution in this wild-and-wooly online world—then they, like Carol, would become my diffusion partners, valuing, teaching, and delivering these "big three." My job would be to open the door to these tools and work together to create new ways for us all to teach.

A day or two later, walking down the hall next to my assistant principal, I waved a copy of the college students' comments and said: "Look, here (shaking the page enthusiastically in front of him): all these college students who just finished a course in library use and skills say that they wished they had learned—in high school—how to search more effectively! What do you say . . . if we lead some professional development that puts us all on the same page in teaching information literacy? What do you think?" He walked silently for a moment, and then turned and said: "Well, what are you waiting for?" Good question... what *was* I waiting for? Approval? Confidence? Truthfully, a lot of both.

I started thinking about how to cast my line: While teachers could see imperfections in their students' work, how do I make a compelling case for *their* professional development? Not everybody needed everything—what would a sequence look like? Was there a best possible framework for this kind of professional development? Honestly, I had more questions than answers.

I have not been trained as a teacher of teachers. Yet, I have often been a presenter, a facilitator, and a participant in professional development events. They have been models, both good and bad, of what works and what doesn't. The most satisfying ones give me something solid to try and something "big" to think about. They make me think about why I make certain teaching choices and what I am learning (Figure 6.1 below). Budget cuts have decimated most professional development in our district. If I could re-create the faculty learning culture that had defined my middle school years, it just might be possible for every high school student to learn my "big four."

---

Figure 6.1: My Criteria for Good Professional Development in Technology

1. **Grounded in real application** so that I see connections between big picture concepts and practical classroom needs

2. **Allows time for practice** integrating the tool into my actual lesson

3. **Makes me feel a bit unsettled**, which enables me to change the way I look at something I thought I knew well

4. **Includes an operational plan** so that I can think with others about what is needed to implement an idea

---

## NEW TOOLS, NEW LEARNING—WITH THE SAME CRITERIA

In 2004 I was thrust somewhat unexpectedly into the role of online professional developer. I had been attending workshops where Web 2.0 tools were being showcased, but I felt overwhelmed by the onslaught of new tools. A colleague from the California School Library Association, Jackie Siminitus, contacted me to take a look at a series of small, hands-on, in-your-jammies, Web 2.0 exercises developed by Helene Blowers for the public library staff of Charlotte and Mecklenburg County. When we tried Learning 2.0, aka "23 Things," (http://plcmclearning.blogspot.com/) we loved how we could absorb an incredible amount of practical information incrementally in a convenient, flexible way. So, with permission, we tweaked the tutorial to include curriculum connections and recruited a cadre of librarians we called the "CSLA 2.0 Team" to support participants. We called our tutorial *School Library Learning 2.0* and offered it gratis as "a summer of 2.0 fun."

Another a-ha. While the online format was different from face-to-face learning, it actually met the technology PD criteria I already knew to be effective:

- Participants could practice and play with tools that relate to their own practical curricular needs but on their own time schedule.

- When participants felt a bit unsettled (and they always did), they could get support from "experts" as well as participants.

- Participants could ask their colleagues questions and share tips about how to implement each tool—social learning with social tools. Since they show their learning on a public blog, other participants "see" them learning, and the transparency made them conscious about doing a good job and finishing.

*School Library Learning 2.0* fueled an explosion of new learning among school librarians all over California, then spread to the country and even the world! Our participants gave us feedback on what had been successful. They gained satisfaction and confidence from learning to use tools that invigorated their own learning and had the potential to catalyze their students' learning. They loved the camaraderie that emerged through their own blogging and reading the comments of peer-learners; it was what they hoped to replicate back at their own sites.

## IN THEIR LINE OF SIGHT

What I learned from promoting the 2.0 tutorials was that many teachers and librarians wanted to learn more about Web 2.0 tools, but just didn't have time to devote to a complete 23 Things program. Back at my own high school, my colleagues were busy grading papers, participating in department meetings, and pursuing their own leadership roles, and while I knew that they were interested in learning more about these tools, there wasn't going to be enough time or interest at this point to participate in the entire tutorial. PD for this faculty would have to be a flexible combination of "teasers," followed by face-to-face coaching, occasional workshops, and even some asynchronous PD online. By demonstrating some of the 2.0 tools from the tutorial in a series of ten-minute segments at our faculty meetings, dubbed "Tech Time" by my administrator, I began presenting myself as the contact for this kind of learning.

For the first Tech Time, I picked the most basic resource—the library website I had created, http://www.phslibrary.org/. Using the LCD projector and a screen, I walked the faculty through the site: teacher pages, databases, class links, and student and parent pages. Ten minutes goes by quickly, but that IS the point: I'm there to highlight a tool or topic, then "get out."

After this quick exposure several teachers dropped by to tell me more about their projects, and we began "what if . . ." conversations. Sometimes I created pathfinders of relevant databases, print resources, and websites; at other times I just listed one or two useful resources; but, as time went by, our collaborations extended. I began to visit the classroom on the day that the assignment was given to show students how to access the site, use the links, and brainstorm search strategies. At other times I studied the teacher's assignment in advance, and then asked clarifying questions so I understood what students would need in order to anticipate roadblocks that they might encounter that the teacher hadn't anticipated. For example, I could ask things such as: "Do you want students to go to sites with critical analysis of the poem, or is this assignment to find examples of the *style* of criticism they're to use in their own essays?" From these discussions we could chart our course and develop lessons that supported student learning more clearly.

If teachers seemed reluctant to use an entire class period to bring students to the library, or if he or she felt that their students "didn't need too much instruction" for a research assignment, I asked for five minutes of class time to give a quick demonstration of available resources. I first asked students to explain their assignment to me. This gave both the teacher and me a quick check of students' understanding. If we saw that the students weren't as savvy as the teacher thought or that some had misunderstood the assignment, teachers usually booked a follow-up library visit during another class period.

## PLAYFUL RE-CREATION

Making the best use of databases and even searching the index of a print source depends on understanding a topic well enough to choose good keywords. I decided to use PD time to show teachers how to *deconstruct* the question or topic they assign so that they could teach students to *construct* keyword searches that get good results from a database or search engine. During Tech Time, I did a short overview of databases available to students and listed a couple of ideas on when and how to use them, but I told my administration that I was looking for a longer period of time for more concentrated exploration. When a PD slot opened up during early-release Wednesdays, I offered to do extended workshops on various library topics, and my assistant principal took the "bait."

I knew I could get the LCD projector out again and do a more thorough overview of the website and show strategies for using different databases, but instead I created a flashy and whimsical scavenger hunt, complete with prizes and interesting questions related to subjects I knew students were researching. I wanted the faculty to see how precise language and the right database improved their own search results. We had a lot of fun, a little competition, and plenty of shout-out sharing, as groups that were progressing more quickly spurred others on. They heard each other asking: "How do you . . . ?" "Where the heck is . . . ?" "Why don't you . . . ?" And, moments later when a group found what they needed, they would cheer and laughingly admit how like their students they really were.

I didn't expect any major overhaul of the curriculum after our "wacky" Wednesday scavenger hunt, but I am seeing baby-step changes in the school's culture. Students are more often directed to use the databases and the library website, and ask me for help. More often than not, I am notified when there's an assignment being developed so I can give my feedback and help teachers identify the most useful databases.

## BAITING A HOOK WITH PRESENTATION TOOLS

Most students had been required to create PowerPoint presentations in their junior high school classes, yet our faculty bemoaned how ineffective their presentations appeared. I thought: why couldn't I use PD time to show teachers how to shake students out of merely moving information into digital posters? Provide some suggestions for ways to capture an audience?

During another Tech Time, I showed Animoto, a flashy, easy-to learn tool that can result in a compelling presentation. I began by playing a couple of book trailers I had made for the library website—effective because they had served to lure students into the library to ask for the books. Quickly I enumerated standards that could be addressed with this presentation tool, and suggested four or five assignments that matched this format:

- To summarize or promote a book in place of a book report
- To present an original haiku poem
- To illustrate a poem that was being studied
- To summarize a topic
- To reveal aspects of a simile or metaphor

For those not yet convinced that academic rigor could be achieved in this medium, I suggested that, rather than replace a traditional essay or assignment, Animoto be added as a visual complement.

I follow up Tech Time sessions with "soft" marketing: Maybe I'll deposit a note in a teacher's mailbox or via e-mail, or drop by a classroom to ask "How it's going?" or to troubleshoot alongside someone who's struggling with a tool, all the while listening for other opportunities to suggest another useful technology application. When an English class was reading historical fiction, I created an Animoto on my favorite historical fiction series, Bloody Jack (Figure 6.2) and passed the link to the teacher. Shortly afterwards, she replied with a link to her first Animoto, http://www.phslibrary.org/book-trailers.html, which I posted on the library's website. She routinely gives her students the option of creating their own book trailers as part of larger projects.

Another teacher wanted her seniors to be able to develop powerful statements that reflected the best of their thinking using presentation tools that they could expect to use in college or business. Rather than focusing on a single tool, I gave a workshop to her class on the characteristics

of presentation tools that were listed on the library's website (http://www
.phslibrary.org/tech-tools.html). After listening to my talk and seeing how
effective different presentation tools could be, she began adding this component to similar assignments in other grades. Like Carol, she took on the
role of peer-to-peer PD mentor to other teachers in her department.

## A BIGGER WORM:
## READING COMPREHENSION AND PLAGIARISM

Note taking and citation are linked tasks that not only teach attribution and
the ethical use of information but can also provide teachers with evidence
that students understand and evaluate the information that they are using.
There are a many note-taking tools available online, but I like the approach
in NoodleTools because it requires students to think about the authority
and relevance of the sources they find and distinguish between quoting or
copying information from a source and paraphrasing or synthesizing ideas
from it.

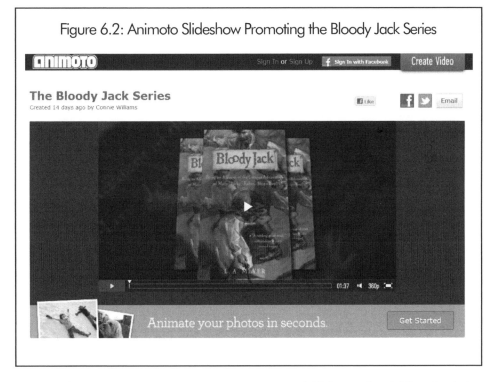

Figure 6.2: Animoto Slideshow Promoting the Bloody Jack Series

Teaching proper citation is an important skill in a school librarian's instructional repertoire, so I'm always "noodling" on how to create a culture
of attribution. On my library website, there is a link to NoodleTools Express so that a student who needs a single citation can create one on the
fly. Express lets them practice citing correctly even for those "gotta turn in

my current event right now" assignments. When I first chose NoodleTools, my inclination was to try to do a whole-staff introduction during Tech Time, but it seemed silly to waste our PD time teaching teachers how to create citations. What I want teachers to know is that they can use NoodleTools to monitor students' progress on a project, assess their reading comprehension by comparing the source quote to the paraphrase, and evaluate how students are synthesizing and organizing material from several sources. Citations today are just too complicated for direct instruction; that's best left to the just-in-time help within the software. NoodleTools helps me focus instead on teaching the "big picture" of research.

Once again, a single teacher's need laid the groundwork for just-in-time, personalized professional development that would seed wider diffusion in the school. While working with an English teacher on cybercitizenship we started discussing Web 2.0 tools, note taking, and citation. She wanted to learn more about how to help her students read and cite effectively without plagiarizing. I gave her a quick run-through of the product and set her up with her own account, which she uses to review her students' notes online. Several more teachers have since bitten the "attribution worm." After they saw how easily they could receive student work in their online "drop boxes" by assignment, they began experimenting with ways to check students' note-taking progress, give feedback on paraphrasing and outlining, and assess student projects more efficiently.

## NEW DIGITAL BAIT

School librarians know that cybercitizenship, media literacy, information ethics, intellectual freedom, and privacy relate to many subjects being taught in high school. Rather than loading the responsibility of teaching them all onto a single teacher's course or elective, during PD I draw connections between content-area topics and how information is created and travels, how data is collected, and what the implications are for students (and adults) when they post and contribute to online content.

For another Wednesday PD, my assistant principal asked me to re-create a presentation he had heard me make to parents earlier in the month at an American Association of University Women (AAUW) sponsored evening on cybersafety. I was on a panel with a law enforcement official, a psychologist, a representative from a local "healthy kids" association, and a school district official. Our unique vantage points resulted in a lively discussion with divergent perspectives. I knew that faculty members, like some parents, made assumptions about their students' level of expertise, which, working with students every single day one-on-one, I know to be inflated. I broadened my parent presentation to show faculty the results of this misunderstanding, whether it showed up on a paper or in students' risky behavior online. The ensuing faculty discussion explored just how much instruction even seniors still need and opened the door to my wider involvement in instruction.

Currently I am working with the teaching team for the Human Interaction classes (which cover big ideas in health topics) to present information to their students on cyberbullying, harassment, and sexting. We are piloting CSLA's *Teen Learning 2.0* (http://teenlearning.csla.net/) in one of the classes to test the effectiveness of teaching information literacy and digital citizenship using online tutorials. The teachers are going through the tutorial themselves to get a broad understanding of these topics so that they can create additional lessons. Sometimes the result of PD is that you work yourself "out of a job" with one team and gain time to work with others.

Unlike my friend who fishes alone, my craft has a social component; I need to communicate the big goals for library PD so that they will come about, albeit incrementally, supported by my administration. I routinely volunteer to serve on committees with administrators and participate in teaching-related opportunities with peers so I can present a library perspective in the discussions. I connect with new administrators early and often, never empty handed. I'll come by with a book on a topic they've mentioned, a report of new research on teaching, or an article that directly or indirectly underscores the value of the library.

Every day I grapple with the uncertainty that I am making a difference. Some days I see tangible evidence that my PD is changing practice. On other days the printer overflows with World War II battle information from Ask.com or write-ups for a science fair project with nary a citation. The crazy thing is, when I ask a teacher if I can help—to create links lists, teach a lesson on citation, or assess students' note taking—most remember Tech Time or wacky Wednesday PD and accept with gratitude. For those who respond with "That's ok, they'll do fine," my Pollyanna spirit kicks in and I come back the next day with another approach. Practice, not just results. Fishing, not just catching.

# Practicing Your Craft With Others:
# Tips for Short Professional Development

1. Do lots of "teacher watching" and listening to find out about assignments and understand learning goals.

2. Connect technology PD to teachers' real needs, assignments, or goals, not how to use a tool just "in case" you ever need it.

3. You don't have to "invent" to be experimental. Reinvent good ideas (like "23 Things") to fit your school's needs.

4. Start small with mini-PD time slots to build your confidence and reputation.

5. Keep PD voluntary, friendly, and even "wacky" if you can manage it.

6. Be ready to claim a longer PD slot when an opportunity presents itself.

7. Focus your teaching on what's important (e.g., deconstructing research questions, evaluating sources, and analyzing information), then find quality software that can help you streamline your teaching of the mechanics.

—Connie Williams

From *Growing Schools: Librarians as Professional Developers* edited by Debbie Abilock, Kristin Fontichiaro, and Violet H. Harada. Santa Barbara, CA: Libraries Unlimited. Copyright © 2012.

# CHAPTER 7
# EMBEDDED LEARNING

*Editors' Note:* Judi Moreillon, a passionate proponent of co-teaching, shares successful collaborative teaching experiences from her career. Her practical stories about co-instruction, a form of embedded professional development, reveal how school librarians can reap important learning benefits for adults as well as their shared students.

## Job-Embedded Professional Development: An Orchard of Opportunity

### Judi Moreillon

If you have never visited an orchard and picked your own apples, you have missed a seminal harvest experiences. In Michigan, where I spent my teen and early young adult years, fall is the season for stunning autumn leaves, hot apple cider, and—donuts. Visiting at this time of year, you may not realize the process that had to occur in order for you to enjoy the bounty of a fall orchard. Way back in the spring, before the Golden Delicious trees could produce their delicate, pale-pink flowers and ultimately their tasty, cider-making fruits, they had to cross-pollinate with other kinds of apple trees. Farmers know that two identical trees won't flourish; they need partners to cross-pollinate each other.

Co-teachers are pollinating partners; two educators with different skill-sets working together to help one another produce learning opportunities for themselves and for their students. The secret of this orchard is that it needs interrelationships in order to grow. Co-teaching has been my pathway to achieve job-embedded professional development. In my teaching career, I have repeatedly blossomed, along with my colleagues, when we have co-planned, co-taught, and co-assessed learning. It's one-on-one professional development that is unlike most professional development relationships because *both* parties benefit equally.

I believe that Vygotsky's zone of proximal development (1978), which articulates that children develop in the company of more proficient peers, is not only for children. We all learn through observation, modeling, and imitating the behaviors of trusted, proficient others. When we engage in interactions with knowledgeable mentors as we attempt new learning (and teaching), we go farther because we have the support of someone who has been there and who is willing to risk with us. We grow and develop more fully and more quickly in the company of our peers. We practice the best kind of professional development—job-embedded professional development—when we co-teach actual students in real time, with the taught curriculum, available resources and tools, and within the supports and constraints of our particular learning environments. Figure 7.1 shows some of the benefits of quality co-planning and co-teaching.

Co-teaching has been at the heart of my career in librarianship. I have been able to share my knowledge and hybridize it with the expertise of my classroom and specialist colleagues. We have grown together and, as a result, became stronger, bolder, and more creative instructional guides for our students. Collaborative teaching is, like the apple blossoms, delicate. It is deeply personal to open our vulnerabilities to another adult. It requires respect between the parties and an intention of melding one another's strengths rather than intending to "improve" the other partner's weaknesses. Damage the blossom, and there will be no fruit.

I know that my own K–12 teaching practices improved as a direct result of co-teaching with classroom teacher and specialist colleagues, and my skillset continues to blossom when I collaborate with my peers. If classroom teachers, school librarians, and specialists remain isolated in our individual classrooms, libraries, and labs, how can innovation and improvements spread throughout a learning community? A school librarian who is committed to building instructional partnerships in order to significantly impact student learning can reach out across the barriers that prevent us from learning with and from colleagues and can break through educators' isolation to implement best practices in instruction and librarianship.

Now, as a university professor, I share my life-long passion for collaborative instruction when I teach a course called "Librarians as Instructional Partners." I love growing a new generation of librarians who will become cross-pollinators in their own schools. As we talk about the values of collaborative teaching both for student achievement and for their own professional growth, I often teach by telling stories from my own experience.

## Figure 7.1: Benefits of Classroom-Library Collaboration Based on Co-teaching

| For Students... | For Educators... |
| --- | --- |
| Better designed lessons | Clarification of goals and objectives through joint planning; co-assessment of lesson effectiveness |
| More individualized attention | More opportunities to work one on one with students |
| Increased opportunity for differentiated instruction | Improved facilitation of differentiated instruction |
| Access to information at the point of need | Literature and information literacy skills integrated in a meaningful way into the classroom curriculum |
| Access to multiple resources, including technology | Shared responsibility for gathering engaging, effective resources |
| More engagement due to fewer distractions | Fewer classroom management issues |
| More material or deeper investigations into concepts and topics | More teaching time (due to fewer management issues and scheduling to achieve student learning objectives) |
| Expanded opportunities for creativity | Expanded opportunities for creativity |
| Acquiring skills for lifelong learning | Personal and professional growth opportunities through co-teaching and co-assessment of student learning |
| Integrated learning | Integrated teaching |

Moreillon (2007, 8; 2012, 8).

From *Growing Schools: Librarians as Professional Developers* edited by Debbie Abilock, Kristin Fontichiaro, and Violet H. Harada. Santa Barbara, CA: Libraries Unlimited. Copyright © 2012.

## THE LAST PART FIRST: WEAVING EXPERTISE AND WEB 2.0 INTO WIKI-BASED LITERATURE CIRCLES

My most recent experience with collaboration occurred when I became the librarian of a joint junior-senior high school: two schools under one roof. Like another variety of apple, I was positioned as a cross-pollinator in this orchard with two different types of trees. At the time, I had been away from daily work in school libraries for five years. During that time, Web 2.0 tools such as blogs, wikis, and podcasts were in their nascent stages as K–12 learning tools. I saw that these tools could offer us flexible new pathways for sharing thoughts and developing collective knowledge. As I returned to working in the field, I did so with a goal of integrating Web 2.0 tools like these. I was excited to put these tools to work!

During the summer before that school year began, I met and started conversing with Jenni, an 8th grade English language arts teacher, on a technology integration grant that she had received. She shared her goals for implementing wiki-based literature circles, and I shared with her how I had used wikis with university students. In our conversations, Jenni and I began to develop shared objectives for the project. We started to build trust in each other and in each other's areas of expertise. We also sensed a shared commitment to students' success and agreed to work collaboratively on this year-long project.

That summer, I also began developing a framework for a library wiki website (http://egjhtvhslibrary.pbworks.com) and launched it when school began in August 2008. In my previous library, I had been required to use Microsoft's FrontPage, a software program that resides on a single computer, to develop instructional Web content. In contrast, this wiki provided our library with a more flexible Web presence since educators and students could contribute easily from any computer. Impressed by my early efforts, my principal asked me to share the school library wiki at one of the first high school faculty meetings. Later I showed my framework to the junior high faculty. At those meetings, I invited teachers to join the library wiki in order to contribute resources and information, but only Jenni did. While I would have preferred that more teachers participate on the library wiki, I understood their reticence. Some were afraid to "mess it up," while others were simply unsure about what they could contribute. Still, in co-planned lessons that used wiki-based pathfinders, collaborating classroom teachers and their students in both schools became familiar with the library wiki as a portal for learning, and they helped me further develop the pathfinders and other resources found on the site.

The wiki-based literature circle project with Jenni's classes took off. Three classes of 8th grade students studied story elements, particularly the impact of setting on the mood and tone of the story, in the books they read and discussed online. Literature circle students developed their group's wiki based on the books they chose to read. Groups were formed across Jenni's three classes, and they conducted asynchronous discussions and wiki work outside of class time. The students flourished in the online environment. Jenni and I co-taught lessons on many topics including netiquette, the ethical use of information, and principles of web design. We also co-facilitated students' guided practice and independent work and jointly assessed student outcomes using rubrics we co-developed.

On their wikis, students used multiple Web 2.0 tools to collaboratively explore and express their understandings. Many students were motivated by the tools and the challenge of collaborating with group mates electronically. With the written archive of their conversations, students returned to discussions with thoughts and ideas that would have most likely gone unexpressed in the classroom. The written documentation also provided Jenni and me with critical evidence and information related to their comprehension of the texts. In their end-of-year reflections, a significant number of students noted that this was the most engaging work of the year because it felt like learning they would continue to use.

Jenni and I had opportunities to share students' learning with grade-level colleagues as well as the entire junior high faculty and the school board. Along with Sara, Jenni's student teacher, we wrote about this experience in an article entitled "Learning and Teaching in WANDA Wiki Wonderland: Literature Circles in the Digital Commons" (Moreillon, Hunt, and Ewing 2009). We learned that having more than one educator, at times three, to co-facilitate students' work supported both the learners and teachers. None of us had previously conducted online literature circles with middle school students. Without willing colleagues, we might not have taken this risk—a year-long project involving many unknowns.

We divided up primary responsibility for groups and consulted with one another regularly. Monitoring the online discussions was important work for us and would have been overwhelming had we not had the benefit of two or three heads reading and pushing students' conversations when needed. With each other's help, we monitored students' learning efficiently and effectively and were able to backtrack and remediate our instruction in time to head off potential pitfalls. One example happened early on when I noticed students were using images and music without attribution or permission. If I had entered the project later on, or if Jenni had worked alone, students might not have learned about intellectual property rights.

As the students learned from one another, so did we. This was my first year teaching middle school students. I knew little about their curriculum or what 8th grade students were capable of accomplishing. Jenni knew her curriculum and had worked successfully with middle school students for several years. I had used college-level literature circle wikis and could share that expertise along with knowledge of many other Web 2.0 tools with which Jenni was not as familiar. Jenni and I both benefited from student teacher Sara's enthusiasm and youthful perspective. We all blossomed as educators, each in our own way, to make a more verdant learning orchard for students.

## ENTHUSIASM SPREADS:
## A POWERPOINT NOVICE BECOMES A CONVERT

Our district had a technology-integration initiative; technology was a focus in faculty meeting presentations and in many curriculum conversations. I learned that Pat, a veteran social studies teacher in the middle school, did not know how to use PowerPoint and had not integrated it into her teaching. Pat and I had begun to build a relationship that same year during a 7th grade interdisciplinary unit in which students studied the early 20th-century time period in social studies and read historical fiction in their language arts classes. In the past, the final product for the unit had been a magazine composed of word-processed articles and historically appropriate advertisements reflecting the culture of the time. Instead, I suggested that students learn to write in a journalistic style and use a newspaper clipping generator to create their final products. The final document, which resembled a primary source, reinforced one of our learning objectives, engaged students, and provided eye-catching displays for the parent open house held in the spring.

Pat was impressed by the student outcomes from the interdisciplinary unit. She approached me at the end of the year about doing a paper poster project about the Great Depression. After describing the Library of Congress's *American Memory Project* (http://memory.loc.gov), I suggested that students could integrate these primary sources into a visual essay using PowerPoint. That was when Pat shyly confessed that she did not know how to make a PowerPoint presentation.

I assured her that it was easy and that she could learn along with the students. We co-planned the content of our lessons, and she left the technology pieces up to me. To introduce the project, I created a four-slide example, and Pat and I invited students to ask questions about these primary source images. Working together and relying on Pat's subject-area expertise, we helped students use their questions to focus their study of particular Great Depression subtopics. As in our sample, students ultimately shared their learning in an oral presentation accompanied by a PowerPoint presentation that included primary source images with captions and citations. During their presentations, students extemporaneously shared their learning, using the images and captions to prompt their oral reports.

I learned more about the Great Depression curriculum from Pat, while she learned how to use PowerPoint and integrate it effectively from me. Our collaborative unit addressed multiple learning objectives, including content-area knowledge, developing questions, locating and citing primary sources, practicing presentation skills, and using technology tools appropriately to meet these objectives. At the end of the year, I asked Pat if she would share her thoughts about the experience. She said this is a videotaped interview:

> We decided . . . each student would be responsible for doing a PowerPoint. . . . I had never done anything like that before. So I was eager to learn and said I would learn right along with the kids. And that's exactly what I did. My school librarian was nice enough to lead me through the lessons as she led the students through them. And by the end of the week, I was helping the students with everything and learning right along with them. This was one good example of what teachers and librarians can do together to help the students learn and become more successful. (Green 2009)

From this experience, I learned that sometimes adults must acknowledge that new learning takes courage. While I have always been supportive of co-learning through co-teaching, I watched, with admiration, as Pat learned with and from the students and me. She was willing to share her vulnerability with her students. I believe this was a great model for Pat's students. Many adult learners would not take such a risk. I was reminded of principles of adult learning for educators that include meeting individual, specific learning needs related to the actual work of teaching. This experience served to help me work more effectively with adult learners. Pat was justifiably proud of her accomplishment, and the students and I celebrated her learning right along with her.

Developing expertise in integrating technology tools to meet learning objectives is a pathway to leadership for school librarians. It requires us to invest in our own learning, to constantly upgrade our knowledge and skills, and to take turns leading and following with colleagues and students who will likely know or discover tools we have yet to try. Such planning with teachers, co-teaching, teaching information and communication technologies (ICT), and providing in-service to teachers are among the library predictors of students' academic achievement on standardized tests, particularly in reading and language arts (Achterman 2008, 62–65). In the 21st-century orchard, technology tools have much to offer as we co-produce tasty, nutritious learning opportunities for ourselves and for students.

## LET'S LEARN IT TOGETHER: CO-TEACHING WITH PUBLISHED LESSON PLANS

Although co-planning collaborative lessons from scratch is ideal, some educators perceive it as overly time consuming or even threatening. A lack of common planning time during the contract day, particularly at the elementary school level, can be a barrier. Middle school and high school classroom teachers and specialists may have additional school duties (such as coaching athletic teams or serving as club sponsors) or family responsibilities that limit their availability after school. While online planning via wikis or other Web 2.0 tools is an option, co-teaching based on standards-based published lesson plans enables teachers and specialists to streamline the planning process.

Using a previously published lesson plan can overcome some classroom teachers' and specialists' reticence to co-teach. It can help educators concentrate on building trusting relationships and comfort with one another's teaching and learning styles. Lesson plans aligned with content-area standards and the AASL *Standards for the 21st-Century Learner* (2007) abound in magazines and journals for school librarians and classroom teachers. In addition, there are numerous books edited or written by school librarians that offer lesson plans, some of which include all of the necessary graphic organizers, rubrics, checklists, and examples of student work necessary to effectively teach the lessons (Moreillon 2007, 2012). Especially in new relationships, it can be less awkward to discuss a third party's lesson plan than to negotiate one another's draft plans. It is also a way for school librarians to overcome our own uncertainties about practicing the instructional partner role.

Another advantage of using published lesson plans is that they have been successfully field tested by teachers and librarians. Although you will undoubtedly adapt any published plan to meet your students' needs and adjust to available resources or tools, you can feel confident that some kinks have already been worked out in trial runs by other teachers, a selling point for educators who need more assurance that lesson plans will effectively promote learning the first time they are implemented.

Preservice and novice teachers are also prime candidates for co-teaching with published lesson plans. A formalized plan, in which students' learning tasks have been carefully analyzed and each step of the lesson is clearly mapped out, provides a certain comfort level. With the added benefit of modifiable graphic organizers, rubrics, and other assessment tools, these lesson plans can be time savers as well as ego savers.

In addition to the sample lesson plans in the professional books I have written, I have coauthored two classroom-library unit plans that were co-planned, co-taught, and co-assessed. Both are hosted on the International Reading Association/National Council of Teachers of English ReadWriteThink .org website. An art teacher and I (serving as a high school librarian) co-taught *Behind the Masks: Exploring Culture and Self through Art and Poetry* unit (Moreillon and Roderick 2004) over several semesters with different groups of students. *Peace Poems and Picasso Doves: Literature, Art, Technology, and Poetry* unit (Moreillon 2003) was a collaborative effort between a 4th grade classroom teacher, the school librarian, the art instructor, and me (as literacy coach). The interdisciplinary nature of the "Peace Poems" unit and the number of educators with different responsibilities in the school who collaborated made it a particularly successful co-teaching experience.

Felicia, the 4th grade classroom teacher who was part of the team, had not, to that point, engaged in significant collaboration with the library. The text set of picture books Diane, the librarian, and I integrated into this study were intellectually accessible to Felicia's second-language learners. Diane and I co-developed comprehensible graphic organizers to scaffold students' reading comprehension, and Felicia provided feedback that was incorporated into the final documents. She especially appreciated our expertise in this regard.

At the end of the unit, we knew we had achieved one of our overarching goals when students' poems reflected their home cultures. Art instructor Tracy's contribution, the simple beauty of students' artwork in the style of Picasso, completed this project. We created a CD of students' poems and paintings that students proudly shared with their families and with a school in Florida. Students received praise from their parents, siblings, and cousins and congratulatory e-mails from their Florida peers. This was the kind of high-impact learning and teaching that is possible when a team of educators works together for kids—each one planting the seeds from her or his areas of expertise in order to develop a rich orchard for student growth.

I have received numerous inquiries and e-mails from educators across the country and a few from around the world who have adapted our *ReadWriteThink* lesson plans for their own teaching. Although I do not know if educators co-taught the lessons as we did, I do know that there is potential for published plans to help school librarians, in particular, prepare fertile ground for co-teaching and to grow a cadre of supportive classroom teacher colleagues and principals who will advocate for the many benefits of instructional partnerships.

In 2007, Pauline and a colleague field tested a lesson plan from *Collaborative Strategies for Teaching Reading Comprehension: Maximizing Your Impact* (Moreillon 2007). In March she wrote:

> The collaboration proved not only to be successful for this project but collaboration in general. I am new to the school and the teachers have never used the library or [school librarian] before. . . . Now I have the entire third grade collaborating with me on their non-fiction units. I want to thank you for allowing me this opportunity to show the school how worthwhile the library can be. (Kola-McVeigh 2007)

Five months later, Pauline wrote, "Because the unit last year was so successful, the principal gave me an entirely flex schedule this year" (Kola-McVeigh 2007).

It is personally satisfying to me that lessons that I co-planned, co-taught, and later developed for publication have positively impacted others' teaching practices and have helped them develop library programs in which co-teaching is a prominent feature.

## PROFESSIONAL DISCUSSION GROUPS

Co-teaching offers one strategy for cross-pollinating in a learning community; professional discussion groups provide a different context for on-site professional development. Principals, librarians, or classroom teachers select a professional book, video, or a series of articles that will be read or viewed and then discussed in a small group or as an entire faculty. Often this activity provides educators with district-level continuing education (CE) credit and is viewed by administrators as a strategy for teacher improvement. School librarians can recommend book titles, serve as discussion leaders, or host discussion sessions in the library or virtually online. The educators who voluntarily participate in professional book study groups are already pre-disposed to lifelong learning and to the goals of professional learning communities. Reaching out to receptive colleagues for collaborative experiences is especially fruitful for new school librarians and for librarians who are new to a particular school.

One of the highlights of my school librarian career came my second year serving at Gale Elementary School in Tucson, when I co-facilitated a faculty book club. Collectively, the participating educators determined the book for our study, selecting *Moon Journals: Writing, Art, and Inquiry through Focused Nature Study* (Chancer and Rester-Zodrow 1997). The principal purchased the books and asked me to co-facilitate along with our art instructor. It was a professional development project made in heaven.

We met in the library once a week for eight consecutive weeks to discuss each chapter. I highlighted children's literature and other resources related to the topic discussed in that chapter. We shared the "moon journals" in which we had written and drawn the previous week and discussed writing and science curricula. We also talked about implementing inquiry learning and shared our philosophies and teaching experiences. I made notes and recorded my colleagues' ideas for later reference.

Then we walked eagerly down the hall where Tracy, our art instructor, who also participated in the discussions in the library, led us in learning the various art techniques described in the book. We laughed; we played; we took risks (especially the least fine arts–oriented of us—me!); we created art; and we learned—together.

These weekly explorations were springboards for collaborative planning and co-teaching. From this book study group, I built a long-term relationship with our art instructor. Over several years, we worked with classroom teachers and students to integrate art, classroom curriculum, and library resources in two different schools. I co-developed and co-taught units of instruction related to many areas of the curriculum, including a six-week writer's workshop with a kindergarten teacher and several science inquiry units with 2nd and 3rd grade teachers. It was a golden opportunity to build relationships with my peers as we explored the interdisciplinary possibilities of science, inquiry, and art. And everyone earned CE units to boot!

Judy, one of the 3rd grade teachers from the group, shared her thoughts about classroom-library collaboration as a result of the book club:

> Having a teacher-librarian to collaborate with has been a very important part of my role as an educator. More importantly, it's very important for the students that I teach. I believe in the philosophy of authentic learning and children finding answers to their questions on their own. Having a teacher-librarian to do this with enables me to take a curriculum which I think has been presented to us by the state at a very superficial level and to take that curriculum deeper—to take the questions that the children have and allow them to learn how to find the answers to their questions. In the 21st century, with the Information Age and information changing on a daily basis, children need to know how to find the answers. (Pickerell 2001)

*Moon Journals* was not the only experience I had in this regard. At another school, I had the opportunity to lead a professional book study of *Life in a Crowded Place: Making a Learning Community* (Peterson 1992). In both cases, and with the encouragement and support of my administrators, I served as a leader in these book discussion groups. [*Editors' Note*: For more on book discussion groups, see Chapter 13.] And through co-teaching with my fellow participants, I had the fortune of putting our professional learning into practice alongside them through co-planned and co-taught lessons. Principals who practice distributed leadership appreciate the contributions of school librarians who can help them nurture and grow a culture of collaboration in their learning community orchard.

## CO-TEACHING WITH ADMINISTRATORS: DEVELOPING EXPERTISE AND PROMOTING CURRICULUM INITIATIVES

As instructional leaders, school principals are often required to enact instructional reform measures instituted at the district, state, or national level. They deliver some of these directives to faculty through on-site staff development inservice, but simply being aware of new strategies, tools, resources, or requirements is not sufficient for change to occur. School librarians can gain traction as instructional leaders alongside administrators, co-leading promising reform initiatives that are compatible with best practices in school librarianship and our personal pedagogy. While the administrator may introduce reforms and evaluate them, he or she rarely has the time to partner with individual teachers to develop lessons and staff capacity in depth. A co-teaching school librarian can fill that need. We can develop expertise, co-lead initial or further staff development on these topics, and, along with colleagues, implement useful new strategies and programs through co-teaching. Partnering with principals or other curriculum leaders in this way can show leaders that we are committed to learning anywhere in the building and may lead to reciprocal support for library-initiated programs.

School librarians can represent the school at district, state, or national trainings. Better yet, school librarians can attend these trainings along with administrators or building colleagues in order to gain a shared understanding of the goals and processes of these instructional initiatives. Bringing this information back to the entire faculty and possessing the expertise to help them understand and implement a new strategy or program can further solidify the school librarian's leadership role in the learning community, creating "an additional layer of leadership within the school" (Zmuda and Harada 2008, 24).

As a high school librarian, I had the opportunity to support a school-wide writing initiative that impacted the learning of 1,800 students. After reviewing standardized test data, our administration and department heads determined that instituting a cross-curricular writing method could help our students better construct their written assignments and earn higher scores on the writing portion of the state exit examination, the successful passage of which was required for graduation.

The English department selected the Jane Shaffer writing method. This method provides a five- or six-sentence structure to scaffold students' writing. After the topic sentence, writers think about what this "shows" about the topic, and compose one or two sentences about that. Then, they think about why this is "important," and compose one or two sentences to address its importance. Writers complete their paragraph with a concluding sentence that refers back to the topic sentence.

The principal invited Ms. Shaffer to come to our school for one full-day workshop. In addition to our entire English department faculty, department heads from all disciplines, language arts teachers and educators selected from our feeder middle schools, and I were required or invited to participate. The goal was to provide a foundational framework to support struggling writers and from which developing and advanced writers could expand their written work in all content areas.

During hands-on portions of the workshop, educators engaged in writing curriculum conversations with and across disciplines and across instructional levels. Educators' fears, such as a concern that students would be restricted to this format, were quieted. After the workshop, the principal in charge of curriculum and instruction asked for a volunteer to share the method at the next faculty meeting. When no one else volunteered, I did, using this as an opportunity to show how I had the expertise to work with colleagues to address this school-wide initiative. I created a PowerPoint presentation to explain the process, shared it at the meeting, and led teachers in writing two or three whole group examples. I added those samples to the presentation and e-mailed it to the entire staff. This principal also asked individual teachers who participated in the workshop to collaborate with departments for which implementing this process would be a paradigm shift. I was selected to work with the fine arts and physical education (PE) departments.

The library program already had a co-teaching relationship with the fine arts teachers. (In the second year of this initiative, both librarians collaborated with classroom teachers.) We had co-taught two long-term projects in which we co-developed rubrics, the most significant feature of which was a self-assessment component (see Moreillon and Roderick 2004). In order to accommodate the Shaffer method, we simply tweaked a few assignment rubrics and provided students with Shaffer paragraph examples for their reflective writing.

Diane, the ceramics teacher, shared this feedback with me:

> For several years, our district has had a focus on writing across the curriculum. Working with the teacher-librarians has helped me more fully integrate the research and writing process into my course. I learned to use rubrics to guide students' written work as well as their artwork and the self-evaluation aspect of the rubric has really been helpful to the students and for me in evaluation. (Roderick 2003)

For the PE department, integrating writing activities into the curriculum was a whole new ball game. I met with all of the PE teachers at their next departmental meeting. Then I asked two approachable members of the team to experiment with me: the girls PE/dance teacher, and the wrestling coach. In both cases, I met with each individual twice to ensure they were comfortable with and confident about the process of teaching the method and co-teaching with me. We brainstormed a few paragraph topics, selected one at each meeting, collaboratively wrote a paragraph using think-alouds, and assessed it with a rubric. We used these same strategies when we modeled the process for their students.

After completing a healthy food unit, the PE teacher and I used the writing method for students' short editorials about the importance of good nutritional habits. Our goal was to submit selected students' writing as letters to the editor to the local newspaper. The students, their parents, and our administrators were thrilled when three of the students' letters were published.

The wrestling coach and I demonstrated a Shaffer paragraph to share what we knew about specific wrestling holds. I knew nothing about wrestling; I learned the content from him while the coach and students learned and practiced the writing method with me. The students drew the names of various holds out of a hat and worked in partners to write paragraphs. In all cases, we used a shared rubric that included aspects of this writing method to assess students' work.

I had not previously had the chance to co-teach with high school PE teachers. While I learned their content, they benefited from integrating writing into their classes through co-teaching. This was also important for students who used writing to share their opinions and demonstrate their knowledge across the PE curriculum. The administrators were particularly pleased and noted our successes at a faculty meeting. Although the message seemed to be "if PE can do it, so can you," we were happy to share our collaborative work because of the positive student outcomes.

Being involved in this school-wide writing initiative gave me an entrée into curriculum conversations that would have otherwise been more difficult to initiate. After my voluntary presentation at the faculty meeting, my colleagues looked to me as the "go-to" person for this initiative. [Editors' note: see also Chapter 2 for a similar outcome.] As a result, I had several invitations to teach in classrooms that had not to that point been open to me. That spring, the students' confidence in their writing and their test scores rose. With the Shaffer paragraph as a foundation, the English language arts teachers introduced additional support for struggling writers and enlisted me to work across disciplines to help reinforce those skills as well.

Similar to professional discussion groups, co-leading a school-wide curriculum initiative is a high-profile leadership opportunity for school librarians. Through supporting classroom teachers and specialists in meeting site or district PD requirements and implementing new teaching practices, we can help our colleagues be successful in actualizing change, which might otherwise seem unsettling or even odious to them. Not only do our principals appreciate our contributions as instructional co-leaders, but our colleagues see us a part of the solution to meeting their needs. Professional development work can be like fertilizer spread in the orchard. It has to be worked into the soil in order to benefit the trees. Through co-leading and co-teaching, we can make sure our administrators' priorities are met. In the process, we build advocates in the front office and in classrooms who will speak up for an integrated library program and the professional work of the school librarian.

## HARVESTING THE BENEFITS OF JOB-EMBEDDED PROFESSIONAL DEVELOPMENT

School librarians can be at the center of a convergence of people, place, and process. We can keep our focus on service—on helping faculty achieve their individual learning goals. We can structure the adult learning environment as a nonthreatening, learner-centered, collaborative, and respectful place of practice. We can maintain a commitment to gather evidence and reflective practice as we share responsibility for improving teaching in order to improve student learning outcomes. Through a self-paced, hands-on, and active process, we can help classroom teacher and specialist colleagues reach their goals through the reciprocal mentorship that comes from collaborative planning and co-teaching.

If you are already practicing instructional partnerships, help stakeholders see this work as job-embedded professional development. Document student learning outcomes that result from partnered instruction. Request that your performance evaluator observe a co-taught lesson. Ask your supervisor to join you and your collaborator in a planning session and a post-teaching reflection. Show your administrator that you are an integral and invaluable member of the instructional program.

"The greatest asset any library has is a librarian" (Lankes 2011, 29). Through co-teaching, we can harvest the benefits of job-embedded professional development and grow a bountiful orchard of expertise for the benefit of the students who depend upon us.

## REFERENCES

Achterman, Douglas L. 2008. "Haves, Halves, and Have-nots: School Libraries and Student Achievement in California." Doctoral dissertation. UNT Digital Library, Denton, Texas. http://digital.library.unt.edu/ark:/67531/metadc9800/m1/ (accessed October 8, 2011).

American Association of School Librarians (AASL). 2007. *Standards for the 21st-Century Learner.* Chicago: American Association of School Librarians. http://ala.org/aasl/standards.

Chancer, Jonie, and Gina Rester-Zodrow. 1997. *Moon Journals: Writing, Art, and Inquiry through Focused Nature Study.* Portsmouth, NH: Heinemann.

Green, Pat. 2009. *7th-grade Social Studies Teacher.* TeacherTube. http://tinyurl.com/testimonial-7th-grade-teacher (accessed October 9, 2011).

Kola-McVeigh, Pauline. 2007. (March and August). E-mails with the author.

Lankes, R. David. 2011. *The Atlas of New Librarianship.* Cambridge, MA: MIT Press.

Moreillon, Judi. 2003. *Peace Poems and Picasso Doves: Literature, Art, Technology, and Poetry.* ReadWriteThink.org. http://www.readwritethink.org/classroom-resources/lesson-plans/peace-poems-picasso-doves-93.html (accessed October 8, 2011).

Moreillon, Judi. 2007. *Collaborative Strategies for Teaching Reading Comprehension: Maximizing Your Impact.* Chicago: ALA Editions.

Moreillon, Judi. 2009. "Co-teaching Published Lesson Plans: A Recipe for Success?" *School Library Media Activities Monthly* 25(5): 29–30.

Moreillon, Judi. 2011. *Making the Case for Co-teaching: An Inservice for Classroom Teachers and School Administrators.* http://voicethread.com/?#u117067.b2178862.i11626726 (accessed October 8, 2011).

Moreillon, Judi. 2012. *Coteaching Reading Comprehension Strategies in Secondary School Libraries: Maximizing Your Impact.* Chicago: ALA Editions.

Moreillon, Judi, Jennifer Hunt, and Sarah Ewing. 2009. "Learning and Teaching in WANDA Wiki Wonderland: Literature Circles in the Digital Commons." *Teacher Librarian* 37(2): 23–28.

Moreillon, Judi, and Diane Roderick. 2004. *Behind the Masks: Exploring Culture and Self through Art and Poetry.* ReadWriteThink.org. http://www .readwritethink.org/classroom-resources/lesson-plans/behind-masks-exploring-culture-395.html (accessed October 8, 2011).

Peterson, Ralph. 1992. *Life in a Crowded Place: Making a Learning Community.* Portsmouth, NH: Heinemann.

Pickerell, Judy. 2001. *Third-grade Teacher.* TeacherTube. http://tinyurl.com/ testimonial-3rd-grade-teacher (accessed October 9, 2011).

Roderick, Diane. 2003. *High School Art Teacher.* TeacherTube. http://tinyurl .com/testimonial-h-s-art-teacher (accessed October 9, 2011).

Vygotsky, Lev. 1978. *Mind in Society: The Development of Higher Psychological Processes.* Cambridge, MA: Harvard University Press.

Zmuda, Alison, and Violet H. Harada. 2008. *Librarians as Learning Specialists: Meeting the Learning Imperative for the 21st Century.* Westport, CT: Libraries Unlimited.

# CHAPTER 8
# LEADING LEARNING COMMUNITIES

*Editors' Note:* While everyone seems to have professional learning communities on their minds, there is need for more literature that describes exactly how PLCs develop at the school level. Carolyn Kirio and Sandy Yamamoto at Kapolei High School in Hawaii capture the evolution of such a community at their high school and their leadership role in helping to shape this initiative.

## Improving Practice Through Professional Learning Communities

Carolyn Kirio and Sandy Yamamoto

Establishing a professional learning community (PLC) is a hot topic on many school campuses. It's fashionable to say that you have a PLC at your school; but quite often, the PLC is probably no more than renamed department meetings that do not deal with improvements over time or use current research to inform and improve practice. In this chapter, we share our discoveries about PLCs at Kapolei High School in Hawaii. We begin with background information on our school and describe our reasons for establishing PLCs. We elaborate on key elements in designing, facilitating, and assessing PLCs and end the chapter by reflecting on what we are learning and how our PLCs benefit our school.

### THE SCHOOL CONTEXT

Kapolei High School was established in 2000 with over 375 9th grade students and 30 teachers. Today, the school services grades 9 through 12 with over 2,000 students and a staff of 117 faculty members. Students work with core teaching teams in grades 9 and 10. Each core team consists of 3 teachers representing English, social studies, and science. As juniors and seniors the students enter into an academy of their choice and select from among 8 different cross-disciplinary fields ranging from graphic arts and industrial technology to business and human services (e.g., public service, social work, and education). Students work independently and collaboratively on a range of interdisciplinary units. All departments and academies emphasize a project-based approach to learning that has also been the focus of our professional development efforts.

## Our Students

Our student population is ethnically and socioeconomically diverse. Over 20 percent of the student body is Native Hawaiian, with other large groups being Asian, Caucasian, and Pacific Islanders. We are not a Title I school although we have students from families that are on welfare as well as students from middle-class households. There are also two homeless shelters in our community. Given the range of cultural and economic differences in our student population, we consider it an accomplishment that as many as 96 percent of our seniors have received their diplomas through regular or alternative education in recent years.

### Professional Learning Communities

Professional learning communities recognize that all members of the school community must work together to focus on improving learning. Richard DuFour indicates that PLCs must address the following critical questions: (1) What do we want each student to learn? (2) How will we know when each student has learned it? (3) How will we respond when a student experiences difficulty in learning? (2004, 8). Such communities encourage open and honest discussions of goals and strategies, and the members experiment with ways to improve practice and share the results. The PLC is a powerful staff development approach that involves both teachers and administrators in a continuous spiral of inquiry and improvement.

## Our Faculty

The 117 full-time faculty members include twelve support teachers (e.g., curriculum coordinators, counselors, teacher mentor, librarian). Most of our teachers have ten or more years of classroom experience with 91 percent being fully licensed. Sandy is one of two nationally certified professionals currently on staff. While Carolyn is also nationally certified, she moved to Kapolei Middle School this year because of budget cuts at the high school.

## EARLIER PD EFFORTS: WHAT DID NOT WORK

In the first four years of the school's existence, we focused on two major approaches to professional development. The first was sending selected faculty to local and national conferences such as those hosted by Model Schools and the Association for Supervision and Curriculum Development. Faculty members were picked based on what they were teaching and the student populations they were servicing. For example, the school was developing a curriculum to assist incoming freshmen with improving their study skills in reading, writing,

---

### Academies

Many high school reform initiatives involve the breaking down of large schools into smaller units, often called academies. In academies, interdisciplinary teams of teachers share the same students and have a common planning time (MDRC n.d.). Academies foster a more personalized atmosphere that encourages a culture of trust as well as accountability among teachers and students. The academy concept at Kapolei High is based on *Breaking Ranks II* (NASSP 2004), a model developed by the National Association of Secondary School Principals. Using this model, the school has integrated different disciplines in real-world contexts. For example, the Hoola Academy brings together science, art, and environmental and cultural studies to address the theme of sustainable living in Hawaii.

---

and math—all critical for success in high school. Consequently, several 9th grade teachers were selected to attend the Model Schools Conference to see how other schools were addressing these issues. Their expenses for the conference were funded through the budget allocated for opening our school.

Our teachers returned from these conferences excited and eager to share their new findings with the rest of the staff. Unfortunately, their presentations to the faculty never materialized in actual implementation. The teachers shared specific strategies for improving writing and critical thinking at one-shot meetings. These sessions were more like overviews with little or no time allowed for discussing how these strategies might be developed in various classroom contexts. There was no real modeling for application and no follow-up sessions. The standard reaction from the faculty was, "I didn't go to the conference so I don't have enough information to make this happen in my classroom."

The administration reasoned that if teachers felt they needed to hear the information first hand, it would be money well invested to bring national consultants to the school. Our second PD approach was hiring coaches from a national consulting firm focusing on the improvement of clinical practice were brought in to help us implement project-based learning (PBL). For three years the visiting team conducted annual workshops that were essentially a week of one-way, lecture-focused communication with minimum opportunities for engagement. In between these visits, the consultants offered assistance via e-mail; however, we discovered that they frequently lacked a clear understanding of our students and they tended to suggest solutions that did not directly relate to the students' cultural environ-

> ## Model Schools
>
> Model Schools targets best practices in professional development, standards alignment, instructional intervention practices, school organizational structures, and teaching impact on student performance. Coordinated by the International Center for Leadership in Education (http://www.leadered.com/resources .html) Model Schools identifies high-performing K–12 school programs across the nation and disseminates information about these programs through conferences, webinars, and publications.

ment and learning challenges. We wound up trying to figure things out for ourselves. For instance, teachers sought strategies to help their students of Filipino descent develop confidence in discussions and debates. Raised in homes where speaking out in front of adults was considered disrespectful, these students were reluctant to participate in verbal exchanges. Consultants suggested that students share in smaller groups until students were comfortable presenting to larger audiences. We realized that this strategy would not work. Instead, we hosted parent and family sessions where we shared the importance of verbal skills and asked parents to encourage their children to practice these skills at home as well as in school.

Alvin Nagasako, our former principal, realized the ineffectiveness of both of these expensive PD approaches, and he assumed a pivotal role in our move to PLCs. A recognized leader among school administrators in the state, Mr. Nagasako attended local and national conferences, read voraciously on school reform, and networked with other educational leaders. He began to realize that genuine change had to be developed from within the faculty and not imposed by experts external to the school.

## IDENTIFYING LEADERS

Mr. Nagasako recognized that the key to establishing PLCs was assembling a cadre of school leaders capable of nurturing the communities. He consulted with his administrative team to identify faculty members who were problem solvers and curriculum leaders. They sought individuals who not only had command of the standards and broad experience with curriculum but sound pedagogical knowledge. Importantly, they wanted professionals with team-building skills. The PLC Leadership Team that was formed included the technology integration teacher, curriculum coordinator, the principal, three assistant principals, and two librarians (us).

---

### Principal Nagasako's Commentary

I read reform documents from the National Association of Secondary School Principals (NASSP) such as *Breaking Ranks II* (2004) and examined online sources such as the Turning Points web site (Center for Collaborative Education, http://www.turningpts.org/work.htm) that advocated for the transformation of teaching and learning from passive and disconnected schooling to something dynamic and relevant. Before Kapolei, I was principal at a school that embraced teaming as the organizational system to foster integrated learning. Teams met and planned curriculum, instruction, and assessment. We provided teachers with additional planning periods to develop units of study that were similar to the project-based learning we were emphasizing at Kapolei. I was impressed with Charlotte Danielson's (2006) advice on how teachers improved practice by learning from each other as they reflected on students' work. I realized that sound pedagogy and action based on reflection had to go hand in hand. This was also a critical part of our restructuring strategy: it wasn't so much that the experts were somewhere out there; we had to honor and leverage the talent within our own faculty and orchestrate opportunities for peer coaching and critical group dialogue. This just made so much sense. I also believed that a critical piece in successful professional growth was to foster teacher leadership.

---

As the librarians, we were thrilled to join the team. It meant that the administration recognized the value of our collaborative curriculum work with the various departments and academies. During his frequent visits, Mr. Nagasako had observed the steady stream of instructional activity in the library. He commended us for initiating and supporting a range of multidisciplinary projects. One example of our work was with a newly formed team of English, science, and social studies teachers. We collaboratively designed and implemented a project that challenged students to examine Hawaii's economy and its dependence on tourism. Focusing on the issue of economic sustainability, the students developed mock businesses for our state that ranged from venues for ecotourism to green solutions such as solar and wind farms. Another project involved the physical education department. We teamed with the teachers on a study titled Hurricane (named after our school mascot) Extreme Sports that combined physical fitness, health, and kinesiology along with proposal writing and oral presentation skills. Students studied the history of different sports and predicted how current technological advances in athletics might lead to alternative forms of current sports.

It was important that we were also active members of committees that affected the entire school community. Carolyn was a lead facilitator on the Senior Project Initiative, and Sandy served as a coordinator of new teachers. In addition, we were both members of the Accreditation Task Force. We recognized the value of keeping up with professional trends and practices in PBL, and we were often invited to administrative sessions where we shared current research and information on topics such as standards-based assessments and inquiry learning. As librarians, we examined resources from the Buck Institute on PBL; subscribed to *Edutopia*, a PBL newsletter; and pulled from different models of critical thinking and co-teaching and adapted these models to our situation. We coordinated the development of a school PBL training guide that could be used in professional development sessions with our faculty. In addition, we invited our principal to attend local library conferences where we were doing presentations and workshops. He appreciated this opportunity to see firsthand how we shared the work we were doing at Kapolei.

## BUILDING A TEAM

Developing trust was the first critical step in working as a PLC leadership team. To be honest, we had initial fears about speaking up in front of the administrators. We were worried that we might offend someone if we gave contradictory feedback. This fear was quickly dispelled by the principal, who set the tone by candidly admitting when he didn't understand something and asking for advice and suggestions from everyone in the group. He stated that administrators often didn't have adequate knowledge of curriculum and pedagogy—it was an area that they hopefully developed on the job. The assistant principals confirmed that their administrative training focused on management issues rather than on curriculum matters.

In our team meetings, we raised tough questions about all facets of the curriculum and our school's direction in terms of overall student achievement. One example of a topic discussed was how to reconcile the testing mandates of the state with a PBL approach. We felt that the high-stakes testing forced teachers to take a fragmented approach to learning while PBL demanded a more holistic, big-picture approach. We wrestled with the concept of rigor and what it meant in terms of expectations for the learner. Were there different levels or types of rigor depending on the discipline? How might we build consensus amongst the faculty members who had varying ideas?

By immersing ourselves in a lot of give-and-take, we learned to appreciate the importance of allowing for different perspectives on various issues and concerns. In short, we were experiencing the type of interaction and discourse we hoped to cultivate with the rest of the faculty. We also knew that we had to do more homework on PLCs and PBL. We had to understand and own the concepts ourselves. Toward this end, the team spent the better part of the 2003–2004 year reading and discussing the literature on PLCs and PBL.

## Defining Professional Learning Communities

We discovered that PLCs are groups of people who have similar goals and interests and collaborate over time to exchange ideas and find solutions (Wenger 1998; Wenger, McDermott, and Snyder 2002). What holds them together is a shared vision, a sense of purpose, and a real need to know what each other knows. In pursuit of these goals and interests, they employ similar practices, work with the same tools, and express themselves in a common language. They collaborate directly, use one another as sounding boards, and teach and learn from each other. They are colleagues committed to jointly developing better instructional practices. They learn by doing, reflecting, and using reflections to refine what they do (DuFour and Eaker 1998; Lave and Wenger 1991). As our team read and exchanged ideas, we realized how important it would be to create environments where people might safely experiment with new practices and strategies and freely engage in collegial reflection. Later in this chapter, we elaborate on how we designed PLC sessions to foster engagement, experimentation, reflection, and action.

> **Rigor in Learning**
>
> Rigor encompasses more than academic proficiency in written and oral communication.
>
> According to Tony Wagner (2008), rigor involves students in grappling with problems, accessing and analyzing information, and socially constructing new understandings in teams. It requires that students adapt and modify their understandings as they are confronted with new challenges and questions. They use their imaginations to consider fresh possibilities and alternatives in dealing with complex issues and reconsider what they know in light of new evidence and information.

## Defining Project-Based Learning

As we mentioned earlier, our school supports PBL as a model that shifts from classroom practices that are teacher centered toward learning activities that are interdisciplinary, student centered, and integrated with real-world issues and practices (Buck Institute for Education 2006; Harada, Kirio, and Yamamoto 2008). To succeed in these types of projects, students actively apply critical skills in project planning, collaborative problem solving, and higher-order thinking. They have to stretch themselves beyond the collection of facts and work toward constructing knowledge that combines facts with the analysis, synthesis, and evaluation of this information. Teaching in PBL, therefore, requires that the instructors guide students in developing thoughtful products. These products

## Essential Questions

Essential questions spark connections with personal experience and prior learning. They engage the imagination and are "poised at the boundary of the known and the unknown" (Clifford and Friesen 2007) Essential questions are broad in scope and perpetually arguable. They are the big ideas or key inquiries of a discipline, e.g., how does one determine an artistic masterpiece? It's essential when the question requires students to consider alternatives, weigh evidence, and justify their answers (Wiggins 2007). It's what Eric Cook (2007) calls an enduring question—one that embeds layers of good ideas that generate rethinking, analysis, debate, and reflection. Jamie McKenzie says that "essential questions cannot be found; they must be invented" (1996).

provide evidence of students' abilities to grapple with the essential questions that serve as the overarching framework for the inquiry. The products also require students to demonstrate mastery of the content standards addressed by the project (Buck Institute for Education 2006).

In our sessions as a PLC leadership team, we shared personal experiences about what was working and what was not with the PBL efforts at our school. We noted that one of the major problems that teachers faced was helping students to formulate essential questions that framed projects. Another challenge was how to develop projects that reflected balanced attention to the disciplines involved (i.e., not having one discipline overpower the others). To help us deal with these types of issues, we examined samples of PBL units developed by the faculty. We analyzed how the essential questions demanded rigorous thinking, how disciplines were integrated, and how learning was assessed. Different members of the team suggested readings and volunteered to lead discussions on topics such curriculum integration, assessment tools, and incorporating rigor. Because Carolyn had worked extensively with different grade levels and departments on PBL, she shared descriptions of essential questions and we discussed how such questions might frame our projects.

## ORGANIZING PLCS

Prior to launching the PLCs in 2004, the leadership team asked faculty members about their satisfaction with the current method of professional development. The teachers uniformly expressed their unhappiness with the outside consultant approach as ineffective in helping them meet instructional needs. They indicated a desire to hear how their colleagues were addressing challenges such as incorporating more challenging questions in projects, creating more relevant learning options, devising strategies for assessing student progress, and involving the community in PBL. Within this context, the team introduced the concept of PLCs as professional development that embraced a collegial, collaborative approach to examining topics of common concern. Faculty members indicated they were willing to experiment with it. They requested that the leadership team organize the PLCs according to grade levels. This made for large communities of thirty to forty teachers. The leadership team realized that this was unwieldy, so within the large communities we invited faculty to form themselves into more manageable discussion groups of four to five people. Some groups organized themselves by teaching teams and others by subject areas. Still others selected partners with whom they shared teaching spaces—for example, a graphic arts teacher who had a classroom adjacent to the grade 9 area joined a grade 9 team. We encouraged self-selection at this point since we wanted everyone to feel comfortable with the composition of the groups. In subsequent years, teachers were willing to form groups based on different criteria such as organizing by subject areas. The PLCs met monthly for about an hour. These meetings were scheduled on Tuesdays or Thursdays at the end of the instructional day in one of the team or academy classrooms. Beyond the monthly meetings, faculty members continued discussions and worked on follow-through tasks through department and academy meetings.

## TOPICS AND THEMES ADDRESSED

In the first year of the PLCs, the communities focused on how well our students were achieving the Hawaii Department of Education's "Vision of the High School Graduate" (http://doe.k12.hi.us/about/intro_vision.htm). A critical component of the vision was students graduating and pursuing post-secondary education. In the exit survey with seniors, we discovered that Kapolei had a 91 percent on-time graduation rate, which was well above the state average of 75 percent. An exit survey was administered to the 347 seniors regarding their post–high school plans—60 percent of the seniors returned the survey. Fifty percent of the respondents indicated that they planned to enter two- or four-year colleges on a full-time basis, while another 17 percent hoped to be part-time students. Six percent responded that they would be entering a trade school, while the remaining 27 percent of the students said they would work or enlist in the military. The PLC Leadership Team also collected informal data on how the students valued PBL. As students returned to visit our campus in the ensuing school year or e-mailed us, they indicated that PBL had prepared them to work in groups, provided them with critical communication skills, and stretched their creative-thinking and problem-solving capabilities. They told us they were able to apply and connect the skills learned to the real world and seriously think about possible career choices.

In subsequent years, we have covered a range of topics and themes under the umbrella of PBL. Based on observed student needs as well as district and state priorities, faculty and administration determine the topics and strive to link the work from one year to the next year. In Year 1, we concentrated on how best to build more rigor and relevance into our curriculum and how this type of learning might motivate our students. In Year 2, we recognized that one of the serious learning gaps for our students was being able to read with understanding, hence our focus on reading comprehension with entering high school students. In year 3, we incorporated critical skills in reading and writing across interdisciplinary projects. In year 4, the state department of education rolled out a new set of content and performance standards, so we spent the sessions realigning our curriculum with these standards. As we continued to work on building critical thinking and basic literacy skills in our projects, we recognized that we also needed to spend time figuring best ways to assess for student learning and interpret the data collected to improve our practices. This became the focus for years 5 and 6. In the last three years, we have concentrated on using assessment data to differentiate teaching and learning. Additionally, while faculty members have been attending workshops and institutes to learn about new technology tools, we are now moving from learning the technology to using the technology for learning. Figure 8.1 summarizes the topics and themes covered.

## Figure 8.1: Examples of Topics and Themes Covered

| School year | Examples of topics and themes covered |
| --- | --- |
| Year 1: 2003–2004 | Forming the leadership team; achieving the state's "Vision of the High School Graduate" and focusing on rigor and relevance in learning |
| Year 2: 2004–2005 | Addressing the reading literacy gap: reading with understanding |
| Year 3: 2005–2006 | Designing interdisciplinary projects that incorporate reading and writing literacies |
| Year 4: 2006–2007 | Connecting the newly revised Hawaii Content & Performance Standards to our curriculum |
| Year 5: 2007–2008 | Assessing for learning |
| Year 6: 2008–2009 | Using assessments to inform teaching and learning |
| Year 7: 2009–2010 | Differentiating learning based on assessments |
| Years 8 and 9: 2010–2012 | Continuing to address assessment and differentiation Moving from learning technology to using technology for learning |

## FACILITATING PLCS

Each member of the PLC leadership team functions as a facilitator for a specific group. One of the three assistant principals also joins each PLC to help with questions or concerns that might require administrative input. We've learned that the following practices are essential:

- Listen with an open mind.
- Appreciate that adult learners have different needs.
- Adapt and differentiate strategies to meet these needs.
- Be flexible and willing to change strategies and plans based on learners' needs.
- Respect different points of view.
- Leverage existing strengths instead of dwelling on shortcomings.
- Keep conversations focused.
- Be patient and persistent.
- Allow everyone to contribute.
- Encourage clarification.
- Probe.

- Reflect.
- Maintain a sense of humor.

As facilitators, we established common expectations and protocols to ensure buy-in from the faculty for our PLC discussions. We realized that we were working with a range of personalities—from teachers who were reticent to speak to those who monopolized conversations. We had faculty who were resourceful problem solvers and those who tended to be naysayers. As facilitators, we are still learning how best to move conversations forward without bruising egos or squelching divergent ideas. The following example describes how Carolyn handled a particular challenge.

---

### Carolyn's Example of Working with a Teacher

Mr. X considered himself to be a master teacher. He felt there wasn't a teaching strategy he didn't already know about or a student he couldn't effectively teach. He initially believed that the PLC sessions would be opportunities for him to expound on his knowledge. With Mr. X monopolizing discussions, the first sessions were pretty miserable for the other teachers. I spent time working one-on-one with Mr. X, explaining the importance of the established guidelines for PLCs, i.e., giving others the opportunity to share and listening with an open mind. I encouraged him to continue sharing, but I also set time limits for all sharing in the group. Mr. X finally began listening to others and discovered that his colleagues had things to offer that he didn't know about. Everyone felt more comfortable about sharing as Mr. X began to listen more and talk less.

---

Sandy dealt with teachers feeling anxious about sharing their teaching with colleagues.

---

### Sandy's Example of Working with a Teacher

Mrs. S was a beginning teacher who was still feeling her way with her students and deciphering the school dynamics. She didn't feel confident about sharing her experiences and opinions with veteran teachers and was often left out of discussions because she was hesitant to share her work. I reinforced the idea with Mrs. S that the PLC was not an evaluation tool but a safe forum for open sharing and learning. I also asked a veteran teacher in her group to provide a supporting and encouraging presence for new teachers. Mrs. S slowly became more comfortable with her group and began sharing her ideas and opinions regularly.

---

The leadership team also received training in facilitative leadership to make meetings effective and productive, to work with different personalities, and to achieve consensus. We listened carefully to faculty feedback and used this data to guide us in determining which resources to provide them and how to present new ideas to groups. As librarians, we also had opportunities to attend workshops that focused on how to offer mentoring support to colleagues. For example, Sandy picked up critical pointers on developing positive relationships with beginning teachers at workshops sponsored by the New Teacher Center at UC Santa Cruz.

## DESIGNING A PLC SESSION

According to Gail Bush (2008), the following points are critical in planning and facilitating PLC sessions:

- Discuss the overarching question and the relevance of the question for the meeting.

- Determine what kinds of evidence would best allow the group to explore specific aspects of the question.

- Follow the agreed-upon protocol for the meeting.

- Reflect on the meeting in terms of the actual learning shared and the process used to reach understandings.

- Discuss what will happen between meetings.

- Plan for the next meeting.

- Document group progress.

In designing a session, our leadership team begins by identifying the driving question and the desired learning outcome. We also indicate how everyone will demonstrate understanding. We outline the session that includes how we introduce the topic or theme. We bring in readings and allow time for faculty to share their experiences with the topic. Figure 8.2 is a planning template for the sessions.

We encourage faculty members to practice and reflect on their experiences so that everyone can bring samples of their work to the following PLC session. Figure 8.3 is an example of an actual session plan.

What happens in between the monthly face-to-face sessions is equally critical. The discussions and suggested assignments are frequently brought back to departments and academies where teachers continue to explore or experiment with a concept. For example, in tackling differentiation, teachers agreed to observe how differentiating strategies were being used in another PLC member's classroom. They brought their observation notes to the following PLC session and shared them using a set of reflective questions.

---

### Figure 8.2: Planning Template for PLC Sessions

1. Driving question for session (what's our focus):

2. Reasons for addressing this topic (why this is important):

3. Alignment to current visions, objectives, and learning objectives (how this fits):

4. Learning outcome for session (what is the desired result):

5. Evidence of learning (how do we show everyone got it):

6. Session strategy (what will the session look like):
   - Introduce
   - Demonstrate/model
   - Engage/experiment
   - Summarize
   - Reflect

7. Post-session strategy (what happens between meetings):
   - Act
   - Reflect

---

To be honest, all teachers do not participate at the same level. There have been times when teachers have not been able to work on samples. As facilitators, we haven't solved this challenge completely. What has helped, however, has been for a facilitator to spend one-on-one time with these teachers. Often, these informal discussions result in clearer understanding of the work being conducted. Frequently, we also discover that teachers have temporary setbacks and just need a little more time to resolve things. We gently stress the importance of working as teams in our sessions and the value of everyone bringing their efforts to the meetings for review and discussion. Teachers also realize that their participation counts as part of the annual faculty review process.

## ASSESSING PLCS

At Kapolei, we assess the effectiveness of our work in PLCs through peer critiques and portfolios. Peer critiques provide opportunities for colleague-to-colleague assessments, while the portfolios allow for self-reflection on accomplishments and areas for future improvement. The leadership team also formed its own PLC to study the results of the peer critiques. We used *Instructional Rounds in Education* (City, Elmore, Fiarman, and Teitel 2009) as a framework for our own discussions on what was happening in our classrooms.

## Figure 8.3: Example of a PLC Session Plan

**1. Driving question for session**

How can we create rigorous and relevant project-based learning opportunities for our students?

**2. Reason for addressing this topic**

Faculty members have diverse expectations as to what is rigorous or relevant. We need a more unified understanding to strive for a consistent level of performance in our classrooms.

**3. Alignment to current visions, objectives, and learning outcomes**

This focus fits with our emphasis on project-based learning. It is critical in realizing the department's "Vision of a High School Graduate" (http://doe .k12.hi.us/about/intro_vision.htm)

**4. Learning outcome for session**

School wide understanding of how to design essential questions at Kapolei.

**5. Evidence of learning**

Everyone will create essential questions and conduct friendly critiques with peers using Bloom's taxonomy and the Model Schools' Rigor/Relevance framework to provide feedback.

**6. Session strategy**
- **Introduce**

  Teachers bring an essential question they have used in the past. They review last year's school wide essential question.
- **Demonstrate/model**

  Facilitators provide samples of essential questions at different levels. Provide each sub-group with three or four sample questions to rank according to Bloom's taxonomy. Have groups share out their rankings. Select one question and revise to improve with group.
- **Engage/experiment**

  Teachers use the Rigor/Relevance framework and Bloom's taxonomy in revising their essential questions to elicit higher-level thinking.
- **Summarize**

  Sub-groups share out their questions and how they improved them.
- **Reflect**

  Groups discuss and provide feedback on this experience.

**7. Post-session strategy**
- **Act**

  Teachers work on a PBL project for the next quarter focusing on the essential questions.
- **Reflect**

  Teachers share their PBL projects at the next PLC session. They also submit their PBL project write-ups to the curriculum coordinator or assistant principal.

## Peer Critiques

Teachers select their own critiquing partners, and they switch partners each quarter to provide opportunities for everyone to work with colleagues from different levels and disciplines. For example, when we were covering research strategies, faculty agreed on the following partner protocols: first quarter: pair with someone in the same subject but different grade level; second quarter: pair with someone from a different subject and level; third quarter: pair with someone within your PLC; and fourth quarter: observe a senior project in progress in one of the academies.

To prepare for a critiquing session, the partners agree on what to specifically observe during the visits. The crucial question is: what should we look for that makes a difference in student learning? The visit lasts for a class period. Teachers try to pick partners that have nonteaching planning periods for the observation sessions. When this is not possible, substitute teachers are hired to cover observers' classes. After the visits, partners meet to exchange specific feedback on observed behaviors. At the following PLC sessions, all partners share their critiquing experiences and how the observations have impacted their teaching.

Our teachers appreciate the critiquing sessions because this form of friendly feedback provides them with credible and specific peer input on what is working and what is not in their classrooms. It also helps faculty members identify areas for further professional development. Importantly, it moves all of us toward a more consistent understanding of best practices.

---

### Teachers' Comments on the Value of Peer Critiquing

**Maria:** I had known Kathy for years. Although she is an English teacher and I am in science, we decided to pair. I was able to observe certain teaching strategies she used that really inspired me. For example, I have always struggled with getting students to understand science concepts. I observed how Kathy broke down chapter text to get her students to comprehend and dig for deeper meanings behind passages. Her strategies reached everyone in class. I applied them in my physics class and got tremendous results: my students connected with the theory of perpetual motion and velocity!

**Jill:** I paired with Lance and we were focusing on using technology in our classrooms. At first I was embarrassed with my lack of tech knowledge but Lance put me at ease. He didn't judge me. Instead, he offered great advice on how to bump up my teaching by making better use of the visual presenter and digitizing handouts for uploading to my class web page. We agreed to keep meeting—this was terrific.

## Figure 8.4: Template for Lesson Plan

Date: _____ Duration: _____

Objective: _____

| Activity | Standards/Benchmarks/ Addressed | Teaching Strategy | Materials Needed/ Preparation Involved | Evaluation/ Assessment | Lead Teacher | Time Allotted |
|---|---|---|---|---|---|---|
|  |  |  |  |  |  |  |
|  |  |  |  |  |  |  |
|  |  |  |  |  |  |  |
|  |  |  |  |  |  |  |
|  |  |  |  |  |  |  |

Reflection:

From *Growing Schools: Librarians as Professional Developers* by Debbie Abilock, Kristin Fontichiaro, and Violet H. Harada, Editors. Santa Barbara, CA: Libraries Unlimited. Copyright © 2012.

The curriculum coordinator compiles and disseminates feedback from the peer critiques. This allows individual departments and academies to also study the data and identify progress being made by their respective faculty members. For instance, the social studies faculty recently focused on connecting learning to prior experiences. The department faculty members were pleased to discover from the peer critiques and self-reflections that almost everyone was using strategies to engage students in making critical connections. This led the social studies teachers to share their strategies in a subsequent PLC session.

## Professional Learning Portfolios

Along with the peer critiques, faculty members compile professional learning portfolios that include their work from the PLCs. Portfolios are also used for national certification, state relicensing, and annual teacher evaluations at the school level. In addition, the PLC facilitators review portfolios, primarily to assess the effectiveness of the sessions conducted and to identify where modifications might be made in the upcoming year's agenda. The portfolio includes lesson plans and samples of student work as well as self-reflections based on the peer critiques. Figure 8.4 is a template for the lessons.

## INSIGHTS AND LESSONS LEARNED

As we enter our ninth year with PLCs, facilitators and participants acknowledge that community building is not without its hurdles. Obstacles and roadblocks crop up and test our perseverance. We discuss some of the challenges below.

## Dealing with Diverse Levels of Experience and Knowledge

With any topic we cover, we have teachers ranging from novices to experienced practitioners. When we geared for the middle of the road, some teachers felt it was too elementary while others couldn't keep up. It was frustrating. We began to incorporate a differentiated approach by offering additional support sessions on certain topics at three different levels (e.g., basic introduction to a topic, support for initial implementation, and support for refinement and expansion activities). Teachers could select which type of session to attend based upon their experience and knowledge of the information being shared. This seems to be working; participants feel the sessions are tailored to their needs.

## Finding Adequate Time to Meet and Plan

Finding time to meet and develop the ideas we share in the PLC sessions remains a continuing challenge. We tackle this in several ways. First, departments and academies have built time in their meetings to extend the discussions covered in the monthly PLC sessions. As a faculty, we are also increasing our use of online options to document conversations. In addition, our administration allows for additional full days of professional development during the school year. These are opportunities to expand on work being conducted in the PLC sessions and invite community guests to join us in these conversations.

## Making Learning Relevant for Teachers

As we mentioned at the beginning, our school's earlier efforts to provide professional development resulted in a huge disconnect for most teachers. However, even with the initiation of PLCs, we still had teachers uncertain about the value of the work conducted. For this reason, the PLC Leadership Team carefully considers faculty feedback and examines peer critiquing sessions and portfolios to ensure that topics and themes selected connect directly with school initiatives that concern the entire school community. In the PLC sessions, facilitators model integration of strategies across both core and elective courses so that all teachers feel connected to the material. Although this is a time-consuming effort, we find it essential. How can we ask teachers to embrace these strategies if we are not able to model them? Some teachers have to be sold on these new approaches, so connections to their classes must be obvious and relevant for them.

## Using Assessment Data to Inform Teaching and Learning

The school collects copious amounts of statistical information on students, from test scores and grades to retention and graduation rates. The faculty realized, however, that standardized test scores provided an incomplete snapshot of student achievement—scores did not identify the individual student's abilities and weaknesses. They recognized that student performance in class work was a critical indicator of actual learning. At the same time, teachers conceded that this was a gap area in their professional learning. Because of this, the PLC sessions in recent years have focused on how to assess for learning and how to interpret the results for data-informed changes.

## Benefits of PLCs for Our Faculty

Most of our faculty members understand and welcome the strategies learned from participation in the PLCs. In their self-reflections, they mention some of the following benefits.

## Meeting and Working with New Faculty

With our staff topping over a hundred, it is difficult to know everyone on campus. PLCs have offered staff members a chance to meet faculty in different subject areas and initiate cross-departmental dialogue about strategies that affect student achievement. Teaming has become easier as instructors got to know faculty beyond their own departments. Working in PLCs has moved our faculty toward a stronger commitment to the vision and mission of the school.

## Assessing for Learning

It is a daunting task to assess for learning and use the data to evaluate the effectiveness of your lessons when you are working alone. By participating in PLCs, teachers receive collegial support in looking at learning together. By sharing and receiving feedback on student work, faculty members identify weaknesses in their instruction and offer constructive and specific suggestions to one another for improvement. In a nonevaluative setting, teachers feel freer to test out different strategies without fear of repercussions.

## Building Capacity Within the Faculty

While the PLC leadership team serves as the core team of facilitators, we have invited more teachers to serve as facilitators for small group work. We identify teachers who consistently share strategies and techniques that their colleagues can adopt or modify and who demonstrate the people skills to encourage the exchange of ideas. By participating in PLCs, more instructors feel empowered to assume leadership roles in group work.

## Value of Being PLC Facilitators

Serving as PLC facilitators has been intensive work but it has also been an invaluable learning experience for us as librarians. We have always embraced a big picture view of the curriculum; however, working with teachers in PLCs has provided us with a deeper appreciation for what the teachers are striving to achieve and how we can collaborate with them. We have also found ways to increase teachers' awareness of the information literacy and thinking skills that are embedded in the *Standards for the 21st-Century Learner* (American Association of School Librarians 2007).

Our perception of the administrators has also changed. Through our PLC leadership team meetings, we gradually recognized their compassion for the students, faculty, and staff. We no longer viewed the administrators as simply our bosses; we appreciated them as people. Meetings often ended with conversations about families, mutual friends, and future plans. In turn, the administrators also saw us in a new light. We were valuable partners they could count on for support and information. One of our former assistant principals, now the principal at a neighboring school, continues to call us for information or to bounce ideas. When another assistant principal became a principal, he encouraged his librarian to assume a greater leadership role and become a more active collaborator with the staff. We believe we changed these administrators' image of what school librarians could do for their schools.

---

## Sandy's Commentary on Developing Teacher-Librarian Relationships

Several years ago, I met a new teacher in my PLC group and learned about his goals and objectives. He had limited prior experience with PBL. I collaborated with him on a project dealing with American life in 1920s that fit his social studies standards. Together, we developed an essential question for the project: "How were the 1920s a cultural, political and economic turning point in the 20th century?" I taught the students search strategies and note taking as well as how to evaluate information and resources. Students ultimately created learning stations in the library on various topics and also made interactive presentations to other classes. The teacher is now a regular user of the library, and we continue to collaborate on projects for his classes.

---

## Carolyn's Commentary on Developing Librarian-Administrator Relationships

One day my principal, Mr. Nagasako, walked in and said, "We need to talk." My gut reaction was "What did I do now?" He entered my office, pulled up a chair across from my desk, and said, "I need to have your opinion on something." He proceeded to describe a problem relating to curriculum that he was wrestling with and wanted to know what I thought. After getting over the initial shock of his surprise visit, I offered perspectives on what I believed might work and debated with him about alternative solutions and their possible consequences. When he got up to leave, he said, "Don't move this chair. I will be back." True to his word, his visits became more frequent. In addition, word got around to the rest of the administrative staff, who also began to frequent my office. As he oriented new administrators to the school, Mr.Nagasako actually made the chair in my office an official stop on his campus tour! This relationship with my administrators became a special bond between us.

---

## CONTINUING OUR JOURNEY

Our ideas about PLCs continue to evolve at Kapolei. In this chapter, we pointed out some of the bumps in the road and the complex nature of professional learning communities. We realize that good teaching and successful learning cannot be separated. As Richard DuFour (2004) points out, schools that are serious about establishing PLCs have to ask persistent questions about what they want students to learn and how they tackle problems when students need help with that learning. He states that every professional in the building must engage with colleagues in the ongoing exploration of these issues for substantive change to happen. Our work at Kapolei affirms the following important insights:

- Staff members must not work in isolation. We must work together to achieve a vision centered on student learning.

- Staffs need supports to work collaboratively. These supports include time to meet and agreed-upon protocols and guidelines to structure and guide discussions and actions.

- Change depends on the identification of clearly defined goals and the gathering of relevant evidence on whether outcomes have or have not been met. It requires that the findings be used to inform specific and meaningful changes.

- Leadership is critical. It starts with a vision-focused administration and extends to the identification of leaders amongst the faculty. It requires growing that leadership over time.

As educators, we feel that being part of the PLC leadership has been richly rewarding.

---

### Our Personal Learning

**Sandy:** I have developed a greater appreciation for the work being done to achieve excellence at my school and my part in it. I also have a clearer understanding of the strengths and weaknesses in our teaching in the classrooms and the library. By helping to develop Kapolei's PLCs, I realize the importance of shared trust, commitment, and accountability. For PLCs to thrive and grow, participants must be willing to share their work and ideas, believe that improvement is possible, and accept and exchange constructive feedback. A school that is starting to develop a PLC should begin with a small group of willing participants. With the support of a committed administrator, even a small village can make a huge difference.

**Carolyn:** I have discovered that professional development can be valued and relevant. When I reflect on what is happening at Kapolei, I note how teachers actually look forward to PLC meetings and exchanges. Over the years, all of us have gained new strategies for teaching and learning. In a large school like Kapolei, teachers often remain strangers outside their own departments and academies. Being part of PLCs has sliced through those silos and created a network of learning and sharing. Because our administrators contribute to the PLCs, they are familiar with classroom activity. In turn, teachers value their assistance. For Sandy and me, being leaders in the PLC initiative has elevated our value in the eyes of our community.

Working together in a more systematic, coordinated fashion is a huge undertaking. It is hard work. The rewards to the entire school community, however, make the journey worth the effort.

## REFERENCES

American Association of School Librarians. 2007. *Standards for the 21st-Century Learner*. Chicago: American Association of School Librarians. http://ala.org/ala/mgrps/divs/aasl/guidelinesandstandards/learningstandards/AASL_Learning Standards.pdf (accessed January 29, 2011).

Buck Institute for Education. 2006. *Project Based Learning Handbook*. Novato, CA: Buck Institute for Education.

Bush, Gail. 2008. "Inquiry Groups for Professional Development and Information Literacy Instruction." *School Library Media Activities Monthly* 24, no.10 (June): 39–43.

Center for Collaborative Education. n.d. *Turning Points: Transforming Middle Schools*. http://www.turningpts.org/work.htm (accessed June 10, 2011).

City, Elizabeth, Richard Elmore, Sarah Fiarman, and Lee Teitel. 2009. *Instructional Rounds in Education: A Network Approach to Teaching and Learning*. Cambridge, MA: Harvard Education Press.

Clifford, Pat, and Sharon Friesen. 2007. "Creating Essential Questions." Galileo Educational Network Association. http://www.galileo.org/tips/essential_questions .html (accessed July 13, 2011).

Cook, Eric. 2007. "Enduring Questions: Why Ask Them?" Big Ideas (e-journal). http://www.authenticeducation.org/bigideas/article.lasso?artid=79& session=Auth:80AB3AF61168f25996lPQ1E59ED7 (cited July 13, 2011).

Danielson, Charlotte. 2006. *Teacher Leadership that Strengthens Professional Practice*. Alexandria, VA: Association for Supervision and Curriculum Development, 2006.

DuFour, Richard. 2004. "What Is a Professional Learning Community?" *Educational Leadership* 61, no. 8 (May): 6–11. http://pdonline.ascd.org/pd_online /secondary_reading/el200405_dufour.html (accessed June 11, 2011).

DuFour, Richard, and Robert Eaker. 1998. *Professional Learning Communities at Work: Best Practices for Enhancing Student Achievement*. Alexandria, VA: Association for Supervision and Curriculum Development.

Harada, Violet H., Carolyn H. Kirio, and Sandra H. Yamamoto. 2008. *Collaborating for Project Based Learning in Grades 9-12*. Worthington, OH: Linworth Publishing.

Lave, Jean, and Etienne Wenger. 1991. *Situated Learning: Legitimate Peripheral Participation*. Cambridge: Cambridge University Press.

McKenzie, Jamie. 1996. "Framing Essential Questions." *From Now On* 6, no. 1 (September). http://www.fno.org/sept96/questions.html (accessed July 13, 2011).

MDRC. n.d. "School-based Reforms in Secondary Schools." http://www
.mdrc.org/subarea_index_29.html (accessed July 12, 2011).

National Association for Secondary School Principals. 2004. *Breaking Ranks
II: Strategies for Leading High School Reform*. Reston, VA: NASSP.

Wagner, Tony. 2008. "Rigor Redefined." *Educational Leaderships* 66, no. 2
(October): 20–25. http://www.ascd.org/publications/educational-leadership/
oct08/vol66/num02/Rigor-Redefined.aspx (accessed July 12, 2011).

Wenger, Etienne. 1998. *Communities of Practice: Learning, Meaning, and Identity*. Cambridge: Cambridge University Press.

Wenger, Etienne, Richard McDermott, and William M. Snyder. 2002. *Cultivating Communities of Practice*. Boston: Harvard Business School Press.

Wiggins, Grant. 2007. "What Is an Essential Question?" *Big Ideas* (e-journal).
http://www.authenticeducation.org/bigideas/article.lasso?artId=53 (accessed July 13, 2011).

# CHAPTER 9
# USING TIME FOR INTERACTIVE LEARNING

*Editors' Note:* Christopher Harris, who leads a School Library System in western New York State, focuses on how to find time for more robust face-to-face professional development. Like many systems and school districts, Harris had inherited regularly scheduled departmental meetings that spent more time on announcements than on professional growth. His solution—to offload less-important, less-urgent agenda items to e-mail, blogs, or discussion forums—gave him and his team the space to grow capacity. Joining Harris is Brian Mayer, who unpacks how the new time allocations made room for librarians to develop PD capacity, supported by the BOCES staff.

## From FYI to PLC:
## How Our System Transformed Meetings Into Productive Conversations

### Christopher Harris

Finding dedicated time for professional development can be a challenge. In an age of increasing demands, declining budgets, and vanishing support staff, it is altogether too easy to succumb to the daily pressures and forget the long-term need for continued growth. At the School Library System (SLS) of the Genesee Valley Educational Partnership, an educational services agency that supports twenty-two small, rural districts in western New York, the solution was to integrate professional development into regularly scheduled meeting times. However, adding professional development into an already-packed agenda meant some things had to go. In our case, we eliminated committees and relegated routine updates to other communication media to provide time for quality face-to-face interactions.

This is not a new concept in education: future principals have this idea hammered home in administrative programs, but new technologies and changed expectations make it a much more viable solution today. Even so, leadership is the critical element that will determine the degree of success or failure of a change like this. In most cases, participants are not going to ask for this change. Sit-and-get meetings, though boring, at least don't require effort or produce additional work for attendees. Changing to a PD-based model requires active engagement and will result in "homework" for everyone involved. Therefore, the meeting facilitator must present a strong vision that emphasizes the importance of professional development and highlights the benefits to everyone involved. And then the leader must deliver on those promises.

As coordinator, I was the leader who would have to deliver. My position is unique: New York State clusters several smaller school districts into regional groups. Each group has an SLS, a library support structure. The SLS provides regional support for resource sharing, program development, and professional development. The SLS is funded by the state as one of three types of library systems; the others support public and academic/special libraries. The SLS of the Genesee Valley Educational Partnership, my responsibility, covers 56 libraries in 22 public school districts and 5 nonpublic schools with a total student population of about 25,000 students. In other words, even though the SLS is spread out over 1,800 square miles and 22 different organizational structures, it has a population similar to that of many large suburban school districts around the country. A single school district implementing our model may actually enjoy greater success due to a single calendar and a single administrative structure.

When it comes to professional development, SLSs enjoy many advantages. State funding provides a revenue stream that cannot be reassigned for other purposes, and the regulations and state reports that guide our work are very clear on the need for professional development. Even so, it can be difficult to find common days among many school districts. Some districts want their librarians to attend district-wide professional development days so they are able to support local initiatives. Other districts struggle to support the unique needs for librarian professional development and so are thankful for regional offerings outside of the district. With current budgets, it can be even more difficult to secure release time (and the associated substitute costs that one hopes go along with an absent librarian). But SLSs have a powerful ace in the hole. The same state regulations that establish and fund the SLS also require that each district identify a communication coordinator and provide release time for her or him to attend a minimum of four regional meetings a year. Given this helpful mandate, it made perfect sense to turn the meetings from information sessions, that is, meetings primarily dedicated to announcements and current concerns, into professional development sessions designed to grow the capacity and programs of member librarians.

Or at least it made perfect sense in my mind when I arrived, bringing a fresh perspective on meetings that did not seem to ever accomplish as much as the agenda suggested. A great deal of meeting time was spent on updates and passing around handouts, but in many cases the information and paperwork never made it back to the other librarians in the districts. Another large section of the meetings were given over to committee meetings for some of the standing committees defined in our bylaws, though it seemed that not much ever came from the committee work. So based on what I saw, I analyzed the problem and developed a solution based on the three goals presented below. In this case, it was a top-down change that I put in place. This is often the fastest way to bring about radical change, but it adds an immense amount of pressure to deliver real results. Compared to more inclusive decision making and change processes, leaders only get a few attempts at this method; failures are not quickly forgiven or forgotten.

For this to work, new structures for information sharing were needed so that we could devote more time to professional development. In my mind, the shift from traditional information sharing meetings into professional development sessions depended on three elements:

- **First, we had to restructure the meeting days** so that more time was available for face-to-face discussion of critical topics and professional development.

- **Then we had to create a new, online tool for information sharing** so that we gave people a new venue for sharing announcements and noncritical information and that permitted librarians who could not attend face-to-face to benefit.

- **Finally, we had to encourage the creation of a regional professional learning community** so that the participating librarians knew that our face-to-face meetings would focus on exploring the issues that mattered to them.

Though this was the order in which we addressed the tasks, they can probably be accomplished in any order. It matters not if it was the creation of an online information-sharing space that freed up meetings for professional development or if the shift of meetings to professional development necessitated the creation of an information sharing portal. The three elements are presented in this order simply because that is how they evolved in this particular situation.

## CHANGING MEETINGS

One of the big secrets of educational leaders is the discovery that leading traditional faculty meetings is as obnoxious and boring as sitting through them. Despite spending hours gathering together updates and creating handouts, I would still see librarians walking out of meetings half an hour early because their contract day was done or find stacks of papers left behind by people who couldn't bother to take them back to share. Even with these frustrations, however, it is difficult to make real changes in the structure of meetings; especially those where the agenda still bears hazy traces from the mimeographed original that has been handed down through history. But change must come. There are too many national initiatives bearing down on our schools to continue wasting time in meetings with one-way transmission of announcements. This is especially true for librarians, one of the only groups in schools that are responsible for the entire breadth and depth of the pre-K–12 curriculum (as well as our own standards!). Any time that can be found for librarians to gather together must focus on meaningful dialogue and professional development.

## Worthy of a Meeting

The first question participants and leaders alike must ask is, "Is this agenda item worthy of a meeting, or could information be shared in another way?" This isn't to say that library meetings can never include a portion of information sharing; it just means that the sharing needs to be two-way. There needs to be a purpose for bringing a topic up during a meeting beyond "letting people know." When one has pulled librarians away from their buildings, there can be tremendous synergy in the room; why waste that human potential on endless announcements? Library leaders need to consider how to maximize the precious face-to-face time. In our SLS, my team and I evaluate agenda topics and information items using a matrix (see Figure 9.1) similar to the important/urgent matrix developed by Stephen Covey and his team in *First Things First* (1994) that I was introduced to during my administrative coursework.

Our matrix asks us to evaluate each topic based on how critical and collaborative it is. Topics that are both critical (e.g., urgent and essential to the continuation of the library program) and collaborative (e.g., needing group discussion, questions, clarifications, or communal decisions) are worthy of meeting time. One recent topic that ranked as both collaborative and critical, for example, was the rollout of the *Standards for the 21st-Century Learner* (AASL 2007), in which the entire group needed to have a deep understanding the standards, the kinds of program changes that may need to be developed, the tension between new standards and a building's current way of doing things, and more. These tough discussions *need* people to be in the same room in order to be tackled.

The other three quadrants, while still important, can be handled just as effectively using online communication tools; in other words, face-to-face interaction is not essential for those issues to be covered. For example, an announcement about an upcoming author visit at the bookstore, while interesting to everyone and useful information to take back to one's school, is not mission critical, nor does it require a collaborative response; hence, it joins reflections, book reviews, and routine updates in the Not Collaborative, Not Critical quadrant.

It must also be noted here that the matrix description of "not critical" was carefully chosen. This does not say that the topic isn't important, just that it isn't *critical*. Developing a plan of attack for the Common Core State Standards is critical. Sharing a change in procedure that involves a new form that must be filled out for health care is critical. Reviewing a new book or sharing reflections from attendance at a conference is important, but not critical. Things would still be okay if you didn't post the information until tomorrow.

---

### Figure 9.1: The Genessee Valley SLS Decision Matrix

|  | Collaborative | Not Collaborative |
|---|---|---|
| Critical | **Meeting**<br>• new standards<br>• new assessments<br>• strategic planning | • staffing changes<br>• procedures<br>• priority updates |
| Not Critical | • best practices<br>• unit development<br>• book discussions | • reflections<br>• book reviews<br>• routine updates |

(adapted from Covey et al. 1994)

---

By their nature, topics that are both critical and collaborative will naturally shift a meeting into professional development mode because they require deep dialogue rather than shallow information sharing. It is the collaborative act of discussing rather than the one-sided telling that engages participants. Unless there is some collaborative aspect to a topic, it is very difficult for any of us to maintain attention, so why bother trying? Instead, focus meeting time on those topics that require engagement. To make sure there is enough time for topics that fall into the Critical and Collaborative quadrant, other topics must be removed from the face-to-face agenda. However, since they are still important, they are not dismissed but relegated to a different communication medium. These other tools will be explored further below.

## Encouraging the Conversation

In many ways, the situation at the SLS of the Genesee Valley Educational Partnership was ideal for shifting from meetings to professional development. State mandates provide release time for four half-day meetings a year for librarian communication coordinators from each district. The job of these communication coordinators is to bring input from other librarians in their districts and then return with updates to share with their colleagues and administrators. Even though I imposed my plan on the group and added new professional development responsibilities, the changes were developed through observations and interactions with our member librarians. Our SLS has a long tradition of librarians in dialogue with the director, so it was much easier to implement the final tweaks to refocus the meetings onto professional development. This was a group primed for engagement rather than passive receiving of information. We just had to come up with a new meeting structure that provided more time for that engagement.

Our first step was to restructure the two-and-a-half hour agenda to condense informational updates into a thirty-minute period (previously, it was over an hour long). During this time, we prioritize items from the critical and collaborative quadrant, as those are the issues for which we need feedback, input, or discussion to help with a decision. Shortening the time for updates means we have two hours that can be devoted to professional development; usually an hour at the start for vendor/product training or a system topic and then a hour at the end for librarian-led topics that are suggested via a call for topics at a meeting or through our online forum. If you are even nominally the leader of PD, don't be shy about using the first hour to impose topics. Professional development, like medicine, is often important even if it isn't fun. This is why our agenda includes two topics per meeting. While the first hour is extremely valuable for the system, the second hour is very important for the librarians attending the meeting. They drive the topic selection, so this is their chance to identify an area in which they need development. System staff then works with librarians to find local experts who can contribute to the conversation.

## Local Expertise

Professional development is a tricky idea. In education, we sometimes think that only so-called experts from outside can provide new answers. In some "stuck" school districts, this may be effective, but it overlooks homegrown capacity and knowledge. Our local colleagues are often the best, and most overlooked, resource. For every topic that has come up in our region, our own librarians have been able to provide local experts. For example, a number of districts had worked on library curriculum documents and were willing to share both the development process and the resulting documents with their colleagues. In other cases librarians have spoken about board policies impacting libraries and how they are implemented in their districts, shared reading club programs, and showcased new tech tools.

The secret to success here is that the librarians feel supported in their sharing. Not only have they become more comfortable as part of a regional professional learning community as detailed below, but volunteers who share during meetings are supported by certified librarians from the SLS staff who facilitate the professional development time and help participants plan their presentations (see Brian Mayer's perspective at the end of this chapter). For librarians new to presenting, it is helpful to have someone help develop materials, make copies, and organize the presentation time. It supports them as new professional developers, gives them a model to follow, and helps them develop skills that they can take back to their local districts so they can grow as building-level leaders. A number of librarians who started by sharing during the professional development portions of our meetings have gone on to present at state and national conferences.

## INFORMATION SHARING

The need to share information—trivial details about programs, upcoming events, changes in procedures, and other bureaucratic minutia—has not disappeared. But it can be relegated to secondary channels to make room for critical and collaborative dialogue during precious group meeting time. Luckily there are many channels available for information sharing. The trick is picking the medium best suited for the message, as shown in Figure 9.2. This section will explore three basic communication tools that can be used to fill out our critical/collaborative matrix.

### Figure 9.2: Forums Selected for Various Kinds of Conversations

|              | Collaborative                                                      | Not Collaborative                                         |
| ------------ | ----------------------------------------------------------------- | --------------------------------------------------------- |
| Critical     | **Meeting**<br>• new standards<br>• new assessments<br>• strategic planning | **Email**<br>• staffing changes<br>• procedures<br>• priority updates |
| Not Critical | **Discussion Board**<br>• best practices<br>• unit development<br>• book discussions | **Blog Post**<br>• reflections<br>• book reviews<br>• routine updates |

(adapted from Covey et al. 1994)

## Critical But Not Collaborative: E-mail

Even though Facebook and Twitter seem to be changing how we stay in touch, e-mail is still one of the staples in our professional communication toolbox. As a "push" method of communication, it ensures direct delivery to each recipient; because of this direct delivery, it is a terrific way to deliver critical but not collaborative updates. Unlike other online communication tools like departmental Moodle sites, discussion boards, or blogs, e-mail doesn't require a reader to take the added step of visiting a site. Do not, however, attempt to engage in collaborative dialogue via e-mail. It just does not work: threads get lost, topics change, replies come out of order . . . in short, it is a mess. To circumvent the dreaded "reply all" cascade that can fill participants' inboxes, consider sending e-mail to large groups through BCC (blind copy). That makes it impossible for anyone to send replies to the entire group, keeping clutter to a minimum.

## Not Critical and Not Collaborative: Blog Post

For routine information or less-critical updates with little anticipated dialogue or conversation, the best method of communication is probably a blog post. (Or, for those situations where "blog" has indeed become a four-letter word and everything that looks like a blog is outlawed or blocked by filters, come up with some other phrase or tool to describe what is essentially a blog post, such as a web or wiki page with dated updates). The idea is to have a section on a website where one can easily post updates in a reverse chronological order so that the newest information shows up first and older information is archived but displayed less prominently. Most modern content management systems such as Drupal, Moodle, or Blackboard provide something like blog posts. Usually they allow comments for basic feedback, but the comments tend to be listed in the order in which they were received. Most blogs lack threaded discussions where comments on a specific topic are all gathered together like in a discussion board, and so they don't really rise to the level of collaborative dialogue.

## Collaborative But Not Critical: Discussion Board

The last quadrant, information that is collaborative but not critical, lends itself to an online forum or discussion board. In the Genesee Valley Educational Partnership, the SLS discussion board has actually become an extension of our professional development program. Though SLS staff occasionally post topics looking for noncritical feedback or to prompt a conversation, most of the discussion comes from librarians asking their peers for help. Recent topics have included a discussion of rearranging library materials in a non-Dewey scheme, a question about using audiobooks, a poll on self-checkout, and a review of library policies and procedures. This is informal, librarian-led professional development. The issues are often not critical, but the resulting collaboration is surprisingly effective and useful. And since this is a discussion board that can be reviewed by any member of the group (unlike an e-mail list where responses may happen offlist), SLS staff can keep watch for topics that are reaching a critical mass and may need discussion during a meeting.

It is the design of discussion boards that make them such an incredible tool for this type of dialogue. They organize discussions into topics that contain the original post and any comments left in response. This means that topics remain on topic more than they might in an e-mail list since each discussion board post has a specific purpose. Furthermore, the responses are available to everyone in the group (our discussion board requires that you log in with a password) so anyone can jump in to a conversation at any point. The board also retains past topics in a searchable archive. Another nice trick is that most forums also "bump" topics with new comments to the top of the list to encourage even more responses.

We went one step further and implemented "participation points" to encourage librarian engagement. For each topic started, comment left, or interlibrary loan request they respond to, librarians get points. The top point earners are displayed on the front page on a leaderboard. At the end of the year they receive a small prize. As a gamer, I know that points and leaderboards can be highly motivating, so as an educational leader I often look for ways to incorporate gaming elements into professional practice. In this case, the participation points provide a small bit of feedback to thank librarians for being engaged. Even without the points, librarians would stay engaged in the dialogue on the discussion board as it has become their regional professional learning community. But in the beginning, the points were a great motivator for encouraging early adoption.

## PROFESSIONAL LEARNING COMMUNITY(ISH)

Professional learning communities (PLCs) are an educational construct that recognizes the importance of the sharing and mutual growth that occurs when professionals engage in ongoing conversations about their practices. While this is not an example of a formal PLC, what we have built shares characteristics with PLCs. Traditionally, PLCs are face-to-face networks, which can make them difficult for librarians across buildings to participate in. Thanks to the many digital communication tools available today, PLCs have become distributed networks of like-minded participants spread across a wide and varied region. This is professional development in its organic form; questions being asked and answered without any artificial constructs. And in the Genesee Valley Educational Partnership, the PLC that has grown from our discussion board is the crowning achievement of our efforts to change meetings into professional development.

## Chicken or Egg

So which came first? The professional development–based meetings or the PLC on the discussion board? Honestly, the answer is lost in the mists of time. The discussion board was around in a crude format for years before we changed the meetings; in those early days, it was being used for questions and answers. It was *how* we used the discussion board, not merely having one, that made the difference. The emergence of a true PLC—an open and honest community of practitioners sharing and growing together—really came from the inclusion of librarian-led professional development at our meetings. The highlighting of librarians as local experts demonstrated the vast knowledge pool available in our region, which gave us confidence that we could successfully shift to deeper, more engaging conversations. Reducing the amount of basic information-sharing elements in meetings also meant that we had to shift to a more robust discussion board (and reconfigure our e-mail and blog efforts). But the change could just as easily occur in the other direction. Creation of a rich online forum for discussion and information sharing could then allow the restructuring of meetings. As noted above, it isn't so much the logistics of modifying the agenda as the leadership challenge of building a PLC that can drive and sustain the change.

## LEADING THE CHANGE

While other chapters in this book reveal the *how* and *why* of professional development, this chapter has explored a new possibility for the *when*. By relegating less-critical and less-collaborative information sharing to other communication channels, library meetings can be freed up as additional professional development opportunities. The precious face-to-face time can be spent focusing on topics that are both critical and collaborative; e.g., those issues that are both timely and essential to the continuation of the library program while also requiring true dialogue. Other information can, based on the critical/collaborative matrix presented above, be communicated via appropriate tools.

For this to work, however, you must step up as a leader and implement change. Look at your current meeting structure and agendas and analyze how much of the meeting is productive and engaging. What are the tangible outcomes? Consider a survey of attendees to see how they feel about the meeting; ask questions that assess their levels of participation in, active engagement with, and connection to topics discussed. And then figure out a plan to address shortcomings.

A few years in, I can report that our restructuring of meeting time has been a huge success. Librarians are engaged in meetings, and our regional website has blossomed into a PLC. Even better, the support we provide for librarian-led PD in our meetings has resulted in librarians presenting at regional and state conferences. One of the greatest joys a leader can have is to see a change that she or he started take root and grow. It makes me so proud to see our region focused on professional development and continued learning. And it is great to receive feedback asking for *more* PD!

## REFERENCES

American Association of School Librarians (AASL). 2007. *Standards for the 21st-Century Learner.* Retrieved December 28, 2011, from http://www.ala.org/aasl/standards.

Covey, Stephen R., A. Roger Merrill, and Rebecca R. Merrill. 1994. *First Things First: To Live, To Love, To Learn, to Leave a Legacy.* New York: Simon & Schuster.

# The Power of Practice

Brian Mayer

There is an imagined barrier for entry into the world of presenting professional development activities that keeps many accomplished and experienced school librarians from sharing back with the learning community. While they may find themselves shut in by a modesty and uncertainty that can seem insurmountable, guidance from mentors and peers with presentation experience can help librarians see these walls as more smoke than substance.

The process begins by helping librarians realize that great things can come from the smallest of places: that the ideas, collaborative lessons, community projects and enrichment activities they create are a valued part of the learning community that will go unseen unless they throw open the shutters and let in the light. As librarians begin to see that their experiences have value to others, the next step is providing opportunities for them to share. This is vital, as the celebrity of the professional presenter needs to be demystified, allowing librarians to understand that most presenters are like them: professional peers with a desire to "share back."

Our catalyst for change has been providing ample opportunity for librarian-led professional development in a safe and supportive environment. One of my roles is to facilitate these PD sessions. I meet with librarians who are going to present and help them develop presentation slides, topic outlines, and handouts. These small sessions give our librarians the first ingredient for presenting: confidence.

The second ingredient, experience, is facilitated by the SLS in two ways. First, we organize an annual Day of Sharing toward the end of each year where we call on librarians to share their accomplishments with their peers. This microconference helps individuals strengthen their presentational skill set and find their voice. From there, we try to encourage librarians to share at regional library and technology conferences either individually, with peers, or in collaboration with a member of the SLS.

As a result of this support structure, you can often find several librarians from the Genesee Valley Region whenever you attend a school library conference in New York State.

# CHAPTER 10
# COLLECTIVELY REFLECTING ON TEACHING AND LEARNING

*Editors' Note:* Tish Stafford presents a detailed account of professional development under district leadership that spans thirteen years. She describes in rich detail how she and her Cecil County librarians in Maryland nurtured a professional learning community based on assessment, reflection, and continual refinement of teaching that helped their students become more critical thinkers and users of information. Tish chronicles a powerful account of how professional development must engage us in close and candid study of how we teach and what students actually learn.

# Using Student Assessment to Drive Professional Development

## Tish Stafford

As school librarians, we share a common goal: we want to ensure that our students acquire the thinking, problem-solving, and information literacy skills necessary to meet the challenges of the future. Our national and state standards provide a description of what 21st-century skills should look like, and projects completed by students give us some sense of their proficiencies. However, if a completed project is all we have to look at, how do we know if students have mastered each step of the research process? If they are weak in specific areas, how can we zero in on them and alter our instructional delivery to address their deficiencies? What are the specific cognitive skills embedded within the inquiry process, and how can we ensure that our students deepen their understanding of them each time they engage in research? These are critical questions for anyone interested in the assessment of student skills, program effectiveness, and instructional efficacy. Professional development within our field must focus on seeking the answers to them.

## BACKGROUND

In Cecil County, Maryland, we have been exploring these questions on several levels. The issues first surfaced in the late 1990s during the early years of my tenure as the program facilitator for School Library Media for Cecil County Public Schools. At that time, I had a vision of what a quality school library program should be and where I wanted Cecil County's program to go. As the supervisor for the program, I was responsible for developing and maintaining a quality school library program, for building the capacity of the twenty-seven school librarians within the system, and for observing and evaluating both the program and the professionals who delivered it. In the fall of 1998, I was asked to submit an implementation plan for the vision I had articulated during my interview. My goals, and the plan I developed to implement them, centered on bringing our school library program into alignment with the changes to school library philosophy promulgated at that time by the American Association of School Librarians. The various draft versions of the *Information Literacy Standards for Student Learning* (ILSSL) posted by the American Library Association on the Internet prior to their publication in *Information Power: Building Partnerships for Learning* (AASL 1998) gave shape and substance to a revolutionary change in approach for school library media programs. Where in the past, we had taught information skills in isolation, *Information Power* advocated giving them context and meaning through a process approach that introduced and reinforced mastery of those skills through frequent research projects integrated into content areas.

### Drafting a New Curriculum

My first goal as supervisor was to draft a new curriculum that would support this process approach. In the spring of 1999, I planned and publicized a week of library curriculum writing during the summer, accepting all school librarians who applied. The group met during July 1999 and included librarians from five elementary schools, three middle schools, and two high schools. We spent the first day together exploring in-depth the rationale behind *Information Power*. Then, using the nine standards delineated by *Information Power* as a frame, the school librarians took our existing curriculum, school library curricula from Baltimore, Harford, Calvert, and Montgomery counties in Maryland, and our state standards, and looked for matches with the ILSSL. Next, in small groups, the librarians analyzed examples of school library curricula from Wisconsin, Utah, Washington, Oregon, Colorado, Texas, and North Carolina and plugged those indicators into our framework. While *Information Power* represented the vision of a curricular framework at the national level, we wanted to ensure that we captured as broad a spectrum of interpretations of information literacy as possible to use as models for our curricular revisions. The result was a rich and resonant document that captured multiple expressions of the best thinking to date on teaching information literacy as a process.

We spent the rest of the week honing in on the essence of the document through thoughtful discussions and fervent debates about the number of broad outcomes our curriculum should have, the best wording for specific indicators, and the appropriate grade level at which indicators should be introduced. Our final product consisted of seven broad outcomes with specific indicators for each. For some outcomes, such as evaluating content, we were able to generate grade-level subindicators while for others, such as questioning that had never been addressed in our curriculum before, we opted temporarily for descriptors of proficiency levels until we had enough understanding and experience to write grade-level subindicators. While still incomplete, the curriculum represented a quantum leap forward in our content and pedagogy, and presaged a radical change in approach to the instructional program in our school libraries. Appendices 10.A and 10.B are examples of the 3rd grade goals before and after the 1999 curriculum work.

We introduced the new curriculum to all twenty-seven school librarians during the professional development activities at the opening of the 2000–2001 school year, meeting with secondary and elementary school librarians on two separate days in August. The writers modeled the process they used to develop the curriculum, and I asked all school librarians to send me constructive feedback over the coming year to help clarify any confusing language or address any shortcomings discovered through implementation. There was little feedback during that year. It surfaced gradually, an indicator at a time, and focused more on precise wording than major overhauls. Since over a third of the school librarians had participated in the development of the new curriculum, their colleagues embraced it enthusiastically, and we concluded each of the two professional days brainstorming the best ways to implement it in elementary and secondary schools.

At our next professional development activity in September, school librarians from all levels examined inquiry models by Kuhlthau, Eisenberg and Berkowitz, Pappas and Tepe, and McKenzie, the models most familiar to those of us in Maryland at that time. After careful consideration, we selected the *Research Cycle* (McKenzie 1999) as the one best suited to the constructivist approach to instruction favored by our school system. McKenzie's cycle began with "Questioning," a more open-ended step than the variations on "Task Definition" found in most other models at the time, and ended with "Reporting," which we changed to "Producing." The school librarians believed that McKenzie's *Research Cycle* aligned well with our switch from a curriculum focused on location skills to one that emphasized using information productively.

## Impact of New Curriculum

With a revised curriculum in hand and our version of the research cycle as a delivery method, I confidently expected to see radical change in school library classes across the county during the ensuing school year as I observed and evaluated instruction. I was naive and overly optimistic. Time and again, the classes that I observed were still caught in the "skill and drill" mode, introducing library skills in total isolation from an authentic purpose. Our written curriculum may have changed, but, clearly, the school librarians' instructional delivery methods had not. Simply introducing a revised curriculum and advocating a process approach to instruction were not enough to change ingrained instructional practices. The librarians needed help understanding the implications of the national standards, their new curriculum based on those standards, and constructivism as an instructional design and delivery model. At the time, Maryland schools were immersed in the Maryland School Performance Assessment Program (MSPAP), an integrated performance assessment program that tested all students in grades 3, 5 and 8, but did not report individual student scores. Instead, the tests assessed the performance of a school's total instructional program. This corresponded closely with my own goal of using assessment to highlight the connection between taught curriculum and student performance. So, in 2001, Cecil County school librarians took a leap of faith and joined me on a journey of discovery, exploring the impact that an assessment of information literacy skills would have on our program and professional practice.

## PROFESSIONAL DEVELOPMENT AT THE SYSTEM LEVEL

To provide some background: in 2000, as I was finishing a graduate program through McDaniel College leading to an endorsement in supervision by the Maryland State Department of Education, I needed to create a project for my practicum that went beyond the current responsibilities of my job. My advisor, Dr. Herbert Phelps, told me to use the time and opportunity to create something unique that would benefit my program. To make the implications of our curricular changes explicit, I knew that our school librarians needed a concrete model of what an information-literate student would look like. Following the principles advocated in *Understanding by Design* (Wiggins and McTighe 1998), I worked backwards from our curriculum to design a performance assessment of those skills that students should master by 5th grade. I selected 5th grade as the optimal time for this assessment for several reasons. Because our elementary program operates on a fixed, weekly schedule, the 5th grade represented the culmination of our elementary instructional program. Testing at that point would give us a clear picture of how much students had learned about the inquiry process and, in addition, help to validate our curriculum and share instructional practices. It would also provide meaningful data to help middle school librarians differentiate instruction appropriately as students moved into secondary school.

At the time, Maryland was conducting statewide performance assessments in 3rd, 5th, and 8th grades that integrated content areas, giving student teams different scenarios to resolve, and then requiring all students to write an explanation of the thinking behind their responses. Because I was interested in how students approached inquiry problems and how deeply they thought about them, I modeled our library assessment on the format of the Maryland School Performance Assessment Program.

## Pilot Assessment

Over the course of three 45-minute testing sessions, the pilot library assessment presented students with a scenario asking them to persuade a business to consider Maryland as a potential location for a new store. Students had to form questions that the business might have about Maryland, brainstorm appropriate resources to answer them, and justify selecting one as the resource most likely to have the information they needed. Next, they were asked to identify keywords within their questions, broaden or narrow a keyword, and demonstrate their understanding of basic Boolean searching. Students were given two short reading selections and, based on their questions, asked to select one and explain how it was relevant, authoritative, and current. They had to take notes addressing their questions and demonstrate their ability to synthesize information from different sources. The assessment stopped short of the production stage although students did have to identify the audience and purpose for the project, then select and justify the best format for their final product. The test concluded with a question that probed student understanding of copyright law.

Since the assessment drew heavily upon social studies content, I shared it with Joseph MacDonald, the county's instructional coordinator for social studies. Joe embraced the assessment enthusiastically and suggested that classroom teachers join school librarians in its administration. In order to accommodate his suggestion, we decided to structure the assessment so that the first and third sessions were given by the school librarians in two consecutive school library classes, and social studies classroom teachers administered the middle session during the intervening week. I selected two schools in our system to sample the range of student responses. We piloted the assessment with over two hundred students in the spring of 2001, and then school librarians met to score them, using a rubric I had designed to accompany the pilot. Appendix 10C shows the original rubric used in 2001 for the question on synthesis.

## Pilot Assessment Results

The results were dismal. Poor test design accounted for many of the problems. I had not isolated specific skills within questions sufficiently with the result that, if a student could not form an effective research question early in the assessment, that failure impacted subsequent responses. Looking at student responses, it was immediately apparent to all of us that students who formed poor questions could not choose appropriate resources to answer those questions nor could they identify effective keywords within them. But even when the school librarians adapted the scoring rubric to compensate for cross-contamination between questions, we were still forced to the inescapable conclusion that our students had mastered few information literacy skills. This was so profoundly disheartening that the school librarians, who had not been involved in the development of the pilot assessment, began to question the point of revising an assessment that made our program appear so ineffective. Several even suggested that our curriculum might not be developmentally appropriate for children. This was a pivotal moment, since it was the first time that open resistance to the curriculum had been voiced by anyone within the group.

I freely admitted to them that it was possible that we had a mismatch between our curricular expectations and children's developmental abilities. However, it seemed just as possible that students could master the skills in our curriculum if they actually experienced them as an integrated part of the research process. To discover which hypothesis was true, I proposed that librarians change their instruction, continue with the assessment, and evaluate the results over time. Since this assessment was not mandated by anyone at the local, state, or national levels, I emphasized that we had a unique opportunity to investigate our impact on student performance, strengthen each other as instructors, and improve our school library program. But, to do so, we had to be brave enough to embrace our student data, accept what it was telling us, and do the work required to make our curriculum and instructional practices better. To their great credit as professionals, the school librarians voluntarily accepted this as a challenge.

## Developing a Culture of Continuous Improvement

I have reflected often upon why the librarians embraced this task. On the macro level, I think that the publication of *Information Power: Guidelines for School Library Media Programs* in 1988 laid a strong philosophical foundation for school library programs, and the subsequent release of *Information Power: Building Partnerships for Learning* in 1998 created a climate for change and risk taking in our field. For the first time, we had standards as rigorous as those in other content areas, even if we did not yet understand fully how to implement them. It was clear at the time that no one else knew much more than we did and that, by enduring a few years of cognitive dissonance, we had the chance to control the direction our professional

# Figure 10.1: Configuration for Library Media Instruction

**Proficiency Level** →

| | | | |
|---|---|---|---|
| Collaboration | Is a proactive, established member of grade or department-level meetings. | Joins department or planning meetings on occasion to develop integrated lessons or units. | Schedules meetings to plan with individual teachers. | Dialogues informally with teachers in the hallway, lunchroom, etc. |
| Integration | Collaboratively develops, instructs and evaluates interdisciplinary units which integrate information skills, Maryland content outcomes, and Skills for Success at all grade levels. | Frequently develops instruction units that integrate information skills with Maryland content outcomes and Skills for Success. | Regularly develops media units designed to introduce media skills in a context that parallels content in the regular classroom. | Develops lessons that sometimes correlate with classroom instruction but frequently teaches media skills in isolation. |
| Instructional Strategies | Differentiates instruction to meet the needs of individual students as they actively explore and construct deep understanding of concepts. | Uses a variety of strategies to help students actively construct understanding of concepts. | Uses varied instructional strategies targeting whole group, small group, and individual work. | Relies heavily on traditional teaching methods, such as lecture and worksheets. |
| Use of Technology | Actively facilitates the ethical use of appropriate technology for accessing, and using information by students and staff. | Regularly instructs students and staff on the use of technology for accessing, retrieving, and using information. | Frequently uses technology to support student learning. | Occasionally exposes students to the use of technology. |
| Information Problem-Solving Model | Regularly designs research modules that reflect recent advances in the science of cognition and engage students in authentic problem-solving behavior. | Occasionally structures research assignments to correspond to an information problem-solving model. | Describes an information problem-solving model to students and staff. | Posts the steps of an information problem-solving model in the media center. |
| Reading | Develops a balanced collection and implements programs and instruction that enable all students to select and read and critically analyze works from a broad range of literary genres. | Develops a balanced collection and implements programs and instruction that enable all students to select and read works from a broad range of literary genres. | Assists students in selecting appropriate materials from a well-developed collection. | Develops a media collection that includes appropriate materials. |

growth would take and validate our program. This was a powerful incentive. So, too, was the fact that classroom teachers at that time were focused on high-stakes assessments and analyzing data. Having data of their own to study clearly increased the librarians' sense of professionalism.

On the local level, I focused intentionally on developing a professional culture in our program when I took over the role of supervisor and used everything at my disposal to do so. First and foremost, I knew that the school librarians had to really own the vision we developed for our program since they were the people responsible for implementing it. At one in-service early in my tenure, I asked them to identify the six most important areas within our program and then, in small teams, create a rubric describing four stages of implementation for each area. The various rubrics they created were displayed on poster paper around the room, and school librarians took a gallery walk, using colored dots to identify the language at each stage that most resonated with them. I used the feedback collected from the gallery walk and the debriefing that followed to craft the final document that school librarians then used to evaluate themselves at a subsequent in-service (Figure 10.1). At that time, I directed them to select three areas as goals for the upcoming school year and to write explicit steps that they could take to improve their performance in each of the three areas. I suggested picking an area of strength, because that was the area that gave joy to their work, as well as their area of weakness and an area in between because I did not want the process of continuous improvement to make anyone feel overwhelmed by perceived deficits. I stressed that it was not important where anyone fell on the rubric; the important part was that we were all focused on growing better at our jobs.

Despite my sincerity, this message was not heard immediately. The first time we used the rubric for self-assessment, there was a disconnect between where many school librarians ranked themselves and the actions they described that would move them forward to the next level. Because I wanted them to discover this disconnect on their own, I developed an activity for our next in-service where I gave everyone strips of paper containing specific goal actions that they or their colleagues had written and asked them to match these statements to the corresponding steps in the rubric. When everyone had sorted and shared their thinking, several school librarians asked to redo their self-assessments in order to write growth plans that were more closely aligned to their own true needs.

From 1999 until 2009, we continued to use this rubric at the beginning of each school year to evaluate the previous year's plan, to self-assess, and to write new personal growth plans for the coming year. In 2010, in a testament to how deeply engrained personal growth has become in their professional ethos, the school librarians decided on their own that the rubric had outlived its usefulness. They asked for the chance to develop a check sheet aligned with the roles identified for school librarians by AASL, which would more closely identify specific actions they needed to address. As a result, they designed a digital form that can now be used interactively to set goals and check on their progress throughout the school year. Figure 10.2 is an example of a librarian's completed form.

While navigating the change process, I knew that it was important to model the dispositions that I wanted to encourage in the school librarians. As their supervisor, I had to voice my opinions clearly, but I tried to do so in an atmosphere that valued their opinions as highly as my own and encouraged open debate. I also surveyed them frequently during the first few years to ascertain their comfort level with the pace of change and adjusted subsequent in-service sessions accordingly (Figure 10.3). As they grew more comfortable with the direction that the program was taking and more confident in their own abilities, the need for frequent surveys abated, although the occasional need to take the pulse of the group never disappeared.

Since the 5th grade performance assessment would force them to critique their own performance, I tried to model openness to evaluation in my own role as their supervisor. Early on, I gave an anonymous survey to everyone asking for feedback on my performance in all aspects of my role and then addressed the results during a professional development meeting. I embraced all criticisms and asked for suggestions of what they would like to see me do differently. I also added some personal observations about my own shortcomings that they did not identify, and we addressed those as well. Then, several times over the course of the past thirteen years, I have shared my performance assessment from my superiors with them and talked about how I planned to address that feedback as we moved our program forward. At all times, I have tried to model my belief that, while positive feedback feels good, it does not push us to improve. Constructive criticism accepted honestly and thoughtfully can help to make us better.

In the end, the school librarians decided of their own free will to adopt the assessment. While I might have suggested this course of action to them, no one imposed it on them. Without their consent, the 5th grade benchmark assessment would have disappeared after the completion of my practicum in supervision. Instead, it became the incubator for the development of a strong professional ethos among the school librarians, establishing a unified learning community in which individual members continually challenge themselves and each other to understand more deeply how to support students as they approach inquiry problems.

Figure 10.2: Annual Goals for School Library Media Specialists FY11 (example)

| Roles | Descriptors | Goals | Strategies |
|---|---|---|---|
| Teacher | ☒ Uses assessments for and assessments of instruction in planning | ☐ Uses assessments for and assessments of instruction in planning | I feel comfortable differentiating for the below level students, but I would like to become more proficient at differentiating for the challenge students. |
| | ☒ Makes connections between instruction and the real world | ☐ Makes connections between instruction and the real world | *This has not been the easiest thing to accomplish. You naturally gravitate to the struggling student. You see the higher ability students finish too quickly but have not yet developed a method to address this. You are reading a book on differentiation and will be applying ideas from that.* |
| | ☐ Consistently differentiates instruction to meet the needs of all learners | ☒ Consistently differentiates instruction to meet the needs of all learners | |
| | ☒ Encourages students to build on prior knowledge | ☐ Encourages students to build on prior knowledge | *Additional suggestions: ask your Challenge Instructional Coach for suggestions; develop pre-assessments of background knowledge for selected units and then use that data to form groups; get reading levels from the classroom teachers and sometimes form groups based on that. You can also tweak assignments so that higher ability students take concepts deeper. Look for one unit per grade level to differentiate at first and use different types of differentiation to see how they work and how much prep they take. Differentiating instruction in 30-40 minute library classes that take place once a week is a difficult animal to capture and tame.* |
| | ☐ Encourages students to construct new knowledge | ☐ Encourages students to construct new knowledge | |
| | ☒ Regularly implements effective instructional strategies | ☐ Regularly implements effective instructional strategies | |
| | ☐ Promotes skillful researching through the use of the Research Cycle | ☐ Promotes skillful researching through the use of the Research Cycle | |

## Figure 10.3: Concerns Form

Name: _____

School: _____

Please be honest in your responses to these items. The information will *not* be used against you. We plan to use it to form groups for future in-service. Once you have addressed each section below, look at each of your concerns and *rank them from 1 (biggest concern at this time) to 3 of least concern at this time)*. Please add any additional constructive comments on the back of this page.

| | |
|---|---|
| Implementation | Where are you having problems implementing? What has been helpful? What parts of the program(s) do you not buy into? How can we help you implement? |
| Skill Level | What do you feel are your strengths? Weaknesses? What skills do you wish you had? On what skills do you need help? |
| Learning | What do you want to learn more about (terms, concepts, other)? What do you want to read in the field? |

## THE DEVELOPMENT OF A
## PROFESSIONAL LEARNING COMMUNITY

In the beginning, I saw the pilot assessment as a means to support two short-term goals of mine: the instructional shift from teaching isolated skills to teaching research as a process, and the development of common expectations for student performance that would standardize the library program across our system. I did not anticipate the effect that our mutual exploration of the intricacies of information literacy would have on the school librarians themselves. Once on board with the assessment, however, they took charge of its subsequent development. Each year, the elementary school librarians have met after the 5th grade assessment to review and revise, if necessary, the scoring rubric and to suggest changes to the test to make it clearer or to better support student thinking.

One of our first debates centered on the precise order of the questions on the assessment. In the pilot assessment, students were directed to choose a format for a final product at the end of test, since that corresponded to where production is addressed in our version of the research cycle. Several school librarians argued vehemently against this placement. They pointed out that, since students must address the needs of the audience in the questions they form as well as in the final product they choose, the audience should be identified at the beginning of the inquiry process. The majority agreed, and the question has been the first one students encounter on the assessment ever since. It has also become a standard part of the introduction to any research project that students complete in library classes. One school librarian objected to the graphic organizer provided in the pilot for students to use as they brainstormed natural, capital, and human resources, calling it "Radio Man" and insisting that its format confused students (Figure 10.4).

She introduced an alternate graphic organizer that she had developed and easily won group approval for it to become part of the assessment the following year, since it was such an improvement over the original. After two years of testing, the school librarians also expressed dissatisfaction with the scenario written for the pilot assessment. They suggested shifting from the generic term "business" to the more specific term "amusement park," arguing that it would be a far more engaging topic for students to consider. Additionally, they decided to begin the assessment with a magazine article on the operation of amusement parks, reasoning that it would help students access their prior knowledge and/or experience of parks as a place to have fun, while forcing them to consider the point of view of park owners (Figure 10.5).

# Figure 10.4: Radio Man Organizer for Resources

Think of all the information that a business would need to know about Maryland before deciding to relocate here. Your project will need to address these information needs. Use the graphic organizer below to brainstorm the different kinds of **natural, capital** and **human resources in Maryland** that a business would want to know about before making such an important and expensive decision.

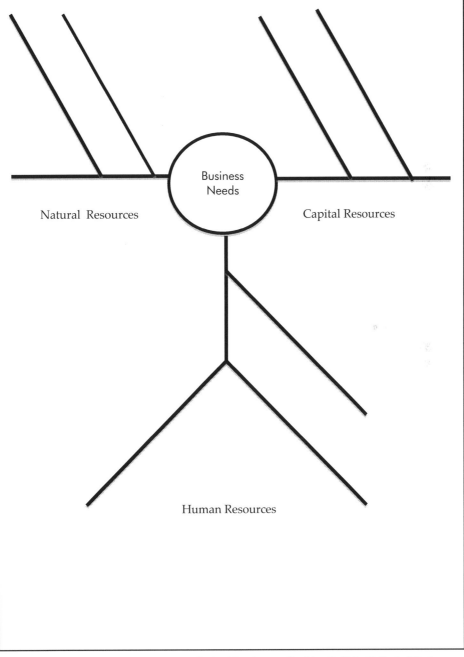

From *Growing Schools: Librarians as Professional Developers* edited by Debbie Abilock, Kristin Fontichiaro, and Violet H. Harada. Santa Barbara, CA: Libraries Unlimited. Copyright © 2012.

# Figure 10.5: Revised Scenario and Organizer for Resources

The amusement park owners would need to know about the natural, capital and human resources in Maryland before deciding to build a park here. Your project will need to address these information needs.

*Natural resources* are gifts of nature that can be used to produce goods and services.

*Capital resources* are the goods that are manufactured by people and then used to produce other goods and services.

*Human resources* are the health, strength, talents, education, skills and effort that humans can use to produce goods and services.

2. **Use the web below to brainstorm** at least **2 natural**, **2 human** and **2 capital resources in Maryland** that any amusement park owner would want to know about before making the expensive decision to build a park here.

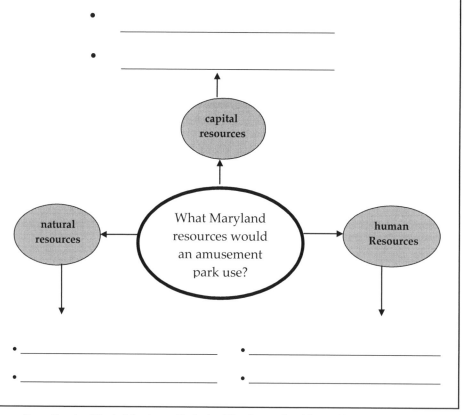

From *Growing Schools: Librarians as Professional Developers* edited by Debbie Abilock, Kristin Fontichiaro, and Violet H. Harada. Santa Barbara, CA: Libraries Unlimited. Copyright © 2012.

Over the years, the school librarians have transferred the lessons they have learned from the test itself to the development of model units and lessons for each grade level designed to support students as they build information fluency over their elementary school careers. Early on, professional development days included time to share and critique instructional activities the school librarians had developed addressing specific skills and grade levels. Over time, this has morphed into monthly meetings where school librarians work in small teams to develop model units for specific grade levels that are shared electronically in Web 2.0 applications such as Google Docs, wikis and Dropbox, then applied and modified, if necessary, until their final format is posted on our curriculum web site. The process has become one of continuous trial, error, and retrial as the librarians use the 5th grade test to assess the success of instructional adjustments they have made.

We were all surprised to discover how quickly students could master higher-level aspects of the inquiry process once our teaching introduced and reinforced these concepts. When the librarians introduced Boolean logic in accessing online databases, they provided constructivist activities in which the students had to discover and explain the effect of the operators. As students continually reinforced this discovery with mnemonics like *"Or means MORE"* each time they searched digital resources, they internalized the reasoning behind simple Boolean searches. As librarians also provided students with scenarios that engaged them in exploring the concept of intellectual property, their students' innate sense of fairness enabled them to grasp the fundamentals of copyright law. If librarians actually used the terms *current*, *authoritative*, and *relevant* instructionally on a regular basis, students applied these criteria to evaluate the quality of the resources they selected.

## DEEPER INSIGHTS GLEANED AND APPLIED

Other aspects of information literacy, however, have proven more challenging for students, librarians, and administrators alike, and have provided the major focus for our professional development activities for the past decade.

### Student-Generated Questions

We collectively struggled with student-formed questions during our professional development activities for several years. Our pilot assessment results indicated that students had difficulty forming effective research questions. We immediately recognized this as a critical problem, since the design of the pilot assessment had proven how a poorly constructed question could derail the entire research process. Our library curriculum included the expectation that students would form effective questions but did not address actually teaching students how to do so. We quickly discovered that the national, state, and local standards of other content areas had similar expectations without instructional guidance.

As we researched the topic of student-formed questions, we found much had been written about open and closed questions, and the importance of asking high-level questions. But, everything we read addressed teacher-formed questions; very little focused on teaching students to form effective questions. We decided to tackle the issue ourselves by devoting more than a year of study and professional development to an in-depth analysis of the questions that our students actually formed on our assessment. Meta-cognitive reflection at this level is an arduous process that severely tested our endurance. While I personally enjoyed the journey from cognitive dissonance to clarity, most of the school librarians were not as comfortable with it, and so we balanced meetings devoted to analyzing student-formed questions with fallow periods during which everyone had a chance to process and integrate what we were accomplishing. In the end, we discovered that research questions have a variety of purposes, that the purposes corresponded to a taxonomy of cognitive skills, and that specific purposes for questions were associated with specific question words or "cue" words. We came to this conclusion about questions as a collective insight. The basic frame came from the "Shared Inquiry" model of Great Books, but we amplified it by breaking it down into cognitive skills and then adding the question words that went along with specific purposes for questions. (See Stafford 2009 for an in-depth look at this process and our results.)

With this insight, we were able to create a scope and sequence for the formation of research questions, infuse it into our curriculum, create graphics to support student understanding and incorporate them as we created model instructional units for each grade level (Stafford 2009). As supervisor, I have shared our insights with other coordinators and principals at the system level and have presented in-service training to key influentials, such as our instructional support teachers, at the individual school level so that they could support and reinforce the work of the school librarians as they collaborate with classroom teachers. Our ability to work through the complexity of this issue until we could articulate clearly how questions function in an inquiry environment and share this understanding with students and teachers alike has increased the level of respect afforded our program across the entire system and has validated for the school librarians the importance of the work they have accomplished collaboratively.

## Broadening and Narrowing Search Terms

The ability to form effective questions is closely connected to the depth of a student's vocabulary and fluency with language. So, too, is the ability to broaden or narrow keywords and concepts. On an early version of our assessment, we asked students to broaden and narrow the term "children" and were shocked to discover how difficult it was for many students. Upon closer analysis, we realized that students could generate subordinate terms independently (e.g., child, boy) but struggled to generate superordinate terms (e.g., family). Curiosity about this led me to the field of cognitive linguistics for an explanation of why this happened (Lakoff 1987) and then to the study of synonyms, hypernyms (broader terms), and hyponyms (specific examples) to find effective instructional strategies we could use to support students as they developed their understanding of categories and the words used to label and classify them. Individual school librarians experimented with various graphic scaffolds and instructional strategies, using Dropbox and other Web 2.0 applications to share their lesson plans and reflections with their colleagues. Over the course of several years, we have fine-tuned the 5th grade assessment by incorporating these scaffolds and strategies into the test itself and then assessing the effectiveness of each. The difficulty that students have with broadening and narrowing keywords has reinforced for school librarians at all levels the need to stress well-developed background knowledge and vocabulary with teachers and students alike throughout the entire inquiry process.

## Synthesizing Information

Synthesis has proven to be another difficult aspect of information literacy for students, and it has taken us several years to craft an effective question to test student ability in this area. In the pilot assessment, I had simply provided students with a list of statements about Maryland and asked them to select two and synthesize them. Not surprisingly, most students copied their selections verbatim, using the conjunction "and" to combine them. The next year, I wrote explicit directions to avoid plagiarism but got the same results, whereupon the school librarians suggested that the statements were too narrow for students to see any connections between them. We brainstormed alternate formats for the question, and decided to limit the topics to two but give students more information about each. However, when we tried giving students two short paragraphs to synthesize, many simply copied the first sentences of each paragraph verbatim and connected them with "and." This forced us to analyze, step-by-step, how we would approach the question and then work in the opposite direction to create a scaffold that would encourage students to replicate our thought processes. (Refer to Appendices 10C, 10D, and 10E to see the modifications we made to the scoring guide for this particular question over time.)

The process we used was time consuming, with everyone contributing a different point of view, discussing these differences, and reaching consensus, but it yielded valuable instructional insight. We discovered that if we required students to generalize first by identifying the main idea of each paragraph and then asked them to synthesize (rather than combine) the two main ideas into an original statement, students were able to demonstrate their skill level and we were able to identify specific deficits that impeded their success. This insight has been transferred from the test to the scope and sequence of our curriculum and from there into instructional design and delivery.

## MOVING FROM PROGRAM TO SELF-ASSESSMENT

The introspective approach to our work that we have developed has become the hallmark of our professional learning community. Even more importantly, our school librarians have demonstrated intellectual and personal courage throughout this process. When the 5th grade assessment began, it provided baseline data that could not be used to evaluate teacher performance in any way. As a result, school librarians willingly embraced the process as a form of ongoing program development rather than as a personal evaluation.

Over the years, however, as school librarians have developed a greater understanding of their curriculum and enhanced their professional practice, assessment results have begun to shine a light as strongly on the quality of teacher performance as they do on student abilities. To encourage true self-reflection while protecting anonymity, I devised a professional development activity several years ago in which we compared average scores on the 5th grade library assessment from across the system, with each school coded rather than identified by name. When asked to hypothesize about the variation in assessment performance, librarians volunteered the usual statements about demographics and students' reading abilities to explain the differences. I then added each school's average scores on our state assessment for reading informational text and asked librarians for additional reflection. Some schools had a clear correlation between both the state and our information literacy scores, but many did not, including the school with the highest reading scores. At that point, one brave school librarian, giving voice to the thought that everyone else tiptoed around, observed that the differences appeared to be related to teacher performance. Her observation opened a floodgate of discussion about personal inadequacies, professional responsibilities, and generalized fear. The emotions released were powerful and demanded balance. Fortunately, I had planned for just this scenario and was prepared to connect the discussion to the culture of personal reflection and evaluation that we had developed over the years. I pointed out that self-evaluation on our configuration had been difficult at first but, over time, had helped to move everyone's practice forward in a nonthreatening way. The data from each school's assessments could prove to be as just as powerful an asset in our continued pursuit of excellence. Eventually, the discussion culminated in a courageous consensus that school librarians have a professional and an ethical responsibility to face hard facts, even those about us, in order to improve our programs.

## SYSTEM-LEVEL SUPPORT

Our assessment program would not have been possible without the support of our school system's leadership, who immediately recognized its potential to drive and document improvements in our instructional program. They have directed that the information literacy assessment be treated as seriously as any other standardized assessment given in our schools. Test and resource booklets are provided for each student. Each school provides accommodators to read or scribe for individual students as needed, and modified versions of the assessment have been developed for students with special needs, including a Braille version of all materials for visually handicapped students. Over time, we have discovered what constitutes the optimal testing environment and which procedures make the administration of the test efficient for teachers and students alike. These have been codified into a checklist (Figure 10.6) that I use to monitor the test administration and to ensure consistency across the system as I visit each school randomly at least once during the testing window.

We continue to enjoy a high level of support throughout the system because student scores on the assessment continue to improve. On our scoring rubric, each question is graded on a scale of 1 to 3, with 1 representing below expectations and 3 representing exemplary performance. Our goal is to have all students scoring at least 2 on all questions. The bar graph (Figure 10.7) shows the average scores for all 5th grade students in our system in 2003 and 2010. Although the graph reveals considerable progress, there is still much room for improvement before all of our students have reached this goal.

Our professional development experiences have taught us how crucial language, higher-level thinking, and metacognition are to the inquiry process. Without them we would not have had the opportunity to delve so deeply into the intricacies of information literacy. The publication of the *Standards for the 21st-Century Learner* (AASL 2007) supported and validated our findings, encouraging us to continue on the journey we began a decade ago. Over those years, school librarians in Cecil County have developed a reputation within our system as the experts on research and higher-level thinking. We have shared our approach to question formation with teachers at the elementary, middle, and secondary levels. We have collaborated with science and social studies as both content areas have explored ways to raise the rigor of the research projects completed by their students. We are currently working with all content areas to explore the Core Content Standards, looking for opportunities to infuse our understanding of the inquiry process into all subject areas.

# Figure 10.6: Library Media Benchmark Checklist

School: _____ Date: _____ Test Monitor: _____

### Test Environment

- ☐ Benchmark test is given in the classroom rather than the media center.

- ☐ Student desks are separated.

- ☐ Lighting is adequate.

- ☐ Temperature is comfortable.

- ☐ Ambient noise levels are low.

- ☐ A "Testing" sign has been placed on the classroom door.

### Test Administration

- ☐ Test materials are stored safely between test administrations.

- ☐ Both forms of the test are distributed in each class.

- ☐ Test directions are read verbatim.

- ☐ Timers are used and displayed.

- ☐ Relevant page numbers are posted for students.

- ☐ The test administrator actively monitors test taking.

- ☐ When students have questions, they are told to reread the directions.

- ☐ Students appear engaged and comfortable with test expectations.

- ☐ Students remain in their desks and quiet until testing ends.

- ☐ All test materials are collected at the end of the testing period.

From *Growing Schools: Librarians as Professional Developers* edited by Debbie Abilock, Kristin Fontichiaro, and Violet H. Harada. Santa Barbara, CA: Libraries Unlimited. Copyright © 2012.

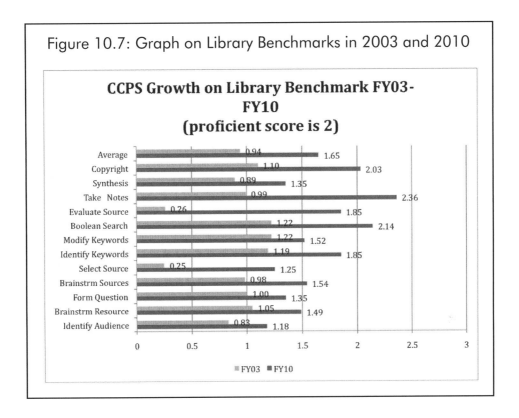

Figure 10.7: Graph on Library Benchmarks in 2003 and 2010

## SHARING OUR INSIGHTS

We have spent a decade using a performance assessment of student skills to develop and improve our school library program. As we meet to score assessments each year, we analyze how students responded to each question, trying to unlock the cognitive steps that lead to success or failure. Then, using successful student responses as exemplars, we have collaboratively developed instructional practices that support all students as they approach particular inquiry skills. When we had no exemplars to share, we actively researched best practices and, if we could not locate a best practice, we used professional development opportunities to deepen our own understanding and then translate what we learned into effective instructional practices. Over the past ten years, we have continuously revised our curriculum, created model units, infused appropriate scaffolding into our instruction, and deliberately planned for the fading of scaffolds so that our students eventually become independent learners.

## CONTINUING IMPACT

Our struggle to create an assessment that would provide a window into student thinking and our close examination of students' responses to our attempts to uncover their thought processes have convinced us that cognitive skills are the common denominator in all curricula. As school librarians, we have a unique opportunity to emphasize the thinking skills that are inherent in the research process. The more clearly we articulate these cognitive processes and connect them to similar processes in the content areas, the more we help our students to think clearly and effectively. The more we contribute to student achievement, the more we legitimize our role in education. Our journey in Cecil County is far from over, for each insight we gain uncovers new questions to investigate and new understandings to develop. The professional learning community that we have fostered provides a strong foundation for continued professional growth, but our journey will not be completed until a fully developed pedagogy for the instruction of information literacy exists.

## REFERENCES

American Association of School Librarians (AASL). 1998. *Information Power: Building Partnerships for Learning*. Chicago: American Library Association.

American Association of School Librarians (AASL). 2007. *Standards for the 21st-Century Learner*. Chicago: American Association of School Librarians. http://ala.org/ala/mgrps/divs/aasl/guidelinesandstandards/learning standards/AASL_LearningStandards.pdf (cited January 29, 2011).

Lakoff, George. 1987. *Women, Fire and Dangerous Things*. Chicago: University of Chicago Press.

McKenzie, Jamie. 1999. "The Research Cycle 2000." *From Now On: The Educational Technology Journal* 9. http://questioning.org/rcycle.html (cited January 29, 2011).

Stafford, Tish. 2009. "Teaching Students to Form Effective Questions." *Knowledge Quest* 38, no. 1 (Sept/Oct): 48–55.

Wiggins, Grant, and Jay McTighe. 1998. *Understanding by Design*. Alexandria, VA: Association for Supervision and Curriculum Development.

# Appendix 10A: Grade 3 (Prior to 1999)

*Bolded skills are taught. Others are reinforced.*
**SKILL** (The student will . . . )

1. Develop appropriate media center behavior.
2. **Understand the organization of his/her media center.**
3. **Use the media center for materials to meet personal needs for independent reading at his/her ability level.**
4. **Demonstrate proper care and handling of print materials, nonprint materials, and equipment.**
5. Develop good listening skills.
6. Properly sign out and return materials.
7. Suggest materials for purchase.
8. Be aware of periodicals on his/her level.
9. Develop literature appreciation appropriate for his/her grade level.
10. **Explain the following types of literature by their definitions: fables, fairy tales, and folktales.**
11. **Be aware of and/or use audiovisual materials.**
12. **Use audiovisual equipment after instruction in the proper operating procedures. (As the need arises and dependent on availability of hardware in each school.)**
13. Be aware of the order of fiction and nonfiction books.
14. Recognize and locate fiction and nonfiction books by the call number.
15. **Recognize the alphabetical arrangement of the card catalog.**
16. Know the location of the nearest public library.
17. Know that the public library is arranged in a manner similar to the school media center.
18. Recognize, identify, and define the following parts of a book: call number, card pocket, cover, place of publication, sign-out card, spine, and title page.
19. Recognize, identify, and define the following parts of a book: acknowledgment, copyright date, dedication, glossary, index, and table of contents.
20. Develop appropriate dictionary skills for his/her level.
21. Locate the reference section of the media center.

# Appendix 10B: Grade 3 (After 1999)

1. Students will access information to address personal or curricular information needs.

   **1.1 Use an information problem-solving model to address personal or curricular information needs.**

   > With assistance, students will apply their knowledge of specific information-seeking strategies as they follow the steps of the research cycle.

   **1.2 Form questions based on identified information needs to guide research.**

   > Sort questions by purpose using the basic question taxonomy.

   **1.3 Identify and be able to use a wide range of information sources.**

   > Identify and be able to use print, media, electronic, and human resources including:
   > - abridged dictionaries
   > - unabridged dictionaries
   > - print encyclopedias
   > - digital encyclopedias
   > - databases
   > - television news
   > - bookstores

   **1.4 Develop successful information-seeking strategies.**

   > Use alphabetical order to locate information in an encyclopedia.
   >
   > Use guidewords to locate information in an encyclopedia.
   >
   > Use alphabetical order and guide words when using an abridged or unabridged dictionary.
   >
   > Describe the general subject arrangement of nonfiction.
   >
   > Explain the purpose and use of an index.
   >
   > Recognize the catalog/OPAC as an index to the library collection.

Define keywords.

Refine keywords by generating synonyms.

Use the catalog to locate information by author, title, subject, or keyword.

Use the index of a book to search for specific information within a text.

*1.5 Acquire information from varied sources that address multiple contexts and cultures.*

Access appropriate resources that address the identified question or information need.

2. **Students will review, evaluate, and select information in order to address identified questions or information needs.**

*2.1 Evaluate content from print, visual, audio, and electronic media.*

Use the copyright date to ascertain the currency of information.

Determine the relevance of information as it pertains to an identified question or information need.

Verify the accuracy of information in more than one source.

*2.2 Select appropriate information.*

Independently recognize and select resources that best address the identified question or information need.

3. **Students will use information effectively to address their identified questions or information needs.**

*3.1 Record pertinent information.*

Paraphrase the main ideas, which address an information need.

Record the author, title, publisher, place of publication, and copyright date of each source used to compile information.

*3.2 Organize information to achieve clarity.*

Independently generate appropriate categories for organizing information.

Independently label categories generated for organizing information.

Select the most appropriate pattern for sorting or sequencing information.

Develop a graphic organizer consistent with the pattern chosen to sort or sequence information.

### 3.3 Synthesize information.

Blend new information with prior knowledge and express using one's own language.

Draw supportable conclusions that address the identified question or information need.

### 3.4 Communicate results.

Independently generate a list of possible formats and select one best suited to audience and purpose.

Working at the level of research rather than reporting, develop a product or presentation that resolves the identified question or information need.

4. **Students will use information and technology ethically.**

### 4.1 Respect intellectual property rights.

Use the title page to identify the author, illustrator, place of publication, and publisher of a book.

Describe how copyright protects the right to control the distribution, performance, display, or copying of original works.

Define plagiarism.

### 4.2 Use information products and technology ethically.
Employ proper etiquette in all forms of communication.

5. **Students will monitor the quality of their own information-seeking process.**

### 5.1 Evaluate one's own information-seeking process and product.
Analyze the impact of each step taken to answer an information need or create a product.

6. **Students will appreciate literature and other creative expressions of information.**

### 6.1 Develop competence as an independent reader.

Select and read works within a limited range of genres.

Retell a literary selection that includes characters, setting, problem, and solution.

Restate an informational selection including a minimum of four details.

### 6.2 Develop competence as an independent listener.

Identify musical elements of literary language (rhyme scheme, rhythm, alliteration, assonance, consonance, onomatopoeia.)

### 6.3 Develop competence as an independent viewer.

Describe how economic factors influence the creation of media.

Explain the producer's choice of form, style, and technique in various media.

Differentiate among entertainment, information, and persuasion as purposes of media.

### 6.4 Comprehend and apply meaning derived from literature and other creative expressions.

Explain the use of literary elements in a story (character, setting, problem, and solution.)

Define the characteristics of a poem.

Define the characteristics of a play (narrator, plot, characters, setting, props, dialog, stage direction.)

Explain the use of rhymes and rhythm in appropriate texts.

Explain the theme in a literary text.

Analyze and evaluate works by the same author.

Evaluate works by different authors based on theme, style, etc.

Recognize and appreciate award-winning books, such as Newbery Medal books, etc.

### 6.5 Compare texts from diverse cultures.

Analyze how culture and social group are represented in literary text and media.

Analyze diverse cultures by tracing the exploits of one character type (e.g., trickster).

# Appendix 10C: 2001 Scoring Guide

Question 12

This question addressed the student's ability to synthesize information from different sources into new and original statements. While the highest quality response will combine information from each source into an original, clear, and logical statement, students at this level may force disconnected facts into an awkward restatement.

There may be some overlap in language between the original source and the recorded facts. However, synthesized statements should not contain flagrant plagiarism.

**RUBRIC**

| Learning Outcome: | Students will review, evaluate, and select information in order to address identified questions or information needs by *synthesizing* information. |
|---|---|
| Performance Indicator: | Integrate new information gathered from a variety of sources with prior knowledge. |

| 3 | 2 | 1 |
|---|---|---|
| Combines elements from both facts, restated in the student's own words, into a clear, concise, and well-formed statement. | Combines elements from both facts, restated in the student's own words, into an awkward, forced statement. | Restates elements in the student's own works with little comprehension or connection to purpose. |

# Appendix 10D: 2005 Scoring Guide

Question 12

This question addressed the student's ability to synthesize information from different sources into new and original statements. While the highest quality response will combine information from each source into an original, clear, and logical statement, students at this level may force disconnected facts into an awkward restatement.

There may be some overlap in language between the original source and the recorded facts. However, synthesized statements should not contain flagrant plagiarism.

| | |
|---|---|
| **Learning Outcome**: | Students will review, evaluate, and select information in order to address identified questions or information needs by *synthesizing* information. |
| **Performance Indicator**: | Integrate new information gathered from a variety of sources with prior knowledge. |

### SCORE GUIDE

| | |
|---|---|
| **Score 3** | • Includes elements from both statements.<br>• Paraphrases.<br>• Forms a clear, concise statement. |
| **Score 2** | • Includes elements from both statements.<br>• Paraphrases.<br>• Forms an awkward statement. |
| **Score 1** | • Includes elements from both statements.<br>• Shows little comprehension.<br>• Shows little connection to purpose. |

---

**TIP FOR SCORING**

*Highlight examples of the same wording in the student's synthesized statement and the original facts.*

---

From *Growing Schools: Librarians as Professional Developers* edited by Debbie Abilock, Kristin Fontichiaro, and Violet H. Harada. Santa Barbara, CA: Libraries Unlimited. Copyright © 2012.

# Appendix 10E: 2008 Scoring Guide

Question 12

Score 3
- Identifies the main idea for each fact box.
- Blends the main ideas into a new statement.
- Maintains the correct level of generality (Maryland rather than Baltimore).
- Paraphrases.

Score 2
- Identifies the main idea for each fact box.
- Combines the main ideas in a restatement, frequently using a coordinate conjunction.
- Maintains the correct level of generality (Maryland rather than Baltimore).
- Paraphrases.

Score 1
- Identifies the main idea of at least one fact box.
- May include elements from one fact box rather than both.
- Attempts to paraphrase but includes significant language from the original.

Score 0
- Plagiarizes

  *OR*

- Shows little comprehension

  *OR*

- Shows little connection to purpose.

Note: The difference between "blend" and "combine" is best illustrated by the following example: You can paint a room red and blue, or you can paint it purple. The first example combines the two colors; the second example blends them.

# CHAPTER 11
# BUILDING CAPACITY FOR
# COLLABORATIVE LEARNING

*Editors' Note:* Kristin Fontichiaro reflects on her growth as a teaching professor and examines how Web 2.0 tools can—but do not necessarily—develop a sense of community among pre-service educators and librarians. Mariah Cherem, one of Fontichiaro's students at the University of Michigan School of Information (UMSI), explains how a Web 2.0 classroom intervention impacted her work both within and beyond the classroom.

## Growing a Community of Learners

### Kristin Fontichiaro

## INTRODUCTION

Many of us grew up with the tale of "Jack and the Beanstalk." Jack, lovably foolish, trades the family cow for five magic beans. Angry at her son's decision, Jack's mother tosses the beans out the window. The next morning, a strong, snaking beanpole has grown up into the clouds. Jack climbs the beanpole, reclaims the goose that lays the golden eggs and the golden harp that plays itself, and outwits the giant and his wife.

Not a bad story to come from a single bean, but it's surprising that when we tell this story to kids, we never talk about what happened to the other beans. A single beanstalk may make for a good story, but it's not the kind of success rate we need in our schools. How can we justify collectively overlooking the 80 percent that did not change?

When we are just getting started as professional developers, it's easy to look up and celebrate the beanstalk. In our early sessions, we often want to be validated as much as we want our learners to grow. We are tempted to focus on giving the greatest talk, doing the most impressive demo, and showing that we have the skills and expertise worth listening to. Especially as librarians, the beanstalk lures us to position our PD primarily as an opportunity to show why librarians and libraries are so valuable. "Look at our great tools, our terrific databases, and how much we can help!" We shoot out our ideas like seed spreaders: a one-way broadcast of our expertise. Sometimes, as in Jack's story, we get one or two seedlings as a result. Sometimes a single colleague decides to change as a result of a talk we've given before the staff, and his beanstalk grows so tall and so strong that we discount those that did not germinate.

Good professional development is about raising the germination rate: thinking about the seeds rather than the sprayer. As we mature into our profession, many begin to recognize that it's not enough for PD to "prove" that we are terrific librarians. When we turn inward, asking ourselves, "What is the impact of what I have just done for the last hour?" the result can be sobering, even more so as the days stretch into weeks and, in looking for seedlings, we see little or no change in our staff's practice. It is in that moment that we recognize that great PD is not showmanship *teaching*; it's about helping our colleagues *learn and grow*. When we transition ourselves from the paradigm of *teaching as talking* ("Did they like what I had to say?") to *teaching as ensuring learning* ("Did they understand, and will they put it into practice?") the job gets a lot tougher. The Happily Ever After patina starts to tarnish as we realize we have achieved only part of the necessary outcome.

And yet, as we survey the landscape around us, we know that educational change is happening swiftly, the responsibilities on the shoulders of our administrators and classroom colleagues are weightier, and, as Jack's mother knows, there is less hope of external rescue from a knightly PD developer galloping in on a white horse. In many school settings, librarians may be among the only staff members who can take on the important ongoing role of building staff capacity over time.

The need for transformative professional development has never been stronger. The ongoing recession has increased class sizes, reduced support staff, and sometimes reduced take-home pay. All of this would be difficult under normal circumstances, but add onto that the imminent rollout of the Common Core State Standards into the majority of America's classrooms, and the clarion call sounds more like, "Fee! Fi! Fo! Fum!" We need to push ourselves, to go beyond saying we "did" PD, as if it is a chore to be completed, and instead move to, "How can the adults I am working with, with my help, achieve and grow more? How do I make the golden goose a reality for more colleagues?"

Let's face it: there are no magic beans when it comes to growing schools. It takes sweat, perseverance, and hard work to plant seeds, nurture vulnerable seedlings, water, fertilize, and guide them toward the sun. Even with the best tools and habits, too much rain or sun—or not enough—can wither the hardiest seedlings. However, like school, farming works in cycles—tilling, planting, nurturing, and harvesting. Each school year gives us a new chance to reflect on the previous harvest, adjusting and making plans for the new crop. Each fall brings an invitation to us to reinvent, reprioritize, and refine.

That yearly RSVP has been my siren song. My PD practice started as a classroom teacher, grew as I became an elementary school librarian, morphed as I took on formal K–12 staff development responsibilities, and led me to my current work with pre-professional classroom and library educators. Teaching adults is a complex navigation of personalities, preferences, past experiences, and priorities: befriending the giant's wife.

In this chapter, I'll share snapshots of my ongoing efforts to grow gardens of community in my classrooms at the University of Michigan. While my learners are pre-professionals, and yours are likely to be in practice already, they are not so different: they want to do well, feel a sense of belonging, and take pride in their work. Sometimes, we harvest a bumper crop; sometimes not. But along the way, I've realized that the more I practice, and the more mindfully I listen, the more successful my efforts are with my adult learners. So while this story begins with a success, you will see that work was rooted in earlier, less-successful ventures that, nonetheless, prepared the ground for future improvements.

## THE GOLDEN GOOSE, 2011: A TOTEM FOR OUR COMMUNITY
*Moral: Persevere, keep trying, and good things can happen.*

> "Hope it's not too late, but can I change my LinkedIn URL for my new website in my chapter? Sorry for the late notice, but I just bought it last night!"

> "You are not the only one who is nervous/excited about this book, I haven't told my Mom until this week and she's already bothering me about when she can see it (and told my entire extended family, yeah). I don't mind people I don't know reading it, but my family is a whole other matter."

> "I'm a former copyeditor. Want me to take a look at it this weekend?"

> "Looks good to me! Start the presses! I wish all my classes left me with a tangible publication like this."

> "We should write an article about this."

> "Nobody panic, but we've hit a snafu."

These are the conversations and e-mails that have recently filled my days. Why? Because we're publishing a book. Or, as several of the students in "Information Literacy for Teaching and Learning" put it, a "real" book. A print book.

Which is funny, because publishing a "real book" is nowhere on the syllabus.

Publishing a class e-book is. And my assignment that each student would report their information literacy field experiences by creating an e-book for the public was the source of my students' top complaints during midterm evaluations. So how did the disliked project become one that people looked forward to seeing completed? And how did it change from digital to print form?

On the surface, the response is that a member of our class works for MPublishing, a division of the University of Michigan Library, which owns a print-on-demand Espresso Book Machine (EBM). She came to me during office hours and laid out how it could be done within our existing timeline. The class voted to publish both in print and online, and suddenly, we were off, voting on Creative Commons images for the cover of *Information Literacy in the Wild*.

But that's too simplistic an answer. We have to pull back the camera angle to see the whole picture. Grades aren't the motivator, as they will receive a single grade for authoring regardless of the number of formats in which we publish. Time isn't the issue: they have precious little as they finish their class projects. Merging our thoughts into a single volume means something that it didn't mean earlier in the term. It means that we have become a team, a community.

But how did that begin? That's the question that sends me to look back in time.

## BASELINE DATA, 2008: NO SEEDS
*Moral: We all begin somewhere.*

A lot has changed since my first UMSI course four years prior, when I was an adjunct lecturer team-teaching Media for Children and Young Adults. I remember how I worried, like Friese in the next chapter, that my students would find out that I wasn't expert in all areas of children's lit, birth to high school. Looking back, I remember feeling that there was almost a line in the classroom: me on one side with the lectern, the students on the other in their chairs.

I remember little spontaneous class discussion. Don't get me wrong. The class received strong student evaluations; we were popular instructors. Similarly, we had strong affection for our students and felt a kind of high after each class. Certainly there were some social elements to the class: a book-talk cocktail party got people moving around the room and talking to one another, students used LibraryThing to track their ongoing reading, and we asked them to engage in conversations on professional listservs. With the exception of the book-talk party, the social activities were designed to engage students with others outside the classroom, not to strengthen the collegiality within the classroom. LibraryThing was an improvement over tracking reading in a Word document, but we harnessed its organizational features more than its ability to connect one class member to another. The listserv assignment asked students to interact with professionals—key for developing a network—but overlooked the network that could be developing within the class itself. Regardless of those activities, it felt challenging to start and sustain conversations.

At the time, this quiet did not strike me as unusual. When we instructors had been students in this same class, we had been quiet, too. Still, I remember being surprised by the vibrant and lively spirit in students' recorded book-talk projects. Such a strong contrast to our face-to-face interactions. The words of the former long-term instructor rang in my ears: "They're quiet, aren't they?" At the time I didn't think it could be otherwise.

My newbie anxiety coupled with my past experiences in that class certainly contributed to the quiet. Another factor was that the class met in a very large room, which meant that the students were able to put distance between themselves and others. This was an accidental factor. Both of us had taken the course when we had been UMSI graduate students and we remembered meeting in a garret-like room, where the conference table was too small to hold all members of the class, meaning that some students took a literal back seat. We wanted everyone to feel included, so our deans agreed to assign a larger classroom. Perhaps, in our efforts to share the conversational beanstalk, we had overshot the target.

## YEAR TWO, 2009: SPROUTS
*Moral: More perspectives enhance, not detract, from our teaching.*

As I entered my second year of adjunct teaching, this time flying solo, something changed. Perhaps it was the small, cozy room in which the class met this time. The room was so crammed with students that when we held our book-talk "cocktail party" later in the term, we had to move some desks out into the hall. The proximity stimulated large-group conversation, although the students sitting closest to me often talked the most.

That was an improvement. Yet another "a-ha" rose from my own anxiety. Worried that I would run out of things to say or that the students in this nighttime course would become restless, I started scheduling small-group discussions or activities into our class time. The tight seating made it easy to move into groups quickly, and I could expand or collapse group time as needed as I adapted to the pacing of teaching on my own. Shifting from direct instruction to whole-class discussion to small-group discussion kept our class momentum going, which helped keep our evening class buoyant. In this way, planning for adult learning didn't differ very much from my work with K–12 students.

I was also motivated by an external decision. There are two ALA-accredited library programs in our state: UMSI and Wayne State University. Like many universities, Wayne State was moving aggressively into hybrid or total online learning degree programs. UMSI, on the other hand, was committed to face-to-face learning and was not moving courses online. Each institution had faced the same choice but reached a different conclusion. If my institution—which had been an early developer of Sakai, the online course management system that could be employed in blended or fully-online learning—was choosing to keep its work anchored in the face-to-face experience, then what could I do to make sure that face-to-face was a superior experience for my students? A lecture-based class was essentially the same face-to-face or online: the student was a listener. But face-to-face teaching meant I had options for more spontaneity: frequently initiating discussions, revising discussion topics as necessary, and shifting students from large-group to small-group discussions rapidly.

As I loosened up the mostly lecture format, and began to listen more, boy, did the class have interesting things to say. The more time they spent talking during whole-group and small-group conversations, the happier and more engaged they became. My first-year misconception that a student's past experiences would show off my weaknesses proved groundless. I realized the opposite: that their personal knowledge *added* to the class experience instead of "showing me up." As a white, middle-class Michigander with college-educated parents who had taught reading, I could only bring one life experience to the table. I couldn't speak with authenticity about searching in vain in the library for books that mirrored my experience. Most library books *did*. Though I had taught in urban settings, I was unfamiliar with the loneliness that might come from being transgendered and seeing nothing in the catalog about me, but a student shared that with us. I had never struggled to read content. I wasn't working part-time in a public library observing how some parents overrode their children's book selections. I didn't have nearly the range of experience of the two former English Language Learners teachers, nor a decade of teaching special-needs students that another participant had. While my weakest children's literature area was manga, I had a student who was immersed in it. The conversations didn't just patch up holes in my experience; they enriched and intensified our learning together. Everyone benefited.

Was everyone enthusiastic about more student talk? Yes and no, just like in your classrooms, though the midterm and final student feedback indicated that the conversations were enriching. The naturally outgoing ones loved having more time to talk with their colleagues. The shy ones needed the practice and could often say more in a small group than they would to an entire class. I knew from my K–12 teaching that more people can share when they are in small groups.

The class was getting noisier, but the connections were getting stronger. We were sprouting.

## CLIMBING THE BEANSTALK: BLOGGING, 2009
*Morals: Good ideas added to good ideas make better ideas. Extending conversation outside the classroom helps everyone learn more.*

Fast-forward to Summer 2009, when I began co-teaching a Teaching with Technology class in the UM School of Education's Master of Arts with Certification (MAC) program.

Previously I had experimented with student blogging in another class and was delighted to realize that this was an established component of my new class. In the past, I had asked students to blog twice a week: once prior to class to reflect on the readings and a second time to reflect on the class discussion. Those reading reflections had helped to prime the pump, guaranteeing that they both read and understood the content, while the discussion reflections helped me know their of understanding and what their key takeaways were, which helped me gauge the effectiveness of my role as conversational moderator. I had loved this experience, but I sometimes felt that I had merely replaced spiral-bound middle-school journaling exchanges with a digitized version. Students would write online, and I would comment online. I might reference their blog post in class, but the rest of the class was likely to be unfamiliar with the content. There were advantages to blogs over passing a spiral notebook between the student and the teacher, but I wasn't using the full social component of a blog's ability to capture the author's thinking, then engage in comments and follow-up conversations.

Based on my past success, we increased the existing blogging project's frequency to twice weekly. But we also kept a past MAC practice, dividing the large class into small cohorts. Each cohort had approximately seven classmates, and each classmate read and commented on their colleagues' posts. A-ha! A missing piece! For years I had worked to build conversations and to engage students in digital tools, but I hadn't united them by using digital tools to host those engaging conversations. Adopting the MAC practice would give us the peer interactivity that I had been grasping for in prior years. It was exhilarating to consider that we could merge successful practices.

By combining successes, we gained a one-two punch that gave us enormous insight into our students. I became addicted to their writing, checking my Google Reader account numerous times a week—sometimes multiple times a day, eager to hear their thoughts. The students did the readings and began discussing them amongst each other in advance. And discuss they did—and in many ways! Most blog posts were remarkably frank about their interactions and showed us how actively they were processing course ideas, framing them against their personal experiences and anticipating the time when they would have their own classrooms. We also saw posts that highlighted the students' individuality and creative preferences. One student regularly included hand-drawn digital comics in her reflection posts. Another imagined herself in a face-to-face conversation with John Dewey about the state of education "reform." One student ended each post with a YouTube video of a favorite Arabic musician. An Oscar Wilde fan used Bunbury as a nom de plume.

Another favorite example of blogging came from a later MAC year. A future English teacher and unabashed fan of *Moby Dick* titled his blog *Call Me Ishmael*. (It should be said that selecting a blog title is serious business for these students, and they often demur and say they will set up their blog at home instead of in class so they can brainstorm the best of all possible titles.) Themes and characters from *Moby Dick* were woven into his reflections in continually unexpected ways. His cohort noticed. When he blogged about his ambivalence for our upcoming conversation about Twitter, one of his colleagues commented that he had nothing to worry about. As a fan of Captain Ahab, continually searching for one particular whale, how could he not like Twitter? After all, when the Twitter servers become overloaded, then, as if in an Ahab dream, the Fail Whale graphic appears, showing birds lifting a huge white whale out of the water. (You can see it at http://www.readwriteweb.com/archives/the_story_of_the_fail_whale .php.)

Our instructions never mentioned how they should structure their formatting, merely that it should show evidence that they had engaged in and were actively reflecting upon the readings and discussions and discussing them. Accidentally, and to our ongoing delight, we opened up room for students to reflect in interesting and individual ways. In cohorts, the students whose posts demonstrated less reflection or evidence of processing inevitably improved the depth and caliber of their posts based on the modeling of their colleagues. By commenting on one another's blogs, they could read and interact with far more diverse viewpoints than would be possible in a face-to-face class.

The students—and we professors—could explore these blogs prior to class. As a result, our in-class discussions could often begin "midstream," without the introductory comprehension checks we needed in the past. If the blogs showed familiarity or comfort with a topic, we could initiate a more refined or sophisticated level of conversation during class. As instructors, we often made last-minute tweaks to our teaching agenda when we recognized that students had a higher (or lower) understanding of a concept than we anticipated. We could also draw upon the students' posts when we introduced a new question or area for whole-class discussion, such as, "Lana raised an intriguing point about Facebook and bullying on her blog. What guidelines might need to be in place to guide students toward productive Facebook use for class?" Our teaching became more customized to their needs. Students often referenced one another's blogs in class when making a point.

Face-to-face class meetings lasted three hours, but discussion continued far into the next week as students began their post-class blog posts. One student's post took the form of reader's theater as he created a scene in which he was pulled over for speeding, claiming that he had been thinking so hard about class concepts that he hadn't realized he had been speeding. (Rest assured: unlike his professor, who had just been pulled over for the same reason, his tale was fiction.) YouTube videos or links to other resources peppered their posts.

Our students took all of their summer courses together, so the blogs added a layer of intimacy to what was already becoming a tight-knit tribe. Although we met with them just once a week, we were connected to them all week long as their stories hit our Google Reader accounts. We often e-mailed posts to one another, saying, "Did you read this?" "Check out the imagery," or "We should really talk about the concept of citation more strongly." Occasionally, we'd write, "Hey—this blog post is all about your love of Dewey," or, "Oh, I am dreading our class talk about Twitter after reading this."

The biggest realization of the power of the blogs came when the formal blogging project ended. Although our course would continue into Fall and Winter terms, we no longer required them to blog. We missed them. We missed their insights. We missed the ambient connectivity that connected us throughout the week. When someone voluntarily blogged, it was a jolt of energy to see their post appear in our RSS feed. The blogs made us see them not merely as students or as preservice teachers. We saw them three-dimensionally, as colleagues to one another—and to ourselves.

Earlier in my teaching career, I might have balked at the idea that someone else might have a better way of framing classroom blogging than I did. After all, when I had first introduced blogging in my class, they had written amazing things. But as I was maturing as an educator, I was realizing the power of combining my good idea with someone else's good idea and, as a result, achieving a hybrid that was far more powerful. Our combined assignment engaged students with one another without losing the student-to-instructor connection. Students probed content and conversation more deeply; classroom discussion was customized to their needs, worries, and concerns; we heard more references to one another's writing in class; and we saw more connections between past experiences and their anticipated futures. Blogging worked in symbiosis with face-to-face conversations: the better our class discussions, it seemed, the more the blogging and commenting in proved. Like Harris in Chapter 9, we learned that offline conversations didn't *replace* face-to-face conversations; they expanded what we could discuss and learn with one another beyond the confines of the meeting time. More seedlings, more learning.

## THE GOLDEN HARP THAT PLAYS ITSELF, 2011
*Moral: Great learning can happen without you in the room if you trust the learners.*

In response to the updated ALA/AASL Standards for Initial Preparation of School Librarians, which were approved by the Specialty Areas Studies Board of the National Council for Accreditation of Teacher Education (ALA/AASL 2010) and anticipated forthcoming revisions to the library media guidelines of the National Board for Professional Teaching Standards (NBPTS 2011), we needed to rapidly restructure SI 643: Professional Practice in Libraries and Information Centers to meet the documents' vision that school librarians play active roles in professional development, an area that was missing from our UMSI curriculum. However, *all* librarians—not just those in K–12—engage in professional development or adult teaching of one kind or another. To rapidly come into alignment, we tweaked SI 643 so that it continued to focus on issues in librarianship while using those issues as a foundation for learning to teach both face-to-face and online. These skills could later be deployed in a variety of settings: professional development of teachers or professors; conference presentations; or programming for adults or children, among others. I wanted the course to give students lots of practice with activities such as:

- creating a podcast interview;
- learning to screencast effectively;
- planning, leading, and assessing a one-shot workshop;
- planning, leading, and assessing a book club or discussion group; and
- planning, leading and assessing a webinar.

In our small library and information science program, some of our courses have large enrollments, which makes it possible to afford smaller, specialized classes. SI 643 was one of the larger classes, with forty-one students.

A challenge emerged: how could students get multiple opportunities to practice if there were so many students waiting for a turn? Even if the students worked in small groups, it would take weeks to get through everyone's one-shot workshop or book club. Meanwhile, the novelty would wear off and the audience would become restless. More weeks of presentations would also mean removing a few of the desired activities from the list. Yet I knew that people became better teachers by practicing *more*. And given the late course redesign, there would not be time to find field placements in which they could get that practice teaching. How could I get students to get *more practice* when the class size was so large?

The real problem was *time*. Not the *class's* time, but *my* time. In thinking back to the presentations I was required to give as a student, from kindergarten up through graduate school, I cannot recall a single time in my learning when my audience was not the entire class *plus* the teacher. What if I took myself out of the picture? And what if they presented to one another in simultaneous groups? With the exception of the few school librarians in the course, most of the rest of the aspiring librarians would never have their teaching formally evaluated. The inauthentic part of the class presentations wasn't the content. It was *me*. If I didn't have to attend every session, then we could book additional classroom space, divide the class into smaller groups, and, like concurrent sessions at a conference, have multiple presentations simultaneously.

Grading was the next challenge. How could I assess their work if I did not see it? The solution was to see the live teaching experience as just one piece of the teaching cycle, which includes planning, presenting, reviewing, adjusting, and teaching again. If I graded their process work (planning and their reflective practice) instead of their product (the teaching itself), then simultaneous presentations would work, and everyone could present in a single evening. We could talk about a teaching strategy one week and practice it the next, with little to no lag time. I would grade the *content* of two asynchronous instructional modalities: individual instructional screencasts demonstrating how to use an online tool, and online webinars, which were scheduled at times convenient to the presenting team and me, then attended by whichever students were available to attend.

As a teacher, I knew this was the solution. As a junior faculty member, I worried that someone would perceive it as abdication of professional responsibility. However, I was emboldened by what I had learned from my MAC teaching colleague: that graduate students flourish when they feel trusted and supported. He was right. Later in the term, a student said, during an office-hours conversation, "Don't worry. We're big kids. We'll be OK without you."

Students had two cohorts that term: a presentation cohort and a blogging cohort. By their vote, they kept the same presentation cohort for each face-to-face presentation. They got to know each of these subgroups well over the term. It is important to me that librarians of all types get to see the similarities among them instead of seeing academic libraries as separate silos from public or school libraries, and vice versa. By intentionally mixing up students instead of congregating them by employment preference, we broke traditional barriers and stereotyped preconceptions. They were continuously seeing other points of view and, in doing so, discovering more commonalities than differences. Members of groups with less interaction focus on the *distinctions* between individuals. Cross-pollination develops our ability to see the harmonies in our groups.

We ended up with two "professorless" sessions. Each discussion group had about 1/3 of the class, or about 13–14 students. For the first activity, we began the week prior by talking about strategies for leading successful book clubs or Socratic Seminars, and an experienced facilitator from our local Ann Arbor District Library talked about her strategies for leading book clubs rich with conversation. For homework, students selected a short reading that was available online without a password and used it to lead a book club. Most of the readings were fiction, but one was a collection of poems written on discarded catalog cards, and one was nonfiction. Readings were announced to the groups in advance, and each member of the book club was required to blog about their reading beforehand and to reflect on it afterwards, as the same blogging format that had been proven successful in previous classes continued here.

While I thought it was a mistake when I accidentally scheduled these book clubs to occur on the first day back from a weeklong break, students reassured me that this was actually one of the most relaxing ways to re-enter the term. Some group facilitators had quiz shows, wrote prompts on index cards, put students into pair-and-share teams, gave out prizes, or sketched. Many used the ideas our guest speaker had introduced the week prior. Always, the presentation ended with written peer feedback, which would later be folded into the individual reflections. Sometimes, a group even brought snacks. If there can be such a thing as a "perfect" book club class day, this was it. Concentration, deep thinking, chuckles, and cupcakes. Following each club meeting, the "participants" responded to their facilitators' evaluation questions. After class, each group wrote collective reflections, added them to their planning documents, and submitted the documents for scoring. Consistently, both the facilitators' self-reflection and the evaluations by their "participants" were high in honesty and low in self-inflation. Like Jack's golden harp, which could play without any hands plucking the strings, my students were teaching and learning on their own.

Their second presentation was a twenty-minute one-shot workshop. Twenty minutes is not very much time, so this activity required a very concentrated focus, such as how to create a Facebook fan page for your library and what to post on it. This activity showed some interesting changes. While engagement was high—and many of the nerves from the first presentation were dampened because they had a better sense of audience—the body language was quite different. Many of the one-shot presenters stood in the small conference rooms where they presented, whereas they had been seated for the book clubs. The presentation tone was more formal, with less group interaction. White boards and projection screens were used frequently. These modifications were to be expected, since the presentation's purpose is different. There was less laughter this time, but the honest responses from "participants" and facilitators were the same.

With good scaffolding, the harp can play itself.

## THE GOLDEN GOOSE LAYS A GOLDEN EGG, 2011
*Moral: Let Go. Make Room For Other Voices.*

Finally, we return to where the chapter began: Fall 2011's Information Literacy for Teaching and Learning. It is four days before Christmas 2011, exam time at the University of Michigan's School of Information (UMSI). The halls are quiet. Many students and faculty have already left for the holidays, but our class is still here, as it is our Information Literacy class's final presentation day.

In the morning, a student stops by to brainstorm an idea for a possible article. We've both been curious about the book project. We suspect that the idea of a print book is what transitioned the class from feeling somewhat apprehensive about the project to more enthusiastic. We both confess to being surprised that at our progressive information school, there is still something magical about print. Is there a publication home for this idea? Maybe we'll check with the class when we see them later in the day. In the meantime, I show her the latest issue of *School Library Monthly* and the "Nudging Toward Inquiry" column, which was filled with the class's suggestions for improving an instructional scenario.

Another student comes to show me her final practicum project for the same class, which, until 10 AM that morning, had been password protected. Now that I don't need her to enter her password so I can view it and assign it a grade, we end up talking for half an hour or so.

She asks me what I plan to change about next year's class. It's been a running joke that we were the class that had eight students enrolled in August and twenty-eight by Labor Day, and so what was meant to be an inquiry-based, participant-driven course has been that but also, at times, a bit less structured than she might have wished. She was the one who, when the class felt anxious that some portions of the course were deliberately not designed in advance, said to me months prior during another office visit, "You know, Kristin, what they're feeling is classic Kuhlthau: we get uncomfortable when the task feels ambiguous." But even as she nudges me into thinking about changes that need to be made, she starts talking about the required practicum; her eyes light up as she tells me everything she learned from shadowing an outstanding campus librarian.

It's a very civilized conversation, and I'm surprised that she is both so open about her concerns and that I have so little defensiveness and that I'm allowing us to dwell on the class's weak points. I am still a *little bit* uncomfortable, but I am so much better than I was years ago during the parent-teacher conferences of my early teaching career.

Together, we walk down to our classroom. Even though we're early, the room is full, and the front table is full of vegetables, dip, cookies, chocolates, and a cake from our resident baker with "Cake Literacy" written in frosting on top. Laptop screens glow with the Skyped-in faces of the students who have already left campus for the holidays. They're joining us remotely, and they are chatting away.

I try to start class, but a student interrupts to thank me for shepherding their work through the print and e-book publishing processes. Then we all applaud the MPublishing student, who spent an unexpected two days wrestling with our book's formatting so it would print properly. Finally, everyone fills a plate, and one by one, they step up to share their final projects.

The projects, developed under a mentor's guidance, represent various strategies for teaching information literacy skills. They range from a nutritional literacy interactive simulation to LibGuides for MLibrary to a class wiki to engage middle school readers to a German class research wiki. Sitting next to me is the university's outreach librarian, who mentored a pair of students and has sat in on many of our classes. While at first I think she is texting during the presentations, I realize she is using her phone to transcribe ideas into her Evernote account.

"That's great," she says over and over. "I'm gonna use that."

"What's the site you used to make that flow chart again?" says another student.

It's a day in which we see the culmination of their field work: the parallels and the divergences. Our course was intentionally structured around active learning and questioning by students. Each student would complete three field experiences: observation, face-to-face teaching, and development of some kind of online learning module. Mirroring the composition of the class, host sites included online classes, middle and high school classrooms, school libraries, the university's Language Resource Center, public libraries, the campus natural history museum, college classrooms, the University of Michigan Library, and a local youth writing program.

We see similarities between middle schoolers' approaches to search and a psychology class of undergrads who grumble that the "why" of databases is taking up too much class time. We see different approaches to the same concern: one group created a learning module about visual literacy and Creative Commons; another discussed how he scaffolded a high school class's first lesson on visual literacy by focusing on primary sources and questioning. A third has inserted a book cover into an online whiteboard to casually drop a visual literacy lesson into a book review site. Between the sugar highs and the great work being shared, I lose track of time. When I realize that we will run beyond the two hours we have set aside for the project presentations, I tell the class that if they need to leave on time, they should. All but those who have to report for work stay. After all, the apex of our "exam" session is our field trip to MLibrary to watch the last of our class books be published.

As the Espresso Book Machine whirs, there are hugs and goodbyes, and one student who stumps us all when she asks how to cite Espresso Book Machine titles. ("Just use the e-book version," a colleague responds. "It's easier to cite.")

I head back to my office, print copies in hand. And as I walk down the corridor, I morph back from teacher to colleague.

"Oh, I heard you were publishing a book," says one colleague. A second helps himself to a copy from my pile to take home.

The class has agreed that we will all announce the book to our social networks, so I do the same, e-mailing our class's seeds to my faculty colleagues and to the professional listservs I am a part of, posting it to the *SLM* blog and posting a Tweet. (Continuing in that tradition, you can download it at http://bit.ly/infowild or https://www.smashwords.com/books/view/115254.)

Then something remarkable starts to happen. People I know start retweeting about the book. And then a few blog posts appear. Within four hours, there have already been over one hundred downloads. A colleague from Italy writes asking me to be sure to tell my students that she's blogged about their project and shared it with her national library association. I e-mail one of our virtual guest speakers saying that a student insisted that she be sent a print copy, so it's in the mail, and she calls back to say that the classroom conversation we had a few weeks back has been on her mind ever since. It is a day when we all hold the golden eggs, where my students can reap what they have sowed, even as their words germinate in readers' minds around the world. And, perhaps most importantly, we have an artifact—the book in print—as a totem for our time together, a physical reminder of our collective efforts.

I have a professional community—I can see it in the tweets and the blog posts, people supporting a book they haven't even read yet.

And I am part of my students' community, too. I start e-mailing the links to mentions of their book, but I quickly realize that this will be as annoying as it is exciting. Instead, I start bookmarking the references into our class Diigo group, which we have used all term.

## The Diigo Group

It's a coincidence that the term ends as it begins, with our Diigo group, which I had implemented as a way to compensate for a syllabus that had to be fixed before the class began. A course organized around questions needs flexibility, and it is difficult to promote individual, inquiry-oriented thinking when the teacher planned the reading list four months ago.

Diigo groups, a feature of the free social bookmarking service Diigo.com, gave us a flexible way to augment the class's core content with additional readings identified and crowdsourced by members of the class. I knew that many of my students read blogs and online content rapaciously, and I hoped that this could provide a solution that would allow us to recommend additional readings to one another.

Each student had a Diigo.com account, the toolbar installed on their preferred browser, and membership in the class group. If they found on-line content that would interest others in the class, they clicked on the toolbar, entered their tags, and clicked to save it to their bookmarks while sharing it with the class. This made sharing easier than pasting a link to a wiki page or e-mailing it to the professor for later distribution (though a few still preferred that method). When I read their weekly reflections, I often referred them to a resource that might help, noting that they could find it in the group. If it didn't interest their classmates then, it might in the future. Settings allowed users to specific how often to receive e-mail updates (immediately, daily, or weekly). From the e-mail, one can click to view the saved site directly or to comment on someone else's saved bookmark. The commenting feature was used more extensively as the term continued. One can also access the group's bookmark collection via the web as shown in Figure 11.1.

Often, when I opened my e-mail after class, I would discover that some-one had, during class, looked up a reference during discussion and post-ed a link in the group. Sometimes, the content was scholarly (research on which ethnic groups would be most affected if net neutrality did not apply to mobile phone users), and sometimes less so (the humorous Tumblr blog http://librarianheygirl.tumblr.com, in which Ryan Gosling repeatedly ut-ters, "Hey, Girl" bons mots about all things library). Occasionally, the link had more to do with being a graduate student (e.g., student loans) than with information literacy.

The group also demonstrated that students were often discovering re-sources outside of their "silo." For example, a future music librarian might post a link about e-books in school libraries, or a school librarian might find a link about teaching in non-K–12 settings. As this had been one of the explicit goals of the course—to look at information literacy holistically, not merely through the lens of one's anticipated future job—it was a pleasure to see.

While Diigo groups were easy to set up and easy to add to, it should be said that not every student contributed actively. However, most did at least once, as we gathered submissions for potential book covers by submitting them to the group. Diigo may not have involved everyone, but usage grew throughout the term in three ways:

- more links were shared

- more people did the sharing

- more comments were left

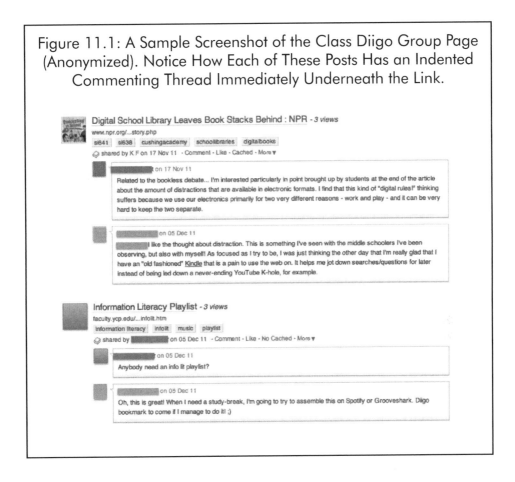

Figure 11.1: A Sample Screenshot of the Class Diigo Group Page (Anonymized). Notice How Each of These Posts Has an Indented Commenting Thread Immediately Underneath the Link.

One of Diigo's strengths, I think, was that it was optional. Had I continued to post resources within our Course Management System, they would have been interpreted as a professor heaping burdensome extra reading on the students. By situating the links in an off-site collaborative space, we democratized the sharing. The professor could share, but so could anyone else. And if the professor shared and it was irrelevant, it was fine to ignore it. This system was effective enough that we voluntarily carried it into two courses the following term as well as into a student-faculty study group.

If Diigo is a digital artifact of the class's collaborative thinking or collective inputs, then the class book they created on the Espresso Book Machine is a tangible artifact of their shared understanding. In the creation of this artifact, we had to have a conversation about copyright. The University of Michigan talks quite a bit about Open Access and Creative Commons, so I assumed that they would want to release the book under a similar plan. We quickly reviewed the possible Creative Commons formats, narrowing our choice down to the most restrictive Creative Commons license, the "CC BY-NC-ND" license, which, according to the Creative Commons website, allows "others to download your works and share them with others as long as they credit you, but they can't change them in any way or use them commercially" (Creative Commons n.d.).

Twenty-seven voted for CC BY-NC-ND.

One did not.

"I know you guys want to do that, but I don't want to give away my content *period.*"

My mind instantly flashed to the Norman Rockwell painting *The Jury* (see it at http://americanart.si.edu/exhibitions/online/tellingstories), where one woman sits confident and arms crossed, as angry male jurors stab their fingers in the air, trying to get her to change her vote.

Just then, the voice of another of our quiet students spoke up. "We all have to agree. This has to be unanimous."

The room exploded into conversation.

"I'm OK with regular copyright," people said.

"It really didn't matter to me."

"I just thought it'd be a cool thing, but it's not that important."

Every one of the twenty-seven classmates changed their vote.

When one person stands up to make sure another isn't hurt, that's a community. When everyone changes their vote to protect the intellectual property of another, that's a community.

## LESSONS LEARNED
### Moral: Nobody Likes a Bellowing Giant

It's taken me a while to think about how community has developed in my classes, and how that community has consistently facilitated better learning experiences for my students and myself. My dean calls it the "secret sauce." And while I'm not sure if he had beans in mind, if I had to make an ingredients list, here is what I have learned along the way.

### Take a Leap of Faith

All of us are in a period of unprecedented technological and pedagogical change. Continuing to do what we always have done is no longer an option. Sometimes, we have to step outside of our past behaviors and try something new in order to impact change. While the idea of novel approaches may appear intimidating, this period of uncertainty also means we have new freedoms and options. Whether it is letting go of the PD leader's traditional "sage on the stage" style by setting up small discussion groups or hosting small concurrent sessions or trying a new tool like Diigo groups or taking up a colleague's suggestion (print book, anyone?), take a leap!

### Have Your Goal Be to Empower Others, Not Prop Up Yourself

In my early college teaching, I spent a bit too much time worrying about what my students would think of me or whether they'd find me worthy to be their teacher. Now, my goal is, "How can I help them become the best professionals they can be?" While I still have a sleepless night before the first day of class, I try to remind myself that I plan my classes and design assignments and tasks to empower others, not flatter myself. Similarly, school librarians can be tempted to use PD sessions as an opportunity to show what the library can do and why the librarian is important to the school. While true, it can be seen as self-serving, while an attitude of empowerment and growth plants seeds that can germinate.

### Recognize That the Librarian (Professor) in the School Doesn't Always Have to Be In Charge

When I was a practitioner, I fell into an occasional trap of thinking I had to be in charge of everything, work on every project, and take on any task. That's what we learn in library school: "BE INDISPENSABLE!" Since then, I have learned two things: nobody likes a know-it-all, and the people we work with (or the students I teach) have perspectives that enlighten the group. Sometimes, backing off is exactly what is needed to empower others. Nobody likes a bellowing giant.

### A Web 2.0 Tool Doesn't Necessarily Make for a Collaborative Experience

Tools mirror the face-to-face culture. A librarian can create numerous discussion boards, collaborative workspaces, or Twitter feeds, but if there is not an underlying face-to-face culture, it can be for naught. Until I started signaling in my face-to-face classes that I was eager to hear my students' opinions, the tools could not be used to their maximum potential. A Web 2.0 tool does not *replace* face-to-face culture, but it can *enhance* or *extend* what is there.

### Adults Love to Feel Like They Are Making a Productive Contribution

Some show their community bonds by writing provocative blog content, some by commenting on it, and still others by bringing baked goods. Some post to a Diigo group, some read in Diigo, and some comment there. These are all signs of community. Similarly, when you ask participants to share ideas, be clear that you are open and eager to hearing their thoughts. Recently, a friend attended an in-service where a new pedagogical vision was introduced with a colorful graphic. The pieces of the graphic were explained by the workshop leaders. Then the staff was broken up into small groups to share brainstorming on how they might achieve each step of the vision. At the conclusion of the brainstorming, the workshop leaders went on to the next activity instead of asking to hear what the groups had discussed. By not asking for the groups to share their brainstorms, they accidentally told the participants that their brainstorming was inconsequential to the vision.

## Tap into Existing Community Bonds Whenever You Can

Do students like one another because we "make them"? Doubtful. They serve in campus clubs together, go to the movies together, and enjoy the occasional Friday night drink together. They bring those bonds to class—leverage them. Similarly, look for existing connections in your classrooms, schools, and districts that you can grow instead of starting from scratch.

## Approach Adult Instruction with Joy

I love class time. I psych myself up to be cheerful and full of good humor even if, inside, I have a raging sinus infection and wish I were in bed. When we love what we are doing, it shows. And it is reflected back to us most of the time with most of the people. In schools, faculty are often tired, overworked, and underappreciated. Librarians don't just talk about lifelong learning—they believe in it and its power to energize and excite us. A school librarian who brings in the warmth and light of the sun will get more germination.

## There Is Always Going to Be Someone Who Doesn't Like What You Are Doing

I am not naive enough to think all of my students' hearts soar when I walk into our classroom. Similarly, librarians often spend time fretting about the clique of nay-sayers who will never collaborate. Librarianship is like a triage unit: support those who can be supported first. You cannot help those who refuse you, but you can burn up a lot of useful energy trying. Invest your energy in those who can return it.

## WHAT WILL YOU DO WITH YOUR MAGIC BEANS?

Each of us has moments when we feel like Jack. We make an investment. Jack gave up his cow; you invest your time. When you get your five magic beans, where will you toss them? How will you help them grow?

## REFERENCES

American Library Association and the American Association of School Librarians (ALA/AASL). 2010. "ALA/AASL Standards for Initial Preparation of School Librarians." Retrieved December 29, 2011, from http://www.ala.org/aasl/sites/ala.org.aasl/files/content/aasleducation/schoollibrary/2010_standards_with_rubrics_and_statements_1-31-11.pdf.

Creative Commons. n.d. "About the Licenses." Retrieved December 29, 2011, from http://creativecommons.org/licenses .

National Board for Professional Teaching Standards (NBPTS). 2011. Home Page. Retrieved December 29, 2011, from http://www.nbpts.org.

A special thanks to my students and to Jeff Stanzler, my MAC teaching partner, for all I have learned from you.

# Collective Bookmarking:
# Using Diigo as a Student in SI 641

## Mariah Cherem

In my return to school, I've found that I'm figuring out all over again just how I learn. The last time I was in college, my reading, note taking and reflection was decidedly paper based. Sure, I'd type up final papers, but most of the ways that I used to organize, track, and process my thoughts were low-tech and private.

When I returned to grad school at the University of Michigan's School of Information in 2010, I was coming directly from working for a tech startup. For the last several years, my "office" had simply been a company-provided laptop. Although I still make paper to-do lists and keep a paper grocery list, there isn't much paper left in the ways I keep track of my ideas, my calendar, and my professional work.

I thought I was pretty darn digital. However, upon diving back into my first semester of school, I realized that I still had some adjustments to make. Printing out one week's worth of reading would have me blowing through my whole semester's print quota. Reading, highlighting, and marking up things on my laptop or Kindle was a habit that I'd need to port from my professional life into my practice as a student. Slowly, I became better at digital note taking in an academic context, as well as marking or bookmarking things and tagging them in a consistent way.

I love the discussion in school—the permission to consider big ideas and to work them out by considering someone else's take. Although many classes offered time for this, the time never seemed to be enough. Sometimes, too, I didn't want a huge discussion—but just to quickly share something I had come across or to see if something I'd read resonated with anyone else in my class/peer group.

This fall, SI 641: Information Literacy for Teaching and Learning gathered together almost thirty graduate students interested in instruction, libraries, and learning. There were some students with classroom teaching experience, some with none (or very little, like me), some who saw their future in public libraries, and some who were attracted to the idea of being an "embedded librarian." There were a *lot* of us and *lots* of material to cover. We had time in class for some discussion, but there would never be enough time to share everything relevant.

Enter Diigo. Kristin, our instructor, set up a 641 Diigo group to help facilitate a type of asynchronous sharing not possible during our limited class sessions. We were all reading for pleasure and for our other classes, and it wasn't uncommon to come across interesting articles and links that applied to our assigned readings and in-class discussions.

Coincidentally, I had begun using Diigo for my part-time job just a few months earlier. In a work setting, it was a great way to share ideas and articles across a distributed team. You could determine the best way to siphon the information flow by setting Diigo to send you every link as it was tagged/added to the group, sending a daily digest, or alternately, just logging in on your own time. I started using it for 641 and throughout the term, noticed a few interesting things.

### Each Group Had to Come to a Shared Understanding about What Was or Wasn't Critical to Read

Some weeks were slow, and some weeks there were a lot of bookmarks. In 641, I would browse the Diigo bookmarks at least once a week (usually every few days), and see if there was something in particular that caught my eye or that Kristin had called out as important. If so, I would spend the time on that article or at least use my "Send to Kindle" Chrome extension to send the text of the article to a platform I could read more easily on the bus or in transit.

Similarly, I had conversations with my work colleagues about our expectations of who would read what and when. We decided that anything critical or urgent would also be communicated more directly than by bookmarking, but that Diigo's searchability would help our group function as a collective reference base for us all. We were welcome, but not required, to read each bookmarked item.

### While Reading, I Often Had the "Other"/My Audience in Mind

Previously, I had thought of reading, even on my laptop, as a relatively private activity. However, now as I read articles, I would occasionally do a spot-check on whether they might be of interest to either my 641 classmates or my work colleagues, since those were my two main Diigo groups. In addition, I started tagging things that I read for another class and shared a link with my Business School classmates where they could follow the articles I had tagged as related to our course.

### Lurking Is Sometimes a Part of Learning. Models are Important.

I think we've all been lurkers at one time or another, either online or in real life. My past professional experience as an online community manager has taught me that even within a simple platform, people often want to wait to get their bearings before participating. There are indeed some sorts of social norms, even within pretty stripped-down ways of interacting. As the semester wore on, more students started posting, responding, and even just clicking through the various Diigo links in our 641 group. As our instructor, Kristin was an important model of that behavior, and I think it was critical (and commendable!) that despite all of her other duties as instructor, she was always bookmarking things for the group and adding some context/commentary with her posts. I was certainly a lurker throughout part of the term, but started posting and reacting more to links as I got more comfortable.

Was Diigo an effective way to share interesting resources and articles with our classmates? Mostly, yes. What more might I hope for when using Diigo in a class in the future? It would be fantastic if Diigo became a place where even more back-and-forth discussion happened, beyond just initial sharing. In a way, it's a shame that our 641 Diigo group will probably end with the term, just as we're getting more comfortable with using it. I can see Diigo being the sort of sharing tool that grows in value over time—perhaps it could be used for discussion/interest groups on particular UMSI-related topics throughout one whole year or among a specific cohort.

# CHAPTER 12
# MENTORING AS A
# CO-LEARNING EXPERIENCE

*Editors' Note:* For the past several years, Beth Friese has taught courses for pre-service teachers and has delighted in their energy and enthusiasm. Here, she shares what she has learned and offers suggestions about how librarians can reach out to their newest colleagues as optimistic collaborators in instruction and professional development. Corroborating these insights, Kim Dority, an experienced consultant in academia, publishing, telecommunications, and in library fields, in for-profit and nonprofit settings, for both established companies and start-ups, confirms that even the most experienced mentors continue to grow alongside their colleagues.

# Always Beginning:
# Welcoming "Beginning Teachers"
# Into a Learning Community

Elizabeth E. G. Friese

## INTRODUCTION

I am a teacher of teachers. Although my education is in school librarianship, my current job is teaching future elementary- and middle-school teachers about children's literature, language arts, and digital literacies as an instructor in the Department of Language and Literacy Education at the University of Georgia. Within months of spending time in my classroom, they will transition into K–12 schools where the school librarian will, in many cases, take over for university instructors as the in-house professional developer. My students will become the teachers anxious to learn in your PD courses. This chapter seeks to build the bridge between my classroom and your faculty meetings so that their learning continues to expand as they gain a foothold in their classrooms.

Scholars and practitioners alike suggest that classroom teachers hear little about the role of school librarians and school library programs during their professional preparation (Asselin 2000; Hartzell 2002). My own experiences working with pre-service teachers bear this out. When students arrive in my classes as college juniors and seniors, few have heard about or seen any meaningful engagement with the school library program during their professional education. During my children's literature and language arts courses, I ensure that they have several opportunities to learn about and work with school librarians. Still, I wonder how university instruction about school libraries, in the rare cases when pre-service teachers receive it, transfers into the workplace. How do librarians welcome them into the school community as fellow continuing learners?

New teachers transition into your school community bringing dreams for success, rich prior knowledge, visions for future growth, as well as fears that they will not measure up. When school librarians can align their professional development to take account of these hopes and fears, they can better tailor professional development so that it is resonant, relevant, and meaningful to their newest colleagues.

## NO EMPTY VESSELS

Traditionally, many of us were schooled in classrooms in which the teacher was the expert and the students expected to absorb the teacher's knowledge. Teachers defined the boundaries of knowledge in a subject area. This practice has given way to another approach: one in which the teacher sees herself as an ongoing learner who models that learning and provides an environment in which students explore, pool their knowledge, and are supported (not dictated to) by the teacher. Although I am nominally "the teacher" in a classroom, I am not the only one with important things to share and contribute. In a room of learners, whether they are youth or adults, no one is the proverbial empty vessel waiting to be filled with teacher-selected knowledge. Rather, research tells us that adult learners bring enormous prior knowledge, biases, learning preferences, and experiences to the classroom. This prior knowledge plays an important role in learning (Bransford, Brown, and Cocking 2000). The teacher may be further along on the learning journey in some regards, but the classroom is full of students who have something to share.

## THE PERILS OF THE "KNOW IT ALL" PARADIGM

Many of us begin our teaching journey with apprehension. Having been students in an era where the teacher tossed out information like softballs for us to catch and retain, as new teachers we may wonder, how can we ever live up to that standard? Can we *ever* know enough to be good enough, especially as we also struggle to learn the ins-and-outs of permanent records, attendance books, grading scales, and the student handbook? I call this approach to teaching the "Know It All" paradigm —a strong, gut-level belief that teaching knowledge is a finite amount of information that can be mastered once and for all—and I see this mindset in many of my students.

In my first semesters of teaching, I felt pressured to try to push out information and "cover" it all. The impossibility of that approach quickly became clear. I read professional journals and listservs while taking academic coursework. In time this evolved into collecting blogs in my RSS feed reader from people who were working in my areas of interest, in "liking" library and literacy professional associations on Facebook, and in developing a group of educators to learn with on Twitter. It seemed as if I was always picking up new tips and tools, engaging with new ideas, and bookmarking new resources—and there was always more. The more I learned, the more I realized what new information was not yet within my grasp. No matter how much time I invested, the more acutely aware I became of what I had yet to learn.

As I worked with pre-service teachers in my classroom, I realized that, without a change in mindset, they, too, would put themselves on this hamster wheel of needing-to-know. In a time of great change, when the content covered in one's formal education is quickly superseded, how was the Know It All approach helping them? And, more importantly, what were the costs of such a mental model? As a result, I started thinking that it was less my job to "teach everything" than to teach them how to continue learning in a sustainable way, long after they've left my courses. I needed to shift from an approach that emphasized skills and content mastery to one that prioritized continual self-learning. My hope is, in turn, they will keep this in mind as they work with their own students.

My thinking coincided with the American Association of School Librarians' 2007 publication of the *Standards for the 21st-Century Learner*, which emphasizes learning habits and processes alongside content mastery. I began to think about my courses as a midpoint in the timeline of my students' careers as learners. Their learning had not started with me, and it would not end with me, either. How could I make their time going forward as learning educators more fruitful and worthwhile?

## FROM THE IVORY TOWER TO THE WHITEBOARD PLAINS

Let's cross the street, for a moment, from the university classroom to your school library. More likely than not, many of the teachers in your building conceptualize the role of teacher as the one who Knows It All (or almost all of it). I certainly see this reflected in the faces of many of my own students: they're bright new professionals clinging to this unrealistic expectation that, if they only read and remember the right set of books, articles, and activities, they can finally and forever master everything. It is no wonder, then, whether in your school or my university classroom, that they may be reluctant to ask questions, since asking questions might reveal what they see as their ignorance or their failed mastery.

However, it is not only new teachers who are constrained by the Know It All mindset. Imagine what it is like to be a longtime teacher who has been relatively successful with her methods and students for a number of years. In some ways, many of these teachers have become very comfortable with the idea of the teacher as one who Knows It All, and may even see that ideal reflected in the mirror. There are always new curricula to adjust to, new initiatives to nod at, but in the end, many veteran teachers may be quite confident and skilled in their instructional approaches. Imagine how they feel when they are greeted (or confronted) with an e-mail or workshop about a proposed pedagogical change, not to mention an introduction to technology tools such as Google Apps, SmartBoards, or VoiceThread. Just like the new teacher, veteran teachers may feel a sense of fear, overload, or confusion at the thought of new approaches to learning, especially those that emphasize inquiry or the potential of interactive technologies. This anxiety may lead to resistance, especially if these e-mails or professional development mandates come from someone whom the veteran teacher feels does not know the content or the classroom as well as she does. Administrators are often at the heart of these new mandates, so teachers may feel less comfortable sharing their vulnerabilities with their supervisors.

In our schools, we are surrounded by professionals at numerous points on the spectrum of comfort with technology, with content, with pedagogy, and with change. Teachers also have different perspectives on what it means to be a teacher, and what it means when a teacher says, "I don't know." It is this last point that sticks with me regularly. If we hold to the Know It All ideal, what do we say to the young teacher who is scrambling to get it all in? What do we say to the veteran teacher who isn't sure how recent advancements fit into their tried-and-true pedagogical approaches? How do we utter "I don't know" without losing face? What do we say to the teacher who is intrigued by the buzzwords of "inquiry" and "student-centered" but is hesitant to change for fear of losing face because he or she was already supposed to know it? It is here that I propose a shift in thinking, and the school librarian as instrumental in that shift. The school librarian, both as a colleague and as a person who loves and invites questions, can create a relationship where it is safe for teachers to seek out information, resources, and advice.

## EMBRACING THE BEGINNER MENTALITY

*"Resolve to be always beginning—to be a beginner."*
*–Rainer Maria Rilke (1975, p. 31)*

I suggest we advocate for a model that celebrates educators as beginners: those who begin new things regularly. By "beginning," I do not mean making changes just for the sake of novelty, but rather as a way of seeking real growth and depth in our instructional practices. Throughout our careers, we will have many "beginnings." School librarians can connect with "anytime beginner" teachers, from the newly hired employee to the veteran teacher learning a new tool or strategy. Part of the transition to lifelong ongoing learning is to embrace oneself as an ongoing learner. We call upon our students daily to begin new things, and creating a school culture in which teachers feel comfortable tackling new challenges and modeling that for their students is powerful. A school community in the habit of beginning can ease the transition for new teachers as well. Thus, these strategies can be adapted to work with any educational community.

When you meet a first-year educator, you may be the first school library contact they have had since their own K–12 school years. Their memory of a librarian's job responsibilities may evoke a bygone, pre-technology era. You may be the first librarian-as-leader they have ever met. Even if they worked with a librarian during a college project, they have most likely only scratched the surface of the learning resources and collegial support that a school librarian offers.

How do we introduce ourselves and start the conversation that will lead to collegial professional learning? In those first days of school, new teachers may feel that many urgent matters are tugging at them for attention as they settle into their classroom. To an outside eye, they may seem preoccupied with trivialities: stapling up bulletin boards, setting up grade books, writing welcome letters to their students, or clustering the desks just-so. Their focus may not appear, at first, to be on the business of teaching and learning. However, as I see recent students post their classroom "set up" photos on Facebook at the start of each new school year, I realize that these early arrangements do much to help novice teachers *feel like teachers*. In their pre-service education classes, they have also likely discussed the role of design and space as enhancements to learning. As they settle into the first weeks and months of school, they will be able to expand their identity footprint beyond their classroom and into the larger school community. Savvy school librarians watch for signals that these newcomers are settling in; in the meantime, they recognize that their most useful role may be in holding up the bulletin board paper while the teacher tacks it to the wall.

## GETTING TO KNOW YOUR OWN COLLEAGUES

In my university courses, I spend a great amount of time getting to know my students, their histories, and their philosophies of education. Some of this learning happens as a result of formal assignments, but a lot of it comes from making room for students to share their ideas and inviting them to participate. I have used simple online surveys to gauge prior knowledge and beliefs about technology use. We've generated numerous products that help me understand their interests, passions, and fears. Most importantly, I try to spend a lot of time listening. All of this springs from my genuine interest in students as people and a desire to learn from them.

This informs the way I design my courses and my ongoing relationships with them as growing educators.

School librarians can do the same. Either in informal conversations or formal meetings, here are some questions that can help you begin those conversations. Notice that these questions *implicitly* communicate that you are aware that they are skilled colleagues and contemporaries.

## What Are You Interested in Learning About?

This question builds on an assumption that ongoing learning is an expectation of your school's culture. When my students leave my courses, their final assignment asks them to think about what they are going to continue to learn, and how they will continue to learn it. Their answers are varied, from interests in learning more about formative assessments to expanding their knowledge of multicultural literature for middle-grades students. I feel it is important to send my teachers out into their jobs with open questions. I would hope that all beginning teachers have a sense of what they'd like to continue learning. Be mindful that some new teachers—especially those at the elementary level or those secondary teachers with multiple "preps"—may say that their goal for the first year is simply to learn the curriculum. The first year is a good time to take their statement at face value. Becoming familiar with a curriculum, its required objectives, and strategies to promote efficient, effective learning *is* professional learning.

## What Resources Do You Need to Get Your Classroom Going?

This question communicates your desire to support their lessons and teaching style. Pedagogically, what mentor texts, read-alouds, multimedia resources, and technology tools are on their wish list? Professionally, what resources do they need to continue learning? Sadly, many teachers across the seniority scale seem unaware that the school library *intentionally* supports classroom and teacher learning. Especially in pre-service programs that emphasize classroom libraries, teachers may be under the misconception that they must purchase many of their own classroom materials out of their own pockets. Librarians can literally save teachers thousands of dollars in their first few years of teaching. For educators who prefer to own their own materials, librarians can offer to put them on a distribution list for review journals such as *Library Media Connection*, *Booklist*, or *School Library Journal*. Especially as the launch of the Common Core State Standards comes nearer, these resources may be of increasing usefulness.

## How Do You Like to Learn?

This question reassures teachers that you would like to tailor your professional development to fit them, not that they will have to adjust to please you. Does the newcomer learn through videos, professional reading, in-person experiences, or discussions? A mix of these? Although formal professional development may not happen immediately, this information can be helpful for the school librarian as she designs future learning and seeks to serve teachers in an ongoing way.

## START WITH WHAT *THEY* KNOW, NOT WITH WHAT *YOU* KNOW

Of course, all of the previous questions ask about the future professional learning of your new colleague. But we cannot forget that new teachers have knowledge that is worth sharing. To address this, final questions you might ask are, "What are the big ideas that you learned in your education courses?" or "What did you learn about in your pre-service university program that you can't wait to try?" These questions acknowledge that a novice teacher's university training may have exposed them to research and practices that would add value to their colleagues' work. Welcoming their expertise reassures them that they have a valuable toolkit to share.

Notice that, in all of these initial conversations, the typical "this is the library and what it can do for you" orientation is absent. While it might be tempting to set up a formal meeting to introduce the new teacher to library resources and policies, consider flipping the situation. Say that you enjoy knowing what's going on in schools of education and would love to hear what they found exciting or invigorating during their time there.

**This "getting to know you" is a way of tapping into your new colleagues' prior knowledge,** a fundamental building block upon which new knowledge is built (Bransford, Brown, and Cocking 2000). By learning what they already know, you may be able to connect new learning to past knowledge. For example, if they reveal that they kept a reflective blog for a college course, you might be able to say later on, "You mentioned that you had kept a blog in college. Our district is moving toward a new web presence—I wonder if the new blogging tool would be a great way for you to keep in touch with parents?" Additionally, you now know that an introductory session on blogging isn't a good match for this new student. And it is quite likely that the recent graduate may have skills that you can learn from!

Beginning by **looking at strengths, instead of identifying weaknesses**, is exactly what I encourage my pre-service teachers to do when they meet their own young students. Instead of meeting kindergarten students and looking first for deficits (such as who can't follow instructions or who doesn't know their letters), we can instead inventory what they already know and can contribute to the classroom. This previous knowledge is sometimes referred to as the students' "funds of knowledge" (Moll et al. 1992, 133), which are key points of personal knowledge and familiarity upon which teachers can draw as they plan learning activities for the year. For example, one of my students in a recent semester had a rich knowledge of life on a farm. I encouraged her to share this interest with students early in the year, relating it to the curriculum in numerous ways. This sharing of personal knowledge was not a way to make the classroom "all about the teacher" but instead served as an invitation to young students to share their areas of expertise as well. Acknowledging these funds of knowledge as a resource is a key step in the development of a rich learning community. We can draw an imperfect but informative analogy between "beginning" teachers and kindergarteners. When new teachers arrive for their first day, we may be tempted to see them in terms of what they *don't* know. But, just as with the kindergarteners, we do these new teachers a disservice if we begin with the assumption that they know little and see them in terms of the gaps we need to figure out how to fill.

New educators are an untapped resource. Although less experienced, they have just completed education programs that shared exciting knowledge about teaching and learning. They are familiar with the freshest approaches to pedagogy and can serve as reminders of the educational ideals we aspired to when we entered the profession. What projects or lessons sparked their interest in college classes? How can the school library make a project like that happen, even enhance it by facilitating connections to another classroom elsewhere in the country? Opening with an invitation for new teachers to share their expertise lets the school librarian learn from this new colleague, which in turn enriches the librarian's own practice and perhaps provides a context for establishing partnerships.

## LEARNING TOGETHER

We know that meaningful relationships with mentors are an important element in successful teacher induction through the early years of teaching. Many times, new teachers are paired with an "expert" teacher in their area to work with and talk to as a mentor. The school librarian, as a learning specialist (Zmuda and Harada 2008), can be another mentor for new teachers and also facilitate other learning connections outside the traditional mentor pairing.

When you ask teachers what they want to learn about, consider connecting new teachers to building colleagues who are also interested in learning the same things. In addition, consider connecting veteran teachers to newcomers who may know new strategies not yet introduced to the building. Perhaps there might be a group working on developing their knowledge about English Language Learners, or technology integration, or inquiry-based science instruction. There is benefit in groups with different levels of experience and different perspectives learning together about topics that matter to them. Instead of outsiders providing professional development (an expense many districts have limited in recent years), teachers can grow their own development within their ranks, establishing interest-based groups who can share their growing expertise. The school librarian can enhance these groups by providing pathways for synchronous and asynchronous communication such as discussion forums, facilitating connections with local and national experts by setting up Skype sessions, and demonstrating ways to collect, archive, and share the growing knowledge of each group via shared Dropbox folders, Google Docs, or password-protected collaboration sites such as Moodle. As Moreillon points out in Chapter 7, the school librarian can be a co-learner, too.

## MODELING TRANSPARENT THINKING: SHOWING PROCESS, NOT JUST PRODUCT

There is always value in attending professional development with someone who has thought deeply about content and created shortcuts, graphical representations, guidance, or other tools to help participants make sense of new material. Part of good teaching is knowing material well and knowing how to scaffold, "chunk," discuss, synthesize, or organize it to help others learn it efficiently, pleasantly, and enjoyably. However, in doing so, we must take care that we do not oversimplify or overpackage content. Making our own searching, finding, and thinking processes transparent can provide useful information and modeling in professional development.

Unpacking our process need not be a laborious task. As an example, my students write and conduct research on topics of personal interest. To get ideas flowing and model how they can help their future students do the same, we engage in activities that spark my students' thinking about their own lives, interests, and curiosity. In my course on middle-school writing pedagogy, we employ a literacy practice that involves creating heart maps: annotated drawings depicting people, places, and ideas we love (Heard 1998). I also use *My Map Book* (Fanelli 1995) as a mentor text for a number of other kinds of maps, such as neighborhood maps. One day, as I talked about these map exercises on Twitter, English teacher Paul Hankins (http://twitter.com/paulwhankins) chimed in with an idea from his own experience. He suggested opening the lesson with a scene from the movie *Jaws*, in which three characters compare their scars and the stories behind them. I loved his idea of "scar maps" and incorporated it into my course.

Earlier in my teaching career, I would simply have shown the clip and attributed the idea to Hankins. The day I taught the lesson, I made a conscious decision that marked a key change in my teaching. I decided to share the story of how I had learned about this teaching strategy. I showed Hankins's Twitter profile and described the experience of learning from him as I set up the clip from the film. I shared that I had never met Hankins, but discovered him through linking, reading, and discovering other teachers on Twitter. I had learned from him, teacher to teacher, by sharing my experiences online. Through this approach, I made my own life as a learner public to my students and illuminated a reason to use the tool at all. Like them, I continue to learn in numerous ways and with numerous tools and strategies of all kinds.

Although the examples above were shared in a classroom setting, it is easy to imagine how we might be transparent about sharing ourselves as learners with colleagues on an informal basis. For example, if I knew a 4th grade teacher was working on inquiry strategies for mathematics, I could locate some resources fairly readily because of the math educators I am connected with through Twitter. It would be easy enough to pass along the resources and feel my job was done. But to push toward transparency, I would also take a moment to share my learning process with the teacher who needed the information. As important as the content is, it is also important to share the process, and even connect colleagues with the kinds of conversations (such as #mathchat or #elemchat, two that I've recently participated in on Twitter) that can enrich and energize their professional growth.

Our lives as educators do not become stagnant or fixed once we have enough lessons to fill 180 days. Instead, we stay fresh with ongoing learning. And the truth is, I enjoy that part of the job as much as many others. I hope my students see my joy in learning and discovering. Shouldn't it be that way in your school as well as your work with your classroom colleagues to build capacity?

## FAILURE ISN'T ALWAYS FAILURE

Creating a library culture—and, by extension, a school culture—that promotes thoughtful experimentation empowers ongoing learners to think of their practice like inventors. I hope school libraries become places where teachers (and students) can not only try and fail, but, in the words of Samuel Beckett (1983), "Try again. Fail again. Fail better" (7). If we are to envision libraries as learning and inquiry laboratories (Kuhlthau, Maniotes, and Caspari 2007), we must be ready to have some experiments that spill, fizzle, or leave an unpleasant smell. But there will also be many moments of unexpected beauty. (*Editors' Note*: View Kelly Ahlfeld's Exploratorium project in Chapter 1 to learn about one strategy that can maximize experimentation while reducing fear of failure.)

When we imagine ourselves as having just taught a successful lesson, the word "failure" is often the last benchmark that comes to mind. Yet, as numerous stories from the world of invention tell us, success often comes only after numerous unsuccessful attempts. The Henry Ford in Dearborn, Michigan, (formerly known as the Henry Ford Museum and Greenfield Village) has a display of numerous nonfunctioning Edison light bulbs, yet few Americans would consider Thomas Edison a failure. Silly Putty didn't solve the problem it was intended to. Penicillin, Coca-Cola, and other "accidental inventions" reinforce the value of inquiry, experimentation, and imagination. Had Edison given up after a single trial, we might be sitting in darkness to this day.

Truthfully, inventors are considered successful not by the number of trials and prototypes but by the ultimate success of just one of them. This is a useful lesson for us to bring to our work with novice and veteran teachers alike. Only stepping beyond our comfort zone can move us more closely to change. Avoiding risk shuts us off from each other as learners as well. Innovation does not happen in a world where we expect perfect outcomes. In my classroom, we celebrate risk taking instead of penalizing students for pushing themselves into unfamiliar territory. I love it when they do this, even if the result is not quite what we had hoped. More often than not, students surprise themselves by creating something magnificent. My favorite examples of this usually involve poetry. Very few of my students enter my classes feeling positively about poetry. I share my own love for poetry by reading and writing it myself, and inviting them to join me if they choose. Final projects of the semester often include haiku, concrete poems, and other forms. I've also had students create websites or wikis for their work. Even if they are not always the most sophisticated pieces of work, they are always meaningful and represent students stretching past what they thought they were capable of. I have never had a student tell me that the risk was not worth it. (But I do wonder if it would have been if the "penalty" for failure were great.) If we are afraid to fail, our learners of all ages may be afraid as well. What have you tried lately that you were unsure about? How have you shared the ways you've challenged yourself?

## FINAL THOUGHTS

In closing, I think again of Rilke's famous quote: "Resolve to be always beginning, to be a beginner" (1975, 31). It is this spirit of the beginner that keeps us energetic and learning, curious and accepting of missteps. Every teacher can (and, I would argue, should) be a beginner. What teacher would not benefit from stepping back and reimagining his or her classroom? What school librarian would not benefit from finding out what teachers themselves are curious about? What established school community would not be enriched by cross-faculty learning that is interest driven and self-managed? It is the mentality of the eager beginner we seek. I will never Know It All, and for that I am grateful. I'm saying out loud that "I don't know" but I, along with my learning community of ever-developing professionals, am working on learning more and sharing. I am enjoying the work, excited for what comes next. When librarians embrace learning's imperfections and resolve to learn alongside the classroom teachers in their building, they, too, can find joy and deep satisfaction.

## REFERENCES

American Association of School Librarians (AASL). 2007. *Standards for the 21st-Century Learner.* Chicago: American Library Association. Retrieved December 31, 2011, from http://www.ala.org/ala/mgrps/divs/aasl/guidelinesandstandards/learningstandards/standards.cfm.

Asselin, Marlene. 2000. "Poised for Change: Effect of a Teacher Education Project on Pre-service Teachers' Knowledge of the School Library Program and the Role of the Teacher-Librarian." *School Libraries Worldwide* 6(2): 72–87.

Beckett, Samuel. 1983. *Worstward Ho.* London: John Calder.

Bransford, John D., Ann L. Brown, and Rodney R. Cocking (eds). 2000. *How People Learn: Brain, Mind, Experience, and School* (Expanded ed.). Washington, DC: National Academy Press.

Fanelli, Sara. 1995. *My Map Book.* New York: HarperCollins.

Hartzell, Gary. 2002. "The Principal's Perceptions of School Libraries and Teacher Librarians." *School Libraries Worldwide* 8(1): 92–110.

Heard, Georgia. 1998. *Awakening the Heart: Exploring Poetry in Elementary and Middle School.* Portsmouth, NH: Heinemann.

Kuhlthau, Carol C., Leslie K. Maniotes, and Ann K. Caspari. 2007. *Guided Inquiry: Learning in the 21st Century.* Westport, CT: Libraries Unlimited.

Moll, Luis C., Cathy Amanti, Deborah Neff, and Norma Gonzales. 1992. "Funds of Knowledge for Teaching: Using a Qualitative Approach to Connect Homes and Classrooms." *Theory Into Practice* 31(2): 132–41.

Rilke, Rainer Maria. 1975. *Rilke on Love and Other Difficulties,* trans. J. J. L. Mood. New York: W. W. Norton.

Zmuda, Allison, and Violet H. Harada. 2008. "Reframing the Library Media Specialist as a Learning Specialist." *School Library Media Activities Monthly* 24(8): 42–46.

# Our Mutual Catalyst for Growth

Kim Dority

Scottish author Kenneth Grahame points out that "the strongest human instinct is to impart information. The second strongest is to resist it." He hit on a universal truth: as adults, it's often challenging for us to admit we don't pretty much know it all. Especially when it comes to our own professional expertise!

When I started teaching a course for the University of Denver MLIS program on Alternative LIS Careers, I discovered one of the most interesting characteristics of the profession: a large part of its members are on second careers. That means that in every class, I work with a highly diverse group of adults in terms of age, demographics, technology mastery, and work experience. Despite—or possibly because of—that, shared information becomes our mutual catalyst for growth.

At the start of each new class I try to discover, for each of the students, two key elements: what are they most proud of in their professional (or student) lives, and what are they most concerned about? No surprise, just about everyone responds that they are most concerned about getting a job. But the interesting—and useful—part is what they are most proud of. Once I have this information, I can start building on that aspect of their self-image to draw their strengths and knowledge into the course, enriching the professional development of all of the other students in ways that I couldn't if the course were only based on what I know. In addition, this knowledge enables me to establish and respect the individual strengths of each student, moving them out of the role of passive note-taker into the role of confident participant—if only because now I know what questions to ask to draw them out!

As a school librarian providing professional development to your teaching colleagues, you're likely to encounter a similarly diverse set of characteristics. The good news: this is great! Who better to step into this key function? School librarians are used to "doing it all," mastering new processes, technologies, and teaching techniques quickly. You may be new to professional development, you may be hesitant about stepping into a leadership role, but your willingness to stretch beyond your comfort zone is the most effective model you could set for your teacher colleagues.

You now have a unique opportunity to model effective communications techniques as part of the learning experience. With your goal being to create a safe and supportive learning environment, you can demonstrate respect for others' knowledge (especially among different generations), responsiveness to diverse learning styles, and openness to learning from participants as your program progresses.

When I first began teaching, I assumed my job was to know everything there was to know about alternative LIS careers. I've since realized my responsibility to my students is to create an opportunity for all of us to learn, and all of us to contribute. My job is to be a learning catalyst, and support knowledge as a change agent.

Your job will be similar as you launch your PD initiatives—you don't need to know it all; you just need to be open to continuous learning. What better role model could your teachers ask for?

# CHAPTER 13
# FACILITATING GRAND
# CONVERSATIONS

*Editor's Note:* In a school-wide program called "Literary Club" for over thirty years, small groups of mixed-age students meet weekly during the same hour for the entire year to discuss books, stories, and, other types of texts.   Marilyn Kimura trains teachers, teaching-interns, administrators, staff, and parent-volunteers to facilitate these discussions in support of the school's literacy goals. She shares her workshop training strategies and her process for assessing the adults, the students, and the program. Marilyn contends that year-round marketing is indispensable in sustaining professional learning of this magnitude and she reflects on how an established program must continually reinvent itself.

By using facilitation skills similar to those taught in "Grand Conversations," school librarians can moderate discussions of thorny school issues, thereby claiming a leadership role in the civic life of their school community. Nancy Kranich is the Convener of the American Library Association Center for Civic Life Advisory Committee and Lecturer at Rutgers University School of Communication and Information. During her American Library Association (ALA) presidency, she learned about deliberative dialogue as an alternative approach to solving problems and recognized the potential of involving librarians as facilitators. She has moderated dialogues on tough issues like immigration, health care, and America's role in the world and, under the auspices of the ALA Center for Civic Life, offers training to librarians at ALA conferences and online. Here she urges school librarians to learn deliberative discussion skills in order to provide opportunities for professional learning that advances civic discourse in their schools.

# Professional Development in Reading:
# A Librarian's Role

### Marilyn Kimura

## LITERARY CLUB

Every Friday morning is buzzing with activity at Nueva, an independent pre-K through 8th grade school in Hillsborough, California. Almost 80 percent of the school's children (330 students from 2nd to 8th grade) can be seen in animated discussion circles for an hour in 33 groups ranging in size from 8 to 12 students. Teachers, specialists, teaching interns, academic advisors, and community parent-volunteers all have been trained to work together. They co-lead small groups in classrooms, offices, the library, and even the business office. Throughout the school year these generally permanent groups will discuss a book, short story, poem, and, occasionally, a film.

The Nueva School was founded in 1967 as a progressive school for the gifted and talented. Our motto, "Learn by doing, learn by caring," reflects our educational mission to create a climate of inquiry and opportunities in which children can construct their own meaning about the world around them. For the most part, the acquisition of skills is embedded in hands-on, authentic experiences, as evident in the Literary Club Goals (Figure 13.1).

Lit Club started in 1982 in one classroom with six children and a charismatic, intense 3rd and 4th grade classroom teacher who began holding small-group book conversations over tea and cookies. Anoth-

---

### Figure 13.1: Literary Club Goals

1. To support each individual in applying critical and creative thinking in order to engage deeply with a text;

2. To inspire each child to take risks by sharing personal responses that spring from reading in order to understand the role of stories in our lives;

3. To have students recognize that, in questioning and tussling and wondering together, a collaborative group can achieve a profound understanding and appreciation of the themes and complexities of a work; and

4. To engender and model a life-long enjoyment of reading both alone and with others.

---

er teacher noticed the benefits of organizing students into small groups by reading interests and asked the school librarian if she would teach a group of high-functioning gifted readers who were restless during her classroom's whole-group book discussions. Not wanting to deal with the logistics of tea and cookies and not interested in "teaching" a book, Debbie Abilock, the school's librarian, experimented with a process modeled on her graduate English seminars with seven highly animated eight- and nine-year-old students. When these children realized that they had both a voice and choice in these seminars, their enthusiasm grew. With my addition as a second librarian, Lit Club expanded rapidly over the next ten years to include 3rd through 6th grade classrooms and, more slowly, to all students in 2nd through 8th grade (Figure 13.2).

---

### Figure 13.2: Reading Statistics from the 28th Year of Literary Club 2010–2011

This year twenty-nine parent volunteers joined twenty teachers and staff to work with students in grades two through six to facilitate conversations. They read more than 160 children's and young adult titles in order to offer appropriate choices to their students!

- 125 2nd through 4th grade students in 14 groups read 72 titles
- 97 5th and 6th grade students in 10 groups read 44 titles
- 103 7th and 8th grade students in 9 advisories read 23 titles

---

Under my administration the program, now entering its twenty-ninth year, is the oldest and largest ongoing teacher and parent-volunteer training program in the school's history. Administered by the library as part of our mission to support literacy across the school and give students practice in applying higher-order thinking skills to their reading, Lit Club is part of every student's curriculum, funded separately from the library budget so that supplies (notebooks, art supplies) and books belong to the students.

So how did we get from tea and cookies to a school-wide community of readers engaged in shared inquiry? Strategic decisions, baby steps, small corrections, grassroots input, and lots of hard work. Since Lit Club aims to empower children to function as independent and collaborative readers, my overriding directive has always been to create dynamic and productive working groups of children facilitated by pairs of trained adults.

## BEHIND THE SCENES: RECRUITING VOLUNTEERS AND ENGAGING FACULTY

Our school has a strong history of volunteerism; parents fundraise, serve on the board, volunteer in classrooms, drive on field trips, and, yes, even shelve and check out books in the library. Faculty is accustomed to having parents share their expertise, interests, and time as mentors and teachers in the classrooms. I must compete with these enticing opportunities in order to recruit between twenty to twenty-five parents from a parent body of approximately 550 people. Along with the classroom teachers, interns, and some administrators, they will co-lead approximately thirty-three discussion groups every Friday morning at the same time from early October to the end of April.

Before school ends in June, I will have touched base, either in person or via e-mail, to thank every leader for their contribution during the year, and urge him or her to commit again the following fall. Our Nueva Parent Association hosts an end of the year Thank You Breakfast for school volunteers to which I personally invite our Lit Club leaders. During the last week of Lit Club, I have written an article for the school newsletter summarizing the number of books read and people involved.

My "marketing campaign" includes information in all school mailings even before the academic year begins and in our weekly newsletter once school is in session. I emphasize the opportunity for "ownership" when I let parents know they will work closely with the same group of students for an entire year. I also find that the chance to work closely with an adult peer over time can be a big draw. I present at six or seven parent orientation meetings and listen for comments like "I love reading kids books" or "I talked with my son about why . . . " Then, much as a fundraiser approaches a potential donor, I personally ask some parents to consider volunteering. While I do not "pitch" to teachers directly since the school assumes they will be Lit Club leaders, teachers also receive these materials and I remind them to "talk up" the program with new parents and encourage previous leaders to recruit among their friends.

Understanding why parents are motivated to make such an extensive time commitment helps me tailor this marketing. Many parents grow to love children's literature as they read to their own children and want to broaden their knowledge both for their own satisfaction and so that they can suggest new books to their own children. Others want to learn how to talk with their own child about a text. A number of parents are former teachers who yearn to be in the classroom again but are not ready to go back to work. Still others feel that interactions with their son or daughter's peers help them recognize what is developmentally appropriate for their own child. One leader wrote at the end of her first year: "I love the discussions with the kids! I also love finding books that they wouldn't have chosen themselves and watching them light up with discovery." If I tailor the training to respond to these needs, I can be sure that leaders will continue to volunteer, sometimes well beyond their child's graduation. One alumni parent has been teaching Lit Club for twelve of the last fifteen years! Teachers express that Lit Club supports their class reading goals and gives them a chance to see how literacy is developing across a larger range of readers.

I want to create good partnerships to lead groups; often this means that I look for different but complementary skills and outlook in pairing co-leaders. Some volunteers, by virtue of temperament and life's experience, may be stronger in creating community and fostering a climate of caring in which children feel safe to risk offering their opinions and insights. Other parents from the business world bring outstanding facilitation skills; they build groups in which children extend and stretch their thinking, see multiple sides of an issue, and provide evidence to back up their opinions. We have had a number of teachers who enjoy teaming with parents over the years, but in general, teachers will most often work with their teaching interns with whom they are likely to be planning with anyway.

This year, we have three groups with two brand-new parent leaders, one new teacher, and three new interns. While novices expect to be paired with an experienced leader, I often pair new leaders so that they grow together as they face the weekly challenges as equals. Over the years, I have had some resounding successes in creating Lit Club pairings; I refer to these as our Lit Club "marriages made in heaven." While the student groups are configured differently each year, almost half of our parent pairs have worked together in prior years, an important element of the program's stability and longevity. Once I'm clear I've created good pairings, I will assign them a group of children that I think will flourish under their leadership.

## BEHIND THE SCENES: CREATING STUDENT GROUPINGS

Nueva has a long history of multiaged classrooms that met the intellectual, social, and emotional needs of gifted children flexibly. With the addition of a middle school and larger lower school homerooms, Nueva converted to single-grade classrooms except for programs like Lit Club, middle school advisories (mixed 5th and 6th grades, and 7th and 8th grades), extracurricular free choices, and weekly academies (interest-driven clubs outside the regular curriculum) in 4th through 8th grades. When our students reach 7th and 8th grades, Lit Club becomes part of the advisory program; currently one hundred students meet with their advisors for weekly discussions. With input from teachers, parents, and the students themselves, I am responsible for creating functioning, cohesive groups in grades 2–6 in which students can develop as individuals and members of a group.

Lit Club affords children the opportunity to practice choosing books that make for good discussion, acquaints them with different genres, and enables them to integrate their reading, writing, speaking, and listening skills within areas of interest. Lit Club enables the library to jump-start reading engagement, amplify community values, and maximize learning beyond the library's walls. My ultimate decisions on placement are based on a sense of a student's ability to profit from an instructional group and to participate productively.

To accomplish this I consider a cluster of criteria: reading ability, speed, preference, and thinking and learning styles. I also look closely at student behaviors and social and emotional considerations such as gender, confidence, and life experiences. Since students remain in the same group for the entire year, I take the time to develop as complete a learner profile as possible. I collaborate with homeroom teachers, advisors, the learning specialist, and the heads of the lower and middle schools to pool knowledge and data about children that I record on three-by-five cards.

Each fall I ask students to profile themselves as readers by reflecting on genres and titles they prefer. Over time fantasy has become hugely popular with all kinds of students, yet there are also a number of students who dislike this genre. In addition to first-hand data about preferences and titles that students have already read, the survey affirms the power of choice and exposes students to the idea that reading may encompass fiction or nonfiction, magazines, newspapers, and online sources. I also ask students to let us know if they see themselves as faster or slower readers.

Initially we sort readers into groups capable of decoding and comprehending selections at about the same "reading level." Since assigning a grade level to a particular text is subject to discrepancies, we use multiple measures including DRA test scores, last year's Lit Club reports, and homeroom reports from the previous and current years. I check in with the current or past homeroom teacher about students I suspect have grown dramatically as readers over the summer as well as those that I worry may be continuing to struggle. We may place weak decoders in a group with competent readers with the understanding that parents will read the selection to the child or provide the book on tape. Or, perhaps, if the child is a slow reader, the parent is more explicitly involved in identifying a regular time and place for the child to complete the homework. I have seen a child who struggles with the decoding process actually relate to the text with greater depth and complexity, and exhibit stronger critical and creative thinking skills than their more adept peers, once the text is decoded.

We don't teach phonics or decoding skills during Lit Club. Nor do we teach dictionary skills. Adult leaders may help a student sound out a word or define it in context, but their primary job is to focus on close reading and meaning-making using skills such as making connections among ideas or texts and seeing the relevance of texts to one's life. That doesn't mean that Lit Club isn't in alignment with classroom reading objectives. For example, I designed a group of 2nd and 3rd graders who needed confidence building before they would choose to read longer books. This group loved the whimsy and wit of Roald Dahl's *The Twits*, *The Enormous Crocodile*, and *James and the Giant Peach*. As they practiced reading and discussing Dahl's shorter pieces, they were building reading stamina for longer and more complex stories.

Teachers and specialists meet frequently during the school year to discuss their students' progress, sort of like IEPs (Individualized Education Plans) for every child, not just students with learning problems. I attend these meetings and keep notes from year to year about issues that could affect a student's growth, either negative or positive. To this I add my own observations over a number of years of a student's general behavior and personality attributes drawn from observations of groups and library visits. I'm interested in the child's attitude toward school tasks, ability to focus in a group, self-esteem, and behavior toward peers and teachers. Is the child independent and perseverant or does the student need step-by-step instructions and regular follow-up? Does this child appear to be "under-achieving" in relation to his or her expected ability? Is this child generally independent? Hard working? Does the student have discernable learning differences that might impact reading achievement in Lit Club?

To gain a three-dimensional view of the child, I seek the advice of the school's social-emotional specialists. Gifted students may be averse to risk and uncomfortable with ambiguity. Others may need peers with whom they already have social and emotional connections. Some children prosper when they interact with older students who are their intellectual peers, while others thrive as leaders when working with students younger than they are. Occasionally, a parent will contact me or the homeroom teacher with input about Lit Club placement. Since traumatic or stressful events have a dramatic impact on learning, I am concerned about anything that might affect a child's successful participation.

I gather data about a student's learning preferences. Sometimes I use that information to form a group of students who need to move around and engage in hand-on activities to focus their attention and work collaboratively. One year I worked with the leaders of a 2nd and 3rd grade group who were discussing *Poppy*, Avi's allegorical fantasy about a small heroine who overcomes the dictator of her community, to design an activity that would channel the physical energy of the group. Students plotted out the setting and action with objects symbolizing ideas or character attributes and created a three-dimensional map of the story during one Lit Club meeting.

I have also grouped highly creative or visual thinkers together and helped leaders design activities in which children can graphically represent their understanding of story, characters, or setting. Assignments with visual options allow less verbally articulate students to share their ideas. For example Figure 13.3 shows a drawing made by a 3rd grader whose massive reading and writing challenges did not prevent her from interpreting a character's view of herself. The assignment suggested that students could use either words (write a diary entry, a dialog between your character and another, or an inner conversation) or visual images to interpret how others saw a character or how the character viewed herself or himself. As we design and evaluate such assignments, leaders learn that they are encouraging visual interpretation, not artistic mastery.

Finally I check for basic balance: Are there positive role models? How many males and females? How many children of each grade, classroom, or advisory group? How many adult- vs. peer-focused children? Toward the end of this process, the lower and middle school heads and executive director review the groupings, bringing their experience with children and families to bear.

Figure 13.3: Drawing by 3rd Grader, Sophie Perl

Sophie
5-22-97
Lit club

Infrequently, I accelerate students beyond their age group. Lit Club is a perfect venue for matching a young child whose reading and thinking skills are sophisticated with intellectual peers who are chronologically older. Sometimes a parent may play a strong role in urging that the school reconsider their child's needs and accomplishments, but ultimately I work closely with our school administration and classroom teachers to choose whether a younger child should be grouped with older children, since social considerations can be as important as intellectual fit.

Last year, I added a 1st grader to a group of high-functioning 2nd graders and a 4th grader to a 5th and 6th grade group based on recommendations from their teachers and administrators. This year, we put a 2nd grader with a 4th grade group after she reported being disappointed that her 2nd and 3rd grade group didn't have opportunities for deeper discussion. When much younger children are accelerated, my charge is to be sure that both the older group and the younger student feel comfortable learning from and with each other. I monitor the group carefully to make sure that the leaders, with my help, choose developmentally appropriate reading material.

When Nueva designed our middle school student-advisory program, Lit Club was tucked under the umbrella of social and emotional learning. Book discussions were to be used by the advisors as a vehicle for students in the same advisory program (who might not be in the same academic classes together) to interact intellectually and emotionally. Given that the groups are formed around a different set of standards, the Lit Club experience in 7th and 8th grades varies as groups are not constituted by either ability or interest, and students are not evaluated. Some advisors (who are also subject teachers) are adept at facilitating literary discussions, but for others, it's a challenge. Book selection can be difficult for teachers whose areas of expertise are outside the humanities. I try to find parent volunteers to co-lead groups with middle school teachers, but we are having increasing difficulty recruiting enough parents. One solution is for me, in collaboration with the middle school humanities teachers, to choose one or two all-group reads and then provide the advisors with questions or talking points to help scaffold their group's productive discussion.

## PROFESSIONAL DEVELOPMENT #1:
## GRAND CONVERSATIONS WORKSHOP

In order to insure the integrity and longevity of a large "extracurricular" program in which many parent volunteers work alongside teachers and other staff, my training must be designed to ground prospective leaders in the program goals and culture. They need to buy in to the common pedagogical assumptions on which the program is based, as well as learn the facilitation techniques that characterize the program.

Literary Club is grounded in two principles:

1. Meaning is created through a continuous, dynamic transaction between the reader and the text (Rosenblatt 1978, 1995).

2. Cooperative discussion results in a synergistic, deeper understanding of a text beyond what one is able to discern alone.

Therefore my professional development goal is to develop Literary Club leaders who can help a child develop a self-image of him- or herself as both a powerful reader and a collaborative learner who is on the road to inquiry and life-long enjoyment of reading.

The original training that Debbie Abilock and I designed and co-led was an all-day professional development workshop called Grand Conversations. It was attended by anyone who wanted to become a Lit Club leader, but it also included experienced leaders who wanted a refresher class, as well as people from other schools who wanted to implement Literary Club programs. I have redesigned this as a four-hour training seminar held in mid-September specifically so that our new leaders understand the big picture: Lit Club's goals and how the program fits into our school culture and curriculum. While the initial training creates a picture and provides some implementation practice, professional development throughout the year will build new and returning leaders' skills and capacities.

## Learners before Leaders

I begin Grand Conversations by inviting new parent volunteers, new teachers, and other new staff to experience Lit Club as readers themselves. We read a provocative adult short story, "The Use of Force" by William Carlos Williams (1984, 56–60), about a rural doctor in the early 20th century who must decide how to deal with a young, uncooperative patient who may have diphtheria. The participants jot down questions as they read, just as leaders might ask students to do. Then I facilitate a discussion, during which we share and group their questions, many of which center on the motivation of the four characters: a father, mother, child, and doctor. There are always a few questions about the story's unusual structure and the undefined setting and time period. Inevitably someone asks a question I've never heard before, a continual reminder to me that there is, indeed, a unique transaction between a reader and a text. By sharing and grouping questions, participants are identifying areas they are interested in discussing, and, inevitably, our conversation begins to take shape. However, since the participants don't know each other yet, they are relatively reserved and watchful.

## Ways of Knowing

Throughout Grand Conversations I emphasize the importance of inquiry—the authentic questions of the reader—as the basis for literature discussions. When children internally question what they read (and good readers often do), they are enacting an imagined dialogue with the author, asking authentic questions that they cannot answer. However since some classroom "discussions" are actually a review of known information or a teacher's oral quiz, children don't necessarily have a model of what makes a good discussion question among peers. If I can train leaders to help children craft thoughtful, open-ended questions that they genuinely want to talk about, their students' Lit Club discussions will become animated and authentic.

In order to create a culture of readers engaged in open-ended inquiry within their group, a facilitator needs techniques that build group process and instill trust among members. As a playful icebreaker, I form adjacent pairs, hand them four flexible, wax-coated colorful "Wikistix," and suggest they form a visual representation of the relationships portrayed in the story. Since manipulating Wikistix doesn't require artistic talent, there is a relaxed camaraderie of learners among learners as participants build and discuss their representation. After I sense that each pair has settled on a particular result (about ten minutes), I ask them to describe their creation to the group while I ask questions about the attributes of their object in order to tease out the ways that one can interpret "relationships" by focusing on visual elements:

- Why did you use that color (or another a physical attribute) to represent that character or emotion?

- What does this show about the characters' interactions?

- How does your creation demonstrate the abstract theme you've identified?

- Can you talk us through the timeline you've shaped?

- How does your object show the setting?

I recorded one team explaining their Wikistix construction (Figure 13.4) as follows:

> We chose to put the child in the center—she's red because she's at the center of all the emotion in the story. The doctor is the link between the parents and the child. We chose yellow for him because it's a hopeful color. The two parents surround the doctor and the child, intending to be supportive of her, but they are not truly connected to her. We turned out the tops of the wikistix to show their disengagement and how they seem to distance themselves from the doctor and child. They're ineffectual.

By using language and strategies that prompt the team to show their collaborative thinking about a nonverbal stimulus, I model for leaders how they can respond to students' visual creations during their own Literacy Club meeting.

Figure 13.4: Two Grand Conversation Participants Explain Their Visual Representation

I am continually gathering both simple and more involved examples of what I call "visual scaffolding" to ground my explanations of teaching strategies to actual practices. For example, I shared a reproduction of a painting of Venice by Canaletto that co-leaders used to help explain Megan Whalen Turner's short story, "Aunt Charlotte and the NGA Portraits" (1995, 45–71), a fantasy about a girl who enters the painting. Or I will read the e-mail of two 5th and 6th grade parent volunteers to their student group, which shows the depth and quality of their preparation for reading John Steinbeck's 1933 novella *The Red Pony*:

> Steinbeck's writing is very rich—almost like poetry. It appears simple, but it conveys many subtle messages. Mark significant words and passages that give you clues about Jody's relationships with the people in his life. Steinbeck also paints beautiful images of the landscape with his words. We are fortunate to live very close to the setting of this novella—on a ranch near the town of Salinas. Feel free to find Salinas, the Galiban Mountains, and Monterey County on Google Maps (or another program of your choice) and look for images on the web. The book is set during the Great Depression of the 1930s.

## Figure 13.5: Asking and Evaluating Types of Questions

| Type | Definition | Example |
|---|---|---|
| Evaluative | Asks for a transaction between the reader's experience and the text. | "Has this happened to you and how did you feel?" |
| Interpretive | Asks for a reasoned response based on evidence within the text. | "What in the story leads you to believe she felt that way?" |
| Rhetorical | Asks for an examination of the author's artistry and craft. | "Why is the story told in alternating chapters?" (structure)<br>"Why does the author repeatedly use that phrase?" (style)<br>"What is the tone of the opening pages?"<br>"What does it mean to say that the 'moon is the North Wind's cookie'?" (figurative language) |
| Metacognitive | Asks for the reader to examine his/her thinking processes and self-regulatory behaviors. | "What did you do to help yourself understand that passage?" |
| Resistant | Asks for the reader to position him/herself outside the text's ethical or social stance. | "Why should Little Red Riding Hood be held responsible for a world in which wolves scheme to attack girls in the woods?" |
| Metaphorical | Asks for a metaphor or image to creatively connect the text and the world. | "What color is this chapter?"<br>"How is this story like a gun?" |
| Factual | Asks for what appears to be simple answer, but which often requires inferencing. | "Why does Jack go up the beanstalk the third time?" |
| Efferent | Asks for nonliterary information. | "What can we learn about the California Indians from *Island of the Blue Dolphins*?"<br>"What does a gold rush town look like in *Adventures of Lucy Whipple*?" |
| Philosophical | Asks for consideration of abstract concepts (nature of courage, nature of intelligence). | "In *The Wizard of Oz*, why does the scarecrow think he doesn't have a brain?" |

From *Growing Schools: Librarians as Professional Developers* edited by Debbie Abilock, Kristin Fontichiaro, and Violet H. Harada. Santa Barbara, CA: Libraries Unlimited. Copyright © 2012.

## Scaffolds, Supports, and Routines

A typical Lit Club homework assignment asks children to read the selection twice, the first time purely for pleasure. During the second reading each child is to write several questions he or she wants to discuss. Novice leaders need a toolbox of practical ways to hone questions, develop consensus on what to discuss, and ways to acknowledge the individual thinking that each student has done at home.

I give leaders a booklet of scaffolds, strategies, and checklists they can use throughout the year. Using "Think about Your Thinking" (Figure 13.6), I model the power of double reading: a quick and pleasurable aesthetic immersion in the story, followed by analytical, close reading. The second reading will enable a student to step back from the power of the story to notice the author's craft, look more closely at ambiguous or confusing elements, or track the breadcrumb clues that mystery authors leave. The checklist reminds leaders of ways to show students how to watch for signals that can be turned into questions.

---

### Figure 13.6: Think about Your Thinking

- Notice when you are confused and ask for clarification.
- Ask yourself what it is you don't know or understand.
- Look for things that can be seen in two or more ways.
- Look for and compare clues.
- Notice when you feel sad, funny, confused—when emotions pop up.
- Think about character motivation.
- Ask yourself if the plot is making sense.
- Ask yourself about the author's purpose.
- Compare things in one story to other stories you have read.
- Listen to the written language for striking words, phrases, and prominent details.

©1998 *Grand Conversations* by Debbie Abilock and Marilyn Kimura. Permission is given to reproduce this as a handout for teaching or training purposes.

---

During a third activity, leaders practice using this bulleted list to develop genuine questions about Leo Lionni's *An Extraordinary Egg* (1994), the story of a friendship between an alligator and some frogs (see Figure 13.3). I ask participants to notice pages that surprise or intrigue them—and put a sticky note on things they would like to know more about in order to understand the story better. After leaders read their notes aloud, they are asked to suggest ways to cluster them. Next we craft a question to represent each cluster. Finally they are ready to vote on a question to discuss it might be the most interesting, the most important, or, perhaps, even their first question.

Figure 13.7: Participants Read *An Extraordinary Egg* in Preparation for the Grand Conversation Discussion

In addition to seeing a strategy for turning individual questions into consensus questions, I want the leaders to understand they can extend an inquiry discussion beyond the content of the story. Therefore I ask why the group has chosen a particular question to lead off the discussion. By prompting metacognition, the thinking about one's own thinking process, I show leaders how they can milk children's questions to move them toward wondering and reflecting about their thinking process. Although Lionni wrote this picture book for children, the story's multiple layers can support a lively adult conversation. After one such discussion, a participant commented, "I found the story sort of boring when I read it. It wasn't until we talked about it together that I realized I had hundreds of questions, and I wasn't bored at all!"

Logistically, if there are six children in a Lit Club and each child brings in three questions, the group has eighteen potential entry points into the discussion. Therefore I quickly outline a number ways to group and refine questions so that the group's inquiry can be both rich and satisfying (Figures 13.8 and 13.9).

## Figure 13.8: Examples of Ways to Group Questions

*The first version of this activity asks each student to think about different aspects of a question they've created for the group to discuss before they bring it to Lit Club.*

Directions for Students:

Choose one question from their homework that is the most discussible and take a position on the question.

1. Fold a piece of paper in half.

2. Record the page number(s) that support the position on the left side.

3. Record the page number(s) that refute the position on the right side.

4. Be prepared to discuss your question using all the evidence you have located.

5. Ask the group to provide additional evidence.

*A variation of this activity asks the entire group to select a common question to discuss. Then, in gradually widening groups, the students discuss all aspects of the question.*

Directions for Students:

1. As a whole group, select a question for discussion.

2. First work by yourself to locate evidence in support of a position on this question.

3. Discuss your findings with your partner.

4. Work with a second pair of students to discuss the evidence you've identified.

5. Be prepared to share your answers and conclusions with the entire group.

The Grand Conversations workshop introduces the Lit Club vocabulary that is used throughout the school. For example, the workshop booklet includes "Asking and Evaluating Types of Questions" (see Figure 13.5) to help leaders identify students' questions during a discussion and over time, the types of questions that each student prefers or avoids. Even the youngest children can label convergent and divergent questions as "skinny" or "fat" *after* they are tested in a discussion if a leader asks, "Why did we have so much to say about this question?"

Figure 13.9: Asking Questions about Questions

- Is this a question with answers in the text? (factual question)
- Is this a question with answers I must find by thinking about the book and my own experiences? (personal or evaluative question)
- Is this a question with no certain answers? (interpretive, metaphorical, or philosophical question)
- Is this a question to clarify meaning? (clarifying question)
- Is this a question about what's coming next or the sequence of events? (predicting question)
- Is this a question about the writer's intentions or voice? (stylistic or aesthetic question)
- Is this a question that pushes against the author's assumptions? (resistant question)

©1998 *Grand Conversations* by Debbie Abilock and Marilyn Kimura. Permission is given to reproduce this as a handout for teaching or training purposes.

How a student begins a question governs the type of thinking that the group will do. Students learn to start with a signal word like "Why" so that they can create a discussable question. One 3rd grade teacher advises: "If you ask 'does,' it will have a yes or no answer. If you ask 'how,' it's open for discussion." Teaching students to select question stems is a way of making explicit the knowledge that students have but cannot yet articulate as a question. For example, although most students have no difficulty *noticing* the voice of author Lemony Snicket in his Series of Unfortunate Events, but they need a frame to help them speculate about the author's tone or choice of words. I suggest that most question starters can relate to the author's craft simply by adding the author's name to the question: "What if Lemony Snicket . . . ?" Over the course of many Lit Club meetings, leaders will become expert at helping students identify types of questions by their effect on a discussion. As students internalize the value of different types of questions, they will learn to orchestrate their own questioning more skillfully.

We know that any well-designed lesson initially engages learners and closes with reflection and self-assessment. Therefore I also describe opening and closing routines. For example, facilitators are asked to open each Lit Club with a general question like "How did it go?" or "What did you think?" I think of these as questions that invite students into the discussion circle and "take the temperature" of the group. If a student hasn't finished the reading, a facilitator can nonjudgmentally move the child outside the circle to finish the reading in class and then rejoin the group. If a student has been disturbed by something in the text, leaders are urged to set aside any planned activity and begin with that issue. I suggest that at the end of class the leaders ask students to reflect on what the group has accomplished:

- How successful were we in seeing different points of view?

- Why did this one question provoke so much discussion?

- Are there other things we might want to do to explore this selection?

## A Fly On the Wall

Although many parents are able to watch teachers when they volunteer in a classroom, facilitation and teaching are not the same. Indeed Lit Club can be hard for adults who are trained as English teachers, especially if they lean toward teaching a certain interpretation of a work. Adults must recast themselves as "a reader among readers," defusing the message that there might be a "right answer" and downplaying their natural position of power among children.

The co-facilitators' role is to create a trusting atmosphere in

### A Reader among Readers

During a heated conversation about *A Wrinkle in Time* by Madeleine L'Engle in a 5th and 6th grade group, in response to a leader's question about evidence the student said, "It's right here on page 220." The leader responded by holding up her book and showing students that she, herself, had highlighted the same passage. As a reader among readers, she could simply share, "I also wondered if this would be significant."

which children develop their own thinking and share their own responses. Throughout the training I provide leaders with transcriptions of sessions (Figures 13.10 and 13.11) and short video clips that show successful and not-so-successful student group discussions that we can analyze.

## Figure 13.10: Transcript from a 3rd and 4th Grade Discussion of "All Ball"

Channing:   "I really don't like this kind of story."

Leader:   "Oh?"

Channing:   "It's not really *about a* ball."

Caroline:   "It's about relationships . . . with the father . . . it's not good."

Channing:   "At the end there's a thin line connected without the ball." (Pause) "I have no idea how I thought that up."

Caroline:   "It's a *good* idea!"

Jake:   "We need to look at the details of why he goes to Korea . . . why they go to Daytona Beach. It was *right* to go because of the war."

Zubin:   "What would have been *better?*"

Sebastian:   "He didn't care about her. Why did he have a child if he didn't care?"

Kelly:   "The ball is like Pandora's box - it contained all the grief until it popped."

© *Grand Conversations* 11/97 Debbie Abilock debbie@abilock.com Marilyn Kimura mkimura@nuevaschool.org

## Learning to be Flexible

Facilitation changes as the year unfolds. At the beginning co-leaders want to create an atmosphere of collaboration and respect so that all students will risk participating. Leaders are cast in the role of traffic control, coaching children into listening and speaking to each other. If they encounter students who feel compelled to offer comments or opinions without waiting for their turn, they can help them practice a "conversation." Do we raise our hands in our group and wait to be called on? Can we learn to anticipate a lull in the conversation and jump in to add our thoughts? Students also need to learn to "piggyback" on a previous comment, to build a conversation rather than simply waiting to contribute the idea in their head. They must learn to disagree respectfully by bringing evidence from the text to the table. Debate is encouraged to reveal many possible points of view, but is never structured to be a win-lose situation.

Grand Conversations can mention but not prepare participants to lead an evolving group over the course of a year. Therefore I have institutionalized a process of giving ongoing feedback to help each pair of leaders reflect on when their group is ready for them to loosen their control. As the year progresses, I expect children to assume greater responsibility for man-

# Figure 13.11: Transcript from a 5th and 6th Grade Discussion of *The View From Saturday*

Readers of E.L. Konigsburg's *The View From Saturday*, a school story told in four alternating voices, need to pay careful attention to character motivation and development to understand the plot. In this transcript the focused co-facitation enables students to look closely at each character, their relationships, and grapple with point of view.

| | |
|---|---|
| Leader 1: | Let's talk some more about Nadia . . . |
| Jeff: | I figured out a contrast between Nadia and Noah. Nadia is a waiter and watcher, Noah is a thinker and doer. |
| Leader 1: | Expand on that a little bit . . . |
| Jeff: | Noah thinks about what he does, and when he finds a good idea that he thinks is capable of making everyone happy, he will do it. Nadia waits for the moment when she's got that leap of courage in her, as she is not a very outgoing, . . . as she is a pretty shy person, not as outgoing as Noah is. |

\* \* \* \* \* \* \* \* \* \*

| | |
|---|---|
| Leader 2: | Can I get back to Jeff's point again? I want to know how you guys respond to that point - support it or disagree with it. Ok, so stick specifically to his point: the idea that Noah is a thinker and doer, and Nadia is a waiter and watcher. |
| Clare: | I think the one thing that's confusing right now is that we are seeing it from a couple of viewpoints. She is not shy with us, but look at the interactions in the book – she is more quiet and shy than she is to us. |
| Leader 2: | Define shy. |
| Alex: | Shy is when someone really wants to say something, but can't do it, because – shy – shy, can't get it out because you're embarrassed. |
| Leader 1: | Ok, does everybody like that definition? Does it seem to be a pretty good definition? Ok, let's go back to Nadia – is Nadia shy by that definition? |
| Clare: | I think she is more quiet than she is shy, but sometimes she can be shy. |
| Leader 1: | Ok, any other thoughts? Who agrees or disagrees? |
| Jeff: | Well, I think Clare is right in the fact that we are seeing it from Nadia's point of view and she may not perceive herself as shy, but if we were looking at this from Margaret's point of view or Ethan's point you'll see that she's not as outgoing . . . |

From *Growing Schools: Librarians as Professional Developers* edited by Debbie Abilock, Kristin Fontichiaro, and Violet H. Harada. Santa Barbara, CA: Libraries Unlimited. Copyright © 2012.

aging the conversation, choosing the reading selections and suggesting activities or changes in the group process. Over the course of many years in Lit Club, students internalize these goals and norms; some Lit Clubs "run themselves."

## Scenarios

Another aspect of flexibility involves being primed to expect challenges. During Grand Conversations I use short scenarios to demonstrate examples of inevitable problems. True stories (with names changed) allow the participants to mentally rehearse what they might do in a similar situation. For example, each year there are a few students who rarely speak in the group at first.

I present the situation of a 2nd grader, new to Lit Club, who listens intently and, as the group disperses, offers a pertinent aside to a leader. I read aloud the actual message his leaders e-mailed me at the time: "After one discussion, John expressed regret. He told us he wished he had shared his ideas during discussion. Because another classmate spoke first, John said, he remained quiet during the meeting."

I ask, "Other than directly confronting the student, how might we encourage participation?"

Leaders brainstorm:

- sit next to a quiet child
- put an arm around or hand on the student's shoulder
- make eye contact and indicate that you're going to address the student
- work to make a special connection just before and just after class
- notify the child explicitly that he or she will be called on next
- say that you'll be calling on students around the circle in order

By discussing practical problems as natural facets of the program, I also convey my expectation that leaders will share their own stories with me and each other during the year, testing their ideas, relating their concerns, and asking their own questions.

I also want to build the capacity of co-leaders to advise each other. We use pairs of leaders so that they can restrain each other during the inevitable moments when one favors a certain child's interpretation or offers their preferred analysis of the selection. Co-leaders can spell each other during a heated discussion or approach facilitation from different angles. If one leader finds certain behaviors challenging, the other leader can step in to work with that child. Practically speaking, of course, working in pairs means that we don't need to worry about finding a substitute when one parent or teacher is sick or at a conference.

## Skills That Enable Powerful Conversations

I delineate the responsibilities for both students and leaders. We expect children to be prepared and to participate. They read the selection twice and bring questions to the group. Since older students may be asked to mark the text, I show examples of how students have annotated their books by underlining, circling words, drawing lines, and using sticky notes in order to develop questions or mark evidence for a discussion.

Leaders are responsible for helping students think more deeply about the content, find evidence to support their ideas, and apply critical or creative thinking as they read and discuss a piece of literature. They are to remind students to look at characters with empathy and keep a flexible attitude and open mind as they read.

## PROFESSIONAL DEVELOPMENT #2: ONGOING TRAINING

### Orientation

The Grand Conversations workshop can be daunting. In spite of assurances that I have a process for getting groups started, I know that some participants will leave the workshop uncertain that they have a handle on what they will be doing when they meet with their student groups. Therefore, during the first week of October, I hold a one-and-a-half-hour orientation for both returning and new leaders. Teachers may leave their classes with a teaching assistant for part of this time or, if they cannot attend, I will catch up to brief them.

I prepare a second packet that includes the Lit Club calendar for the year, their co-leader's name, names of students in their group, and a meeting place. I include a schedule for their first and second meetings (Appendix 13A) that helps them settle groups into familiar patterns of behavior, and materials that summarize important ideas from Grand Conversations (Figure 13.12).

Since I have a broad knowledge of the literature that will be both discussable and appealing, and I know quite a bit about individual children, I include a sure-fire selection for each group to discuss at the first meeting in order to buy leaders some time to learn about their group members before they choose a reading.

I set up a blog for each Lit Club so that students and their parents can get homework assignments and other announcements electronically. Over the last few years I have seen leaders use these blogs to set up assignments, suggest ways to approach the next reading, report an answer to a factual question that needed additional research, and invite students to post early comments and questions as they do their next

## Figure 13.12: Ten Guidelines for Successful Leaders

1. Respect unusual questions and ideas ("divergent thinking").

2. Encourage and model high-level questions.

3. Expect responsible behavior and delineate natural consequences.

4. Build and model respect for others.

5. Do your homework. Set aside planning time with your co-leader to discuss the selection and to communicate concerns and questions about the group, the process, or a particular child.

6. Acknowledge children's work promptly. Research shows that feedback is most useful and powerful when it is given immediately. Some leaders have used sticky notes to make comments within the child's book, in addition to notations on the child's homework.

7. Value the group's work together. Close each meeting with the group's self-assessment of how "we" did today. Did we have many ideas? Was this an interesting discussion?

8. Talk to or e-mail me regularly to elicit or provide teachers with information about children.

9. Call your co-leader if you will be absent, and contact me regarding a substitute.

10. It's OK to tell kids you don't know. Enjoy yourself!

"Reading is a privileged pleasure because each of us enjoys it, quite complexly, in ways not replicable by anyone else. But there is enough structured common ground in the text itself so that we can talk to each other, even sometimes persuade each other about what we read; and that many-voiced conversation, with which, thankfully, we shall never have done, is one of the most gratifying responses to literary creation, second only to reading itself." From Robert Alter's *The Pleasures of Reading in an Ideological Age* (New York: W. W. Norton, 1990, 238).

From *Growing Schools: Librarians as Professional Developers* edited by Debbie Abilock, Kristin Fontichiaro, and Violet H. Harada. Santa Barbara, CA: Libraries Unlimited. Copyright © 2012.

reading, which the leaders use to shape the next discussion. This has been used with great success for one 5th and 6th grade group that had trouble sustaining focus for an hour face-to-face.

Probably the important messages that faculty, staff, and volunteers need to hear at this meeting is that parents are assuming a new role in the school community. Although their friend's child may be in their group, I emphasize that parent leaders should not contact that parent directly with concerns. When questions or concerns arise about a specific child, I have developed a process with classroom teachers and the heads of the lower and upper schools to troubleshoot and problem solve. A Lit Club leader once sheepishly confessed that she had met her friend, parent of one of her Lit Club students, in the parking lot, and blurted out, "What is the matter with your child!?" She confessed, "I couldn't help myself—her child was unprepared for several meetings and I was at the end of my tether." Clearly a better approach for the parent, the child, and the school is that I work with the child's teacher to identify when the teacher can remind this student to do the assigned reading during school or at home.

## Mini Sessions: How We Choose Books for Lit Club

Over the course of the school year I schedule four or five 45-minute sessions right after Lit Clubs to address important topics and practice facilitating both process and content. I use the leader blogs to make a blanket announcement and send out links to materials that are archived electronically. Whether or not there is a mini-PD session, leaders habitually gravitate to the library to socialize or share interests, including what happened in their groups. They may approach other leaders about books they're using or browse the shelves for books their students have suggested. Leaders aim to select three to five paperback titles from which their group will choose one or more to discuss. Lit Club leaders express that book choice is probably the single most difficult and time-consuming part of facilitating their group. However, imagine the effect on a community when over forty teachers, specialists, teaching assistants, academic advisors, and community parent-volunteers are reading and discussing two hundred or more titles cumulatively over the course of a year!

I routinely schedule book shares in which leaders chat about books that went well (or didn't) and we keep an on-going list of paperbacks examples of which are in Figure 13.13, that have been successful in discussions.

## Figure 13.13: Selections That Are Too Good to Miss

Aiken, Joan. "Think of a Word." In *The Last Slice of Rainbow and Other Stories*, 128–144. New York: Harper and Row, 1985.

Avi. *Poppy*. New York: HarperTrophy/HarperCollins, 1995.

Ehrlich, Amy. *When I Was Your Age, Volume One*. Somerville, MA: Candlewick, 1996.

Ellis, Deborah. *The Breadwinner*. Toronto: Groundwood /Douglas & McIntyre, 2000.

Farmer, Nancy. *The House of the Scorpions*. New York: Atheneum/Simon & Schuster, 2002.

Feiffer, Jules. *A Barrel of Laughs, a Vale of Tears*. New York: HarperCollins, 1990.

Lionni, Leo. *An Extraordinary Egg*. New York: Dragonfly/Alfred A. Knopf, 1994.

Rodda, Emily. *Rowan of Rin*. New York: Greenwillow, 2004.

Sachar, Louis. *Holes*. New York: Farrar, Straus and Giroux, 2008.

Satrapi, Marjane. *Persepolis: The Story of a Childhood*. New York: Pantheon, 2004.

Speare, Elizabeth George. *The Sign of the Beaver*. New York: Yearling/Bantam, Doubleday, Dell, 1983.

Steinbeck, John. *The Red Pony*. 1933. Reprint, New York: Penguin, 1993.

Turner, Megan Whalen. "Aunt Charlotte and the NGA Portraits." In *Instead of Three Wishes: Magical Short Stories*, 45–71. New York: Greenwillow, 2006.

Van Draanen, Wendelin. *Flipped*. New York: Borzoi/Knopf, 2001.

White, T[erence] H[anbury]. *The Sword in the Stone*. New York: Philomel, 1993.

---

Informally sharing books with each other helps leaders analyze the character of their group and the potential for using another group's successful selection. "*Flipped* went really well for our [5th and 6th grade] group," said one leader, "because the boys have been lobbying for a boy book and the girls were holding out for a girl main character." A coming-of-age story told in alternating voices, *Flipped* satisfies the needs of both groups because it addresses how the relationship between a boy and girl changes as they enter their teens.

Since teachers don't attend these post-session meetings because they must return to their classrooms, they share their suggestions electronically, as this 7th and 8th grade advisor did:

If you are looking for a good Lit Club book, my group is loving the graphic novel *Persepolis* by Marjane Satrapi. There are some uncanny connections between the Iranian evolution of '79 and what is currently happening in Tunisia and these helped us to have one of our best discussions ever. It turns out my group couldn't put communism and fascism on the left-right political spectrum and really enjoyed learning about this as well.

In case you opt for reading this with your kids, here are some good extension websites. And, hey, there's a movie and we've now got a copy for the library.

Unlike Literature Circles, where books are presented to the class and small groups are formed (and reformed) by the choices they make, I want a consistent group of children to make choices and build a collaborative working relationship over time. Although I already know a great deal of information about the reading interests and abilities of the students, I ask leaders to survey their group for suggestions several times a year. Even if books are not chosen, peers' suggestions will influence pleasure-reading choices.

Based on what I know children have already read in their classrooms or previous Lit Clubs and what the leaders report, I will present co-leaders of a group with ten to twelve titles that are available in paperback. Once selections are made, I order personal copies for the students and leaders from the Lit Club budget. I ask leaders not to use a title if someone in the group has read it. This can become a huge challenge. Recently a leader reported that out of twenty-five potential titles, only three had not been read by someone in the group!

A title read in one Lit Club often sparks interest among others. Last year, we saw a run on Jules Feiffer's whimsical tale of a flawed hero, *A Barrel of Laughs, A Vale of Tears*. Several years ago in our 5th and 6th grade groups, five of our nine groups read Nancy Farmer's compelling dystopian novel, *House of the Scorpions*. When the process goes well, I hear comments like this one from a 3rd grade student: "I like Lit Club because I get to learn about books I never even took a second glance at."

I counsel co-leaders to not take it personally when kids tell them they "hate" a selection, because experience tells us that the books or readings that students dislike engender provocative discussions. I once led a group of 3rd and 4th grade boys who loved sophisticated fantasy. We culminated our year's work with T.H. White's *Sword in the Stone*, the story of Merlin's mentorship of a young Arthur. Students complained weekly that "nothing ever happens" in the story, but my co-leader and I had to chase them out at the end of each hour, still tussling with the lessons Merlin had chosen to guide the future king.

On the other hand, there are genuine mismatches between a child and a specific book. For example, this year, 3rd grade Rebecca's parents reported that her current book, *Rowan of Rin*, a hero's quest fantasy by Emily Rodda, was too difficult for her. A concrete and literal reader, Rebecca was not grasping the thematic content and couldn't keep track of the characters. Rebecca's Lit Club leaders reported that they saw a child with her head on the table, disengaged from the conversation and often seeking to divert the attention of her friends. Rebecca's teacher and I determined that we needed to move Rebecca to a group that was reading shorter, lighter material, and the conversations were more tightly structured, in order for her to feel successful.

Choices must fit the leaders' inclinations as well. I tell leaders not to do a particular title or genre if they, themselves, object to working with it. When Louis Sachar published *Holes*, the story of a boy sent to a work camp for juvenile delinquents, it spread like wildfire among the students. They loved the offbeat characters and zany plot. At the same time, a number of Lit Club leaders professed to hate the story; "It's about child abuse—forcing children to dig holes in the desert all day long as punishment."

## Observations and Feedback

In order for adult learners to grow, they need coaching. Like students, they need specific information to affirm what they are doing well and to reflect on areas to grow or improve. I monitor groups and support leaders continually once Lit Club is underway. I observe as many groups weekly as I can, looking for collaboration between leaders and growth for students. As I observe, I ask myself questions like these:

- Who is facilitating?
- Who is taking notes?
- Do leaders look as if they are enjoying themselves?
- Do leaders make eye contact with individual students?
- What kinds of questions are leaders asking?
- Do the students and leaders appear to be collaborating?
- Do students offer comments backed by evidence?
- Are students making eye contact and responding to each other?
- Is anyone dominating or hiding out?
- Is that quiet or fidgety student focused on the discussion or "spaced out"?
- Does the discussion focus on one subject at a time?
- Does the discussion build or are ideas merely repeated?
- Are leaders using collaborative language?

Some weeks I will pick five or six groups and rotate through them, rapidly assessing the atmosphere and fixing a visual image of the group in my mind. At other times I will target one or two groups and do an in-depth observation, specifically looking at how the discussion develops and assessing the strengths and weaknesses of the group. Am I hearing thoughtful comments from students I know are capable of generating ideas from their reading? Is the discussion truly a conversation, with students working with each other's ideas? When I spend more time observing one group, I transcribe a portion of the conversation to see how ideas develop and grow in a discussion.

For example, during a discussion about the quality of the sophisticated short fantasy story "Think of a Word," from a collection of short stories by noted children's author Joan Aiken (1985, 128–44), I noted evidence that Elissa, a 3rd grader, had recognized the story's complexity. After listening to comments made by various members of the group, she was attempting to synthesize their discussion. I transcribed the following to share with her leaders and teacher as evidence of her growth in thinking and conversational skills: "Going back to about five minutes ago, this story is kind of good from one point of view because it's bringing up a huge conversation about confusement and unconfusement [sic] and what makes sense and what doesn't. So it can add up to a big conversation. So it's one point of view that the story is kind of good."

Afterwards, I meet with co-leaders to debrief these observations. I read the transcript to them and share my notes (Figure 13.14). By working from evidence collected during specific observations, I can help co-leaders apply abstract ideas presented in Grand Conversations to their actual practices within a group. We can identify what is working and pinpoint what they might tweak in order to achieve a better result. Early in the year, when leaders are establishing their group culture, I will frequently point out that the way a group is seated around the table could be a key to growing group cohesion. If two leaders are sitting side-by-side, the visual "weight" of two adults can convey unwonted authority, or that the adults are nervous in the midst of their students! If all the boys sit across from all the girls, the atmosphere can become one of debate instead of collaboration. At another time I might list how the leaders begin questions or word choice so that they hear how small changes effect inquiry (Figure 13.15).

During a forty-five-minute debriefing period each week in the library, I balance feedback sessions about the groups I've observed with other kinds of problem solving, so that I can reflect with leaders on the growth I inevitably see over time in them and their students. Co-leaders may seek a moment to discuss a behavior issue or cognitive question about a particular student. Probably one of the most significant concepts leaders need to understand is not to attribute intent to a behavior. A parent leader complained that 5th grade Adam, who had not been keeping up with the homework, was "lazy

---

### Figure 13.14: Observational Notes on a Discussion of *Watership Down* in a 5th and 6th Grade Group

Group is attentive and alive with discussion about issues in story— lots of smiles, hands up, eye contact with one another.

| | |
|---|---|
| Leader: | Who's the hero here? |
| Amanda: | The whole group is the hero (lists out characteristics and names of rabbits that match). Rabbits are communal animals. |
| Jon: | (Disagrees) It says right here, "What would we do without Big Wig." He's the strength of the group. |
| Cameron: | We forgot the single most important thing about heroes—they have leadership. Hazel has leadership. Fiver has insight, but not leadership. |
| Leader: | Can the hero use the strengths of the others? |

*Question for leaders: Hannah, Ethan, Ginny—silent but watchful. Are they listening?*

---

and uncooperative." After talking with Adam's teacher, it became apparent that Adam was struggling with time management in all his classes and needed major support by his teachers and parents to create a schedule for completing all his work. Working parents may have to leave immediately, so they may wait until they are home to shoot off a quick line or two about each member of their group—concerns, commendations, or observations. I forward this information to teachers or, when appropriate, to an administrator and archive a comprehensive record of all interactions, oral and written.

Transparency goes a long way toward building a culture of learners among learners. Rather than sidestepping an issue, I may ask directly when one leader appears noticeably "on" and the other "off" or if I notice strain between them. Other co-leaders openly seek help in defining an equitable balance of responsibilities. In some teams one leader will assume a role for the entire year—book choice, homework assignments, note taking, and facilitation—while in other groups, co-leaders may rotate those tasks. There is never just one right way to create a working team, just as there are many aspects of an interpretive question. Cultivating a working team takes thought and practice.

---

### Figure 13.15: Words That Set a Tone for Inquiry

Be clear with yourself about the distinction between inquiry (investigation) and interrogation (one right answer, yes or no answer). The more we use inquiry language, the more obvious it becomes that we value a discovery process.

- **Use invitational prompts:** "As you wondered about . . ." "What are your thoughts . . . ?" "How did you . . . ?" "What led you to think about . . . ?"

- **Use conditional language:** "How might you . . . ?" "Is it possible . . . ?" "If you are . . . ?"

- **Use collaborative language:** "How should we . . . ?" "Does our group . . . ?"

- **Use plurals:** Goals, connections, reasons, hunches, answers.

---

Nonetheless there have been times when two leaders realize they don't mesh well. Co-teaching can be tough, and teaching style, as well as adults' perception of children (and each other), can differ enough to cause a breakdown in collaboration. With one set of leaders, I held several problem-solving sessions attempting to help the leaders see each other's point of view about differences that had surfaced. One leader was directive in the discussions, feeling she needed to keep the group tightly controlled in order to stay on topic and progress toward conclusions. The other felt her co-leader stifled the students' insights and limited the conversations. I was unable to help them break down the polarization that had built up over time, and the only solution was for the leaders to agree to disagree. As a result they agreed to alternate leading discussions and taking notes without interacting each week in order to finish out the year together with their group.

For several years, we invited a parent who was a professional videographer to film Lit Club sessions in their entirety every week. I would watch the taped sessions, take notes, and ask the leaders to debrief with me after they had watched the video. When I asked leaders what they saw as they reviewed their tapes, I was often gratified to hear that they identified many of the same strengths and weaknesses in their own facilitation that I had seen. One leader was surprised to see that, just by repeating verbatim a comment made by a child and suggesting ways to follow up, she had deepened the group's discussion. By reviewing the discussion on video, she was able to appreciate the nuances of group dynamics that went unnoticed in the heat of facilitation. I continue to use a video or still camera to document what I'm seeing, but I find that the mechanics of filming keeps me from really "hearing" the conversation and thinking actively about it in the moment.

Over the years this program has accommodated different styles of teaching, various school initiatives, and even larger educational trends by keeping the channels of communication open with teachers. While some teachers whole-heartedly support specialist programs, others are more reluctant to give up class time, especially with struggling students, even if they believe that these programs enrich their students' learning. I have seen a steady trend among the teachers and the administration toward leveling books and emphasizing measurable comprehension skills in classrooms. When teachers look to measure the "right answer," inquiry can be stifled. In order to continue getting teachers' support, I am acutely aware that the program needs to provide teachers with clear evidence their students are making progress in both intellectual and student skills.

## ASSESSMENT, SELF-ASSESSMENT, AND EVALUATIONS

I encourage leaders to give feedback, verbally and in written form, to their students weekly. This can be as simple as allowing five minutes at the end of each session to recap with the students where the discussion went and how successful the process of conversing and exchanging ideas was. Leader Cathy, working with 2nd and 3rd graders on their reading of Elizabeth Speare's *Sign of the Beaver* (1983), asks her students, "Well, how do you think it went for us today? I wonder how many ideas you can remember that helped us understand the relationship between Matt [a thirteen-year-old white boy] and Attean [a Native American boy]?"

At the end of each session many co-leaders collect students' books and materials, write a sticky note commenting on their students' homework or ideas that they generated during the discussion, and return these materials by the end of the morning. They might suggest goals to the child about preparation or participation. One leader, commenting on a noticeable lack of student participation, wrote, "We missed your voice today. We hope you will take the time to catch up on your reading assignments so that you will be fully prepared to join in next week!" Leaders learn from each other's commenting techniques and strategize about documenting children's growth both face-to-face and through e-mail. One leader shared with others that she routinely wrote a short, pithy comment on a sticky note directed to each student, stuck the notes to a single sheet of paper, copied it, and had an archived weekly record of her impressions of her students—invaluable data when it came time for writing her evaluations.

For over twenty years we have used the same rubric (Figure 13.16) with every grade level to identify the key skills and to document how students grow throughout their years in Literary Club.

The leaders fill out a copy of the rubric for each child midyear and at the end of school. While groups will frequently reflect commonalities of thinking styles and cognitive skills because of the placement decisions we've made, students differ radically in their work habits and ability to focus or contribute to conversations. The rubric identifies exceptional cognitive behavior, such as the ability to reason abstractly or to see commonalities across the readings; creative attributes, such as the bringing a divergent point of view to the group's understanding; and social-emotional characteristics, such as respecting others' ideas and building group collaboration.

In addition, leaders in 2nd through 4th grade Lit Clubs write a short narrative evaluation that describes in nonjudgmental language each student's individual strengths and accomplishments, delineates challenges, and suggests attainable goals for growth. Writing evaluations can be challenging for teachers as well as parent volunteers. Who is the audience? Student evaluations are read by the student's classroom teacher, his/her parents or guardians, and hopefully, by the student. Evaluations paint a portrait of engagement shaped by the complexities of the material and the parameters of the group. Often, the fall semester schedule is choppy, interrupted by unexpected events. Therefore I suggest that leaders create a general statement that prefaces their specific comments about individuals, such as this statement prepared for a 2010–2011 second and third grade group:

> "We had only seven Lit Club meetings this semester and are still working with this young group to promote inquiry, and to learn to ask good questions as they read. This semester we have concentrated on the comprehension strategies of schema (making connections to the text), making predictions, and visualizing."

The goal is to create a vivid picture of the year for the child, the parents, and the teachers. When a student reads the evaluation, he or she should recognize the successes and see ways to improve. Parents should recognize their own child within the context of age-appropriate skill acquisition. Classroom teachers should acquire a three-dimensional but focused view of their learners in a different setting. After they finish individual evaluations I suggest that leaders complete the rubric (Figure 13.16) for their group as a whole since it acts as a benchmark for the second semester. By the time evaluations are completed in January, the picture of individual children and the entire group provides a roadmap for the second semester.

## Figure 13.16: Literary Club Rubric Grades 2–8

| | | | | | |
|---|---|---|---|---|---|
| **PREPARATION** Student has read and prepared for discussion. | Rarely observed | Exhibits *variable* reading and preparation for discussion | Exhibits *regular* reading and preparation for discussion | Exhibits *careful* reading and preparation for discussion | Exhibits *thorough* familiarity and *thoughtful* preparation |
| **PARTICIPATION** Student participates in discussion. | Rarely observed | Exhibits *uneven participation* in discussion | Exhibits *consistent participation* in discussion | Exhibits *relevant and reasonable questions and interpretations* in discussion | Exhibits *critical analysis and insightful interpretation* in discussion |
| **EVIDENCE** Student provides evidence that advances the group's understanding in the discussion. | Rarely observed | Locates *factual evidence* in text | Locates *evidence to support an idea* under discussion about the current reading | Uses *evidence* in text *to expand on an idea* or *draw relationships* among ideas across readings | *Consistently* uses evidence in the text to *focus group's understanding* of bigger themes or ideas |
| **INQUIRY** Student asks questions that advance the group's understanding in the discussion. | Rarely observed | Asks *relevant* questions | Asks questions that *provoke* others to respond at a deeper level in the current discussion | Asks questions that *relate* the current discussion to previous discussions | *Consistently* asks questions that *connect* the current discussion to bigger themes or ideas |
| **CONTRIBUTION** Student makes comments that advance the group's understanding in the discussion. | Rarely observed | Makes *relevant* comments | Makes comments that *deepen* the current discussion | *Draws connections* that *relate* the current discussion to previous ones | *Consistently* makes comments that *connect* the current discussion to bigger themes or ideas |
| **ANALYSIS** Student reasons analytically and logically, which deepens the group's inquiry in the discussion. | Rarely observed | Contributes *opinions* and *reactions* | Contributes *reasoned opinions* and *reactions* about the current reading | Contributes *reasoned opinions* that demonstrate *logic* and *relate* one idea to another | *Consistently* offers *reasoned analysis* that *deepens* the group's inquiry |
| **CREATIVITY** Student exhibits creativity, which deepens the group's understanding in the discussion. | Rarely observed | Contributes *creative* comments, images, or responses | Contributes *creativity* and *unique perspectives* to deepen the current discussion | Draws *creative connections* between the current and prior readings | *Consistently* contributes *unique* and *creative* approaches to deepen the group's inquiry |
| **COLLABORATION** Student helps build collaborative culture of the group in the discussion. | Rarely observed | *Focuses* respectfully on discussion | *Builds* on current discussion | *Synthesizes* current and previous discussion, which advances group's progress | Takes a *leadership role* in building group's collaborative search for meaning |

©1998 *Grand Conversations* by Debbie Abilock and Marilyn Kimura. Permission is given to reproduce this as a handout for teaching or training purposes.

From *Growing Schools: Librarians as Professional Developers* edited by Debbie Abilock, Kristin Fontichiaro, and Violet H. Harada. Santa Barbara, CA: Libraries Unlimited. Copyright © 2012.

Lit Club leaders' completed evaluations are considered drafts. I read and edit 126 evaluations for students in grades two, three, and four every winter and spring to assure consistency within each group and throughout the program. I critique each set of rubrics and evaluations in order to help leaders match their narrative to the rubric. My comments help leaders recognize that they cannot "see" motivation, only report on observable behaviors. While leaders can set a goal for a child to "read more slowly" in order to track the rising and falling action in the plot or notice how a character changes, they cannot ask children to "read more deeply" or be "less literal" if they have not facilitated the thinking that enables deeper reading or clarified the steps needed to acquire a skill (Figure 13.17). As leaders reflect together on student accomplishments in light of their abilities, skills, attitudes, and behaviors, they are assessing their own growth as facilitators and teachers.

The process of assessing students has been strengthened and simplified by technology. Leaders of the 2nd through 4th grade groups e-mail their assessments to me along with a completed rubric. After a cycle of editing and formatting, leaders receive final copies via e-mail. The library retains electronic copies and deposits copies in students' permanent files on the school server. Finally, Lit Club evaluations are sent home electronically to parents as part of the midyear and final reports.

Evaluating students gives Literary Club curricular authenticity. When Nueva's middle school was reconfigured to include 5th and 6th graders, the head of the middle school made the decision to drop written evaluations in 5th and 6th grade Lit Clubs to match 7th and 8th grade advisory Lit Clubs that are not assessed. I can see the effects of this lack of accountability. Whereas you would expect that older students' participation would grow stronger and their preparation become more autonomous, frequently I must follow up with advisors to counteract the low priority students give to a once-a-week class. Their attitude, stemming from the "weight" they perceive Lit Club is given, demoralizes the leaders who put their heart into their teaching and undercuts the students who yearn for a more enriching learning experience.

## THE LONGER VIEW

Literary Club serves the needs of many. While some participate to gain insights on their own children, others say that they are gratified that they can help students practice a set of academic skills and lifelong strategies that build inquiring minds and creative thinking. When asked about what was most personally satisfying about facilitating Lit Club, a volunteer who had just completed her first year wrote: "The kids! They are so bright, fun, funny, engaged—it was a pleasure and a privilege to hang out with them this year. I also found the challenge of thinking like a teacher (or attempting to!) a welcomed change from the other volunteer opportunities I generally take on. It felt like an important and valued way to contribute to the Nueva community."

# Figure 13.17: Examples of Student Evaluation Comments That Clarify Responsibility and Scaffold Improvement

**STUDENT IS RESPONSIBLE FOR:**

**Preparation: Reading and other assigned homework**

"Our goal is that _____ come to Lit Club each week having read the material and completed any additional assignments. This will give him the fuel for participating in our discussions."

"We recognize that the amount of Lit Club homework may feel like a lot to _____. We urge her to create a schedule for herself so that she can accomplish her tasks in small increments over the week."

"We suggest that _____ create a system for remembering to bring his book and binder to class each week. This could take the form of a plan book, or a note to himself on his desk or door."

**Participation: Listening attentively to others and adding own voice to conversation**

"Although _____'s comments indicate she is following our discussion, she often looks down as she doodles during class. Making eye contact as she listens and volunteers her insights will help her to have a stronger presence in our group."

"We urge _____ to practice active listening, using attentive body language, making eye contact, and acknowledging and working with the comments of others."

"_____'s enthusiasm can lead her to impulsively talk over or interrupt others."

"_____ is a quiet member of our group who rarely volunteers to join in our discussions. We urge _____ to jump in and add his voice to our collaborative work."

"We challenge _____ to volunteer comments at least 3 times each Lit Club."

"His insightful comments spark good discussion and his enthusiasm acts as a catalyst for our group."

**LEADERS ARE RESPONSIBLE FOR:**

**Facilitating process: Creating safe atmosphere so student can risk participation**

"_____ is a valued member of our group. We notice that when he comments, others listen. We want to hear more from him, and will work with the group to ensure that he has the time and space to contribute."

**Facilitating content: Asking follow-up questions, helping student refine and zero in on insights, thoughts, ideas**

"_____ contributes valuable insights to our discussion. We would like to see her develop her thoughts more fully, and will try to follow up with comments to prod her to go further (or deeper) with her ideas."

"_____ contributes valuable insights to our discussion. We would like to see her develop her thoughts more fully, and will try to give her the time and opportunity to go further (or deeper) with her comments."

From *Growing Schools: Librarians as Professional Developers* edited by Debbie Abilock, Kristin Fontichiaro, and Violet H. Harada. Santa Barbara, CA: Libraries Unlimited. Copyright © 2012.

As education theories and practices change over time, my professional development remains fiercely focused on consistent, long-term goals and simultaneously flexible about choosing and implementing practices. That tension is at the heart of being a community of readers among readers engaged in grand conversations.

## REFERENCES

Alter, Robert. 1990. *The Pleasures of Reading in an Ideological Age.* New York: W.W. Norton.

Rosenblatt, Louise M. 1978. *The Reader, the Text, the Poem: The Transactional Theory of the Literary Work.* Carbondale: Southern Illiniois University Press.

Rosenblatt, Louise M. 1995. *Literature as Exploration.* New York: Modern Language Association.

Williams, William Carlos. 1984. "The Use of Force." In *The Doctor Stories,* compiled by Robert Coles, 56–60. New York: New Directions Books.

---

### From a 9th Grade Alumnae Panel

**Moderator:** "Did you guys feel well prepared [for high school] . . . ?"

**Thomas:** "Lit Club was something I despised at Nueva, but if I had to name a single thing that was really, really helpful, it was Lit Club. Being used to the dynamics of a discussion environment, when to keep silent, and when to share your thinking . . . really helped."

**Natalie:** "I called English 1 'Lit Club with papers'. We would read a book, discuss it, annotate, annotate, annotate and then you go back and write a paper about it. Lit Club really prepared me for English."

# Appendix 13A: Leaders' Checklists

**Checklist 1: First Meeting with Children**

☐ Introductions of children and leaders: create community

☐ Introduce purpose of Lit Club: to discover new books and to enjoy discussing them together

☐ Discuss and brainstorm additional group rules to facilitate process

☐ Brainstorm strategies for remembering to bring:
- Supplies (binder, story, pen or pencil, highlighter)
- Homework

☐ Introduce skills of Lit Club:
- Careful first reading
- Second reading as assigned where appropriate for group, the material, or a particular task
- Dialoging with text as a way to develop questions and mark the path for discussion
- Asking questions that come from real curiosity
- Vocabulary strategies: get from context, look up definition, or ask an adult

☐ Set stage for Lit Club discussions:
- Discussions come from the questions we have
- The role of adults is to help everyone get a chance to speak and to help everyone listen to each other

☐ Ask students to bookshare their favorite titles from their own pleasure reading

☐ Introduce the first selection:
- Set purposes for reading
- Leaders begin reading selection aloud
- Pause to discuss at appropriate places

☐ Assign homework:
- Assign remainder of reading and homework "response," if appropriate, in written form
- Ask students to complete Homework Log
- Ask that parent or guardian read, sign, and return the parent letter to you via the child

☐ After your meeting with children:
- Provide feedback notes to the students
- Prepare written assignment for the following week
- Post assignment on your Lit Club blog

☐   Library will photocopy your short stories or order your books

**Checklist 2: Second Meeting with Children**

☐   Check attendance, homework, and signed parent letter

☐   Inventory students regarding their time management:

- Reward honesty, curiosity, confusion
- Ask for ideas regarding different methods of preparation (reading selection, written work, plan book, binder)

☐   Inventory students regarding the story:

- Explore ideas brought up by assignment
- What might have gone on in their heads as they read (dialoging with text)?
- Did a second reading (if assigned) make reader notice other things?
- Remember to use facilitation techniques

☐   Closure/Resolution:

- "Anything new to add?"
- Summarize discussion
- Acknowledge active listening and thinking
- Evaluate process: "How did we do today?"
- Reevaluate group rules developed at first meeting if necessary

Remember: Lit Club is a place where children feel comfortable in expressing different opinions and where "Rights, Respect, and Responsibility" are valued. Your goal is not agreement on one idea but to develop the group's ability to interact, deeply and thoughtfully, with what they are reading and with each other.

**Checklist 3: After Each Lit Club**

☐   Give out homework:

- Go over written assignment
- Remind students to fill out homework log
- Remind students to bring back signed parent letter if they haven't already

☐   Give feedback promptly:

- Provide feedback notes to students
- Return binders same day
- If you were unable to give out assignment during class, put in students' binders before returning them. (Let them know homework will be put directly in binder)
- Post assignment on your Lit Club blog

# Deliberative Dialogue:
# Changing the PD Discourse

## Nancy Kranich

Like many of you, I yearn for authentic, civil, productive discussions that create and accelerate meaningful change. I simply want to flee when discourse becomes hostile and polarizing or professional dialogue elicits discord and wheel spinning rather than collaboration. This frustration with the state of both political and professional discourse prompted me to seek another way to talk and a different way to act.

Deliberation is a highly structured discussion process moderated by a facilitator in which a group, faced with a difficult problem, weighs the costs and consequences of various options for action. Deliberative dialogue builds the group's capacity to think, talk, and act together as they grapple with tough choices. A facilitator guides participants in developing a shared understanding of critical issues in order to decide on a course of action (Figure 13.18). Unlike rancorous debates, deliberation encourages listening for deeper understanding. Indeed, under facilitated discussion, participants discover that their individual values and concerns overlap with those who hold very different perceptions.

A facilitator uses or develops a discussion guide framed around three or four general approaches, each reflecting a different diagnosis of the problem or conclusion about what should be done. For your initial work with faculty, you might want to experiment with published guides such as ALA's "Who Do I Trust to Protect My Privacy?" (Appendix 13B), which frames one aspect of digital ethics. Other relevant topics for deliberative dialogue that you can create based on this model include evaluating a filtering policy, responding to a challenge to materials, or weighing curricular options.

You will guide your faculty through a discussion of each approach, during which participants see new possibilities, as well as potential costs, consequences, and trade-offs for different courses of action. As the trained and neutral moderator you are a professional leader, helping participants fully understand the impact of various approaches as well as empathetically listening to the experience and circumstances of others. When participants recognize that their most favored approach may inadvertently affect others in negative and unacceptable ways, they learn to take a more inclusive stance. By joining together to peel back an issue, the group reveals the "problem behind the problem," ensuring that one person's solution is not another's curse. Deliberative discussions foster greater understanding, inform decision making, and will help your faculty find common ground for action. And, they let people disagree without being disagreeable.

## Figure 13.18: Moderating a Deliberative Forum

A deliberative discussion:

- Gives each approach a fair hearing;
- Examines the costs and consequences of each approach; and
- Provides a space for trust and respectful listening.

The discussion timeline:

- Welcome, Charge, Ground Rules, and Personal Stake (15% of time)
- Deliberate three or four approaches for equal amounts of time (65% of time)
- Personal and Group Reflections (20% of time)

The moderator's tasks:

- Understands the issue in order to present the overall problem neutrally and each approach in turn.
- Keeps track of time.
- Recruits a recorder who will summarize what people say on a flipchart that everyone can see.
- Makes sure that no person dominates the conversation and everyone participates.

Asks a starter question to turn the work over to the group, such as:

- How has this issue affected you personally?
- When you think about this issue, what concerns you?
- What is appealing about this option or approach?
- What makes this approach a good one—or a bad one?
- How did you come to hold the views you have?
- Lets the group work on the issue by sharing knowledge and perspectives with each other.
- Raises perspectives that the group is avoiding.
- Zeros in on tensions by probing trade-offs.
- Asks what differing viewpoints and positions would mean to everyone if they became policy.
- Listens carefully for shared concerns where people might work cooperatively or in a complementary fashion.

Leads final reflection:

- Considers how people's thinking about the issue has changed.
- Determines if a shared sense of direction or purpose (common ground for action) has emerged.
- Consider tensions, what people were really saying, and what they are still struggling with as a group.
- Weighs which tradeoffs people are willing to make to move in a shared direction.
- Discusses what was learned and what people will do with what they learned during the forum.

Along with the National Issues Forums Institute (NIFI) Teacher's Forum that helps educators integrate deliberative dialogue into K–12 classrooms and the Democracy Imperative that focuses on higher education, the American Library Association Center for Civic Life is committed to building the capacity of librarians to learn these skills. In my own journey in search of more productive civil discourse, I have learned how thoughtful decision making, moderated by an inclusive leader, can solve difficult problems. When colleagues are able to listen to perspectives that are very different from their own and work through the emotions that tough decisions raise, they can make better decisions, participate in and own solutions to common problems, and learn together with civility and mutual respect.

# Appendix 13B. "Who Do I Trust to Protect My Privacy?"

# Who do I trust to protect my privacy?

## What concerns people about privacy?

When asked about their privacy concerns, people responded that privacy is a right necessary to human dignity and individual integrity – a right they consider personal and individual. They often judge privacy within a family and especially between parent and child differently.

Many commented on the gossip culture that pervades media and affects our concept of privacy. Others expressed fear that partial and misinformation will result in them being misjudged. Several people revealed that they use new technologies to learn more about others to protect themselves. At the same time, they recognize that these same new technologies heighten their awareness of privacy implications.

Some say privacy is a lost cause because we no longer know how to protect it. Others question, "What are you trying to hide?" A number were willing to trade privacy for convenience and convenience for security. Still others believe that privacy is connected to financial security, health care, and employment prospects. Those who want government to protect their privacy do not trust the government's intentions or its ability to foil hackers. Though they invoke public safety and national security in opposition to privacy, many recognize security as necessary to protect privacy.

## Approach 1: the marketplace

The marketplace is the source of innovation in security and privacy protection technology and it also has a vested interest in privacy that secures the integrity of financial data.

**Actions to Implement**
- Purchase security measures
- Use spending to reward business that respects privacy
- Use public opinion, boycott against intrusive business
- Adopt and distribute strong company privacy policies and procedures

**Supporters Would Say**
- Innovates to protect privacy
- Keeps up with new threats
- Is motivated to please customers
- ID theft threatens profits

**Opponents Would Say**
- Targeted marketing is invasive
- Data mining is profitable
- Susceptible to government pressure
- Public has limited leverage

**Tradeoffs**
- Savings through targeted sales
- Escalating security expense

## Approach 2: the government

The government has a responsibility to provide for public safety which includes identity protection and to secure the rights necessary to a free society.

**Actions to Implement**
- Set up an office like Canada
- Use courts to enforce checks/balances
- Enact comprehensive legislation that protects privacy
- Publicize existing privacy laws and regulations

**Supporters Would Say**
- HIPAA, library, financial, and other confidentiality laws protect privacy
- Privacy implied in First Amendment
- Protecting rights is a government role
- Clarifies public value for public servants

**Opponents Would Say**
- No universal definition of what's private
- Susceptible to demagoguery
- Cannot keep up with changing threats
- Always tempted by secrecy

**Tradeoffs**
- Public safety & national security
- Complex bureaucratic rules

## Approach 3: my self

I, my self, recognize that privacy values are individual and varied and that no one cares more about my needs than me.

**Actions to Implement**
- Monitor personal credit, stay informed
- Join privacy organizations to demand transparent processes
- Pay cash, avoid EZ-Pass
- Opt out of participating in data collection when possible

**Supporters Would Say**
- "Who will watch the watchers?"
- Privacy desires vary among individuals
- Individual carelessness is main threat
- I'm the only one who can detect/correct errors or theft

**Opponents Would Say**
- Too hard, too much work
- Public is lazy, won't demand privacy
- Individuals powerless and ignorant
- Can never be sure you're safe

**Tradeoffs**
- Time, effort, and inconvenience
- No one to blame but self

From *Growing Schools: Librarians as Professional Developers* edited by Debbie Abilock, Kristin Fontichiaro, and Violet H. Harada. Santa Barbara, CA: Libraries Unlimited. Copyright © 2012.

# CHAPTER 14
# GROWING INFORMATION
# LITERACY SCHOOL-WIDE

*Editors' Note:* In a nondenominational independent school in Silicon Valley (CA), the library director and site-based librarians gain administrative support to create a whole-school initiative that positions information literacy as essential learning for every student from kindergarten through high school. Then a faculty team, representing all curricular areas in the school, designs and implements a process for identifying and incorporating relevant information literacy skills into disciplinary content classroom-by-classroom. After seven years of sustained work and focused goal setting, the school community sees the librarians as their key professional developers, facilitators of PLC groups, and valued co-teachers and learners among their peers.

## Professional Learning Communities in an Information Literacy Odyssey

### Susan Smith

## THE SCHOOL CONTEXT

School librarians often teach only as invited by classroom teachers to collaborate on discrete projects; however, under the right leadership and with a capable faculty, the library program can become a catalyst for curricular change. Such has been our experience at the Harker School. Our K–12 independent college prep school in the heart of Silicon Valley, now the largest independent school in California, is a nonsectarian, college-preparatory, K–12 school with approximately 1,800 students and 200 faculty members. The school is descended from Miss Harker's School and Manzanita Hall, two "feeder schools" for Stanford University dating back to the turn of the 20th century. The school program features a traditional content-packed curriculum with conventional assessments, including extensive Advanced Placement (AP) offerings. The library program similarly has traditional roots that include storytelling, creative dramatics, and basic library skills. Our high school program was added in the late 1990s, providing an impetus to update the program to prepare students for an increasingly complex information universe. The student population reflects the rich diversity of Silicon Valley.

## AN INFORMATION LITERACY INITIATIVE

In 2004 the previous library director, Enid Davis, had a vision for a school-wide information literacy initiative that would be developed in departmental professional learning communities (PLCs) led by a team of librarians and instructional technology teachers in this technology-rich school environment. Through strategic thinking and hard work Davis had grown the program from a single campus K–8 library to three campus libraries staffed with professional librarians and support staff, in order to begin the outreach she imagined. The school also hired a director of instructional technology, Dan Hudkins, who placed learning ahead of the technology and yet saw the value of using 21st-century tools to promote learning. Recognizing that the information literacy initiative would require the understanding and backing of her administrators, Davis began by interviewing lower school teachers to gather data about the problems they faced in teaching research projects in language arts and social studies. Armed with an expansive list of issues ranging from identifying what is important to include in a paper, to how to take notes, to finding appropriate information, she gained approval from our head of school for the creation of a K–12 Information Literacy Committee, composed of the library director; director of instructional technology; the lower school, middle school, and upper school librarians (including the author); and the academic dean of curriculum, charged with creating and implementing a systematic approach to the research process.

As the campus librarian at the upper school, I had just completed my MLIS from San Jose State University after spending twenty-three years in the electronics industry, working in a company that used Deming's quality circles and continuous improvement process (Plan, Do, Check, Act) to manufacture high-quality components. Now in education, it seemed clear to me that we needed to develop a similar approach to quality control that would ensure that every student graduated with the same set of information literacy skills, regardless of the teachers they had or the courses they chose. However, we lacked an information curriculum or a methodology to teach every student within each discipline to find, evaluate, and use information. This provided the motivation to create a more collaborative teaching environment.

When we embarked on this journey, students in grades 5–12 received library skills instruction if and when teachers solicited our help, usually when they needed supplemental resources. We ran a fixed schedule in the lower school, where our K–4 students had one library period each week that included library skills, creative dramatics, storytelling, and genre studies. Individual teachers had their annual research projects, but information literacy instruction varied widely depending on a student's classroom teacher or, in the upper school, their course of study. As librarians we know that 21st-century learners must be prepared to find, evaluate, and use information in all of its forms, in order to achieve success at college and indeed, to be lifelong learners; an inconsistent approach was simply not good enough.

## TOWARD A COMMON UNDERSTANDING OF INFORMATION LITERACY

When we began our information literacy initiative, our focus was on finding a way to map the curriculum, or at least the projects or units that already included opportunities to teach information literacy skills. Since we didn't have a curriculum map, we decided that interviewing teachers—especially in language arts, social studies, and science, could be a first step. Davis's exploratory interviews at the lower school exposed some disconnects between and among grade level expectations, for example, a 5th grade social studies teacher might expect incoming students to understand how to cite sources, but the introduction of the skill was not in the 4th grade curriculum, so it may have been introduced by one teacher but not by others.

It was clear that initially, our faculty did not understand what information literacy was. As we contemplated how to begin our information literacy initiative, the "to do list" seemed endless, and concerns abounded. We chose to begin with three objectives: 1) figure out a K–12 scope and sequence, 2) identify a methodology we could use to teach it, and 3) survey the faculty about what they thought the students knew based on what they were teaching.

The scope and sequence would help us define exactly what skills we would teach, and later we would determine how we would teach it. Working from the California School Library Association's scope and sequence (Abilock 2004), the Information Literacy Committee prioritized and adapted key skills that fit the existing Harker curriculum and could be mastered by a Harker graduate; this became the "what." While the scope and sequence defined the skills, it was rife with information science terminology that was not intuitive to teachers. Since the committee did not have an inventory of school-wide projects, we could not determine where and how the required skills could be taught. We briefly considered a departure into curriculum mapping, but after some cursory evaluation of the current research and available products, the administration decided that the return on investment for the faculty was low. We were back where we started, asking "How can we help the faculty understand what we want to help them teach?"

Unlike subject teachers, we did not have our own curriculum. Even if we had an information literacy curriculum, other than in grades K–4, librarians lacked predictable access to students in order to teach it. We realized that we could not be successful unless we connected the need for information literacy with learning objectives teachers already understood. In order to understand the gaps, we needed to identify where information literacy skills were taught, with or without librarians, through existing projects. Then we needed to convince the K–12 faculty to work collaboratively with the librarians and information technologists to teach these skills seamlessly across the curriculum. This would inevitably require professional development.

A common vocabulary and a framework were needed. We had to help teachers understand how accessing, evaluating, and synthesizing information could improve student learning. The committee began by surveying the teachers about where they thought they were teaching information literacy skills. We did this at one of our annual faculty retreats, when we were given ninety minutes to survey teachers in their department breakout groups. We provided them with a list of selected skills from our newly adapted scope and sequence, and asked them to indicate whether, in their grade and course, the skill was introduced, reinforced, or mastered the skill. Teachers could also indicate if they felt a skill was neither taught nor practiced in their course. Even though this approach was indirect—teachers reported only what they thought students knew—and lacked any direct assessment of students' abilities, it raised consciousness among faculty about information literacy and initiated discussion of department-specific information literacy skills. Librarians were available during the survey to answer questions like "What is a Boolean operator?" and teachers were encouraged to ask about skills they did not understand. We began to build a common vocabulary of key terms.

Shortly thereafter, we selected the Big6™ information problem-solving model as a framework, which helped us develop a common understanding about the process steps. While the Big6™ for elementary and above and Super3™ for primary students do not incorporate all of the curricular skills and values we defined (e.g., the ethical use or appreciation of literature), the strength of its information problem-solving methodology and excellent promotional materials made it an easy choice to begin our campaign to roll out information literacy to our community (Eisenberg 2011). We purchased Big6™ and Super3™ posters, videos, bookmarks, and workbooks to help everyone learn the steps and use the same terms when communicating with students and each other. Davis, who excels at writing parody, even composed a song incorporating the steps for our elementary division, which was published on the Big6™ website (http://www.big6.com/2006/12/10/sing-a-song-of-research-turning-the-big6-into-a-tune/).

## THE LIBRARIANS' ROLE IN PROFESSIONAL DEVELOPMENT

As the upper school campus librarian and charter member of the Steering Committee, I did not initially foresee a professional development component as critical to our success. It simply grew out of my desire to comprehensively teach information skills to our students. I was frustrated with the historically uneven approach to information literacy that depended on in-dividual teachers coming to the library or librarians, asking us to help with classroom projects. Students' experience with information literacy instruc-tion was a function of the teachers or projects they were given, rather than an integral and consistent element of the curriculum. Our students were getting into elite colleges that would expect them to be able to conduct independent research, craft an argument, and write thesis-driven research papers.

I knew by this time that professional development was valued at Hark-er, but I did not initially see the Library Department as playing a particu-larly strategic role. Other than the obvious responsibility to introduce new information products and tools to teachers, I did not picture librarians as leaders of any broader initiatives. However, the work on information lit-eracy in the first two years put the librarians face to face with a professional development challenge with our faculty.

Professional development is a priority for administrators who value their teachers. Every teacher and staff member at Harker, whether full- or part-time, is given a professional development budget each year, with the expectation that it be used. Jenifer Gargano, our assistant head of school, promotes professional education each year by disseminating information on general education workshops as well as discipline-specific seminars. She defines professional development broadly, believing that teachers must be free to decide how they will grow best. Gargano describes her professional development philosophy as combining the best of three types of opportunities for teachers: (1) external workshops, (2) top-down obser-vation and evaluations by department chairs and administrators, and (3) inside resources such as librarians, instructional technologists, and global education specialists along with peer observation. While she recognizes the importance of conferences and seminars, Gargano believes the richest experiences often come from sharing within our own school community: "Teachers must model life-long learning; there is no place for teachers who are content to stand still!"

Each Harker teacher develops his or her own professional goal for the year, including a project plan to ensure completion, and submits it to the department chair. These goals must relate to the school's expected school-wide learning results, and department members can choose to align their goals for the year, under a broader objective. These goals can remain con-fidential between teacher and department chair, or be shared with all de-partment members, which is particularly useful when a goal shared by multiple teachers can create synergies. A professional goal can be as gen-eral as "improving my repertoire of warm-up exercises" or as specific as "publishing an article on our summer reading program in a professional library journal." Goals set by librarians have included topics as varied as how to facilitate conflict resolution, e-book collection development strat-egies, media literacy curricula, and integrating Web 2.0 tools for library instruction. While teachers are commended on presentations and publications they produce, neither is expected nor required. Teachers are encouraged to pursue their passions and improve their professional practice in ways that are most stimulating to them as individuals. Every year a few teachers now choose as their goal the integration of information literacy into their teaching and select a librarian to help them with project design and instruction.

In addition to personal goals, each February the entire K–12 faculty gathers for a one-day "retreat" when Gargano hosts a nationally acclaimed keynote speaker followed by breakout sessions to discuss how we might apply the material in our teaching or within the school community. Faculty-taught workshops are often included, where we learn from each other about new tools or pedagogical approaches in a discipline. Peer sharing is further reinforced when division heads ask teachers to observe two other teachers—in disciplines other than their own—at least once during the year. Yet another opportunity to share is at the Instructional Technology Department's Summer Institute, held each June. Harker teachers present new tools or strategies and submit topics throughout the year. Harker librarians participate as presenters every year. These diverse professional development activities contribute to an atmosphere of collegial cooperation.

## FINDING OUR PROFESSIONAL DEVELOPMENT ROLE

In the second year of the initiative, Davis had expanded the Steering Committee to include interested teachers of science, music, history, and English, who brought an understanding of their subject areas. We now had assembled a "critical mass" of teachers interested in infusing information literacy into curriculum. In the third year we created campus committees in the lower, middle, and upper schools, under the leadership of its campus librarian. The Information Literacy Steering Committee now consisted of the library director, instructional technology director, the academic dean, and me, the librarian on the upper school campus. By this time we had hired a second full-time librarian, Lauri Vaughan, for the upper school. With the Campus Information Literacy committees in place, the Steering Committee was now free to spearhead such initiatives as developing a scope and sequence for paraphrasing as it relates to plagiarism prevention, or other projects that span more than one division or that require administrative approval or K–12 faculty meeting time. On the other hand, the lower, middle, and upper campus Information Literacy Committees were free to study the age-appropriate skills, identify best practices, and discuss deficits they observed among students in their division. As requested, Harker librarians began to conduct short subject-specific workshops on information literacy skills (e.g., how to teach image citation, introduction to new subscription databases, or new features of NoodleTools) during the staff development days of fall orientation. In subsequent years, these sessions have been used by departments to refine their information literacy goals for the year, perhaps deciding to emphasize a particular skill like source evaluation, over another skill that seems to have been mastered.

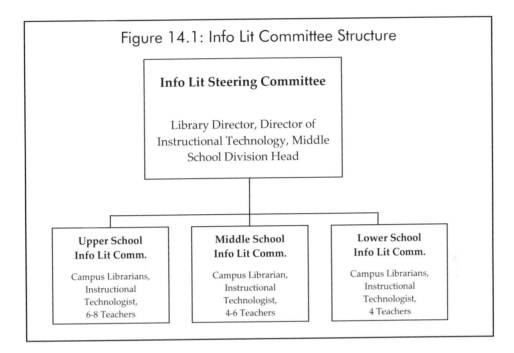

Figure 14.1: Info Lit Committee Structure

**Info Lit Steering Committee**

Library Director, Director of Instructional Technology, Middle School Division Head

**Upper School Info Lit Comm.**

Campus Librarians, Instructional Technologist, 6-8 Teachers

**Middle School Info Lit Comm.**

Campus Librarian, Instructional Technologist, 4-6 Teachers

**Lower School Info Lit Comm.**

Campus Librarians, Instructional Technologist, 4 Teachers

We had begun to institute changes, but still had not directly assessed our students. We lacked a baseline from which to measure our progress with students, and there were few tools available. At the time, Educational Testing Service was introducing their ETS iSkills™ Assessment, which we evaluated for use with our high school students. Technical considerations and logistics led us to look for other options, and we ultimately chose to determine baseline proficiencies of our 6th and 9th graders using the no-cost TRAILS: Tool for Real-time Assessment of Information Literacy Skills (http://www.trails-9.org/) developed at Kent State. While we would have preferred a more authentic scenario-based instrument, the TRAILS results allowed us to identify strengths and weaknesses of our students at these two grade levels. We asked faculty to take this online test as well, so that they could better understand what was expected of their students. History and social studies teachers gave us class time to administer the tests and also took the test themselves. They were given feedback about their own scores as well as the aggregate scores of their students. By this time the faculty, having realized the limits of their own understanding, were anxious to learn more about how to teach these valuable skills to their students. Another professional development opportunity was born!

Teachers increasingly began to solicit librarian assistance with projects. An open dialogue grew between teachers and librarians, and teachers began to trust that librarians would work as full partners in design, instruction, and assessment. Requests for collaboration came pouring in! Teachers seemed to be eager to incorporate what they saw as essential skills and now felt comfortable asking for help. They began to see us as partners in instruction and allowed us to develop and score our own assessments to be included in the final project grades. For example, what had previously been a simple 3rd grade report on a famous African-American woman in history could now be infused with web evaluation and database search skills that culminated in a critical thinking question about legacies of these important figures in history. At the high school level, a 12th grade term paper on a modern international issue was transformed into a policy position paper that required evaluation of international and alternative media sources with consideration of bias and perspective.

Quantifying librarians' contributions to student learning is critical, especially to administrators. Each librarian tracks his or her collaborations using a simple Excel spreadsheet that includes subject, teacher, and time spent on preparation, teaching, and assessment. Tracking yearly increases in collaborative activity continues to help justify staffing. As we became more involved in the planning of the projects from start to finish, the librarians were able to use their instructional design expertise to co-create engaging lessons and identify specific information literacy learning objectives for each step of the process, determine which skills can be best practiced through each assignment, and help teachers construct better rubrics. We found that improving task definition alone (Step 1 of the Big6™) improved the quality of the projects, particularly in a collaborative environment when teachers and librarians had to agree on components such as how many primary, secondary, or scholarly sources should be used. It forced us to be clear about specific requirements for a successful project. Similarly, we developed models for project elements like detailed outlines and annotated bibliographies so that students saw the end-state. Planning sessions with teachers at the beginning of the semester began to supplant those "hallway meetings" just before the lesson was taught. Together we determined project timelines and milestone assessments. Participating at this level in lesson design continues to be one of the most gratifying aspects of our collaborations.

## SO HOW WERE WE DOING?

As librarians, we wanted to know how the teachers were experiencing our newfound partnerships, so my colleague, Lauri Vaughan, and I created a collaborative evaluation worksheet to review with teachers what worked and didn't work. We asked: "Did the library have enough resources to support this project?" "Did the librarian's instruction add value to the unit?" "What should we change when we do this next year?" Now we are asking students these same questions. We use this input to revise future lessons, buy better resources, and refine our teaching techniques. This helps formalize our continuous improvement process; teachers expect us to want to "autopsy" each collaboration (Figure 14.2), and their assumption is that we would repeat the project the next year, even if in a completely revised form.

## Figure 14.2: Harker Upper School Library Collaboration Plan

| **The BIG 6™**<br>http://www.big6<br>.com/index.php | Teacher: | Librarian: |
|---|---|---|
| | Class: | Today's Date: |

| | Lesson Title or Description w/ Objective: |
|---|---|
| **1** task definition<br><br>**2** information seeking strategies<br><br>**3** location and access<br><br>**4** use of information<br><br>**5** synthesis<br><br>**6** evaluation | Project Description (circle):  Paper  Presentation  Web Page<br>Other<br><br>Length:<br><br>Due Date:<br><br>Minimum of Number of Sources:<br><br>Source type(s): (circle)  books   articles   scholarly websites<br><br>NoodleTools required? (circle):  Yes    No<br><br>Notecards required? (circle):  Yes    No<br><br>Was a rubric given to the students? (circle):  Yes    No |

| | Preparation or Activity  (Check all that apply.) | # of hours |
|---|---|---|
| | Discuss objectives and needs with the teacher: | |
| | Prepare a list or sources for the teacher: | |
| | Prepare a lesson for the students: | |
| | Select books for student use: | |
| | Prepare a pathfinder: | |
| | Conduct research on behalf of a teacher or class: | |
| | Select titles for purchase on behalf of a teacher: | |
| | Assess student work: | |
| | Other: | |
| | Total Hours: | |

continued on page 312

From *Growing Schools: Librarians as Professional Developers* edited by Debbie Abilock, Kristin Fontichiaro, and Violet H. Harada. Santa Barbara, CA: Libraries Unlimited. Copyright © 2012.

Activities:

Assessment:

Lesson materials used or created:

## Collaboration Evaluation

What worked well in this lesson/unit?

Suggestions for improvement:

Was this lesson/unit enhanced by collaboration? Yes/No/Why?

Was the lesson/unit successful enough to warrant doing it again in the future?

How well did the library <u>collection</u> support the unit objectives?

Scale: 5=excellent   4=above average   3=average   2=below average   1=poor

Enough materials for entire class? _____

Quality of resources? _____

Variety of formats (electronic/print/media)? _____

Reading level appropriate to students? _____

Comments:

Collaboration content adapted from David V. Loertscher and Douglas Achterman, *Increasing Academic Achievement Through the Library Media Center: A Guide for Teachers.* Salt Lake City: Hi Willow Research, 2003.
The "Big6™" is copyright © (1987) Michael B. Eisenberg and Robert E. Berkowitz. http://www.big6.com.

One experience is particularly memorable for me. In the first year of our information literacy initiative I taught a one-period lesson on research skills in a senior elective on international issues. The teacher, Ramsay Westgate, told me I delivered too much material; I needed to slow it down and let the kids practice each skill. I knew he was right; I had a seventy-five minute PowerPoint presentation that must have felt to the students like a graduate-level search class. After several semesters working with him, and several collaborative reviews, I admitted to Westgate that I was initially afraid I wouldn't see the kids beyond a "one-shot" lesson, so I threw everything I knew at them in hopes they'd be armed to write his ten-page paper! Westgate, who had wanted to increase the emphasis on the research component of this course but did not feel qualified to teach advanced skills, revised his lectures and course content to allow the students to have class time to practice the advanced search skills I teach, like evaluating new information formats and identifying bias and perspective within complex and controversial international issues. At Back to School day he has grown accustomed to introducing me to parents as his "co-pilot" as I teach six to eight class periods with him each semester.

As our initiative expanded, we became busier. When my fellow upper school librarian, Lauri Vaughan, and I crossed paths between classes, we shared our successes and failures as we experimented with new lessons, she mostly in English classes and I in history. We kept a notebook (Figure 14.3) we titled "Info Lit A-ha's" to record our reflections. For example, when one of us noticed how search behaviors seemed to differ when students were presented with electronic reference formats, we developed a presentation to faculty on how teachers and librarians must recontextualize sources for students who are faced with, in effect, miscellaneous results from a keyword search.

As time permitted, we would revisit our observations. For example, we once revised a game she created to make searching different resource "containers" (e.g., the open web, subscription databases, Google Scholar, library catalogs) to make it more competitive and fun by dividing students into teams, timing them, and adding a collaborative bibliography as a culminating group project; we called the lesson "The Race for the Perfect Source!" Although this was the first time either of us had journaled professionally, we felt this accelerated our learning and ultimately helped us to develop a core set of lessons on information access, bibliographic citation, and annotation that we could customize to various courses.

The Campus Information Literacy Committees grew as interest among the faculty grew; librarians also recruited new members strategically, so that more departments were represented. Teachers met twice a year to discuss issues and specific skills that would be targeted at the divisional level. Increased teacher participation on the Campus Information Literacy Committees meant that discussions about information literacy carried over to department meetings, so some departments moved toward developing a discipline-specific information scope and sequence.

## Figure 14.3: Excerpts from Professional Journaling between Lauri Vaughan and Susan Smith

Vaughan 11/8/2006: "Why did Noodle Tools notecards work so well in Susan Nace's [Study of Music] class and not in Mailien Nguyen's [US History] class? Some guesses:

- Music students were given more time to complete them.

- Music students selected their own topics; more buy-in on the front end?

- Susan Nace sent students urgent reminders reminding them of the point value of the notecard assignment.

- The research process in Study of Music has been broken into a greater number of smaller "packages."

Smith 11/4/2007: "Maybe we need to sue more class time for 'labs' instead of lecture, especially for discerning scholarly journals from the rest [of the sources]. Deemphasizing the editorial process in favor of tactical strategies like 'Look for the long titles' or 'titles that start with "The Journal of . . . "'."

Smith 2/7/2007: "After reading Judi Moreillon's article 'Two Heads Are Better Interventions During Participants' Pre-service Education' and suggestions for collaboration, I am thinking about how free choice topics do not <u>ensure</u> that the student asks an essential question. In fact, perhaps that is not what students should be asked to do in 9th or 10th grade. Essential questions are abstract, conceptual, and require a deep understanding of the topic."

Vaughan 10/22/2008: "We are beginning to specialize our instruction—not so much for content area of discipline (which we've always done)—but for the most necessary elements a class needs for a particular project. Most of our instruction so far this year (and it's still early) is less 'throw the kitchen sink at them' and more depth on particular skill sets. Along with that, I think we are developing lesson plans that deal with more abstract elements of research, e.g., search term identification and paraphrasing. We still find information about the concrete aspects powerful (Boolean, limiters, citation, etc.)."

Although the campus committees continue to establish their own annual agendas for each division, the Steering Committee can see that discipline-specific information literacy initiatives will evolve uniquely, perhaps guided only by the Steering Committee. Each department would focus on skills best taught within its discipline, e.g., science would focus on searching citation and abstract databases, or English might address literary criticism as secondary sources. With oversight from the Steering Committee, we believe all information literacy skills can be taught seamlessly across disciplines, K–12.

Our three campus instructional technologists and their director, Dan Hudkins, participate on the campus committees and also play an important role in supporting information literacy. Their role is to discover and test 21st-century tools for teachers to employ in the classroom. They recently began to develop their own scope and sequence to teach a range of applications, patterned after the process we used for information literacy. Hudkins's vision has always been to use technology to improve learning outcomes; he sees technology as primarily a tool for learning. Although we are known as a science and technology school, our enthusiasm for the latest tools is tempered by sound consideration of how they increase motivation or overall understanding of the material. The teacher, librarian, and information technologist function as a team: the teacher presents the content, the librarian helps to design and teach information-rich inquiry-based projects, and the information technologist introduces tools to heighten motivation and develop effective production. This approach makes the most of our joint expertise, and provides students with engaging learning opportunities.

## OUR FIRST PROFESSIONAL LEARNING COMMUNITY

The first of the departmental initiatives involved the upper school history department; this became our first Professional Learning Community (PLC). The history department was a likely place to begin since many of our traditional research projects were already being assigned by its teachers. Donna Gilbert, the upper school history department chair, felt that multiple iterations of the required junior year research paper assignment had all met with disappointing results; students consulted weak sources, didn't cite properly, and the burden of dealing with suspected plagiarism had worn the teachers down. She felt it was "time to take responsibility for teaching kids how to research properly." A recent information literacy workshop by the librarians coincidentally occurred at the same time that the school approved a three-year history requirement for graduation, planting the seeds for reform. Gilbert remembers thinking, "I knew that we needed to develop a more carefully articulated set of skills into a scope and sequence, and that research is the foundation for the entire discipline of history, not just a construct but the staple ingredient."

We began with a systematic evaluation of all current projects and term papers in light of what history teachers had identified as the discipline's critical information skills—source selection and evaluation of sources. I was invited to department meetings where information literacy and its component skills were on the agenda. Although previous information literacy lessons had been related to each assignment's content (e.g., which databases to choose for a debate about individual civil liberties vs. national security and how to search them), we learned from the teachers that students did not transfer what they learned from these assignments to longer essays, papers, or projects. The team concluded that these small changes in pedagogy weren't making much of a difference in learning. Our nascent PLC was grappling with how to more effectively teach research skills and writing in history. In order to teach students to authentically research and write thesis-driven papers, we knew that ultimately we needed to give students more time both in and out of class, to learn the requisite skills.

Over the course of many discussions with teachers, we jointly recognized that bigger changes in how we taught research skills were going to involve real time trade-offs. If we were going to have the time to teach the research process effectively, individual faculty members would have to give up some unique projects that they loved, for example, a contemporary African newspaper project that had become a staple of the Modern World History course and a favorite among students. Finally, at one meeting, a world history teacher said, "You can't learn how to write a research paper unless you do a research paper—start to finish." This was the turning point; the department agreed that they all would teach the entire research process explicitly through one paper each year, so students could practice and hone these skills. I really respect the teachers for deciding to assign research projects; this would mean making tough decisions on other projects and content and the additional work of grading all the papers every year. I assured them I would help teach the process, and create and assess the milestone assignments like bibliographies, outlines, and annotations. Some teachers had never taught research skills before. Gilbert herself admitted, "I know I needed a refresher course on contemporary research procedures and strategies since many of us last did serious research in the 80s or 90s, and in a variety of other disciplines." Others had reservations about the increased time and burden of grading papers. Still others were so concerned about the content they had to cover that they really believed there was no time for such assignments.

Over the course of the next two years, course content concessions were made as I advocated for more deep research within our otherwise traditional curriculum. I forwarded articles suggesting the importance of student choice to foster intrinsic motivation, and teachers began to understand that teaching the research process effectively meant that class time must be devoted to guided searching on topics of individual interest, to practicing writing, to facilitating thesis statement discussions, and to collaborating on products like group bibliographies and concept maps.

The teachers discovered that coaching students through a research paper could be implemented in a variety of ways, each with its own advantages and problems. For example, the 9th and 10th grade history teachers decided to spread the process out over five months (October–March) to minimize the impact on the existing curriculum. For 9th grade World History I classes, students could choose one of five compare-and-contrast questions created by the teachers and librarian that involved topics that they had either already covered or that would be studied later in the course. World History II classes in 10th grade were given the freedom to define their own essential question under one of five broad topics. Several class periods were added in each grade so that the librarian could teach search skills, evaluation of sources, creation of citations using the *Chicago Manual of Style* (it was the first year the department made this change), and note taking using NoodleBib's online notecards. Annotated bibliographies became a new standard requirement as the teachers learned the value of asking students to critically evaluate each source with regard to relevance and authority and identify its unique contribution to arguing their theses. I learned that requiring and assessing the bibliographies early in the process ensured that students were reading deeply and with purpose.

Though both projects included many milestone checks such as notecard assessment, preliminary annotated bibliographies, and outline checks, student research just didn't seem to gain traction. In department meeting discussions, teachers reported that our younger students were struggling to remain focused over such a long period, especially since they were simultaneously learning new material in class and attempting to work on their papers as time permitted. Some teachers argued that the research questions must be about material already covered in the text so that the learning curve would not be so steep. In retrospect, I realized that we could not accomplish meaningful change in teaching research without much bigger content trade-offs and changes like substituting research papers for unit assessment grades.

Yet another challenge was how to add research assignments to content-packed AP courses (European, World, and US History) taught in sophomore and junior year. It had been historically acceptable to refrain from assigning research papers in all AP classes except US History, where students research Supreme Court cases, and non-AP US History students research topics in the Civil War. However, in all other history AP classes, teachers had heretofore insisted that there was too much content to cover to add a research project. The first concession was made in the AP European History course. I proposed that, if the teachers devised the essential questions, I would compile sources for each question, and we would ask students to create a very detailed outline, including their thesis statement and evidence (with citations). This works perfectly in the years when the test is given early within the "AP season"; students have a couple of weeks for the research. In years when the test falls later in the "AP season," students can write the paper during the additional week of class time. In both situations, teachers create the questions and I identify sources so that students focus on note-taking and synthesis (the outline or paper), rather than finding sources.

The first year we made this change, we only had time for the outline. The following year I encouraged the teachers to create very specific and engaging questions. I borrowed books from San Jose State University's library, which I put on reserve in classrooms to support these questions.

I taught lessons on thesis statement development and how to construct the outline, to which we added a requirement for Chicago-style endnotes, since we wanted students to practice this skill for their junior year paper.

This was the first time that students had learned how to write what they termed a "formal outline," containing detailed section headings, thesis statements, and evidence cited for each assertion. When asked to reflect at the end of the project, they said they could "see" their paper even though they did not actually write it! Apparently the logic of outlining, necessary to the structure of a linear research paper, wasn't clear when students used concept mapping and spider web graphic organizers in elementary school. Students also told us they actually enjoyed being able to read, synthesize, and organize the scholarly sources given to them (without having to search for them!), and to study deeply a topic covered only superficially in this survey course. We all rejoiced in what was initially an experiment to see if we could practice selected research skills with a limited amount of time in an AP course.

Instrumental to the success of our History PLC were frequent team meetings. I met with the 9th and 10th grade teachers periodically to assess what was and wasn't working, to try new ideas and report back. Meetings were ad hoc, sometimes called by the teachers to make sure they were all at the same point with a project, and sometimes called by me, especially when I saw a need for group consensus on, for example, how to teach annotations. As I taught lessons on targeted skills, e.g., how to search for primary sources or how to paraphrase, I learned from students and was inspired by the creativity and insights of the teachers who knew just what their classes needed when I was struggling. Julie Wheeler, an experienced 9th grade teacher, sensing that this five-page research project was overwhelming to some of her students, coached them along with encouragement: "We will help you through each step—don't be scared!"

We got much-needed support from the department chair, Donna Gilbert, who was always available when we needed to make major decisions, such as shortening a unit to provide more in-class time for research. She kept us focused on our goal of developing a process by reminding us that "these might not be great papers, but this will be a learning year." Of course, Gilbert did more than cheerlead. She set aside significant amounts of time during monthly department meetings to continue these discussions. Her administrative support helped this collaborative group of history teachers evolve into a professional learning community with time for focused practice and reflection, regular conversations on shared goals, and a commitment to try new things and collect evidence of learning. This practice has been extended to include 6th grade through 12th grade teachers from both the upper and middle school campuses and the librarians from each division who meet to make curricular decisions transparent and create a seamless articulation of skills and goals from grade to grade.

Some members of our history department PLC made individual commitments to improve their craft. For example, Dr. Ruth Meyer, the 9th grade history team leader, applied for a Harker Technology Summer Grant, which funds teachers to work on curricular enhancements, usually with a strong technology component. Despite her doctorate in history from Oxford, she wanted to learn more about how to build note-taking skills using Noodle-Tools, our web-based citation and note-taking tool. She also wanted to know more about the student's perspective. Her grant enabled her to learn Noodle-Tools notecards and do library research with my support, using one of the compare and contrast questions we actually assign to the students. Both of us agreed it was a valuable learning experience. She chose a topic she knew the least about, in hopes of making the learning authentic. I guided her as if I were working with a class, recommending resources and providing choice in the direction her topic might take her. As a true historian, she began with primary sources, yet found it difficult and confusing to vet sources and cross-reference her findings as she made her notecards. She decided to model for students how using one source can lead to the next, and she chronicled her questions in the My Ideas portion of the notecard, as her understanding of her topic deepened. At the end of the week, she and I developed a rubric (Figure 14.4) for teachers to use to grade student notecards, and our work led to a revision of some questions to narrow the focus for students. The rubrics and revised questions were presented to teachers at orientation and used with students during the next year.

As the 9th grade project drew to a close and the students began writing, some students reported a fear of beginning to write; anxiety prevented them from knowing how to turn their notes into an essay. The team tried tactics to jumpstart writing, tactics that students told us they wished had been introduced earlier. For example, several teachers required that students write their outline in class. One teacher, without warning, announced that the first two paragraphs of their paper were due at the end of the class. When their outlines or writing had unsubstantiated claims, I helped them review their sources to locate evidence to match the claim. When we didn't understand the logic of the outline, I taught them to analyze and sort their subtopics using NoodleTools outlines according to conventions history teachers had presented, like PERSIA categories (political, economic, religious, social, intellectual, and artistic).

Despite coaching, multiple checkpoints, and a guided research process, most of the 9th grade World History I students did not find their focus until they were actually writing. Despite our scaffolding, students did not begin writing papers on their own. The spontaneous assignment by an experienced teacher was just the fix because it helped them push through the anxiety of starting to write by doing it in class together. In reading a reflection piece that students completed after the project, we were particularly struck by the number of students that reported that it wasn't until they began to create an outline or even write their paper that they really thought about their thesis and what they were going to say. At that point they had to go back and fill in gaps in their research, rethink their thesis, or change their position. As a team we must identify what might have been missing in the design or teaching or how we can scaffold the synthesis earlier.

| | Exemplary | Proficient | Partially Proficient |
|---|---|---|---|
| **Title** | Your title captures the main idea of the quote and is relevant to the prompt. | Your title captures something of the main idea of the quote, but it may be a little too general to be really helpful. | Your title is too general. It needs to relate more directly to the prompt and the quote. |
| **Direct Quotation** | Your quote is important. It shows that you have been reading thoughtfully and have extracted a key idea about your subject | Your quote may not be entirely relevant. It may not be entirely clear how this quote fits into the research project. | Your quote is either not relevant or consists of well-known facts that need not be cited. |
| **Tags** | Your tags are descriptive keywords that capture key concepts. They describe the themes and concepts that are key to your research. | Your tags are appropriate, but may need to be made a little more precise. They may need to be linked in more directly to the overall content of your notecard. | Your tags are either too general or misleading. It is hard to see the connections between the tags and the themes behind your research. |
| **Paraphrase** | Your paraphrase captures the author's entire idea and point of view in your own words. | There are some problems with your paraphrase. It is either incomplete or contains some of the author's own words. It may not entirely capture the author's point of view. | Your paraphrase is either incomplete, contains too many of the author's own words, or adds content not in the original. It either does not capture, or misrepresents, the author's point of view. |
| **My ideas** | My ideas offer insight, analysis, and original thought. They evaluate the source and relate it to other sources. They clearly link the source to the prompt and to the overall research process. | My ideas offer some insight, analysis, and original thought. They offer a partial evaluation of the source. The link to the prompt may be somewhat unclear and connections to other sources may also be somewhat unclear. | My ideas are either incomplete or too simplistic, for example: "Gladiators were originally people of the lowest class." This statement may simply be restating the direct quotation. |

Figure 14.4: NoodleTools Notecard Rubric, Dr. Ruth Meyer, August 2010

From *Growing Schools: Librarians as Professional Developers* edited by Debbie Abilock, Kristin Fontichiaro, and Violet H. Harada. Santa Barbara, CA: Libraries Unlimited. Copyright © 2012.

## USING PROFESSIONAL RESEARCH TO INFORM
## TEACHING PRACTICE

I began to investigate the current scholarship on information literacy, partly as a result of my growing awareness of these studies through my membership in the Association of College and Research Libraries (ACRL). I came to realize that many of the decisions we were making were being supported by recent studies, and I began to act as a conduit for that research to our faculty. I shared Head and Eisenberg's preliminary findings about how college students do online research (2009) with departments, explaining that many challenges and behaviors of older students paralleled those of our high school students.  The preliminary model of the contextual foundation for the research process that Head and Eisenberg created has helped us think about how to build the contexts—understanding the big picture, learning the discourse, knowing the teacher's expectations, and conceptualizing the relevant information landscape—that college students report missing as they work on research.  We now require students to search resources in a prescribed order (general reference, specialized reference, monographs, and primary sources) and introduce the search for primary sources (as opposed to just providing sources to analyze) at different stages of research.

I summarized a second study that reported that college students did not stop to evaluate sources even when they told the interviewer how important they knew this to be (Hargittai et al. 2010). Our faculty could feel confident that our decision to emphasize assessment of authority in students' annotated bibliographies was on target.

Another finding that supported our integration of more research into the curriculum was Paul Rogers' Stanford Study of Writing (2008). He followed undergraduate writing assignments from 2001 to 2006, and found that students were assigned 60–100 pages of various types of writing in their first year. Such reports remind us that we must give students time to practicing research skills and identify the professional development that will enable teachers to implement this integration.

Understanding these studies and reporting on them during team discussions supports my own growth as well as my colleagues. For example, I emphasize note taking in part because we learned that a large body of educational research shows that note taking, summarizing, and paraphrasing are strategies highly correlated with student achievement (Marzano 2001, 78–87). Since paraphrasing is necessary for synthesis, the library team focused their minilessons and guided practice on using the three-part graphic organizer in NoodleTools to scaffold students' thinking process from cutting and pasting a quote to paraphrasing, and from paraphrasing to active processing and inquiry thinking.

Coupled with my role as a conduit between the faculty and the current research on information literacy, I began to understand that increased time in the classroom offered me extended opportunities to watch students practice search and discovery. My colleague, Lauri Vaughan, calls these hours a "time-consuming but very effective" way to understand how students think and to identify their stumbling blocks. Although we had used the CSLA standards early on to guide our initial integration of information literacy skills, we now find the ACRL information literacy standards (2009) offer more discrete and measurable guidance than either the AASL *Standards for 21st-Century Learners* (2007) or the California Department of Education's Model School Library Standards (2010). We often turn to these college standards when assessing whether our students are prepared to compete academically at the most rigorous institutions to which they matriculate. For example, ACRL Standard Three says that "the information literate student evaluates information and its sources critically and incorporates selected information into his or her knowledge base and value system." It includes performance indicators and specific outcomes that can be observed.

1. The information literate student summarizes the main ideas to be extracted from the information gathered.

   *Outcomes Include:*

   A. Reads the text and selects main ideas;

   B. Restates textual concepts in his/her own words and selects data accurately;

   C. Identifies verbatim material that can be then appropriately quoted (2009).

## PROMPTING THE SHARING OF PRACTICE

As the librarians continued to co-teach in classrooms, it occurred to me that I could support reflective teaching by encouraging teachers to share practices that they were testing in their classrooms. I have the privilege of observing these inspired moments in the classroom, but teachers are too immersed in their own teaching to recognize their value to others. Further, teachers hesitate to share what they feel is merely experimental. At one of our 9th grade meetings I urged a teacher to describe why she had asked students to create a visual representation of their current thinking about their compare and contrast research topics. She explained to our team how a Venn diagram or chart could show her which students were successfully developing a thesis and which were using superficial or irrelevant sources. When a learning community builds trusting professional relationships and supports risk taking, teachers become willing to share their experimental work, and mistakes as well as their successes. They seek advice from peers and feel more confident making "on the fly" changes when something isn't working. Librarians can facilitate the sharing of best practices that promotes quality assurance often lacking in even the best schools.

Now in our fourth year, I believe we have created a spirit of openness and experimentation for our PLC. The frank discussions that I sometimes uncomfortably facilitate have allowed teachers to examine practices in an atmosphere of acceptance; we are all focused on creating the very best learning environment for our students. This open culture has enabled new teachers to easily share fresh ideas and contribute to our ongoing improvement efforts, even as they are relieved to find a honed process in place.

Early on I realized that each collaborative project cycle benefits from both student and teacher evaluation. I believe this promotes individual growth and is an essential ingredient of successful PLCs. Student feedback informs subject teachers about content and librarians about their understanding of the research process. Teacher feedback informs the PLC about specific pedagogy and further helps me, now the library director, to support the growth and refinement of our program's overall information literacy objectives (Figure 14.5).

Teacher evaluation has grown to be largely informal, occurring in one-on-one discussions with teachers in the classroom, at the team meetings, or at department meetings. Sometimes I bring such findings or decisions back to the high school history department and chair for their input, because I am mindful that the changes made to a project at any grade level will affect the entire scope and sequence. An example of one such outcome is the decision to differentiate between task definitions for the honors and regular classes in 9th grade by allowing honors students to choose topics not yet studied in the curriculum. We added the same criteria to the 11th grade US history paper so that AP students can write about Supreme Court cases not covered in classes while non-AP students write on Civil War topics covered in the first semester.

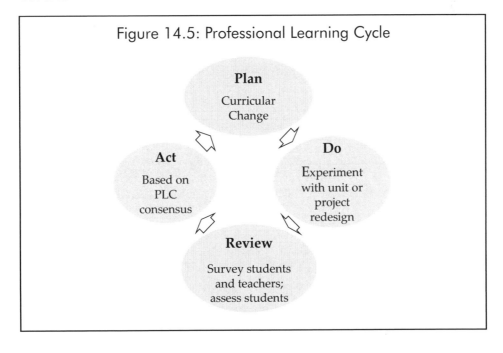

Figure 14.5: Professional Learning Cycle

**Plan**
Curricular Change

**Do**
Experiment with unit or project redesign

**Act**
Based on PLC consensus

**Review**
Survey students and teachers; assess students

Equally important is the opportunity for students to evaluate their research experience (Figure 14.6). Once the papers are turned in, students respond to a series of open-ended questions about their process: Was there a turning point in your research? What do you wish you knew at the beginning of the process? How did you grow as a researcher? As time permits, we have a follow-up class discussion so that students benefit from their peers' observations. Students recognize important information literacy strategies, thereby providing us with, perhaps, the best evidence that they are monitoring their own learning. They offer insights like, "I wish I had started my research with books because the databases were too hard to search and the Internet had too much information, some of which was erroneous." In addition to almost unanimous confessions of procrastination and failure to correctly estimate the time that the research would take, most now realize that they will need to read so much more than they ultimately use in their future papers. Most gratifying is the increased student confidence we see each year as they begin the next project another year wiser.

Although research papers are now mandated by the history chair for 9th, 10th, and 11th grade classes, the teachers are encouraged to implement the process in their own way and to collaborate with the librarian on teaching the skills they believe most important to their own classes. Giving both students and teachers the permission to experiment—and to fail—results in diverse and rich understandings of how students learn to do research. Though the papers are indeed not perfect, the professional learning community that has developed is impressive. Characterized by generous amounts of time devoted to collegial discussion, reflective practice and transparent accountability, this PLC is serving as a powerful template for other departments. Although the librarians are consultants, we are also learners.

We have developed a far more complex mental model (for an example, see Figure 14.7) of how to teach the research process as a result of our PLC's efforts. The basis of our future work together is our knowledge that students do not understand the iterative nature of research: they must read first for background information to contextualize their topic, then delve into the specifics to answer an essential question and take notes, then organize their ideas and arrive at a thesis, and finally double back to fill in gaps, ask deeper questions, and even change their argument.

## CAN PLCS LEARN FROM ONE ANOTHER?

The PLC that developed in the upper school History Department has expanded to incorporate history and social studies teachers and the middle and lower school librarians. All the teachers in 3rd through 12th grade meet least once a year to discuss articulation of information literacy skills as part of our ongoing curriculum review. Strands of the information literacy scope and sequence, like paraphrasing, are discussed and integrated

## Figure 14.6: Student Research Reflection

1.  How do you think you have grown as a researcher as a result of this project?

2.  What would you do differently next time?

3.  What did you learn that you wish you knew at the start of the process?

4.  What areas did you feel you already knew and didn't need instruction on? Did any instruction or activity seem like a waste of time?

    a) Librarian coming to class

    b) Going to the library

    c) Librarian making a list of books on the topics

    d) Peer editing

    e) Teacher editing

    f) Other

5.  What was especially helpful?

6.  What was the hardest part of the process?

7.  What was the easiest part?

8.  Note taking: did you feel that this was effective in gathering and organizing your research, or were you just "making those fifteen cards for [teacher's name] to grade"?

9.  Did you need more help with search strategies? What worked best for you?

10. Where did you get stuck?

11. When did the light bulb go on?

12. What had you never done before?

From *Growing Schools: Librarians as Professional Developers* edited by Debbie Abilock, Kristin Fontichiaro, and Violet H. Harada. Santa Barbara, CA: Libraries Unlimited. Copyright © 2012.

---

### Figure 14.7: Revised Information Seeking Strategies

**Big6™ Step 2: Information Seeking Strategies**

2.1 Determine the range of possible sources (brainstorm)

2.2 Evaluate the different possible sources to determine priorities (select the best sources)

**Harker's Revised Information Seeking Strategies**

2.1 Present "order of operations" and types of sources (reference/monographs/primary sources/scholarly articles)

2.2 Search for reference sources; add keywords to search list as knowledge expands

2.3 Present search strategies and limiters unique to subscription databases, library catalogs, and open web

2.4 Practice searching and gathering background information

2.5 Identify source type from citation (identify from "hits") —assessment;

2.6 Present criteria for evaluation of sources

2.7 Write annotations for selected sources (summary, authority, relevance)—annotated bibliography assessment

---

into each level of the subject curriculum. The expanded PLC works together to identify the best opportunities to integrate skills, and to make sure skills are refined as students mature.

Our second scope and sequence initiative and new PLC is developing with the Science Department. While many of our students opt to enroll in a fourth-year science course, they must first complete three years of requirements. Unlike history, every student takes the same sequence: physics as a freshman, chemistry as a sophomore, and biology as a junior. This provides obvious advantages when integrating information literacy, since all students take courses in the same order and all students in, for example, physics, are freshmen. Over a series of three department meetings, the upper school department chair, Anita Chetty, and upper school campus librarian, Lauri Vaughan, led the teachers working in grade-level teams to develop a scope and sequence of information literacy skills for their science courses. Though not all science teachers were initially enthusiastic about the new initiative, the teachers of each subdiscipline (physics, chemistry, biology) could work with like-minded colleagues to find skills that best fit their content, and the more or less uniform developmental level of their students.

We began a process that had worked for the History Department of giving teachers a list of literacy skills, including summarizing, paraphrasing, using citation and abstract databases, reading scholarly scientific (original) research, and detecting bias, which were tailored to scientific content.

Teachers sequenced the skills, and then picked those they believed they could incorporate into their own course. Reading scientific articles in the popular press might be suitable for freshmen physics students, while locating and evaluating scholarly scientific research would fit better into the investigation of coral reef ecology that juniors are assigned in biology. Many of our students do original scientific research, under the supervision of mentors, to compete in external competitions such as Intel or Siemens; but we want to make sure all Harker students graduate knowing how to find, evaluate, and use scientific information. By the end of the three-month scope and sequence development, the entire department seemed more enthusiastic about how information literacy skills could promote more critical thinking and authentic inquiry in science. A chemistry teacher even chose as his professional goal to learn skills to integrate into his chemistry course the next year!

## Assessment Data

- Interviews with faculty to inventory the skill gaps based on their expectations
- Survey of faculty about where they thought they taught info literacy skills
- TRAILS (an information literacy assessment) for 9th grade students—scores given to teachers
- TRAILS for 9th grade teachers—given their own scores
- TRAILS for 6th graders—given their own scores
- Excel spreadsheet tracking of librarian collaborations
- Models for project elements: mind maps, notecards, annotations, outlines
- Rubrics for notecards, annotated bibliographies, outlines
- Collaboration Evaluation worksheet —teachers rate experience
- Student reflections to rate learning experience
- Professional journaling by librarians

The upper school English Department is the newest group to ask the librarians to facilitate a scope and sequence workshop. This work will be a rich addition to that of the History Department; information literacy skills will be integrated throughout the humanities. As more departmental initiatives coalesce, students are developing discipline-specific information skills. In spring 2011, the upper school Campus Information Literacy Committee held a small focus group of graduating seniors, to discuss research across the curriculum. This was a mostly elite group of students who had taken AP US History and AP English Literature, and one of whom had also been an Intel Science Competition national semifinalist. They shared insights about the kinds of research they had done while at Harker. Most memorable were the projects where they researched a compelling question that was part of a larger topic and contributed to class-wide learning. They enjoyed research most when they were given lots of individual feedback along the way (that highly inefficient type mentioned earlier!), and they valued opportunities to learn how to research and write in different disciplines, especially English and history. They longed for more independence in the research process as they grew to be upper classmen, suggesting more freedom from producing required notecards and fewer graded benchmarks as they progress. We agreed that this is important preparation for college.

In addition to the reactions of our students, we track our own progress quantitatively including how we are assessing students. In addition, each year we track the number of collaborations among librarians and teachers has grown. Between 2006 and 2010, the lower school's percentage of research periods increased by 68 percent. The middle school librarian taught every middle school student (almost six hundred) during one collaborative research project, approximating the kind of quality assurance we hope to implement school-wide. Upper school collaborations tripled in the same time period. The formula for Harker's information literacy program has many ingredients: librarians who have the time to educate administrators and teachers; tools and guideposts like the Big6™ and a scope and sequence that are adapted to the school's culture and needs; and teachers who are pleased with the results of collaboration and pass the word around to other colleagues. That this program became a forum for the development of several professional learning communities has been an unexpected bonus.

## REFERENCES

Abilock, Debbie, ed. 2004. *Standards and Guidelines for Strong School Libraries*. Sacramento, CA: California School Library Association.

American Association of School Librarians. 2007. *Standards for the 21st-Century Learner.* http://www.ala.org/aasl/standards.

Association of College and Research Libraries. 2000. "Standards, Performance Indicators, and Outcomes." http://www.ala.org/acrl/standards/informationliteracycompetency#stan (accessed June 7, 2011).

California Department of Education. 2010. "Model School Library Standards for California Public Schools, Kindergarten through Grade Twelve." http://www.cde.ca.gov/be/st/ss/documents/librarystandards.pdf.

Eisenberg, Michael. n.d. "Big6 Resources." http://www.big6.com/ (accessed June 7, 2011).

Hargittai, Eszter, Lindsay Fullerton, Ericka Menchen-Trevino, and Kristin Yates Thomas. 2010. "Trust Online: Young Adults' Evaluation of Web Content." *International Journal of Communication* 4: 468–94. http://ijoc .org/ojs/index.php/ijoc/article/view/636 (accessed June 7, 2011).

Head, Allison J., and Michael B. Eisenberg. 2009. "Finding Context: What Today's College Students Say about Conducting Research in the Digital Age." *Project Info Lit* (February). http://projectin folit.org//_ProgressReport _2_2009.pdf (accessed June 7, 2011).

Marzano, Robert J., Deborah J. Pickering, and Jane E. Pollack. 2001. *Classroom Instruction That Works; Research-Based Strategies for Increasing Student Achievement*. Alexandria, VA: ASCD.

Moreillon, Judi. 2008. "Two Heads Are Better than One: Influencing Preservice Classroom Teachers' Understanding and Practice of Classroom-Library Collaboration." *School Library Media Research* 11. http://www .ala.org/aasl/aaslpubsandjournals/slmrb/slmrcontents/volume11/moreillon

Rogers, Paul. 2008. "What Is Student Writing Development?" Stanford Study of Writing. http://ssw.stanford.edu/research/paul_rogers.php (accessed June 7, 2011).

# CHAPTER 15
# NOURISHING ONLINE COMMUNITY

*Editors' Note:* Delivering professional development through webinars is an increasingly popular alternative. Michelle Luhtala describes her Emerging Tech series that has attracted participants from across the nation and almost twenty countries. She provides practical tips for designing and facilitating webinars and makes a passionate case for librarians to take the lead in merging technology with learning in 21st-century schools.

## Becoming a Webinarian: Designing a Webinar Series and Facilitating a Professional Learning Community

### Michelle Luhtala

## THE BEGINNING

It was my worst nightmare. It was the last time slot of the last day of the Consortium of School Networking's 2010 annual conference (CoSN). My talk was lumped into a group of similar presentations, but the other panelists dropped out, so there I was on my own. I was standing before an audience of thirty people, ready to deliver a presentation I had been working on for months. I had checked and rechecked my audio, my connectivity, and my wireless access. I was ready to go. It was show time. It started well, but fifteen slides in, my computer crashed. Sweat pouring off my forehead, I stumbled through apologies as I tried to reboot. Within minutes it froze again. As I initiated the restart process a second time, I heard someone in the audience shout out, "Just tell us about what you do!" So I did, and while I was initially nervous, nodding heads and broad smiles from the audience encouraged me, and I soon found my groove.

By March, it was my third time delivering a variation of the same presentation in six months. The objective was to illustrate the value of using mainstream social media and collaborative tools for K–12 instruction. I knew what I had to say. I believed it. I could see that participants shared my enthusiasm. Their questions focused on replicability rather than obstacles—always a positive sign. When I finished, one participant (Lisa Schmucki) approached me and said, "I don't know if you'd be interested in being compensated for this kind of presentation, but I would like to talk to you. I run a professional learning network for educators. I am in New Jersey, and I would love to meet with you to discuss presentation opportunities sometime soon."

On the way home that evening, I looked up the network and joined. I was intrigued by its collaborative prospects and by each community's focus. Thus began my career as a professional learning community facilitator at edWeb.net. It was March of 2010, and the concept was innovative. Lisa Schmucki, the founder and CEO of edWeb.net, had done some research and observed that of all the educator groups in the network, school librarians were among the most tech-savvy and participatory. She also observed that educators including school librarians were often too busy to keep the conversation going on their own. She recognized that those who joined were enthusiastic; however, it was clear that they were not forming communities. Lisa suspected it was a combination of lack of time and lack of experience with networking technologies. She believed that the school librarian community needed a moderator and a coach—someone to carry on the conversation and engage the members with stimulating content. She believed that I possessed qualities critical in a webinar facilitator.

## THE MECHANICS

Over the next few months, Lisa and I met to set goals, discuss pedagogical strategies, and evaluate webinar platforms. We experimented with Webex, GotoMeeting, Elluminate, Wimba, and DimDim. We tested each system, compared pricing, and reviewed system requirements. Cost was an important consideration, and so was software downloading—a factor that might prevent teachers from participating, particularly on school campuses. Finally, we settled on InstantPresenter.com, which met all of our criteria for friendly interface, reliability, reasonable cost, no downloads, and archived recordings. By June 2010, we had developed *Using Emerging Technology to Improve Your Library Program* as a series of twelve interactive webinar sessions that I describe later in this chapter. Although it was designed for librarians, through large-scale mailings we were able to enlist membership from a broader community. Our webinars now include educational technology leaders, administrators, consultants, academics, graduate students, private industry professionals, and instructional coaches. It was the first facilitated community with regularly scheduled webinars in edWeb.net.

To participate in this free webinar series, participants from around the world first join the edWeb community. Membership is free. edWeb.net has a partnership with MCH Strategic Data, the owner of a K–12 database of educators. It is primarily funded through education companies who use the platform to create online communities and professional development programs. edWeb.net also offers professional services to assist organizations in using edWeb.net more effectively. Its community portal stimulates communication and collaboration among participants through a blog, a discussion forum, a calendar, document sharing, messaging, live chat, polls and quizzes, wikis, bloglinks, and weblinks.

## WEBINAR STRUCTURE

Each month I present a webinar followed by a live chat discussion that is continued asynchronously through a community blog and discussion forums. My formal presentations last thirty-five to forty-five minutes, and each session lasts an hour. Although I do not follow the chat during the presentation, I join the conversation via audio feed during the last portion of each session. I use a wiki for the development of collaborative policy and practices. I also conduct polls to clarify the perspectives and opinions of the group using both synchronous (PollEverywhere.com and Instant-Presenter.com) and asynchronous (Google Forms and edWeb.net interface) tools. The webinar recording, supporting documents and research, and bibliographic material are archived for reference in the community.

Participants receive continuing education (CEU) credits. For this purpose, I create a short quiz (strictly factual—five multiple-choice questions that can only be answered by viewing the presentation) for each session. The quizzes are created in Google Forms, which feeds responses into a spreadsheet. I configure the form's notification so that the administrator receives an e-mail each time a quiz is completed. When a quiz is received, the administrator e-mails a certificate to the recipient.

Because I develop and deliver the monthly webinars, I provide continuity for the ongoing conversation. A consistent presence gives me the experience and institutional memory needed to refocus, redirect, and sustain momentum. During the weeks between sessions, I introduce new ideas using the technology tool best suited for delivery. I build on previous sessions and take audience needs and interests into consideration. For example, the conversation evolved over time when I introduced tools such as Voice-Thread, Shelfari, and GoodReads along with strategies to engage students in reading. Initially, we explored social technologies that promoted literary appreciation by motivating learners to participate in online conversations about books. This grew into a more philosophical dialogue about the kind of reading we wanted to promote and additional exchanges about reading formats (print versus digital). Finally, the conversations included posting book trailers online and the mechanics of using social features in library management software. This example models the kind of participatory, responsive learning that participants are trying to incorporate into their K–12 schools.

There is a rhythm to the monthly webinar cycle. I post a blog entry on the community blog page to introduce an upcoming webinar topic about a week before the session occurs. I suggest a few resources for those who want to read ahead, and I generally initiate several threads in the discussion forum as well. The thread topics usually originate in the webinar chat or its evaluation, but others emerge from questions sent directly to me, or from an active school-library-related Twitter topic (#tlchat). Thread posts are delivered to community member e-mail inboxes (options include instant delivery and daily or weekly digests). Participants respond in the forum. Then come the webinars themselves—they are scheduled on Wednesdays, so I call that day Webinednesday. After the webinar has concluded and I have reviewed the chat transcript, I post a follow-up blog entry responding to residual questions, reflecting on new learning shared by the participants, and highlighting connections between prior and forthcoming sessions.

## WEBINAR CONTENT

The content for *Using Emerging Technology to Improve Your Library Program* emerged from an eight-year campaign to build the school library program at New Canaan High School. What evolved has been a blended online/ face-to-face program that supports an inquiry approach to learning. In conducting research, students select from an array of online resources, ranging from detailed text narratives to task-specific video tutorials. Students assume an active role in project discussion forums and other activities that engage them in collaborative problem solving, communication in different formats, and self-assessment. This program provided many of the examples of technology for learning that became an integral part of the webinar series.

Based on my work at New Canaan, I highlighted what the six following technologies had done for our program, our students, and our colleagues in terms of differentiating and embedding 21st-century learning across disciplines:

- **VoiceThread**—freeware for online book discussion
- **Moodle**—open-source course management system
- **Google Apps**—cloud access and collaboration
- **Facebook**—library news and updates including photos and videos and allowing for student comments
- **Twitter**—posting tech support tips and updates
- **YouTube**—instructional tutorials dealing with lessons and "how-to" tips

I featured only free or open-source technology, stressing how incorporating these technologies into our library's instructional program had impacted student learning and strengthened the library's credibility. I emphasized how it had elevated librarianship to leadership by demonstrating to faculty that librarians were knowledgeable about using technology to improve student learning and that we were purposeful in our choices. Many districts blocked the applications I featured in my presentation, but Lisa was intrigued by our district's willingness to embrace them—a decision that the district made in 2006, when it became apparent that (1) students were skirting the proxy server to access them, and (2) Facebook, Twitter, and YouTube were terrific vehicles for teaching digital citizenship. She asked that I incorporate this discussion in the webinar series.

Lisa and I planned and published a syllabus in order to secure funding for the edWeb.net series. Follett Software Company agreed to an exclusive sponsorship, but allowed us complete editorial freedom. New Canaan Public Schools had recently migrated its records to Destiny, Follett's Library Management System, but Follett never articulated expectations for product endorsement. In the webinars, I introduce a range of products from different vendors because the platform is critical for service delivery.

The first sessions established the philosophical and pedagogical groundwork. Then we built on those principles with specific instructional strategies and applications, and we concluded with solutions for dissemination and advocacy. This delivery helped to organize the curriculum in a natural instructional sequence that continuously built on previous sessions. It lent itself to bringing participants back for subsequent installments once they attended a session. The twelve sessions focused on the following:

1. **Overview of and Rationale for the Series**

   Discuss the impact of social media on the library program's success; highlight the need for open access, the reticence among technology directors, and solutions that benefit all stakeholders.

2. **Millennials and Digital Brains**

   Explore ways in which the millennial brain is evolving, what instructional opportunities this transformation presents, and how librarians can capitalize on this shift to improve learning environments in our schools.

3. **Best Instructional Practices for the 21st Century**

   Draw connections between best instructional practices (e.g., Responsive Teaching, Differentiation, Understanding by Design, and the Partnership for 21st Century Skills) and emerging technologies. Explore how using social media for instruction improves student learning outcomes.

4. **Hybrid Programming**

   Demonstrate the advantages of offering a hybrid online/face-to-face program for library instruction. Feature a walkthrough of the New Canaan High School Library's instructional portal and discuss how it was designed to support best practices and enhance learning (and retention) for today's students.

5. **Communication, Collaboration, and Cloud Computing**

   Demonstrate how online communication and collaboration tools help support the framework of the Partnership for 21st Century Skills, embedding them into core curricular areas and the school library instructional program. Discuss the role of the informational authority in the new millennium, i.e., is expertise still relevant if the most widely consumed information is considered the most authoritative?

6. **Evidence-Based Practice and Data Collection**

   Show how data on student learning can inform instruction and improve school library programs, build collaboration, and streamline instructional focus on identified areas of need. Also, demonstrate how polling and its applications can be used for library program development.

7. **Social Capital**

   Focus on leveraging adolescents' social and self-involved nature to engage them in online discussion tools for new learning, with emphasis on promoting literacy, recreational reading, and book discussion.

8. **Visibility and Advocacy**

   Use social and static media to increase the school library program's visibility, retain faculty and staff in harsh economic climates, increase budgets, and promote school library programs.

9. **Microcommunication**

   Share how the 140-character message can change instructional delivery by making it timely, widely accessible, and concise, but also disposable. Discuss what this form of information exchange means for libraries. Explore the value of microblogging for professional development.

10. **Productivity**

    Focus on taking advantage of the onslaught of new thinking, new products, and new research without being overwhelmed. Share devices and applications that can help users streamline efficiency and productivity.

11. **Partnering with the Larger Community**

   Discuss strategies to build stronger community support by partnering with other libraries and community organizations and pooling resources to expand services.

12. **Earning Recognition**

   "If you build it, share it!" Highlight ways to share your library's successes and reap the benefits of your hard work and innovation through conference presentations and awards.

## DESIGNING A WEBINAR

As a professional development series delivered online, *Using Emerging Technology to Improve Your Library Program* reaches a diverse and shifting audience. Although there is a core group that attends every session, we also have a growing number of newcomers each month (I elaborate on the demographics of participation later in this chapter). Our continued growth poses some interesting challenges. During any session, we can have anywhere from thirty to over two hundred attendees. Of those participants, 30 percent are very familiar with the program, but the rest may have limited past experience. This presents a dilemma: do I rehash the basics each time or do I plow on as if everyone knows what I am talking about? Much as I would design a lesson for a heterogeneous class, I devised the following template for each webinar.

### Warm-up

The programs begin with housekeeping, which includes announcements. I couch this segment in context by reviewing what we already covered in a previous session and how an announcement for a resource or workshop might be connected and relevant to it. This allows regulars to reconnect, chat their hellos, and update one another. It also makes newcomers aware that they are joining a series-in-progress, and that many participants have been involved since the beginning. This often prompts new members to ask if they can access and stream past recordings. For this reason, we include the link to the Emerging Tech landing page where the recordings are archived with an explanation of the content in the introductory slides. In addition, Lisa and her assistant Erin participate in each session, fielding technical support questions and clarifying content points for newcomers.

## INTRODUCE CONCEPTS

I introduce or revisit important and fundamental ideas in this segment. For example, we discuss the following concepts and skills defined in the "Framework for 21st Century Learning" (Partnership for 21st Century Skills 2004). Community members share how they integrate these concepts in their own teaching. I encourage them to communicate and contribute through threads, blogs, and weblinks, and to collaborate using wikis.

Accountability
Adaptability
Collaboration*
Communication*
Creativity*
Critical thinking*
Cross-cultural skills
Flexibility
Information literacy
Initiative
Innovation
Leadership
Media literacy
Problem solving
Productivity
Responsibility
Self-direction
Social
Technology literacy

We focus most frequently on the four asterisked Cs, collaboration, communication, creativity, and critical thinking, often adding a fifth C—curiosity. We also identify some of the major theorists and researchers in educational innovation (e.g., Howard Gardner, John Palfrey, Urs Gasser, Tony Wagner, Ross Todd, David Loertscher, Carol Gordon, and Carol Kuhlthau) and discuss their fundamental assertions about the millennial generation such as their liberal attitude toward information disclosure. This is where the chat component is critical because regulars often answer questions posed at this juncture. Two themes that invariably resurface are administrative censorship (districts that block social media) and teacher buy-in. Returning participants are adept at addressing these issues. For instance, they might provide a response that was incorporated in an earlier webinar, explain an acronym, or refer participants to a resource that might provide additional guidance.

## Provide a Hook

When I plan a webinar, one of the first things I develop is the "show piece." I try very hard to make it visually appealing to engender the "wow" factor. Usually, it's a visual in a slide, but sometimes it is informational. In the session on social capital, for example, I compared results from student and parent surveys about Facebook (Figure 15.1). There were many similarities, but also some glaring discrepancies that made the data compelling. In this example, 60 percent of responding parents said they often talked to their children about Facebook activity, but only 6 percent of responding students indicated their parents talked to them about their Facebook activity.

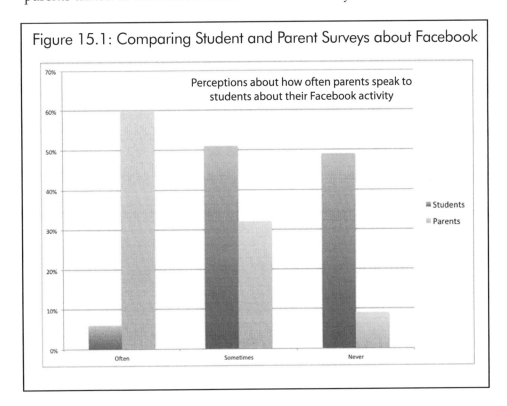

### Figure 15.1: Comparing Student and Parent Surveys about Facebook

## Connect Prior and New Learning

This is the segment where we link prior knowledge with new concepts. Sometimes, I delineate connections for participants, but depending on the subject, I encourage them to generate their own learning in the chat. The chat offers a great forum for participants to flesh out issues, and it is recorded so that I can recap takeaways later. For instance, in an e-book webinar, we discussed the impact of formats such as ePub on the acquisition and distribution of information and the influence on learning in K–12 education. One knowledgeable participant followed up by providing advice and resources for the group to broaden its knowledge. I featured this discussion when I joined the chat.

## Provide Example

I provide examples for each concept, often drawing from my experiences at New Canaan High School. In the session on cloud computing, I included an example of how we used YouTube, e-mail, and Google Docs to promote an author visit in honor of Teen Read Week.

## Propose Implementation Strategy

It is important to address replicability of the strategies shared in a webinar. I am particularly sensitive to this concern given that I teach in a well-funded, high-performing school, and I realize that many schools have fewer resources than we do. Platitudes and words of encouragement, particularly the "You can do it!" message are seldom enough and can even engender resentment. Presenting a practical plan for participants to implement the session's key concepts is critical. In the session on hybrid programming, for example, I recommended a three-year rollout and suggested small-scale starter posts. I stressed that it would not be a spiffy product in the first year but rather it would be rather rudimentary. However, the programming would become richer and more robust as one added content and multimedia in subsequent years.

## Wrap-up and Reflect

I end the session with constructive suggestions. At the same time, I acknowledge the challenges our participants face with serious budget and personnel cuts that impact library services in many districts. Figure 15.2 provides a plan for one of the webinar sessions.

## GUIDING CHATS

I recently described the series' format to a colleague. When I explained that participants chatted online while I presented, she was appalled. To her, the idea of participants "talking" during a presentation was a sign of disrespect, not engagement. In reality, that's the best part because it gives the audience a voice in their learning. By chatting, participants engage one another in discussion about the presentation in real time as questions and comments arise. This experience in participatory learning demonstrates the value of social media in learning. It comes back to the old adage about two heads being better than one. Try over a hundred! For example, during a webinar on social capital, one of our participants, Lisa Nielsen, technology and innovation manager for the New York City Public Schools, who blogs as *The Innovative Educator*, enriched the webinar by contributing a substantive body of evidence to the chat conversation with links to articles, blog posts, and other relevant resources. As a result, I adopted the practice of appointing a *chatter* to facilitate each chat while I presented. Chatters often have a special interest or expertise in the topic for that session. Often they are Emerging Tech community members, but I have reached out to non-edWeb.net members as well.

## Figure 15.2: Example of a Session Plan for the Webinar on eBooks, eReaders and Mobile Learning

| | |
|---|---|
| Warm up | Introduce our chat facilitator, the Twitter hash tag for edWeb.net, and a personal anecdote about my own shift in reading format preferences. |
| Introduce concept | Focus on five aspects of the eBook discussion. Introduce new learning by defining each concept and explaining its context in our program: eBook vs. Codex, eTexbooks vs. Learning, Ownership vs. Lending, Devices vs. Cloud, and Applications vs. Browser. |
| Provide a hook | Provide an A-Z list of factors in comparing print and digital formats. Make it catchy by challenging participants to ponder the ambiguities associated with digital content delivery—few of the listed considerations fall neatly into the pro or con categories. Classification is contingent on learning objectives among other factors. |
| Connect prior and new learning | In an earlier webinar, we had discussed eTextbooks in the chat. I revisit parts of that conversation, using the chat transcript to describe our earlier position on this topic. In this session, I ask participants to assess their current thinking: Has it changed? |
| Provide examples | Share how we were rolling out eBooks at New Canaan High School on iPads, discussing the advantages and disadvantages of the tablet as an eReader, and describing configuration challenges. |
| Propose implementation strategy | Since eBooks are still in their infancy, this session's implementation piece focused on raising questions. What should you ask yourself before purchasing eBooks and eReaders? How should you define your objectives? How answers to those questions should guide implementation. |
| Wrap-up and reflect | Close with possible evidence or implementation outcomes. Highlight the impact of mobile apps on database usage at New Canaan High School, thus eliciting a "larger lesson" about millennial learners. |

From *Growing Schools: Librarians as Professional Developers* edited by Debbie Abilock, Kristin Fontichiaro, and Violet H. Harada. Santa Barbara, CA: Libraries Unlimited. Copyright © 2012.

After the webinar, I join the chat. In truth, if I never joined the chat, the regulars could easily facilitate this, particularly now that we've added the chatter. Returning participants are adept at coaxing the newcomers along, happily reconnecting with one another and picking up conversations that occurred asynchronously online during the past month. This occurs naturally, without prompting. They are eager to fill in newcomers on previously covered content, often sharing links and referencing specific webinars or discussion threads.

Originally, I worried that the chats would turn into gripe fests, but they didn't. Participants attend the sessions to learn. I preface my webinars with carefully chosen lead-ins—links, blog posts, and threads—that help participants solidify their personal learning objectives for each session. I avoid editorializing, and allow the conversation to flow naturally. I ask probing questions to encourage participants to reflect about their own practice and consider applications for the session's new learning. Participants chat by typing into the software's chat function. I use a headset microphone to provide answers, which allows me to respond to more questions in the limited time. I don't panic about replying to everyone in real time because I upload a follow-up blog post within the week, after carefully reviewing the chat transcript, in which I address unanswered questions from the webinar. This allows me to study the chat for gaps in my instruction. In a webinar about using video for library instruction, for example, the chat transcript revealed that I hadn't mentioned recording equipment. I made sure to cover this in the follow-up blog post.

## THE PARTICIPANTS

*Using Emerging Technology to Improve Your Library Program* started as a librarian community on edWeb.net in late 2008. Membership increased from 8 to 123 in its first year, then by only 1 in the first quarter of 2010. After hiring me in April 2010, Lisa began promoting the series through her partnership with MCH Strategic Data. Membership since then has increased on the average by 20 percent each month (Figure 15.3).

Connecticut librarians comprise the largest participant pool among the regulars. Michigan and Canada are also well represented, but the rest of the core group is scattered across the United States, and they teach at every grade level. Every state is represented. We also have members from almost twenty countries (Figure 15.4).

Sixty percent of our members are practicing librarians. Another 7 percent supervise librarians in their role as instructional leaders. Support staff and classroom teachers form an additional 10 percent of the Emerging Tech community. Figure 15.5 details the occupational breakdown of those who are not librarians. Nonlibrarian chat participation deepens the dialogue by adding diverse perspectives to the conversation. Webinar attendance increases when the topic focuses on technology integration as opposed to librarianship.

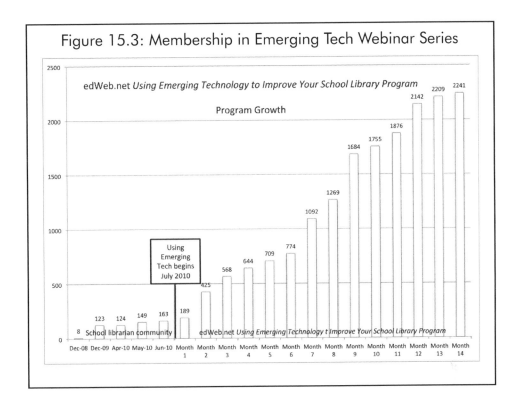

Figure 15.3: Membership in Emerging Tech Webinar Series

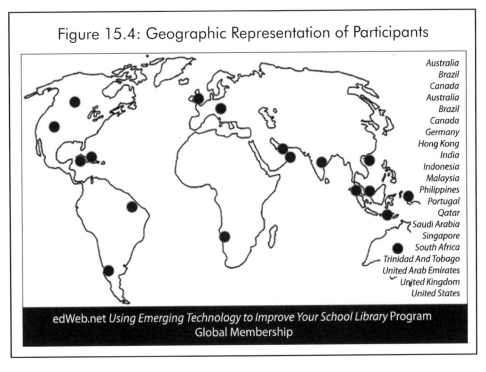

Figure 15.4: Geographic Representation of Participants

Australia
Brazil
Canada
Australia
Brazil
Canada
Germany
Hong Kong
India
Indonesia
Malaysia
Philippines
Portugal
Qatar
Saudi Arabia
Singapore
South Africa
Trinidad And Tobago
United Arab Emirates
United Kingdom
United States

edWeb.net *Using Emerging Technology to Improve Your School Library* Program
Global Membership

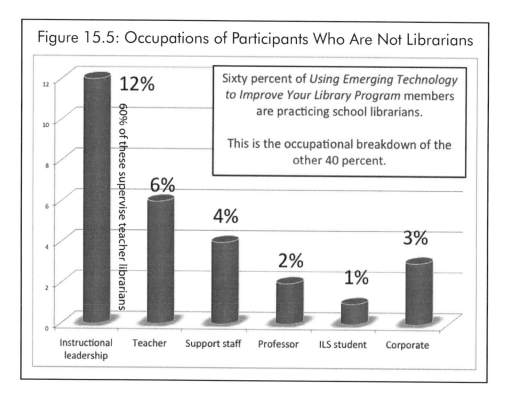

Figure 15.5: Occupations of Participants Who Are Not Librarians

## THE RESOURCES

The program syllabus identifies recommended resources for each session. When it became apparent that the reading list was limited by my preferences and knowledge base, we opened a bibliography wiki in the Emerging Tech community where participants were invited to add their favorites. This editable web space allows all members to contribute to a continually expanding resource.

Since the focus of the series is emerging technology, I highlight software applications regularly, but as with the reading list, featured products were originally limited by my tastes and experiences. We opened several "cool tools for..." discussions where participants could add to the applications list. This has been particularly helpful for K–6 educators since I typically focus on high school students. We plan to include more K–6 chatters in future webinars to further support educators who teach younger learners.

The edWeb platform is plentiful in its offerings; however, because of the platform's security settings, I can't embed external code for streaming video, slide shows, or iframes into the site. To handle this issue, I constructed an external blog, Bibliotech.me, to host what I could not post to edWeb. The blog also informs the external community—my Twitter and Facebook colleagues among others—about edWeb.net happenings. It is a public vehicle for communication and marketing between the edWeb.net community and the rest of the world.

## TIME INVESTED

Preparing and facilitating the series takes time. I spend twelve to sixteen hours building each webinar and an additional two to six hours facilitating the in-between discussions and blog posts. Because I have a proclivity toward working under pressure, I concentrate most of my monthly hours into one ten-day period. I would not recommend this approach—it is stressful. It would be far more relaxing to spread the work over the entire thirty-day period. I devote time on weekends to this work, and I couldn't do it if I didn't love it. I also do it because I believe teacher librarians must distinguish themselves as leaders in education. We have a long tradition as progressive thinkers, but this is not a consistent public perception. Professional learning communities, and webinars in particular, provide us with a platform to promote what librarians offer learners, and give us a chance to articulate our role, underscore its necessity, and interact with like-minded educators.

## MEASURING SUCCESS

One measure of a webinar's success is the ensuing online discussion. Asynchronous participants take the quiz mentioned earlier, but that only tells us whether they saw the presentation, not what they learned. The number of threads is one quantifiable measure; the thread content is an equally important measure of success. We look for quality—depth of insights—to help us gauge new learning. If community members open two or three new threads in the discussion forum after a webinar, this indicates that they were engaged and that they want to continue the conversation. We also added a standard professional development evaluation form to the follow-up blog post to get feedback on the specific presentations (Figure 15.6).

## TAKEAWAYS

Webinars are exploding in popularity. Almost daily, I find a new webinar invitation in my e-mail inbox. It's no wonder: they are cheap, they can be archived and rebroadcast, and they eliminate travel complications and real meeting time. Here are several things I have learned about the technical aspects of developing a webinar.

- Have up-to-date equipment. After my CoSN debacle, I upgraded to a new computer with an up-to-date processor. This is a critical investment, and it is cheaper than face-to-face conference travel.

# Figure 15.6: Evaluation Form

## edWeb.net Session #9 Feedback

Please take a moment to complete this brief session evaluation form

**Please select the number that identifies the response that best describes your experience in the most recent session**

| | strongly disagree | disagree | agree | strongly agree |
|---|---|---|---|---|
| The presenter was knowledgeable about the topic | O | O | O | O |
| The presentation was well organized | O | O | O | O |
| The presentation was engaging | O | O | O | O |
| The presentation was visually appealing | O | O | O | O |
| The presentation was timed adequately | O | O | O | O |
| The presentation met my expectations | O | O | O | O |
| The chat during the presentation was informative | O | O | O | O |
| The chat that followed the presentation was informative | O | O | O | O |
| I will be able to apply what I learned today to my practice | O | O | O | O |
| I would recommend this presentation to a colleague | O | O | O | O |

**Please share what you liked best about the presentation**

**Please share your recommendations for future presentations**

**Do you have anything else to add?**

Submit

Powered by Google Docs

From *Growing Schools: Librarians as Professional Developers* edited by Debbie Abilock, Kristin Fontichiaro, and Violet H. Harada. Santa Barbara, CA: Libraries Unlimited. Copyright © 2012.

- When uploading slideshow presentations into webinar software, avoid animations. This is very important for the following reasons: (1) The larger file sizes tend to freeze presentations. (2) If the presentation is uploaded into the webinar content manager, animations won't work the way you intended. This is software where the audience logs in to participate and where I show the webinar, where the chat occurs, and where the session is recorded and archived. (3) They slow up slide advancing. (4) They often distract from webinar content. (5) They don't transfer well from computer to computer. (6) Different browsers display animations differently. (7) Some webinar software packages do not permit animations.

- Add a second monitor to your computer. This allows your presentation to run on one monitor and your notes to display on a second computer. Craigslist.com is a great source for inexpensive monitors.

- If possible, use screen share and run the presentation from your own computer as opposed to uploading slides to the web host's presentation tool. By doing this, you can read your notes online and view your graphics display as you intended.

- Write a script. While some presenters feel comfortable ad-libbing in a live webinar, this strategy is not effective for me. Instead, in the notes field of my presentation software, I write out every word (a forty-minute presentation usually amounts to three thousand words) I intend to say, and I stick to my script.

- Rehearse so you sound natural and relaxed. Don't read the slides! Use graphs, charts, images, anything to NOT read the slides.

- Although I admit to obsessing over graphics, I recommend spending the time on your content first and saving visual aesthetics until later. I script all three thousand words before adding images to the presentation.

- Keep backgrounds clean. I have tried images, even faded ones, as backgrounds, and they invariably end up looking cheesy. My colleague, Cathy Swan, advises me to use dark slides and light letters. Green does not project well, and while that isn't a factor in the webinar, I avoid green. I work from a master but always include blank, white slides in my slide layout repertoire for image slides. Backgrounds tend to detract from images, so I alternate between the designed layout and the blank one, depending on slide content. I tend to shadow my fonts, to highlight contrast. I work in PowerPoint, even though I am an Apple enthusiast.

- When you blog, be genuine, conversational, and succinct. There are many bloggers out there, so it is important to distinguish your voice and content from other writers vying for busy librarians' attention. I strive to be amusing, informal, and catchy.

## IF I KNEW THEN WHAT I KNOW NOW

It was important to create a syllabus at the program's inception. It helped to secure an audience and funding and provide continuity. But going forward, I would prefer to deliver more "hot topic" content, and I would enjoy the flexibility of introducing new tools and accompanying pedagogical strategies as they become available instead of waiting until the next webinar series to discuss them. For example, new tools often trend in Twitter conversations, and I would like to move nimbly to introduce our participants to these trends. I would like to engage the Emerging Tech community in those conversations, and also poll participants at each webinar's conclusion about possible topics of interest for the next session. On the other hand, I have to consider that this user-driven approach might demand additional planning and preparation time to bring myself up to speed on those requested topics. I have also learned not to make assumptions about perspectives in the Emerging Tech community. For example, my school district permits mobile phones in school. Although I realized that mobile phones were not allowed in other school districts, I was not prepared for the strong feelings for and against this policy that emerged during a chat session.

## PERSONAL REFLECTION

I never imagined how much I would learn from facilitating the webinar series. By exchanging questions and ideas with participants in such a range of educational contexts, I am gaining a new understanding about where my own school program falls on the spectrum. The webinar experience forces me to reexamine my assumptions, consider alternatives, and reflect on how to frame future sessions.

I am learning about elements that are critical in establishing and maintaining a virtual presence. Not only do I gain knowledge from participants, but I also glean new ideas and perspectives to include in upcoming webinars from the external community of teacher librarians and experts in educational technology. I frequently solicit input from the Twittersphere, which serves for me as an unofficial connection between edWeb.net and other professional learning networks (PLNs). This cross-PLN communication enriches the community's experience and mine as well by including other educators in our conversations. I can't imagine functioning without this interaction.

## CONCLUSION

Participatory culture is a key component in our online lives, but has yet to transfer into many schools. My Emerging Tech webinars invite participants to join an online community where they may freely initiate questions, contribute experiences and observations, and develop connections with ideas and people. The goal is fostering a community of invested professionals who construct new learning together. As a professional development facilitator, I continually wrestle with how participants might be encouraged to apply the ideas and applications introduced in the webinars to their work environments. I want participants to consider how they might extend their learning by engaging their colleagues and students in dynamic, interactive learning experiences. Participants have the potential of assuming leadership in their schools by moving from being adopters and adapters of the technologies to serving as mentors. This is the long-range goal we are striving toward in this edWeb community. We have made a promising start, and the future possibilities excite us.

## REFERENCES

Partnership for 21st Century Skills. 2011 "Framework for 21st Century Learning." http://www.p21.org/index.php?option=com_content&task=view&id=254&Itemid=119 (cited June 10, 2011).

## RECOMMENDED READINGS

American Association of School Librarians. 2009. *Empowering Learners: Guidelines for School Library Media Programs*. Chicago: American Association of School Librarians.

Bibliotech (blog). n.d. http://bibliotech.me (cited June 6, 2011).

Casey, Michael E., and Laura Savastinuk. 2007. *Library 2.0: A Guide to Participatory Library Service*. Medford, NJ: Information Today.

Chubb, John E., and Terry M. Moe. 2009. *Liberating Learning: Technology, Politics, and the Future of American Education*. San Francisco, CA: Wiley & Sons.

Courtney, Nancy. 2007. *Library 2.0 and Beyond: Innovative Technologies and Tomorrow's User*. Westport, CT: Libraries Unlimited.

Drayton, Brian, and Joni K. Falk, eds. 2009. *Creating and Sustaining Online Professional Learning Communities*. New York: Teachers College Press.

Fadel, Charles, and Bernie Trilling. 2009. *21st Century Skills: Learning for Life in Our Times*. San Francisco, CA: Jossey-Bass.

Harlan, Mary Ann. 2009. *Personal Learning Networks: Professional Development for the Isolated School Librarian*. Westport, CT: Libraries Unlimited.

Jue, Arthur L., Mary E. Kassotakis, and Jackie A. Marr. 2010. *Social Media at Work: How Networking Tools Propel Organizational Performance*. San Francisco, CA: Jossey-Bass.

Kroski, Ellyssa. 2008. *Web 2.0 for Librarians and Information Professionals*. New York: Neal-Schuman Publishers.

Luhtala, Michelle, ed. n.d. "Using Emerging Technology to Improve Your School Library Program." http://edweb.net/emergingtech (cited June 5, 2011).

Ross, John D. 2011. *Online Professional Development: Design, Deliver, Succeed!* Thousand Oaks, CA: Corwin Press.

Toor, Ruth, and Hilda K. Weisburg. 2011. *Being Indispensable: A School Librarian's Guide to Becoming an Invaluable Leader*. Chicago: American Library Association.

# CHAPTER 16
# RETHINKING ONE-SHOT WORKSHOPS

*Editors' Note:* D.C. al Coda is an abbreviation for "dal Capo al Coda," an instruction written by the composer on his music directing the musician to return to the beginning and play it through to the end.

# D.C. al Coda

## Debbie Abilock

Our professional development journey has taken us across the United States mainland, and to Hawaii and Canada. We've visited a variety of school communities ranging from a rural K–6 school to a large urban system; from public schools and districts to private and religiously affiliated schools. We've heard echoes from one story to another: common pedagogical strategies, intentional learning goals, and learners actively shaping their own understanding and what they are able to do. Even so, differences emerge from the specific context of the professional learning, pedagogical preferences, and the beliefs of the PD leaders themselves. Thus some initiatives are fashioned by backwards design while others emerge as variegated beads on a necklace, each unique but united by the goal of changing the instructional skills, knowledge, attitudes, and beliefs of the faculty in order to improve student learning. We conclude this book with some advice for the road since, to paraphrase a Taoist maxim, your journey begins with a small step: a single workshop.

## BEFORE

### How Do I Learn about My Potential Participant?

The most effective way to understand what an adult learner knows, believes, and is able to do is to ask. Don't treat this conversation as a collaborative planning meeting where a fellow teacher has come to share and build upon what he or she knows in order to co-design, implement, and evaluate a lesson or a unit. Your intention is to listen for this teacher's preferred modes of teaching and learning. In this listening role, you are not the school librarian with expertise to offer. Use an approachable voice with tentative language including plurals (hunches, ideas) and exploratory words (possible, might) to clarify. Ask questions that invite the teacher to go beyond prescribed standards, goals, and methods to personally held professional values and beliefs. Don't proffer advice, redesign the assignment, or promote the library skill you know is missing. Rather, by listening with empathy, asking rather than interrogating, you hope to peel away the trappings of the assignment to gain insights about the teacher's own learning affinities, capabilities, and gaps in knowledge. Below the surface you may notice reluctance to use a particular technology tool or to participate in cooperative work groups. And beneath that you may recognize personal convictions about oneself as a learner (Figure 16.1) manifested as a growth mindset or fixed mindset (Dweck 2000).

Design a plan to support, rather than "train," your faculty. In the long run, your goal is to initiate a process of learning rather than polish a discrete event—and because you are a member of the faculty rather than an outsider, you can focus on long-term growth even as you plan a single experience. Effectively supporting adults through a process involves scanning the landscape: understanding their concerns and appreciating the intensity of their feelings. Learners begin at different stages of concern and progress at different rates; your interventions will adjust to their needs.

Your adult learner will filter the professional development that you offer through these lenses. Therefore your instructional design must be shaped by your learner's specific characteristics and needs, and your instructional delivery must monitor the responses of those individual learners.

When I first suggest this, school librarians will tell me that teachers are "too busy." They are. And yet when these formal or informal conversations do occur, almost without exception the teacher expresses gratification that you have listened to an in-depth explanation of something that he or she has been teaching and thinking about. (Psst, have you noticed that administrators who take time to have these conversations are lauded as instructional leaders?) For a school librarian, it's the beginning of a collaborative relationship we refer to elsewhere as "concierge PD," but for now it's about understanding your potential learners.

# Figure 16.1: Mindset Chart

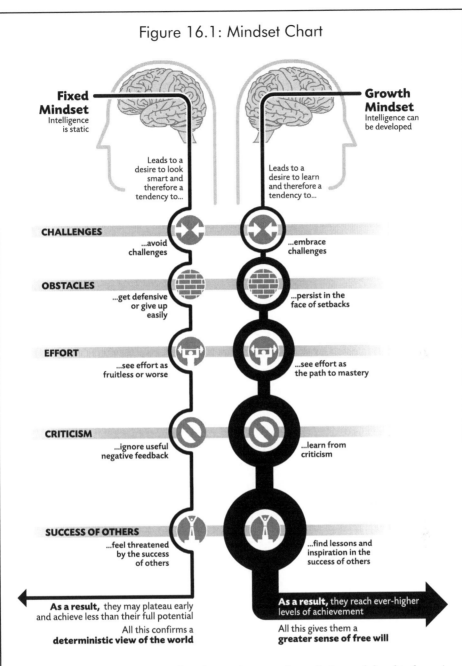

**Fixed Mindset**
Intelligence is static

**Growth Mindset**
Intelligence can be developed

Leads to a desire to look smart and therefore a tendency to...

Leads to a desire to learn and therefore a tendency to...

**CHALLENGES**
...avoid challenges

...embrace challenges

**OBSTACLES**
...get defensive or give up easily

...persist in the face of setbacks

**EFFORT**
...see effort as fruitless or worse

...see effort as the path to mastery

**CRITICISM**
...ignore useful negative feedback

...learn from criticism

**SUCCESS OF OTHERS**
...feel threatened by the success of others

...find lessons and inspiration in the success of others

**As a result,** they may plateau early and achieve less than their full potential
All this confirms a **deterministic view of the world**

**As a result,** they reach ever-higher levels of achievement
All this gives them a **greater sense of free will**

An adult learner who believes that she can improve is ready to work hard to learn in spite of challenges, while one with a "fixed mindset" worries about looking smart and making mistakes, and so avoids risks and copes poorly with setbacks. (Dweck 2000). Graphic by Nigel Holmes, reproduced with permission.

Of course you'll also be gathering other data over time by people watching, just as Connie Williams (Chapter 6) identified faculty needs by examining student projects coming through the library printer. Sniff out common misconceptions, irritations, or challenges. Have you heard teachers despair of ever teaching students to summarize? Or did a teacher confess that he clicked on a link in a phishing e-mail from his bank and has to change all the passwords on his accounts? Cloaked within these stories are the adult learner's needs and challenges: to learn how to teach students to do honest work or to learn how to shrewdly evaluate one's own information sources. These become opportunities to initiate brief workshops-on-demand, one-shot PDs to meet the needs of small groups of learners among your faculty. Of course, when an administrator offers you a PD gift in the form of time at a whole faculty meeting, say "yes" and follow up with a quick poll of interests (theirs, not yours) or three choices for faculty to prioritize. However you choose to spend those thirty to sixty minutes, don't use it as an opportunity to broadcast what you need to tell everyone. That, as Chris Harris (Chapter 9) learned, belongs in an e-mail. Focus on their needs. Not yours, not the library's.

## How Can I Relate Their Learning Needs to My Library Goals?

Once you have some hypothetical ideas for your one-shot PD lesson, you're going to want to take Mike Eisenberg's advice to align them with your school's priorities, since this will boost their relevance and transferability. Is your school focused on an initiative such as technology infusion (Geiger and Arriaga, Chapter 2), Lesson Study (Stokes, Chapter 3), assessment (Kramer and Diekman, Chapter 4), school reform (Kirio and Yamamoto, Chapter 8), or literacy (Kimura, Chapter 13)? What might your teachers—with their unique profile of goals, prior knowledge, and gaps—need to know, understand, and be able to do in order to fully support your school's objectives as well as the library's learning goals for their students? These priorities have much in common. Just as you hope to teach students to extract evidence from their source notes to answer a research question, the English teacher wants students to learn to use evidence to support claims in writing assignments, and the science teacher is engaged in showing how to gather experimental evidence for a hypothesis. The math teacher's "guess and check" strategy functions much like a "predict before you click" search strategy. At the same time, honor the unique inner logic of each discipline: "Every discipline has a gestalt, an internal logic, a patterned way of relating to the great things at its core" (Palmer 1998, 122).

## During: What Does a One-Shot Look Like?

Design criteria for a one-shot lesson:

1. Focus on outcomes that are important to the participants.

2. Consider "flipping" your instructional design (i.e., sharing a short, pre-workshop how-to tutorial or provocative reading) so that your faculty comes to your PD event ready to experiment with a new tool or discuss the application of an idea rather than learn about the basics.

3. Engage adults as learners first so that the pull and thrill of transformative learning sells them on compelling instruction that they can replicate with students.

4. Differentiate tasks so that all participants are challenged. For example, comparing two technology tools is more demanding than exploring the features of one, while choosing a tool to address a teaching problem and then designing a lesson that actually solves it is more difficult than just investigating how a tool works.

5. If this PD involves changing teachers' practices, anticipate and plan how you will address the possible concerns and varying needs for information, assistance, and support both during the PD and afterwards.

The "Menu of Workshop Strategies" (Figure 16.2) outlines the possible flow of a one-shot workshop for your faculty. It was inspired by a menu of strategies that Kristin Fontichiaro created for her pre-service librarians.

# Figure 16.2: Menu of Workshop Strategies

*Appetizers*

- **Welcome and logistics**
  - Do I sit anywhere?
  - How do I get online? (Or do you want my laptop closed?)
  - Are there snacks?

- **Introduce yourself** (even if they know you) **and your goal**
  - Why are we here and you there?

- **Icebreaker** can be more than a "cute" activity.
  - **Facilitate introductions.** Place an index card on the chair when you arrive with a thinking question, word, or phrase on it. Walk around; find the person with the same index card as yours. Sit with that person and talk about why this might be interesting to learn. For the moment, this is your learning buddy (breaks up chatty cliques).
  - **Assess prior knowledge.** Here are three straws and masking tape (or use Wikistix as Marilyn Kimura does in Chapter 13) to create a model of what your group thinks they know about this topic already.
  - **Facilitate an environment of learning.** Share and record what members of the group want to learn.
  - **Energize a late afternoon workshop.** Brainstorm with a partner . . .

- **Establish participation or discussion norms** (if appropriate and relevant).
  - We accept all ideas during brainstorming.
  - If you want help . . .

*Salads: A Healthy Taste of New Information*

- **Connect to prior knowledge and build on what participants already know**
  - "As a group, what words come to mind when you think about . . . "
  - "Take a minute on a piece of scratch paper to . . .
  - "Turn to your neighbor and talk about . . . "

- **Provide handouts for reference and to structure note-taking**
  - **Jigsaw regroups groups to build and diffuse learning.** Provide a number of short readings about your topic. Divide into the same number of groups, mixing people from different grades and subjects. Give each group a different piece to read and discuss. Re-sort groups one or more times so that one person from each original group is represented. The new group members pool their ideas to build their knowledge which is then shared out to the entire group.
  - **Direct instruction.** Talk for ten minutes, asking people to listen but not take notes. Then have participants take turns summarizing what they've learned for five minutes each or ask individuals to jot down what they learned on paper. Then open the floor for clarifying questions. Repeat.
  - **Peer-led discussion**. In small groups a key discussion source is read either silently or aloud. Using a graphic organizer or questions appropriate to the thinking task, the group discusses the topic. All members take notes then pool ideas so that one person can report out for the group. Collect handouts or access digital notes to assess the depth of table discussions so you can modify the handout for a future workshop.
  - **Demonstration** Role-play an example, show a video or read a scenario. Participants write observations, questions, and interactions and then share with a neighbor. Leader adds ideas and other perspectives (e.g., expert, coach, administrator, parent) that the group hasn't considered.

From *Growing Schools: Librarians as Professional Developers* edited by Debbie Abilock, Kristin Fontichiaro, and Violet H. Harada. Santa Barbara, CA: Libraries Unlimited. Copyright © 2012.

## *Main Courses: Processing New Information*

- **Individuals think alone, then process with another person, and finally share out**
  - Think Pair Poll or Tweet (from Mary J. Johnson)
  - Think Pair, then Merge into a Quartet
- **Individual or small-group work time**
  - Rotate through random, level, cross-level, and disciplinary groups on application of ideas to genuine teaching problems or concerns
- **Interactive activities of different challenge levels to test/build skills** (online tools, games, role-playing, etc.)
- **Case studies as generators of new practices or opportunities to apply new learning** (not recipes to follow)
  - "What would you do if . . . ?" "How do you make sense of . . . ?"
  - Provide one assignment with an example of student work and ask the group to redesign the assignment based on what they have learned and how the student responded to it.
  - Provide a rubric and have participants apply it to an assignment.
  - Ask participants to create a rubric to guide a lesson design.

- **Frame and facilitate a discussion using a hook or a structure**
  - A well-chosen image or film clip to evoke tacit knowledge or unstated feelings
  - A protocol for evaluating evidence (Easton 2009)
  - An issue map to manage a hot topic (Kranich, Chapter 13)
  - A backwards planning framework to design curriculum units (Wiggins and McTighe 2011)
  - An acronym like SCAMPER (Substitute, Combine, Adapt, Magnify, Put to other uses, Eliminate, Rearrange) to encourage creativity
  - A strategic planning matrix like a SWOT analysis (Strength, Weakness, Opportunity, Threat) to evaluate a proposed change.

## *Desserts: Reflect, Invite and Assess*

- **Reassess the learning objectives**
  - Pair-up to organize and summarize learning. Decide who is A and B. A tells B everything he/she has learned today. At half-time B tells everything he/she has learned without repeating what A said. Share-out one learning your partner gave with the entire group.
  - Create labels for imaginary file folders that hold reminders of your learning today. Share one file folder with the group and explain why it was important for you.
- **Take your learning pulse**
  - Fold a paper in half. On the left write what you've learned. On the right identify your feelings and new questions. Share an idea from the left side of your sheet and its corresponding feeling or question on the right.
  - Map your learning as a timeline with rising peaks for high points. Explain to a partner why you have a peak or a valley at a certain place.

- **Assess impact and value**
  - Ask participant to fill out a short evaluation (or an online survey), including suggestions for another PD workshop, as the "ticket out the door."
  - Ask a walk-away question that motivates participants to reflect or self-assess as they leave.
  - Suggest that participants imagine a destination and list the help, support, or information they could use to reach it.
  - Send out an e-mail asking participants to give you feedback on the workshop and suggest next steps and future workshop topics.

## AFTER

All learners go through evolving stages of concern about change (Hord et al. 2006) during which they have differing needs for information, assistance, and support and varied capacity to reflect. Your next step is to find out about and understand their concerns so that you can respond with an appropriate intervention (Figure 16.3). Some may return to their classroom feeling inadequate because they had never heard about or didn't follow what you presented. Others may wonder whether they'll be capable of managing their classroom in light of certain changes that may affect their students' behavior. At different times in their professional lives, when teachers perceive that they are being asked to change the "houses" they have carefully fashioned for student learning, they respond as resisters, accessorizers, redecorators, or renovators (Brighton and Hertberg 2004). While some will embrace remodeling, a few of your faculty may treat your PD as an earthquake threatening their home.

Overt or covert **resisters** may refuse to consider changes for various reasons:

1. A dysfunctional match between their teaching beliefs and practices and those embedded in your PD training.

2. A lack of agency—feeling they had no choice in being involved in this PD.

3. An absence of systematic, long-term focus in the school—they see your one-shot as just one more example of lurching from one professional development initiative to the next.

4. A lower priority on what they've learned in your PD than other mandates or initiatives already on their plate.

5. Little or no connection between their own professional interests and what you've presented.

Some of their resistance is out of your purview; you can understand their feelings but, quite possibly, are unable to change the thrust of what you've presented. Ideally it would have been useful to discover these barricades before you began, but since you're just beginning to learn this role, your knowledge and skill are developing hand-in-hand. The first and, to some extent, the second factor can be addressed by you in future planning for professional learning, especially if you invite resisters to explore their behavior using the techniques described at the beginning of this chapter. With understanding and empathy, your ability to anticipate and differentiate for resisters and renovators will grow.

## Figure 16.3: Supporting a Learner's Stages of Concern about Change

1. If I've **never even heard** about this, your support might include:
   - Acknowledging that ignorance is normal and questions aren't foolish
   - Encouraging discussion about the change
   - Providing a modest amount of information to arouse interest
   - Matching novices up with more knowledgeable faculty
   - Correcting inaccurate information sharing

2. If I only **know superficially** about this, your support might include:
   - Sharing clear information in various ways
   - Encouraging sharing among faculty with different levels of knowledge
   - Identifying similarities between the change and what they already do
   - Being enthusiastic and talking about others who have tried the innovation

3. If I'm not sure if I'm **capable** of doing this, your support might include:
   - Affirming that this is a natural response to innovation
   - Affirming specific strengths and capabilities
   - Connecting anxious learners with those whose concerns are fading
   - Mapping a possible sequence of baby steps
   - Encouraging but not insisting

4. If I'm not sure of **how to manage** the change, your support might include:
   - Helping teachers sequence components, activities, and a timeline
   - Providing "how to" and "when to" logistics for practical problems
   - Focusing on now, not what might happen in the future

5. If I'm worried about the **consequences** of the change, your support might include:
   - Finding opportunities to see other teachers or schools
   - Celebrating even the smallest accomplishments
   - Encouraging discussion of strategies, skills and implementations
   - Sharing what you've seen

6. If I'm wondering if **learning with others** might make this change easier, your support might include:
   - Encouraging discussion of potential collaboration
   - Advising collaborators to begin with modest goals
   - Generating opportunities for faculty to work with each other

7. If I'm thinking of **experimenting** with other ways to implement this change, your support might include:
   - Listening carefully to novel ideas and alternative suggestions
   - Affirming that there are many paths through innovation
   - Encouraging faculty to test and report back
   - Asking questions to help refine ideas and plans

These intervention suggestions are correlated to the Concerns-Based Adoption Model (Hord, Rutherford, Huling, and Hall 2006)

From *Growing Schools: Librarians as Professional Developers* edited by Debbie Abilock, Kristin Fontichiaro, and Violet H. Harada. Santa Barbara, CA: Libraries Unlimited. Copyright © 2012.

Figure 16.4: Visualizing a Learner's Stages of Concern

## Visualizing Stages of Concern

**Unaware**                                    **Creative Synthesis**

- - - - - - - - - - - - - - - - - - - - - - →

7. What if I modify of refine it by . . . ?

6. Might I learn to do this better by working with others?

5. What consequences will result from my making changes?

4. How do I implement and manage this change?

3. Am I capable of learning to do this?

2. Tell me more about it?

1. What is this?

Based on stages in Hord, Shirley M., William L. Rutherford, Leslie Huling, and Gene E. Hall. 2006. *Taking Charger of Change*. Austin, TX: Southwest Educational Development Laboratory.

**Accessorizers** make superficial changes to their houses, adding to their repertoire of "tricks" by purchasing new curtains or moving a lounge chair. Brighton and Hertberg (2004) postulate that they are likely to be un-reflective teachers who lack a conceptual understanding of the underlying purpose and pedagogy of the changes you've presented, and thus might not see a conflict with their own educational beliefs, nor recognize a need for structural changes.

> Often, accessorizers' strong sense of professional competency was reinforced by their colleagues. Many were held up by their districts as model teachers and were frequently asked to be mentors or to take on other leadership positions in their teams or schools. Their reputations as master teachers often resulted from the fact that, from the outside, their classrooms looked impressive and well-run. These teachers generally possessed strong classroom management skills that kept their students on-task and orderly. (Brighton and Hertberg 2004, 7)

While a one-shot workshop gives accessorizers little more than another decorative touch for their living rooms, you need these learners working by your side because they are influential and generally respected as leaders. They can help to advance your goals. To impact their instruction and beliefs, provide time for them to reflect during your one-shot. If these teachers mull over problems that they can no longer ignore in their teaching or in student learning, they are more likely to integrate their learning into their practice.

When your teaching matches the educational belief system of your participants, **redecorators** will reflect on their own instruction and assimilate changes into their practices. They will identify some teaching problems that they can address by implementing the learning you have proffered. Brighton and Hertberg describe these as experienced, traditional (rather than cutting-edge) teachers who will be model learners, accurately implementing improvements to their teaching. While you can anticipate no revolutions in their classrooms as a result of your professional development, you might notice that their instructional practices will improve student learning by increments. The changes they make will help you build your reputation as a trusted teacher, coach and mentor.

If and when you can provide the last group—the risk-taking **renovators**—with a compelling case for instructional changes that will have major benefits for all their students, these are the learners who will gut their homes and rebuild their instruction and beliefs from the inside out. They range from beginning to expert teachers but, as learners, they share a reflective openness to ambitious challenges. These are the risk takers that will demolish the practices and beliefs that frame their houses if they believe that it will result in significant student learning. "These teachers seemed to realize that ambiguity is a natural part of the process of learning; they recognized that discomfort is necessary for growth" (Brighton and Hertberg 2004, 12). In your workshop, these are the participants who will expect you to paint a picture of student learning worth the struggle, to inspire them to risk and strive, rather than simply provide them with clear and orderly explanations of decorative elements.

The "Desserts" in our Menu (Figure 16.2) suggests ways to assess the immediate impact of your training. While the feedback will help you gauge the comfort level and engagement of your learners, it won't provide information about whether they will be able to retain and use what they've learned. Use your people-watching skills and empathetic close listening to find tangible evidence of learning, such as changes in attitudes, skill level, or instructional behavior, to alert you to new prospects for professional development.

Planning multifaceted professional learning with the scope of institutional change may seem a far cry from a one-shot PD workshop. Truthfully, it is. Changing teachers' practice is a function of both intensity and the number of hours spent (Smith, Hofer, Gillespie, Solomon and Rowe 2003, 119), typically close to fifty hours to improve teachers' skills and student learning (Darling-Hammond, Wei, Andree, Richardson, and Orphanos 2009, 5). And yet, like the framework of a cottage, even your first modest design can contain the essential elements and functions of a master architect's breathtaking skyscraper. Each of our narratives of embedded, content-focused teaching and reflecting, observing, and assessing had a beginning. And so, my invitation to you is to begin. Intentional planning can make your first baby step a meaningful commitment to professional learning. Won't you begin your first house for adult learners?

## REFERENCES

Brighton, Catherine M., and Holly L. Hertberg. 2004. "Reconstructing the Vision: Teachers' Responses to the Invitation to Change." RMLE Online 27(2): 1–20. http://www.amle.org/portals/0/pdf/publications/RMLE/rmle_vol27_no2_article5 .pdf.

Darling-Hammond, Linda, Ruth Chung Wei, Alethea Andree, Nikole Richardson, and Stelios Orphanos. 2009. *Professional Learning in the Learning Profession: A Status Report on Teacher Development in the United States and Abroad*. National Staff Development Council. http://www.nsdc.org/news/NSDCstudy2009.pdf.

Dweck, Carol S. 2000. *Self-Theories: Their Role in Motivation, Personality and Development*. Philadelphia: Psychology Press.

Easton, Lois Brown. 2009. *Protocols for Professional Learning*. Alexandria, VA: ASCD.

Hord, Shirley M., William L. Rutherford, Leslie Huling, and Gene E. Hall. 2006. *Taking Charge of Change*. Austin, TX: Southwest Educational Development Laboratory.

Palmer, Parker J. 1998. *The Courage to Teach: Exploring the Inner Landscape of a Teacher's Life*. San Francisco: Jossey-Bass.

Smith, Cristine, Judy Hofer, Marilyn Gillespie, Marla Solomon, and Karen Rowe. 2003. "How Teachers Change: A Study of Professional Development in Adult Education." NCSALL Reports #25, November. Cambridge, MA: Harvard Graduate School of Education. http://www.ncsall.net/fileadmin/resources/research/report25.pdf

Wiggins, Grant, and Jay McTighe. 2011. *The Understanding by Design Guide to Creating High-Quality Units*. Alexandria, VA: ASCD.

# INDEX

# ABOUT THE EDITORS AND CONTRIBUTORS

DEBBIE ABILOCK is the co-founder of NoodleTools, Inc., an online platform for teaching academic research. She speaks and consults in schools in the United States, Europe, and Asia based on over thirty years as a school administrator, curriculum coordinator, librarian, and ICT director. As a K–8 school librarian she taught a range of high-potential students, from learning-disabled gifted to profoundly gifted, and developed differentiated curriculum in collaborative faculty teams each year for most grades. She is currently President of BayNet, a multitype library network in the Bay Area, and has worked on numerous local, state, and national boards and committees. Founding editor of *Knowledge Quest*, the journal of the American Association of School Librarians (1996–2010), she also edited *Standards and Guidelines for Strong School Libraries* (2004) for the California School Library Association. She has authored over fifty articles and chapters, most recently "True - or Not?" (*Educational Leadership*, March 2012) and co-authored "Sea Changes in Technology Services and Learning" (*Independent School Libraries: Perspectives on Excellence*, ABC-CLIO/Libraries Unlimited, 2011). Debbie has been honored as a *Library Journal* "Mover and Shaker" in the library community, appointed a Library of Congress American Memory Fellow, received the CSLA President's Award for curricular leadership, and won Grand Prize for innovative online curriculum from *Time* magazine. "My favorite 'prize' is a school consulting job that included a opportunity to teach 3rd graders to evaluate information."

KELLY AHLFELD is Librarian and Technology Coordinator for the Mettawee Community School, a small, rural elementary school in West Pawlet, Vermont, in the Bennington-Rutland Supervisory Union. She earned her BA from Smith College, and since earning her MLS from Simmons College, Kelly has worked in libraries for over fifteen years. She loves to work with technology and teachers, and her favorite pastime is developing lifelong readers in unexpected places. Kelly serves on her school district's Instructional Leadership Team and has presented on a variety of topics, including professional development, media literacy, and reluctant readers. When she is not spending time with her favorite people (husband Peter, and two sons, Russ and Henry), she likes running, reading, cooking, writing, and cheering on her boys.

ANNE ARRIAGA received her BA from Bowdoin College and her MLIS from San Jose State University. Soon after being accepted into San Jose State University's School of Library and Information Science, she began working as a library assistant at Moreau Catholic High School and two years later became co-librarian. During her final summer as a graduate student, she served as the Exploratorium's Learning Commons and Teacher Institute intern where she supported a cohort of math and science teachers from around the country. At Moreau Catholic, Anne developed the *Live from MCHS* program and the MCHS Library's 24 Hour Read-a-thon. She has presented on a variety of topics, all of which fall under the broad category of librarians serving as student- and teacher-support specialists in 21st-century schools.

JENNIFER BLOOMINGDALE graduated from the College of St. Rose in 2006 with a bachelor's degree in Childhood Education. In 2011 she completed her master's in Educational Technology and became a New York State–certified Educational Technology Specialist. Jennifer was a 5th grade teacher at Mettawee Community School in West Pawlet, Vermont, for four years. It was through her teaching experience and master's program that Jennifer developed a passion for integrating technology and assisting others in doing so. Jennifer lives in upstate New York with her husband and son. In her free time she likes to knit, read, and spend time with her family.

MARIAH CHEREM holds an MSI degree from the University of Michigan's School of Information, specializing in Community Informatics and Library and Information Science. Before returning to school, she served in a variety of communications, outreach, publicity, and program/event-planning roles for a collegiate art museum and a children's publishing house. Most recently, she applied her outreach and engagement experience to launching and building Yelp's community and brand in Southeastern Michigan. Her main questions upon returning to school focused upon online social interaction. However, she has found herself increasingly intrigued by the shifting roles of libraries and museums, and how such institutions were seeking new ways to connect with the public. She serves on the organizing committee for Ann Arbor Ignite, and continues to work on projects for organizations from 826National to the Ann Arbor Film Festival. Mariah's primary interests revolve around the intersection of communities, technology, and learning. She is particularly interested in the social side of tech and how various tools, platforms, and ideas about technology and collaboration can both support and constrain teaching and learning.

LINDA DIEKMAN is Director of the Learning Resource Center (LRC) at Glen Grove Elementary School in Illinois, working with 3rd to 5th grade readers and researchers. She was a participant in the *Here's the Evidence* project while she was the library media specialist at Central Elementary School in Lake Bluff, Illinois. Diekman holds a Certificate of Advanced Study (CAS) in Library and Information Science from the University of Illinois at Urbana-Champaign. Her 2009 research project titled "Exploring Research: Lessons Learned from Library Assessment" expanded on her *Here's the Evidence* work on assessment. She has an MS in Library and Information Science from the University of Illinois at Urbana-Champaign and a BA in Personnel Administration from Michigan State University. Diekman currently serves as an adjunct professor at the University of Illinois at Urbana-Champaign's, Graduate School of Information Sciences, teaching Information Books and Resources for Youth. She also teaches Collection Development and Teaching Research to Children and Adolescents at National Louis University's College of Education School Library Media Program. A frequent lecturer on assessment and collaboration, Diekman has presented at numerous professional conferences. Along with Pamela Kramer, she published "Evidence = Assessment = Advocacy" in *Teacher Librarian* (2010).

KIM DORITY is the founder and president of Dority & Associates, an information strategy and content development company focusing on research, writing, editing, information process design, and publishing. She has consulted in all types of organizations to design, build, and execute effective information strategies. During her career, she has worked in the academic, publishing, telecommunications, and library fields, in for-profit and non-profit settings, for both established companies and start-ups. In addition to her work with Dority & Associates, she is on the advisory board of the University of Denver's Library and Information Science graduate program, where she created and teaches a course on alternative career paths for LIS students and practitioners. She is the author of numerous articles and several books on library and information science career topics, including *Rethinking Information Work: A Career Guide for Librarians and Other Information Professionals* (Libraries Unlimited, 2006). She created and manages the LinkedIn "LIS Career Options" group, which now includes more than 1,700 members from 30 different countries commenting on roughly 200 discussions. She received her MLS from the University of Denver.

MIKE EISENBERG is a professor and founding dean of the Information School at the University of Washington, serving from 1998 to 2006. During his tenure, Mike transformed the school from a single graduate degree program into a broad-based information school with a wide range of research and academic programs, including an undergraduate degree in informatics, master's degrees in information management and library and information science (adding a distance learning program and doubling enrollment), and a doctorate degree in information science. Mike's current work focuses on information literacy (Project Information Literacy) and information problem solving in virtual environments (funded by the MacArthur Foundation), and K–20 information science education. His "Big6 approach to information problem-solving" is the most widely used information literacy program in the world. Mike is a prolific author (nine books and dozens of articles and papers) and has worked with thousands of students—pre-K through higher education—as well as people in business, government, and communities to improve their information and technology skills.

KRISTIN FONTICHIARO is a clinical assistant professor at the University of Michigan School of Information, where she coordinates the school library media program. She teaches courses in school librarianship, instructional librarianship, and media for children and young adults. In addition, she co-teaches Teaching with Technology in the UM School of Education. Formerly, she was an elementary school librarian and professional development facilitator for the Birmingham (MI) Public Schools and a secondary English teacher in Tennessee. She is the author of several professional books, including *Active Learning Through Drama, Podcasting, and Puppetry* (2007) and *Podcasting at School* (Libraries Unlimited, 2008), and co-author of *Story Starters and Science Notebooking: Developing Student Thinking Through Literacy and Inquiry* (Libraries Unlimited, 2009). She contributed the "Pride and Prejudice and Technology Leadership" chapter to *The Many Faces of School Library Leadership*, edited by Sharon Coatney (Libraries Unlimited, 2010). With Buffy Hamilton, she co-edited the 2011 crowdsourced eBook *School Libraries: What's Now, What's Next, What's Yet to Come*. She edited of *21st-Century Learning in School Libraries* (Libraries Unlimited, 2009) and was co-guest editor, with Judi Moreillon and Debbie Abilock, of the Professional Practice issue of *Knowledge Quest* (Nov–Dec 2009). She also writes informational texts for middle grade readers, has written for *Principal Leadership*, *ASCD Express*, *Teacher Librarian*, *Synergy*, and other publications, and given webinars for *Booklist* and *LMC Connection*. Named an Emerging Leader by the American Library Association, Distinguished Alumna by the Wayne State University Library and Information Science Program, and a *Library Journal* "Mover and Shaker," she blogs at fontichiaro.com/active-learning and writes the "Nudging Toward Inquiry" column for *School Library Monthly*.

ELIZABETH E. G. FRIESE is a PhD candidate in Language and Literacy Education at the University of Georgia. She received her master's in Instructional Technology with certification in School Library Media in 2006. Her research interests include literacies in school and public libraries, creativity in research and representation, and resources for children and youth. Beth's professional goal is to bring the library and literacy communities closer together in their common work toward enhancing a wide range of literacies for young people. Beth's work has appeared in *School Library Monthly*, *School Libraries Worldwide*, *Library Media Connection*, and *Voices from the Middle*. She has shared her ideas at local, regional, national, and international conferences. In her spare time, Beth enjoys learning new technologies, reading poetry and graphic narratives, and spending time with family and friends.

SUSAN GEIGER is the lead librarian at Moreau Catholic High School, a 1:1 laptop school in Hayward, California. Susan holds a master's degree in Library and Information Science from UCLA and began her career as a children's librarian at Hayward Public Library. She also held the positions of Young Adult Librarian and Branch Manager at Hayward Public. She is a member of ALA, AASL, and has served as President of BAISL, the Bay Area Independent School Librarians Association. She has presented on information literacy in electronic environments and organizes and moderates the Internet@Schools West Conference in Monterey and Internet@Schools East in Washington, DC. She and her support team collaborate extensively with the teachers and students in her school to create engaging and relevant learning experiences. Her interests include participatory citizenship in a digital age, application of Web 2.0 tools in a learning environment, and the use of social media with students.

CAROL A. GORDON is Associate Professor in the School of Communication and Information at Rutgers, The State University of New Jersey, and the Associate Director of the Center for International Scholarship in School Libraries (CISSL). She holds a doctoral degree in Education from Boston University, a master's degree in Library Science from Western Michigan University, and a master's in Secondary Education from the City University of New York. She has worked as a teacher of English Language Arts in the New York City Public School System and has been a school librarian in public and private schools, including elementary, middle, and high school grades, in the United States and Europe. Dr. Gordon served as Director of Library and Information Services for the Frankfurt International School, Germany, and participated in a teacher exchange program for one year at the American School in London. Her consulting has brought her to Europe, Asia, Africa, Australia, and Central and South America where she works with schools on curriculum, instruction, school libraries, technology, literacy, and action research as a tool of evidence-based practice. Before coming to Rutgers, Dr. Gordon was Head of the Pickering Educational Resource Library and Education Bibliographer for the Mugar Library at Boston University and an associate professor in the School of Education. Dr. Gordon's research interests include adolescent information behavior, the information-to-knowledge connection, and 21st-century literacies.

VIOLET H. HARADA is a professor of library and information science in the Department of Information and Computer Sciences at the University of Hawaii. She has been a secondary teacher, curriculum writer, elementary school librarian, and state specialist before joining the UH teaching faculty. In addition to her teaching duties, she coordinates the school library specialization for the Library and Information Science Graduate Program. Her major areas of research involve inquiry-based approaches to information seeking and use and the study of teacher and librarian collaborative partnerships. She examines how K–12 students learn best and teaching practices that help students achieve their learning goals. She works closely with school librarians and teachers to bring these "best practices" into classrooms and school libraries. She has published articles and books on these topics and is a frequent speaker at state, national, and international conferences. Violet says: "Working as a librarian and as an administrator in lower education and now as a teacher and researcher in a university graduate program, I have a fresh appreciation of both worlds. I maintain close ties with field practitioners and strive to involve them in the research and scholarship of our profession."

CHRISTOPHER HARRIS is Director of the School Library System for the Genesee Valley Educational Partnership, an educational services agency supporting the libraries of twenty-two small, rural districts in western New York State. In addition to blogging about "E-Content" for *American Libraries Magazine,* he is a regular technology columnist for *School Library Journal* talking about "The Next Big Thing." Christopher was the co-author of *Libraries Got Game,* a book on using curriculum-aligned modern board games in school libraries written with Brian Mayer and published by ALA Editions in 2010. Christopher was a participant in the first American Library Association Emerging Leaders program in 2007, and was honored as a Library Journal Mover and Shaker in 2008. Since then he has been involved with the ALA Office of Information Technology Policy Committee and numerous ALA e-books and digital content task forces and working groups. An avid gamer as well as a dedicated reader of both digital and print formats, Christopher lives with his wife, a K–12 school librarian; daughter; and four cats in Le Roy, New York.

MARILYN KIMURA has worked at the Nueva School since 1985 and became the head librarian in 2002. During that time Nueva, a pre-K through 8th grade independent school for gifted children in Hillsborough, California, has nearly doubled in population, and added a middle school. She supervised the design and new construction of a 7,200 sq. ft. library to house a 17,000-item collection, a media lab, small teaching spaces, and workspaces for students, teachers, and parents. In addition to teaching library classes and administering Nueva's twenty-nine-year-old Literary Club program, she is also a 5th and 6th grade advisor and tours prospective parents for admissions. Marilyn is passionate about keeping the library as the "heart of the school" and literacy at the forefront of students' lives. Her library motto is "We are a community of readers!"

CAROLYN KIRIO is currently the librarian at Kapolei Middle School in Hawaii. She began her library career at Waianae High School and moved to Kapolei High School where she opened the library in 2000. Kapolei High Library was recognized as a National School Library Media Program of the Year (SLMPY) in 2006. Kirio earned her National Board Certification in 2002 and was selected as one of *School Library Journal*'s "Top Ten Librarians to Watch" in 2003. She is a past president of the Hawaii Association of School Librarians and has been honored with the organization's Golden Key Award for her exemplary leadership in the school library profession. She and Sandra Yamamoto have jointly presented at state and national conferences. Along with Sandra, she authored *Collaborating for Project-based Learning in Grades 9–12* (Linworth Publishing, 2008). She continues to promote the importance of school librarians assuming a leadership role in professional development at the school level.

PAMELA KRAMER retired in 2010 as Director of Educational Services at the DuPage Library System, Geneva, Illinois, where she was responsible for consulting and support to school, youth, and academic librarians and coordinated the continuing education program for the DuPage System. Kramer and Sharon Ball jointly managed *Here's the Evidence: School Librarians Help Students Achieve*, an LSTA-funded project. From 1993–1997 Kramer served as Deputy Executive Director of the American Association of School Librarians (AASL). In this leadership capacity, Kramer worked with the National Guidelines Vision Committee that developed the information literacy standards for student learning and updated *Information Power*. She was also the AASL consultant on videos created by World Book and Great Plains National ETV illustrating collaboration and information literacy. Active in the Illinois School Library Media Association (ISLMA), Kramer was the principal writer for first edition of *Linking for Learning, the Illinois School Library Media Guidelines* (Illinois School Library Association, 1999) and served as a consultant on updated editions of the document. In addition, Kramer worked with ISLMA and the Illinois State Board of Education on the development of the certification standards for school library information specialists. As a "retired" librarian, she serves on the Friends Board for the local public library and as a trustee on the Friends of the City Museum Board. She also does school library consulting under the corporate name of Pamela K. Kramer & Associates, Inc.

NANCY C. KRANICH served as President of the American Library Association in 2000–2001, focusing on the role of libraries in democracies. Since that time, she founded and chairs the ALA Center for Civic Life and ALA's

Libraries Foster Civic Engagement Membership Initiative Group. Formerly Associate Dean of Libraries at New York University and a public librarian in Bridgeport and Windsor, Connecticut, and Madison, Wisconsin, she now teaches at the Rutgers University School of Communication and Information, and works on special projects at the RU Libraries. An active proponent of dialogue and deliberation, she served on the board of the Kettering Foundation's National Issues Forum Institute (NIFI), participated in Kettering's US/Russia Dartmouth Conference dialogues, convened and moderated deliberative forums, participated in the naming and framing of the privacy dialogue for ALA, trained moderators, and chaired the NIFI local affiliate in State College, Pennsylvania. Nancy earned a master's degree and studied for her doctorate in Public Administration from NYU's Wagner School of Public Service, and an MA in Library Science and a BA in Anthropology from the University of Wisconsin–Madison.

CATHERINE LEWIS is a distinguished research scholar at Mills College, where she directs two federally funded studies of "lesson study"—a collaborative, teacher-led approach to improving instruction. Lewis hails from a family of three generations of public school teachers, and her writings and videotapes, including *Lesson Study Step by Step: How Teacher Learning Communities Improve Instruction* (Heinemann, 2011) and *Can You Lift 100 Kilograms?* (Mills College Lesson Study Group, 2000) have introduced educators on four continents to lesson study. Information on these resources can be found at the website of the Mills College Lesson Study Group (lessonresearch.net), a nationally known resource on lesson study that was selected for publication in "Essential Websites for 21st-Century Educational Leaders." Trained as a developmental psychology researcher at Stanford University (PhD) and Harvard University (BA), Lewis speaks and reads Japanese and is the author of more than forty publications on elementary education and child development, including the award-winning book *Educating Hearts and Minds: Reflections on Japanese Preschool and Elementary Education* (Cambridge University Press, 1995).

MICHELLE LUHTALA is Department Chair of New Canaan High School Library, which won the 2010 National School Library Program of the Year Award, the 2010 Connecticut Library Program of the Year Award, and 2010 honorable mentions for collaboration from ISTE and CoSN. The Connecticut Library Association also named Luhtala its Outstanding Librarian in 2010. Luhtala was one of the recipients of the 2011 I Love My Librarian Award, initiated by the American Library Association and sponsored by the Carnegie Corporation of New York and the *New York Times*. This award gives the public an opportunity to nominate a librarian who has made a difference in the lives of the people they serve. She was one of ten librarians from around the country who were selected for this award from more than two thousand nominations. Luhtala serves on the AASL Board as

Region 1 Director-Elect, the Connecticut Digital Library Advisory Board, and its database subcommittee. In addition, she is Co-chair of the CoSN Awards Committee. Her program has been featured in *District Administration* (March 2011), *Technology & Learning* (February 2011), *The CoSN Annual Compendium* (2010), and *Intel's Blueprint Solutions* (2010). Luhtala facilitates a 2,300+ member online professional learning community for school librarians called Using Emerging Technology to Improve Your Library Program at edWeb.net, an online professional learning network for educators, where she presents monthly webinars. She is co-authoring a forthcoming book for ABC-CLIO, *Relevant Librarian: A 21st-Century Guide to the Responsive Library*. She has also published articles in *Teacher Librarian* and *School Library Monthly*. Credited with launching #bannedsites Day, a celebration of students' freedom to read and learn online, and its website BannedSites. info, Luhtala is a passionate advocate for free-range media and Bring Your Own Device (BYOD) policies in K–12 education. She blogs at Bibliotech.me.

BRIAN MAYER is Gaming and Library Technology Specialist for the Genesee Valley Educational Partnership as well as an independent library consultant. The focus of his work is on the use of modern board games in school libraries as a way to engage students, build literacy, strengthen social skills, and reinforce the curriculum. He has been critical in the growth of designer games as a resource in school libraries and is the co-author of the book *Libraries Got Game: Aligned Learning through Modern Board Games* (2010) from ALA Editions. His work in developing a nationally recognized model for games as resources is available for viewing at the Genesee Valley School Library System's Game Library (sls.gvboces.org/gaming).

JUDI MOREILLON is a literacies and libraries consultant. She serves as an assistant professor in the School of Library and Information Studies at Texas Woman's University. She teaches courses for school librarians, including librarians as instructional partners, school library administration, storytelling, and multimedia resources and services. In addition, she teaches library materials for children, an undergraduate course for pre-service classroom teachers. Judi earned her master's degree from the School of Information Resources and Library Science at the University of Arizona and her doctorate in education at the same university in the Department of Language, Reading, and Culture. During her thirteen-year tenure as a school librarian, Judi collaborated with classroom teachers, specialists, and principals at the elementary, middle, and high school levels to integrate literature and information literacy into the classroom curriculum. She has also served as a district-level school librarian mentor, a literacy coach, a classroom teacher, and a pre-service classroom teacher educator. Judi chaired AASL's School Librarian's Role in Reading Task Force and served on the AASL Guidelines and Standards Implementation Task Force. Her current research centers on the instructional partnership role of school librarians and the factors that influence pre-service and practicing classroom teachers' understandings and practice of classroom-library collaboration. She is the author of two professional books for school librarians and classroom teachers: *Collaborative Strategies for Teaching Reading Comprehension Strategies: Maximizing Your Impact* (ALA Editions, 2007) and *Coteaching Reading Comprehension Strategies in Secondary School Libraries: Maximizing Your Impact* (ALA Editions, 2012).

JACQUELYN (JACKIE) SIMINITUS describes herself as a library advocate. Most recently, she is Vice President for Communications and Web 2.0 Project Manager for the California School Library Association (CSLA) and sits on a number of boards and advisory councils. She previously worked for AT&T in Consumer Affairs and the Education First team for twenty-one years. Prior to working in the telecommunications industry, Jackie was Vice President and Director of Library and Publications for HRN, a Philadelphia-based public affairs/social responsibility consulting firm for Fortune 200 companies. She has a master's degree in Library Science from Drexel University and taught a class on "Marketing Libraries in a Networked World" at San Jose State University Graduate School of Library and Information Studies. In 2010, she helped develop the public awareness campaign, the California Campaign for Strong School Libraries (library campaign.csla.net) and the Campaign's Library Store with Illustrators galore at cafepress.com/csla. She publishes articles and blogs at Library Advocate (advocate4libraries.csla.net) and manages CSLA's online professional development tutorials for educators; opens her local middle school library each morning; teaches senior citizens in using computers; and takes graphic design courses to add more visual elements to her work. Jackie says, "It is fun to meet new people of all ages and learn creative ways to advocate for strong libraries."

SUSAN SMITH is Library Director at The Harker School in San Jose, California, where she has worked since 2001. Prior to her librarianship, Ms. Smith enjoyed a twenty-two-year career in the electronics industry, managing a worldwide sales team. She holds an MLIS from San Jose State University, and a BA (magna cum laude) from Duke University. She has also completed MBA coursework at University of Minnesota. Smith has a passion for teaching research skills and frequently speaks at Bay Area conferences, including Internet@Schools West. She chairs the Information Literacy Steering Committee at Harker and teaches research skills at the Upper School.

TISH STAFFORD worked as a reference librarian for public libraries in Jackson, Mississippi, and Anniston, Alabama, after receiving her MLS from the University of Maryland at College Park. She began working for Cecil County Public Schools when she moved to Maryland, starting out as an elementary school librarian and later moving to a high school position. After twelve years, she was selected as Program Facilitator for Media, assuming responsibility for the library program in all twenty-seven schools within the system at a time when information literacy was redefining the profession, revolutionizing our instructional focus, and creating exciting opportunities for integrating inquiry skills into all content areas. A fervent advocate of collaboration and continuous growth, Tish has modeled and fostered a culture of continuous professional improvement during her tenure in her current position. Together, she and the school librarians who work with her have challenged and supported each other as they have pushed their understanding of the inquiry process to ever-deeper levels and then shared their insights within the school system and across the state. Twice in the last three years, a Cecil County school librarian has received the Mae I. Graham Award, given annually by the Maryland Association of School Librarians to the best library program in the state. Cecil County's school librarians are taking active roles in local and state professional organizations and have attained National Board Certification in large numbers. Intensely proud of their program, they continue to nurture the professional learning community that they have developed, knowing that it has been the incubator for their growth and success. Stafford is taking the insights she has gained over the years as a part of this learning community and is sharing it with graduate students at the University of Delaware.

ANNE STOKES is the librarian at the Edgewood Elementary School in Scarsdale, New York, where she has worked since 2002. Prior to becoming an elementary school librarian, Ms. Stokes had worked as an elementary classroom teacher as well as at the Westchester County Archives. She holds an MLS from the Palmer School of Library and Information Science, an MTS from Bank Street College of Education, and a BA from Vassar College.

JUDITH SYKES has served as a secondary language arts/drama teacher, teacher-librarian, school library specialist, assistant principal, and principal for the Calgary Board of Education. She is currently School Library Services Manager, Alberta Education, and is leading the Alberta Education *School Library Services Initiative*. Sykes has led associations, published, and presented locally, provincially, and internationally on school libraries and leadership including co-chair/principal writer of *Achieving Information Literacy through Quality School Library Programs: The Vision and Standards for School Library Programs in Canada*. She is the author of *Library Centers: Teaching Information Literacy, Skills, and Processes K–6* (Libraries Unlimited, 1997), *Action Research: Practical Tips for Transforming Your School Library* (Libraries Unlimited, 2002), *Brain-Friendly School Libraries* (Greenwood, 2006) and *Engaging in Action Research to Study Your School Library* (Libraries Unlimited, 2012). Sykes says: "Action research has influenced the breadth and depth of my work in multidimensional levels; guiding my learning through living in a question, reflecting and studying not only the wisdom that has come before, but living stories and events inherent to the questions I have pursued, culminating in answers that propel actions and reflection in my work and study. These actions ultimately aim to guide other educators and improve student learning."

ROSS J. TODD is Associate Professor in the School of Communication and Information at Rutgers, the State University of New Jersey. He is Director of the Center for International Scholarship in School Libraries (CISSL) at Rutgers University. CISSL fosters the transformative role of school libraries in 21st-century schools, their integral role in the learning fabric of schools, and their role in ongoing school improvement and reform. His scholarly work primarily focuses on the engagement of people and their information worlds, and understanding how this engagement can facilitate professional action and change and make a difference to individuals, organizations, societies, and nations. Current teaching and research interests center on adolescent information-seeking and use. The research is multifaceted and includes: understanding how children learn and build new knowledge from information, how school librarians and classroom teachers can more effectively empower student learning, and how the development of information and critical literacies through guided inquiry and constructivist learning approaches leads to deep knowledge and deep understanding.

CONNIE WILLIAMS has been a teacher-librarian in the Petaluma City Schools for the past twenty-three years both in junior high and high school. She has a BA in Geography from Sonoma State University, and received her MLS from Emporia State University. She is the co-developer of the CSLA 2.0 tutorials and co-producer of a CD, "Circulate This! Stories from the School Library," that is also the name of her blog (circulatethis.posterous.com) in which she writes about libraries and posts audio stories. She is the author of several articles for *Knowledge Quest*, *LaVoz*, and the *CSLA Journal* and presents at state and national conferences on topics such as school library advocacy, creative lesson design, and marketing your library. Williams is past President of the California School Library Association (2008–2009); Chair of the AASL Legislative Committee (2011–2012), and Chair of the California Campaign for Strong School Libraries. She is an adjunct reference librarian at Santa Rosa Junior College. She is studying Spanish and hopes to be fluent someday soon.

SANDRA YAMAMOTO is the librarian at Kapolei High School in Hawaii. Kapolei High Library was recognized as a National School Library Media Program of the Year (SLMPY) in 2006. She has also been the librarian at Waianae High and Pearl City High Schools. Sandra earned her National Board Certification in 2007 and is active in the Hawaii Association of School Librarians. She and Carolyn Kirio have jointly presented at state and national conferences. Along with Carolyn, she authored *Collaborating for Project-based Learning in Grades 9–12* (Linworth Publishing, 2008). Sandy is heavily involved in building professional learning communities that include implementing school reform initiatives, mentoring new teachers, and facilitating professional development.